Creating the National Park Service

Creating the National Park Service

The Missing Years

By Horace M. Albright
and Marian Albright Schenck

Foreword by Robert M. Utley

University of Oklahoma Press
Norman

Also by Horace M. Albright

The Birth of the National Park Service: The Founding Years, 1913–33 (Salt Lake City, 1985)
Oh, Ranger! (with Frank J. Taylor) (Stanford, 1928)
The Mather Mountain Party of 1915 (with Marian Albright Schenck) (Three Rivers, Calif., 1990)

This book is published with the generous assistance of
The McCasland Foundation,
Duncan, Oklahoma.

Library of Congress Cataloging-in-Publication Data

Albright, Horace M. (Horace Marden), 1890-1987.
  Creating the National Park Service : the missing years / by Horace M.
  Albright and Marian Albright Schenck ; foreword by Robert M. Utley.
    p.   cm.
  Includes bibliographical references (p.   ) and index.
  ISBN 978-0-8061-3155-9 (paper)
    1. United States. National Park Service—History.   2. Albright, Horace M.
  (Horace Marden), 1890-1987.   3. United States. National Park Service—
  Officials and employees—Biography. I. Schenck, Marian Albright, 1921-   .
  II. Title.
  SB482.A4A3688   1999
  353.7'8—dc21   98-43916
                                                                    CIP

The paper in this book meets the guidelines for permanence and durability of the Committee on Production Guidelines for Book Longevity of the Council on Library Resources, Inc. ∞

*My father wanted this book dedicated to "the Greenies"—
the National Park Service rangers in the field, the
dedicated, hard-working, backbone spirit of the service.*

Contents

Illustrations

Photographs are from the collection of Marian Albright Schenck
unless otherwise indicated.

MAP

Foreword

by Robert M. Utley

I first met Horace Marden Albright on an autumn day in 1968. I was chief historian of the National Park Service, he a venerated icon of the formative years of our service. Also a passionate student of history, he dropped by my Washington office to get acquainted. For three hours, this spare, soft-spoken, kindly man reached deep into his incredible memory to pour forth a chronicle of the origins of the National Park Service. Expressed in the animated and lucid detail that marked his conversational style, Albright's fascinating stories yielded new insights into my professional antecedents.

Beginning on that day, I formed a lasting friendship with Horace Albright, one grounded in respect, admiration, and shared interests and values. After I left the government in 1980, we continued to exchange letters until his death in 1987 at the age of ninety-seven.

Horace Albright's significance in the early years of the National Park Service can hardly be overstated. As the second director, 1929–33, he expanded and diversified the National Park System and solidified the canons of its management. Greater and more lasting contributions, however, marked the first years of his service. In the painful birth of the National Park Service itself, and in the adoption of a creed to guide the infant agency toward maturity, Horace Albright played a decisive role.

Albright was twenty-three and a graduate student at the University of California when he went to Washington in 1913 to take a position on the staff of Secretary of the Interior Franklin K. Lane in the new administration of President Woodrow Wilson. Stephen T. Mather was thirty years his senior and a man of great wealth when he arrived in 1915 to oversee the national parks. The extraordinary bonds of friendship, admiration, and respect cemented between these two took an agonizing turn when Mather suffered periodic episodes of manic depression.

Near the end of his long life, Albright and his daughter Marian came increasingly to term the formative period of the National Park Service, 1917 and 1918, history's "missing years." For this Albright himself bore some of the responsibility. So solicitous was he of Mather's significance and reputation that he blurred or withheld vital information. In his last years, however, his daughter persuaded him that he owed posterity a true accounting of the missing years.

These were the years when the newly established National Park Service was organized and placed on a firm foundation of policy, principle, and tradition. These were also the years in which Mather suffered what then passed as a "nervous breakdown" but now is seen as the fluctuations of manic depression.

Mather's illness left his young assistant with daunting political and administrative responsibilities, hidden from public view because Mather's condition had to be kept secret. Earlier publications have contained hints of Albright's pivotal role in the congressional passage of the National Park Service Organic Act in 1916; in the formulation of principles and policies to govern the management of the national parks; in the defense of park resources against exploiters using the cover of World War I to gain entry for cattlemen, sheepmen, lumbermen, and miners; and in other issues critical to the future of the fledgling parks. Until his last years, however, Albright persisted in hovering outside the spotlight that bathed Mather.

Albright enjoyed a phenomenal memory until the day of his death, and he kept nearly every scrap of paper that recorded his life—correspondence, reports, news clippings, little pocket diaries, and even railway ticket stubs and the menus of special dinners. He and his daughter set forth to tell the story of those years. They wrote, in Albright's characteristic style, a virtually day-by-day chronicle of the missing years, as well as the preceding years. The result was a huge manuscript of more than two thousand pages.

Much reduced for publication, here is Albright's story, assembled with the devoted help of Marian Albright Schenck. This book restores Albright to his proper place in history without diminishing the significance of Mather and reveals, in incontestable detail, that the momentous events that gave birth to the National Park Service were a joint achievement. Stephen Mather was the public-relations giant of sweeping vision, exceptional ability to persuade and move people, and unswerving dedication to a splendid system of parks for all Americans—talents tragically crippled by mental illness. Horace Albright was the young, able, self-effacing, hardworking lawyer who made certain that the grand visions of his chief were carried into reality. It was a crucial partnership; neither could have achieved the outcome without the other.

Albright's memoirs close at the end of the missing years. Newly married and with an infant son, he had intended to return to San Francisco and practice law. Instead, in July 1919, he moved his little family into the big stone commanding officer's quarters at Fort Yellowstone and became the first National Park Service superintendent of Yellowstone National Park. His health restored, Mather assumed his duties as the first director of the National Park Service. During the decade of Mather's tenure, Albright served both as Yellowstone superintendent and as "field assistant director," a post in which he continued to aid his chief in the political, budgetary, policy, and management activities of the service. He was Mather's obvious successor and served as second director from 1929 to 1933, when he resigned to embark on a corporate career. He retired as president of the United States Potash Company.

Although it is a significant historical document, Horace Albright's book stands out as a story of compelling human interest. In addition to his distinctive relationship with Stephen Mather, he lays bare his own feelings and self-doubt as he confronts demands almost overwhelming to one of his youth and inexperience. He also relates without reservation his love for Grace Noble, the tortuous course that led at last to marriage, and the influential role she played in his career.

Throughout, Albright tells engagingly of his dealings with political leaders in the Wilson administration, the Congress, and state and local government; with eccentric but potent figures of the conservation movement; with luminaries of the scientific community; with corporate functionaries and media giants; and even with walk-ons such as Buffalo Bill Cody, Franklin D. Roosevelt, Thomas A. Edison, and Orville Wright. Personalities are vividly drawn and forcefully judged. Conflict and harmony are set forth candidly and incisively. Humorous anecdotes abound.

Finally, Albright exposes graphic fragments of the social history of the United States in the years before and during World War I. The ways in which people thought, behaved, dressed, lived, and traveled are implicit in the narrative. In particular, a continuing theme is travel, by mule back and wagon, by railroad and auto, coupled with the magnificent American scenery that unfolded before the eyes and emotions of a young idealist from California. Here is a virtual travelogue of the United States in the second decade of the twentieth century.

In the years since World War II, America's national parks and monuments have suffered a variety of crushing impacts. Millions of people in millions of automobiles demanding ever-expanding road networks; proliferating campgrounds, lodges, and hotels; rampant development crowding against park boundaries; air, noise, and water pollution; and a host of destructive special uses severely damaged the very qualities that gave the parks national distinction. At the same time, shrinking appropriations and new scientific insights into the vulnerability of delicate ecosystems severely impaired the ability of the National Park Service to cope with the challenges and, as commanded by the Organic Act of 1916, preserve the parks "unimpaired for the enjoyment of future generations."

Against this backdrop, modern critics fault the Mather-Albright administration for laying the groundwork for some of these afflictions. Mather and Albright organized a massive publicity campaign to lure people to the national parks, championing automobiles, roads, luxury hotels, and other amenities of comfortable travel. They adopted measures to afford visitors maximum opportunity to view and even interact with wild animals. Albright himself lived to see their knowledge of the natural world outmoded by scientific research.

Such criticism not only unfairly disparages the reputations of two great men but egregiously distorts history. It judges Mather and Albright by the conditions, knowledge, and experience of today; it ignores the social, political, and economic realities of the early twentieth century. Mather and Albright knew that Congress would not create any new parks or fund existing parks unless people visited them. Without publicity, roads, comfortable accommodations, and relaxed enjoyment at the destination, people would not travel to the parks in numbers sufficient to prompt action in the Congress. That the United States today boasts a National Park System at all testifies to the validity of these Mather-Albright policies.

Most national parks display a bronze tablet bearing in bas-relief the likeness of Stephen T. Mather. The text reads: "He laid the foundation of the National Park Service, defining and establishing the policies under which its areas shall be developed and conserved unimpaired for future generations. There will never come an end to the good that he has done."

As Horace Albright's chronicle makes plain, a truer tribute would read, "There will never come an end to the good that *they* have done."

Introduction

by Marian Albright Schenck

Some people will ask what this book is, and why Horace Albright, approaching his century mark, chose to undertake another narrative about the National Park Service. Hadn't enough been written about Stephen Mather, Horace Albright, and the history of the National Park Service? In a way, the answer is yes. But in another way, the answer is an emphatic no. What he called "the missing years," 1917–19, had never truly been examined.

This book is not an autobiography in the precise sense. An autobiography is a biography of a person written by himself. Instead this is a book conceived, planned, and for the most part overseen and checked, page by page, by my father. I did research, meticulously copied his spoken words as we discussed the events of his life, followed his directions in locating material, and then wrote the narrative for his correction and final approval. He died on March 28, 1987, before the last section of the text had been completed, although the outline had been created and important parts had been written.

My father took on this chore in his nineties because for many years he had been concerned that the early years of the National Park Service had not been chronicled in sufficient depth. He realized that he had been partially to blame because of his reluctance to discuss this period. He had overseen, corrected, and approved all three books published about Stephen Mather and himself (plus an unpublished one). They contained much the same material and presented history as he wanted it told at the time. He feared that a full disclosure might harm Mather's reputation. My father worshiped Mather and wanted to do nothing to damage his name.

As the years went by, however, my father grew increasingly worried about the rising criticism of early Park Service policies and actions. He considered some of the criticism unwarranted and disparaging of Mr. Mather's reputation. He decided that the time had come to write about these "missing years," to explain how the policies were formed, and to emphasize the serious difficulties that had to be overcome.

But my father faced a terrible dilemma. Since 1916 he had kept files of these early days in his home. He allowed access only to such documents as he chose. These files contained sensitive material about Mather and other matters. He agonized that laying out the detailed history of the years 1917–19 would do more harm than good. He treasured the memory of Mr. Mather and felt that his daughter, her husband, and her family had to be protected, for he loved them all as his own family. He wavered over whether he should destroy these records for the sake of the Mather descendants, but was held back by the belief that, as a historian, he should save them.

Finally, because these events were so far in the past and because some modern writers were distorting the true history, he believed that his personal documents and memories were needed, as he called it, "to put the record straight." He was uneasy with the writers' reluctance to use primary sources and with their simplistic and revisionist tendencies. He concluded that if he could set down the factual history it would throw needed light on those shadowy years. He wanted to clarify the context of that eventful time and place. He would relate the development of the National Park Service, but he would also show how profoundly Mather had suffered and how he had emerged through his own strength to return to years of brilliance that benefited the service.

Even as we worked on other projects (*A Trip to Paradise 1920*, *My Six Trips with Ickes*, and *The Mather Mountain Party*, the last for the centennial of Sequoia National Park), my father began to formulate the story of "the missing years."

First, my father read every document and letter in his old Phoenix File boxes, sorting out what would be pertinent to the narrative. He intended to start with meeting Stephen Mather and end with Mather's return to Washington after his prolonged illness. He then made a general outline of the narrative he wanted to write.

Next, my father and I combed the material that he and Frank Taylor had used to write a biography of Mather several years after his death in 1930. My father had written to more than four hundred people who were close to Mather, asking them for anecdotes or anything else they could recall about the man. I don't know how many responded back in the

1930s, but quite a few answers remained in his files. There were also chapters from their uncompleted book *Along Came Steve Mather*. In addition, there were more than a hundred pages of my father's handwritten or typed information prepared for that book but as yet unused. Much of this Robert Shankland used when my father asked him to start afresh on the biography later published as *Steve Mather of the National Parks*.

For the period we were writing about, my father had retained his personal files, his pocket diaries, my mother's diaries, and his scrapbooks. There were files with data provided for Donald Swain's *Wilderness Defender*, as well as oral tapes and transcripts for Robert Cahn when he was working on *The Birth of the National Park Service*. My father also had four or five transcripts of tapes he had made for Columbia University, the National Park Service, and other organizations and individuals.

After we had culled all these sources for the years through 1919, my father sent me to the University of California at Los Angeles, to which he had donated personal papers. The research assistant there helped me check these out and made copies of items I thought useful. Historians from many parks combed their libraries for material. I might add that a few years after the death of my father, the Park Service's bureau historian, Barry Mackintosh, introduced me to the early records of the service in the National Archives, where I double-checked some of the details.

Now the work was to start. By this time, my father lived at the Chandler Convalescent Home near Los Angeles. But he spent much of his time at our home, a drive of about ten minutes. In a study my husband and I had set up for him during the years he had lived with us were his books, files, photograph albums, and my computer. We spent hours here as we began to put the book together.

As my father grew older, he remained at Chandler more of the time. A different routine became necessary. We would discuss the work on the book. I would take down his instructions and conversations, go home, check out details, write a section, and take it to him to read, correct, or make additional suggestions. Another rewrite or more might be necessary until he was satisfied.

At some point in this process—I don't remember exactly when—my father decided he wanted to tell the whole story of his life before the missing years. I believe my daughter asked him to do that, not for the book but just for family history. He got out some manuscripts he had written years earlier, a partial autobiography. Publisher Alfred Knopf, his friend and a longtime park supporter, had asked him to write this and intended to publish it. However, my father never got beyond the years from his birth to his move to Washington in 1913.

This was a turning point for him, because he decided that he wanted every possible detail about his early life written down. The planned book would still cover only 1915–18. Later he decided to extend it into 1919 to include his appointment as superintendent of Yellowstone National Park. Of course, the narrative now burgeoned well beyond the original concept, but my father said the part for the book could later be cut down to size. Meantime, we were going to write every fact that we could find and he could remember. As he worked over the primary source material, the photograph albums, and his old scrapbooks, the narrative kept growing as my father's fabled memory clicked in, providing an incredible amount of detail. It turned into an extraordinary marathon.

We found it fairly easy to bring his original manuscript up to the creation of the National Park Service in 1916. From that time on, however, especially with Mr. Mather's breakdown in January 1917, it was a slow, meticulous task. It's hard to describe how painful much of this was for my father. He wanted to skip lightly over Mather's illness, and sometimes he would say that certain facts couldn't be included, or he would want to gloss over them, always trying to protect the Mather family. Then he'd come around to feeling that the story had to be written, that it had to be true history this time. Occasionally tears slowly coursed down his cheeks as memories became too vivid.

We worked for several years in this manner. Then in the summer of 1986 my father nearly died. When he returned from the hospital, he seemed to feel that he wouldn't live much longer. He had to finish his projects as rapidly as possible. From that time until March 1987, when he left forever, we finished his *Six Trips with Ickes* and polished *The Mather Mountain Party* for publication. But he always pushed ahead with this book too. Believing that his time was getting shorter, he fortunately insisted on skipping ahead to get down the facts on Mather's problems at the end of 1918, his own conflict with Interior Secretary Franklin K. Lane, his resignation and ultimate settlement with Mather, and his assumption of the superintendency of Yellowstone National Park in 1919.

In the years after my father's death, I worked on this project whenever possible. To finish the last section myself, I followed the same procedures we had used for so many years. My husband and I made trips to places that figured in my father's life, down old roads to destinations bypassed or forgotten and on to modern parks. I spent hours in various national parks going through the archives with the always helpful ranger-historians. Few people still lived who were involved in the missing years, but I corresponded or talked with most or with their relatives, many of whom I had known as a child.

Finally, this monster of a manuscript, close to two thousand pages, was wrapped up. And then the question arose of what to do with it. My father had often said he would have a National Park Service historian look at it. So I hesitantly asked our friend Bob Utley, a retired chief historian of the service, if he would do this. He kindly read the whole thing and felt that, with careful editing, it could be offered for publication. At his suggestion, a "prequel" of my father's life from birth to 1915 was included as an introduction to the main story.

To pare the manuscript down to publishable dimensions, many large segments had to be cut out altogether. To connect what remained and preserve continuity, "bridges" became essential. My father, of course, could not oversee these; I created them, using his distinctive first-person style and his own words and thoughts where possible. I am confident that he would have changed virtually nothing in these connecting paragraphs. They are set in italics to distinguish them from the body of the text.

It is impossible to state the debt we owe to Robert M. Utley. His place as a historian of America's past is well known and honored. His face and voice are recognizable through his appearances in and contributions to fine television documentaries, such as *Real West* and *How the West Was Lost*. But only those who know him personally can appreciate the man who is kindly, intellectually brilliant, and devoted to his country and the National Park Service. I also owe him my humble appreciation and gratitude for his endless hours of plowing through thousands of pages of manuscript to pull together a clear and concise narrative while leaving my father's original words and actions intact. As for me, I learned an encyclopedia of information on editing, punctuation, and writing discipline from his patient teaching and sage advice. More than that, I learned about a man who is in many ways a "clone" of my father: a fine-honed mind with an understanding, gentle, humorous, optimistic, and idealistic soul.

In conclusion, let me say that my father and I tried to produce a narrative as historically accurate as possible, using almost entirely primary source material along with his memory of dates, places, and events he had experienced. His age precluded his writing the text, but he read and approved all except the last chapters. His death left me with only a short period to cover, a time for which he had already supplied the salient facts.

This, therefore, is neither a personally written autobiography nor a personal memoir. It is an effort on the part of a man who loved his National Park Service and Stephen Mather and wanted to tell the history of both to the best of his ability in a factual historical manner.

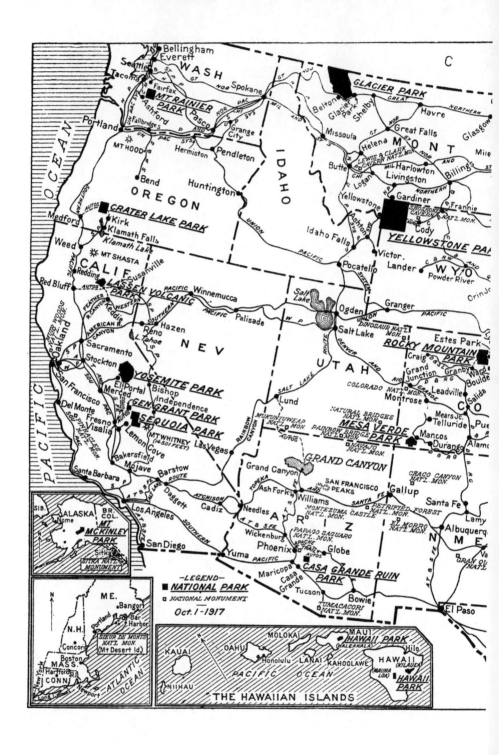

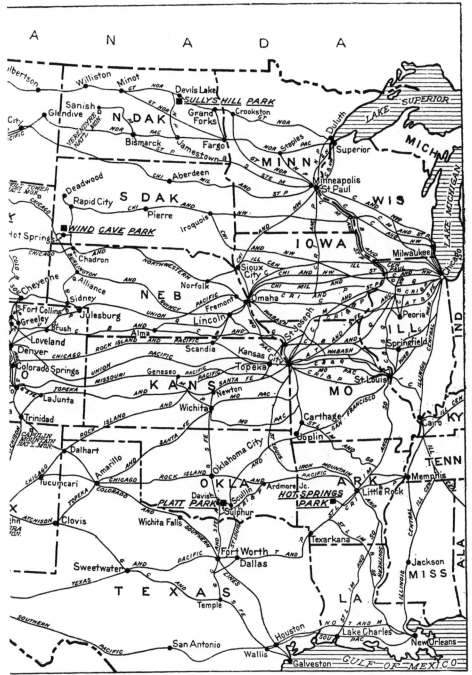

National Parks and Monuments, October 1, 1917. Seventeen national parks containing
9,773 square miles or 6,254,508 acres and twenty-two national manuments containing
143.4 square miles or 91,824 acres. Courtesy National Park Service.

Creating the National Park Service

Maybe it's like constructing a house. I'm at the stage where I am laying the foundations. They are what everything else is built upon. I have no blueprints and no architect. Only the ideals and principles for which the Park Service was created—to preserve, intact, the heritage we were bequeathed.

HORACE M. ALBRIGHT, SEPTEMBER 1917

CHAPTER

1

Boyhood Days in the Owens Valley
1890–1908

Beyond the High Sierra and near the Nevada line lies Inyo County, California—big, wild, beautiful, and lonely. In its center stretches the Owens River Valley, surrounded by the granite walls of the Sierra Nevada to the west and the White Mountains to the east. Here the remote town of Bishop hugs the slopes of towering Mount Tom, 13,652 feet high, and here I was born on January 6, 1890. When I went to college, I discovered that most Californians did not know where Bishop was, and I had to draw them a map.

My birthplace should have been Candelaria, Nevada, for that was where my parents were living in 1890. My father was an engineer in the Northern Belle silver mine. I was often asked, "Then how come you were born in Bishop?" and I replied, "Because my mother was there." The truth was that after losing a child at birth the year before, she felt Candelaria's medical care was not to be trusted.

The decline in the price of silver, the subsequent depression, and the playing out of the mines in Candelaria forced the Albright family to move to Bishop permanently.

We had a good life in Bishop. I loved it, was inspired by its aura, and always drew strength and serenity from it. I have no recollection of ever having any bad times. There weren't many special things to do, but whatever we did, it was on horseback or afoot. Long hours were spent in school. We had only one elementary school and one high school, the only one in Inyo County, which was as big as the state of Massachusetts.

We didn't think we were poor, didn't know we were poor, but we certainly were. Bishop had no autos, no power, no lights, no sewers, and no water systems, but we never missed them because we never had them. I don't remember anybody complaining about it either. They were good people, and nothing really bad happened. We never locked doors, and I don't remember any stealing. Once in a while we had a killing, but somehow I don't recall who was killed—or why!

My parents were very different people. My dad, an immigrant from Canada in 1873, had only completed a sixth-grade education before he was apprenticed to a cabinet maker. He later utilized his talents as a millwright and an engineer in mines from the Comstock Lode to Aurora to Candelaria. In Bishop he bought a mill and put up his sign, which read: "Contractor–Builder–Planing & Feed–Undertaker." He made it plain he was not a mortician. "All I do is make a coffin, get the body as soon as I can, and bury it." He had learned this trade in Candelaria, where he and Chris Zabriskie, the local Wells-Fargo man, had operated an undertaking business on the side, which advertised: "A to Z–Albright to Zabriskie. You kick the bucket. We do the rest."

My mother, Mary Marden Albright, was something different. She was born in Mokelumne Hill and had been honed in tough times in the rough mining camps of California and Nevada. However, she was a rare woman of that period. She had gone to college in Napa.

My mother ran the family with an iron hand. After her three sons spent long hours in school, there were chores around the house and tough physical work outdoors, washing windows and dishes, scrubbing floors, beating carpets, chopping wood, and doing the gardening. Every other waking minute was devoted to education and learning. And because my father was such a gentle, kindly man, she felt she had to be more aggressive.

My dad was a very popular man in town because of his involvement in local activities and his endearing personality. He was a quiet fellow, very gentle, very, very friendly, and awfully hard working. He was a handsome man, fairly tall, always lean but muscular. He had a mustache but was getting bald at an early age.

Besides working hard from dawn to dark, Dad belonged to every society and lodge in town and conducted most of the rituals at them because of his unusual memory. My mother used to say to him, "You belong to so many lodges you never lodge at home."

My parents were bent on education for their children. Both had phenomenal memories. Because they realized the value of this extraordinary gift, they trained their children. While we were waiting to have breakfast, Mother made us recite poetry. My brother Leslie and I used Sundays (when we were forbidden to indulge in nonreligious activities) to play a game. One would start reciting some poetry or work of an author and keep going until he ran out or made a mistake. The other picked up at that point. I don't remember if there was a reward or penalty attached to the winner or loser. It was a great game, and we could recite whole sections of *Idylls of the King* or cantos of Virgil's *Aeneid*—in Latin!

Mother started us on "the classics" at an early age. It was my twelfth birthday when she gave me *David Copperfield* and soon afterward the James Fenimore Cooper books and the books by the English author G. A. Henty. Each Henty book had a boy hero who participated in nearly every historical era, including crossing the Alps with Hannibal or campaigning with Clive in India. When I was about thirteen, my parents probably went into debt to buy the *Encyclopaedia Britannica* from the Sears & Roebuck catalogue. What a feast of reading that was!

We enjoyed music in our home. My mother played the small organ we had in the living room and had us sing along with her. She also encouraged her boys to try musical instruments, but Dewey and I were hopelessly tone deaf. Leslie was musically gifted, teaching himself the piano, organ, and most stringed instruments. He was especially fine with the mandolin.

One more item about that organ. There were no banks in Bishop in those days. Our family "banked" in an old stocking that, when filled with the Albright savings, was tied tight and hidden in the organ through the foot pedal.

One thing we missed was a phonograph, but there was no money for it. Happily, we lived next door to a widow who had one and was pretty deaf. When her phonograph was playing, you could hear it all over town.

My father did not go to church. He said he had been reared in the Church of England and heartily disliked ritual. Sunday was his only day of rest, so he stayed home, reading his *San Francisco Chronicle* or *Argosy Magazine*. My mother, however, attended the Methodist Church, until the Presbyterian Church was built around 1900. She insisted her boys go to Sunday school, starting at age five. Our teachers gave out cards every Sunday with a biblical picture and quotation on it. My mother made us memorize these, and then we had to recite them by the month of the year.

In the summers, most boys who were old enough worked in the hay fields, as this was farming country before the water rights were bought up by the city of Los Angeles. Before I was old enough to do this, I made many outings in the Sierras. When I was ten years old, I went with some relatives and friends up to Ten Big Trees camping area and the old ghost town of Pine City, in the shadow of Mount Humphreys. Here the crumbling houses built around 1870 had walls papered with old newspapers. Brother Leslie and I loved reading "history" off them.

The next year, my dad took me camping to Twin Lakes along with two other men and a boy my age named Billy. When Billy and I set off to fish on the lake, the boat proved to have holes in it and nearly sank. Fortunately, we made it back to shore. I couldn't swim then and, though afraid of water ever after, never did learn to swim.

While up near Mammoth Lake, we met Robert L. P. Bigelow, a ranger for the old General Land Office in the Sierra Forest Reserve, which extended south from Yosemite Valley to the Tehachapi. There was, as yet, no United States Forest Service. In 1904 Bigelow took me along when he made his inspection trip north into Yosemite National Park. We went through Mono Pass and Bloody Canyon into Tuolomne Meadows, but never reached, or even saw from above, the Yosemite Valley. We saw the beauty of the Minaret–Devils Postpile region, an area that was removed a year later from the park. I never forgot that and tried all my life to get the lands restored to Yosemite.

We camped at Red Meadows, near Devils Postpile, with U.S. cavalrymen detailed to protect Yosemite Park from trespass by sheepherders and their flocks. They had just put fifty to seventy-five miles between some shepherds and their sheep. I remember noting some objects high in the pine trees. I asked what they were and was told they were sheep that had been "dressed out" in sacks and hoisted high in the trees to keep the meat cool and fresh. The sergeant said he thought they had enough sheep meat to last the rest of the summer.

Perhaps more than to either of my parents, I looked to my maternal grandfather, Horace Marden, as a model. He was born in Maine in 1832. Like thousands of others, he set off to find gold. He crossed the Isthmus of Nicaragua and arrived in California before his twentieth birthday.

Finding business more profitable than mining, he engaged in the freighting business throughout California's Mother Lode and the mining country of Nevada.

For nearly forty years, he retained his transportation business while operating stamp mills in Aurora and Bodie. He served in the Nevada Legislature and saw six of his nine children die. At last he pulled up stakes in Nevada and entered the logging business in northern California. I spent several summers working at his camps, where we had long talks, and he transferred his strength, courage, and philosophy to me. This, in turn, shaped my ideals and determination to reach the high goals he had set for himself.

Granddad Marden was a rugged old character. As we drove along together in the mountains of northern California, we would discuss the affairs of the time or he'd tell me about the old days of the gold rush and life in the mining camps. We'd talk about the forest—the magnificent stands of timber clothing the slopes of Mount Shasta. It bothered him that these beautiful places were being so ruthlessly destroyed, and yet people like himself had to make a living from doing it. I especially remember our emergence from the Sacramento Canyon to see the astonishing view of Mount Shasta. Its majesty swept the whole horizon. We stopped and just silently absorbed its beauty.

Large areas of these woodlands had been cleared of commercial timber, and there had been some destructive fires that swept over the slashings and young trees and shrubs. As we stood there and looked at the old cut-over areas, my granddad again talked of the wasteful destruction of the timberlands. He regretted that nothing seemed to be done about it, although it was apparent from his conversation that he was familiar with new government publications regarding forests and the ideas of Gifford Pinchot. As young as I was, I believe I got my first feeling for conservation from this trip with my old granddad.

In 1903, when I left Bishop and saw the outside world for the first time, I not only went to visit Granddad Marden, but later joined my mother and brothers for a tour of San Francisco. Although most of the city was a mass of ramshackle wooden shacks, the heart of it was truly impressive. Later I thought how lucky we were to have seen San Francisco before its destruction in 1906.

The first thing my mother did in San Francisco was to take her three sons to a barbershop. The barber circled me and, completing his study, said, "My boy, where did you get your last haircut? You haven't two hairs on your head the same length."

I replied, "Mears Creek with horse clippers."

One morning Mother read that the army transport *Sherman* would sail for the Philippines the next day right after noon. She decided to take us to the dock to see her sail. We were disappointed with the soldiers, who wore dungarees instead of blue uniforms with brass buttons. Some regiments did appear, one of which was a colored regiment. It was most impressive, as we had never seen black people.

Then more soldiers arrived. Among these were two outstanding officers in blue uniforms with maroon stripes down the legs of their trousers. They were tall and handsome, straight as a ship's mast, walking in perfect cadence to board the *Sherman*. I found out the next day when their pictures appeared in the newspaper that they were Lieutenant Douglas MacArthur and Lieutenant U. S. Grant III, just out of West Point and on their first assignment as officers to the Philippines. I determined then and there that I would be an officer in the army.

I was excited about the possibilities of army life from reading books and from recollections of the Spanish-American War, especially the exploits of Colonel Theodore Roosevelt and his Rough Riders. I decided I wanted to go to West Point, and for the next three years I bedeviled our congressman, Sylvester Clark Smith of Bakersfield, for an appointment. Finally, in 1906, he gave me an appointment as first alternate, which meant that, if I passed the examinations and the principal failed or for some other reason did not want to go to West Point, I would go.

Actually, I had a problem. Bishop High School was not accredited at this time. After I finished two years there, Mother decided I should go to high school in Stockton, where I could live with an old friend of hers from Aurora. In April 1907 my appointment as first alternate candidate for a West Point cadetship came through. This meant that I had to take the examinations for the academy at the Presidio in San Francisco. Shortly thereafter I took the night boat from Stockton down to the Bay City to face the tests.

In the morning I was shocked to see the panorama of ruins from the earthquake and fire of 1906. I had the bad luck to arrive in town just as a streetcar strike began, and my cheap old hotel was four miles from the Presidio, a long walk to the army fort and back every day to take the exams. From May 1 through May 5, 1907, I was examined, mentally and physically, by a board of army officers. I passed the physical exam and all of the academic tests (geometry only conditionally). It didn't make any difference, however, because I was only the first alternate. The principal appointee passed everything and took his place at West Point in the summer.

Realizing that West Point was probably a remote chance, my mother had urged me to take a look at the University of California at Berkeley as long as I was in the vicinity. I did this and was overwhelmed by the beauty of the campus and by its buildings and history. I immediately decided that I'd like to attend this college if my West Point appointment fell through.

In 1908 I finished high school in Bishop and was admitted to the University of California for the fall semester. Because my high school was still not accredited, I was placed on probation until I passed my first-semester freshman exams. I worked my summer job until the last day before I left for Berkeley. I needed every cent I could earn, as my family could not afford to pay my way at college.

The last rays of sun were disappearing behind Old Tom, casting a glow across my beloved mountains. Inwardly, I was somewhat sad to leave this beautiful, serene valley, but I realized how lucky and how happy my life had been in this little Sierra town. Paradoxically, my youth and eagerness to experience life outside this sheltered existence sent a tingle of anticipation through me as I hurried home. I always remembered that last lovely day as a resident of Bishop, Inyo County, California. I never again came home except as a visitor.

University of California
1908–13

On August 26, 1908, I registered at the University of California in the College of Commerce. Although my father and grandfather had encouraged me to study mining engineering, I knew I did not want to be an engineer, but then again I didn't know what I wanted to be or do. Commerce looked good, as it covered many lines of activity, and my high school courses fit the college curriculum in that field.

Of course, I had to find work. My father could only spare twenty-five dollars a month for my board and room, and even this had to be discontinued all too soon. I had to earn money for everything else, including books and uniforms for the military. I worked for the real estate firm of Mason-McDuffie putting up rental and "for sale" signs, digging postholes, and erecting billboards. (I have hated billboards ever since.) I was a mailman at Christmas and a logger in the summer. Occasionally I worked in a bookstore, which I liked very much, and sometimes even earned $2.00 or $2.50 a day. I had to watch myself because I saw too many books I wanted to buy.

I was never much at athletics. After toying with football, track, and rowing, I came to the conclusion that there were too many fellows far better than I and I really didn't have the time, as I had to work whenever and wherever I could. Anyway, in those days, being a successful athlete brought you only local fame and could get you flunked out. I decided to limit my activities to military science, which I really liked.

The military was a good experience for me, for I was really a very shy fellow, inclined to hold back, and found it hard to get acquainted with strangers—especially women. Military work gave me confidence, most particularly when I had the duty to command even a squad.

I became a cadet in the University of California Cadet Regiment and, by graduation, rose to the rank of captain. I commanded a company of one hundred men and served as an instructor to freshmen cadets. I added to my interest in military tactics by joining the First Company Field Artillery, California National Guard, at the Presidio. I was made a second lieutenant and could now wear a sword at drill time.

I went home for the summer of 1909 and again worked for my father doing carpentry work, shingling, and nailing clapboard on buildings. My father came to realize during the summer that I was not interested in engineering, contracting, and especially undertaking. My brother Leslie was even more of a student than I and would certainly become some sort of a professional man. Our father needed us, as he was nearly sixty years old, had suffered back trouble for years, and had lost an eye while making a windlass for a mine about the time I was finishing high school.

Before I left to go back to Berkeley, my dad and I had a talk, and he, in his gentle way, said he knew he could not count on me and did not blame me for wanting to follow a different path in life. He also understood that Leslie had great promise in the academic field. He smiled and wryly added, "I guess that leaves me with Dewey." And then we grinned at each other, for Dewey was the least likely to try for a higher education. Girls were more his pursuit. As it turned out, he was the one who took over Dad's business—at least the undertaking side of it.

In the spring of my freshman year, I had been "rushed" by Del Rey, a local fraternity or club. Its fun-loving, hard-joshing, rough-and-tumble living and fellow poverty-stricken members brought out the hidden qualities of a mixer in me. I agreed to join, but stated that I couldn't live in the house until my finances improved. My summer paychecks made this possible.

On returning to the university in August 1909, I went to live at the Del Rey Club at 2203 Atherton. There I was more the exception than the rule. There was much time wasted and too little attention to studies. The rating of Del Rey among the fraternities was low, not far from the bottom of the list. Also, the Dellers resented compulsory military courses, which the Morrill Act governing Land Grant Colleges required. Consequently, those of us who enjoyed them were tormented to some extent and our uniforms were kicked around. Of course, the dissidents treated their own uniforms much worse.

In the second semester of my sophomore year, the most memorable event of my entire life occurred, although I didn't recognize it at the time and nothing came of it for a few more years. One day a girl I had met once or twice, Ethel McConnell, telephoned to ask me to come to "a little party" at her home a few nights hence. There would be dancing and refreshments. She said she also needed two more boys and asked if I could bring a couple from my house. I accepted with thanks and promised the two boys. When we arrived, we were admitted to a spacious parlor with folding doors opening to a large dining room, both cleared for dancing. There were about two dozen couples by the time everyone arrived.

I was no more inside the door of the McConnell house than I spied a beautiful girl, the most attractive girl I had ever seen. She was a brunette—lovely, genial—and wore a red dress with flowers on it. Above all, she had the most beautiful brown eyes I had ever seen. When introduced to her, I found she was a classmate and her name was Grace Noble. She was with another classmate, Elton Charvoz, a premedical student.

Now this girl was obviously popular, for she was dancing all the time with different men. What a beautiful dancer she was, too. I somehow got a couple of dances with her, but she was constantly worried about Charvoz, who was suffering from asthma. Although I admired her concern, I felt it unlikely that a college sophomore would be overly worried about another classmate unless he was badly injured or dying. Each time I managed a dance with her, I became more uneasy. Her compassion for Charvoz, although admirable, began to make me think she might be engaged to him. And already I did not want her engaged to anybody. Something had happened to me. I had fallen in love almost instantly. Grace Noble, this striking brunette with her big brown eyes, taller than an average woman, seemed to be my ideal girl.

The following Monday afternoon, I was walking with Beverly Clendenin across the campus when Grace Noble approached us. She smiled and spoke to Bev, but never even noticed me. What a blow! Anyway, I felt snubbed and did not again approach her until I was a graduate student. Then I found Grace Noble again, and I never looked at another woman for the rest of my life.

At the end of the 1910 spring semester, elections had been held for vice-president and manager of the Del Rey Club. One group, who felt that alcohol should be limited to banquets and more attention should be paid to scholastic achieve-

ment, nominated me and labeled me the "dry" candidate. The "wet" candidate, Bill Janicke, saw no reason to put any limitations on anything (especially beer). I won by one vote. My term was for one year (later affirmed for another), and I was to receive free room and board.

Because our old clubhouse needed repairs, I decided that I had better stay in Berkeley that summer of 1910 to oversee the work. I also took a few typing and stenography courses and got a job as a dishwasher in a restaurant.

The year 1910–11 at the University of California began on August 30 and marked quite a change in my life. My mother, pleading a heart condition, which was a panacea for having things her way, rented a house in Berkeley for herself and my two brothers. Leslie was now enrolled at the university and Dewey in Berkeley High School. Although he joined Del Rey, Leslie remained with my mother until he graduated, finished his master's degree, and left for Spain in 1916. I often used to wonder how my dad got along in Bishop, alone and with the extra financial burden of two homes to keep up. No one volunteered this information, and I never dared inquire.

When the new semester started, I was pretty sure that I wanted to be a lawyer, so I loaded up on three jurisprudence courses as well as Latin, economics, history, and the military. Being house manager of Del Rey was a tough job because the limit for room and board payments was twenty-five dollars per member per month. Right in the middle of the semester the boys would decide to have an extra dance without additional levies. Some fellow would invariably shout, "Aw, pay it out of the deficit." This would overrun the budget. Then I had to use my imagination to reduce the debt by having the butcher throw in a liver or two for a customer's dog. I told him we had six dogs, so I received a lot of extra liver for the boys.

I had taken a great interest in the 1910 campaign for governor of California. My granddad Marden was happy when Hiram Johnson won the governorship and invited me to go with him to Sacramento to see Johnson inaugurated at noon on January 1, 1911.

Shortly after this, I celebrated my twenty-first birthday and could vote for the first time, in a special election to determine whether women should be allowed to vote. I believed that my mother and the other women of my acquaintance knew just as much about political affairs as most men I knew (and a lot more than a mighty lot of them). I have always been proud of the fact that I cast my first vote for women's suffrage.

In the spring of 1911 ex-president Theodore Roosevelt, back from his safari in Africa, came to Berkeley to give the Charter Day address and the Earl Lectures at the university. I was in the Greek Theater to hear him deliver his Charter Day address. The next afternoon he was Colonel Roosevelt the Rough Rider when he reviewed the cadets. I also attended the Earl Lectures and was honored by being one of the undergraduates introduced to Roosevelt and given the chance to shake his hand.

Accompanied by brother Dewey and a fellow Deller, I spent the summer at my granddad Marden's lumber camp in northern California. My job as a loader of Big Wheels was back-breaking work during the day, but most evenings I went over to my granddad's cabin. We spent these evenings together, talking about logging, the waste of it, the economics of the timber industry, and politics. I especially soaked up his yarns of the early days in California and Nevada. They were music to my ears, and I never got enough of them.

I left the logging camp a little early, as it was quite a job to organize the new house before registration on August 29, 1911. I settled into my career choice of jurisprudence by taking six courses in that field.

In my senior year there were all kinds of splendid balls and fraternity dances. The most glamorous one was the military ball, to which I took a lovely Copa de Oro girl, all the time wishing I could have asked Grace Noble. I did see her there, and she was beautiful. In 1912 the ladies had fancy cards that were filled out by writing in the name of a partner for each of the dances. I tried to get a dance with her, but she referred me to her escort. I never did approach him, as we had crossed swords at a drill exhibit once. I knew he'd never let me have a dance with her anyway.

In my last semester, I heard that Professor Adolph Miller, the head of the Department of Economics, was seeking a reader for the following year. A reader was usually a graduate student assigned to a professor to monitor classes, check attendance, run errands, give examinations, and correct papers—a "man Friday." I went to see Miller, a most unpopular professor, and asked for the reader job. He reminded me that he usually went through two or three readers a semester, as they always quit in short order. I assured him I would stay. He scowled and sternly asked why I thought I would stay when others never did. My reply was: "Because I need the job badly and I'll just have to stay. And I assure you I will do the work no matter how hard it is—or you are." Miller hired me at fifty dollars a month, which was big money for me.

May 15, 1912, was graduation day at the University of California. My whole family, including Granddad Marden, was in the audience. Instead of a cap and gown, I proudly wore my ROTC uniform and was given my diploma by the university's president and my commission by Governor Hiram Johnson. Sadly, I knew I might have been the colonel of the regiment instead of second in command had I not been hospitalized for mumps in the spring. Not only did I lose out on this honor, but my eyes had been damaged to the extent that I had to wear glasses for the rest of my life.

After a miserable summer in Chico, working as a carpenter's helper in a shop with a tin roof and a temperature of around 120 degrees each day, I came back to Berkeley a week or so before the university opened on August 28, 1912, to take up my duties as reader for Professor Miller. I worked for him my whole graduate year, although I knew he was imposing on me at times. Then a lecturer or assistant professor, Sol Blum, was stricken with tuberculosis, and Miller assigned his sections to me. It was extremely hard to manage these extra chores and keep up with the difficult law course and all my other responsibilities. In the long run, it paid off and changed my life.

Among other courses, I studied the law of mines and waters under Professor William E. Colby. This subject was right down my alley, for my family background had given me a good knowledge of the technical features of mines and mining. Colby and I became great friends because of our mutual interest in mining and our love of the Sierra Nevada. He was the best friend and right-hand man of John Muir, then president of the Sierra Club. One night I accompanied Colby to a meeting of the Sierra Club in San Francisco and had the opportunity to meet and talk with Muir, who died shortly afterward. The old man, who looked like a disreputable shaggy dog, made an enormous impression on me with his discussion of the Hetch Hetchy problem in Yosemite.

And again there was politics. Shortly before we graduated in the spring of 1912, Woodrow Wilson, governor of New Jersey, came to the campus to deliver the annual Phi Beta Kappa lecture. I attended the lecture and was so fascinated by it that I went to the library and began reading up on the man and the issues he had raised.

The time came to vote in November. Hating myself for abandoning "TR," I cast my first presidential vote for Wilson. Being young, I wanted that first vote to be for a winner.

Of course, I worked hard on my Republican relatives to vote as I did. My parents refused as well as my old granddad Marden. He had never voted for a Democrat since 1852, when he was only twenty years old. If a man had a mustache or beard, no one prevented him from voting in California gold rush days. All he needed was a signature and an address, so he couldn't vote twice. In 1852 Granddad voted for Franklin Pierce, which he said proved that he was incompetent to vote.

To save money this year, I lived with my mother and brothers and walked the mile to my classes four times a day. Going across the northwest corner of the campus, I often passed Grace Noble, who was in the graduate School of Education. By now I was getting some smiles and a word of greeting. She even invited me to a party at her home. When I had to refuse because of an engagement with a law group, I wrote her a formal letter on Del Rey engraved paper. She regarded it as a real insult to her attempt to be friendly.

Woodrow Wilson was elected president of the United States and appointed Franklin K. Lane of California as his secretary of the interior. Although Wilson had never met him, it was known that Lane would promote San Francisco's interests in construction of the Hetch Hetchy dam, a project uppermost in Democratic Party objectives. Lane asked Adolph Miller, a close friend from UC Berkeley days, to be one of his assistants in Washington. Miller agreed, as he was wealthy and tired of university work, and the challenge of the new administration was enticing. His only request was that he wanted to bring a young assistant along with him. Lane agreed to that, and Miller threw the proposition to me. I agonized between his offer of twelve hundred dollars a year as his confidential clerk and giving up my goal of finishing law school. But my family and Will Colby convinced me I should grab this opportunity.

Miller advanced me the fare to Washington and added: "You'll need formal attire back there. You can have an old outfit I don't use anymore, and if you need some alterations, go to my tailor and I'll foot the bill." His gift was nineteenth-century sartorial elegance. I used it time and again in Washington and wore it when I got married.

Just before I was going to leave for the staff of Secretary of the Interior Franklin K. Lane, I was walking across campus and met Pearl Lutzi, the sister of a club brother. Who should be with her but Grace Noble. Pearl stopped me and said, "We heard you are going to Washington. We'd like you to come over and have dinner with us."

Before I could say anything, Grace spoke up: "Pearl, it's not any use trying to get him, he's always too busy." Pearl laughed and repeated her invitation, and I accepted. We agreed on a date for that. Then she threw out a dare to me by asking, "Aren't you going to see Grace before you leave?"

She really shocked me with that, and, not looking at Grace, I answered, "I have no date with her, but I wish I had one." And I astonished myself even more when I turned to her and asked, "Can I see you some evening before I go?" I was stunned when she replied that she would be glad to see me, and we agreed on a night for me to come to her home.

With this encouragement and my newly found self-assurance with the Washington position, I thought I was cool and calm as I walked up to her front door to keep our date just two nights before I was to leave Berkeley. There was only one problem. I was so excited that I showed up on her doorstep almost a half-hour early. I must have run part of the way or I was very nervous, for she later told me that I was perspiring so profusely that I took the varnish off the chair I sat on all evening.

I met her parents and sister, and then, almost on cue, they quietly withdrew, leaving us alone in the parlor. Grace was genuinely friendly and cordial. I was hardly myself, I was so thrilled just to be with her. I felt as if I either babbled or sat as silent as the sphinx and gaped at her. For me, it was an enchanted evening. All my dreams were coming true. Grace Noble was more beautiful than ever. She was even more charming, intelligent, and delightful than I had imagined. The hours flew by. It was after midnight when her mother appeared to suggest that I might be getting too tired, what with my long trip ahead.

As I left Grace, she expressed hopes for my success and added, "Drop me a line sometime, Mr. Albright."

I managed to blurt out, "Thanks for a lovely evening and good-bye, Miss Noble." I cursed myself all the way home for being such a clod. I knew I was already deeply in love with Grace, and here I had probably wrecked any hope I had to make a good impression on her.

Several days later, at 9:00 A.M. on Tuesday, May 27, 1913, as I was about to leave for Washington from the Oakland Sixteenth Street Station, I discovered that my train was late, so I used the time to phone Grace and asked once again if she really meant it when she asked me to write her. She assured me she did. When my train stopped in Ogden, I mailed my first postcard to her, and when I changed trains in Chicago, I sent her another one. After I arrived in Washington, I wrote a sixteen-page letter postmarked June 1, 1913, 11:00 P.M.

Washington, D.C.
1913–14

My train trip across the continent of the United States kept me spellbound at the immensity, diversity, and complexity of this vast, beautiful country. Arriving in Washington on the morning of May 31, 1913, I checked my suitcase at the station, bought a guidebook, stopped off to have my one and only suit cleaned and pressed while I sat with a rug over me, and then headed for the Interior Department in the Old Patent Office Building between Seventh and Ninth and F and G Streets.

A few minutes after nine I presented myself at the office of the secretary of the interior, Franklin K. Lane. His fine, large office was on the corner of the building, on the first floor. After being welcomed by Secretary Lane and introduced to the appointment clerk, Ronne Shelse, I was sworn into my office as confidential clerk to the secretary and informed that my salary was sixteen hundred dollars per year. I was stunned, as I had understood from Miller that I would get only twelve hundred. This was an astronomical boost for me.

Overwhelmed by this surprise salary, I promptly lost two days' pay by not working that day, Saturday, and thereby forfeiting pay for Sunday also. But I had to find a place to live. I had passed the Young Men's Christian Association on the way to the Interior Department. So when I left the office, I headed back there and was lucky enough to get a room on the sixth floor in a relatively new wing at just sixteen dollars a month. A new acquaintance here advised me of a nearby rooming house owned by a Mrs. Travis that provided breakfast and dinner for thirty-five dollars a month. There were plenty of quick-food places for lunch where a sandwich, a piece of pie, and some milk could be picked up for twenty-five cents.

Through the summer of 1913 I fulfilled a wide assortment of jobs. I was a real jack of all trades. My position as confidential clerk to the secretary called for me to do anything that he or Assistant to the Secretary Miller requested. And for the first month I had to fend for myself, as Dr. Miller did not check in for work until July 1. Miller's and my office was connected with Lane's and his secretary's—not directly, but with doors to each. So I moved the furniture to facilitate our work, organized files, and then read everything available about areas of Miller's responsibility.

When Miller did arrive, he quickly found that his job of overseeing national parks, eleemosynary institutions such as St. Elizabeth's Hospital for the Insane, the territories of Alaska and Hawaii, and the departmental inspectors wasn't all that interesting. He found a lifesaver in Bertrand Acker. This wonderful individual was an assistant attorney assigned to head the Miscellaneous Section of the Chief Clerk's Office, the division of the Interior Department charged with procurement of supplies, payment of vouchers and salaries, and supervision of mails, files, and personnel. Among other things, Acker had to watch over the bonding of disbursing agents, prepare the annual report of the department, and oversee the national parks and monuments.

Acker was devoted and faithful to the interests of the parks, although they were a loosely grouped bag of miscellaneous units. He was a terrific worker, a master of department procedure, and a strict conformist to principles and practices of administration. It was he who, over the years, had worked out the contracts for operation of park concessions and had developed the rules and regulations for the care and protection of these parks. When projects were submitted to the secretary that seemed to Acker to be out of line with basic principles laid down by Congress for the protection of parks, he promptly killed them if possible.

So when Miller quickly showed his interest in few things except the parks (and no detailed work with those), Acker was fortunately standing beside him and was allowed to continue his work as before, shaping policy and advising on matters of legislation. One important thing that Miller did was to appear with J. Horace McFarland before the Public Lands Commission. They made a fine presentation for a national parks bureau, but as usual it was premature.

WASHINGTON, D.C.

As Miller pulled away from his Interior Department job to advise on economic matters, most of his work devolved on me. And I in turn became a devoted student of W. B. Acker. He was a kind, thoughtful, intelligent person who grounded me in departmental affairs, encouraged me to attend law school, and was always ready to help when I was overwhelmed by work or ignorance.

In 1913 the Interior Department was small. I did everything imaginable, covering a wide range of items scattered over the forty-eight states and the territories. We had only eight departmental inspectors, troubleshooters, to keep an eye on these areas. However, many troubles arose that didn't call for one of these inspectors but did call for me to make decisions about them. One of these was a stagecoach robbery in Yellowstone National Park. I spent two days reading up on the park and meeting with personnel from the War Department to settle this problem. The park was in the Interior Department, whereas the army supervised and protected it. I always remembered this as my first real contact with a national park.

In a small way I was involved in the Hetch Hetchy controversy. Secretary Lane had been city attorney of San Francisco and had fought for a grant of rights to the Hetch Hetchy Valley, which was a magnificent, deep, glacier-carved gorge through which flowed the Tuolumne River. It had many features similar to Yosemite Valley—granite walls, waterfalls, unique domes and spires. John Muir called it another Yosemite, or more often a "yosemite," a term he used for all these glacier-cut gorges, including those of the Kings and Kern Rivers. Secretaries of the interior from 1900 on had consistently refused to grant rights to dam Hetch Hetchy to provide water for San Francisco.

Franklin Lane's appointment to the cabinet was made specifically for the purpose of pushing this project through, the so-called Raker-Pittman Bill. There was tremendous opposition from John Muir and the Sierra Club, newspapers, magazines, and just plain citizens who realized that the loss of Hetch Hetchy would be irreparable. Letters came into Lane's office by the thousands and had to be answered. I, along with several other secretaries, had to learn to counterfeit Lane's signature and sign letters in reply, trying to explain why the grant should be made or saying "careful attention" would be given to the protest. I hated this job, for I was in sympathy with the protests. However, Lane and the Congress prevailed, and President Wilson signed the grant into law on December 13, 1913.

It is possible that something good came out of this because Lane now gave some attention to national parks. These were floating orphans in the department, not attached to any bureau. Bills had appeared in Congress time and again to create a bureau to administer them, but were ignored or died in committee. Congressman John Raker had again introduced a bill in 1913, and Lane suggested that Miller be responsible for dealing with members of Congress to try to get this bill passed. Miller did testify, talk to a few friends, and entertain a few at dinner parties, but the legwork was assigned to me. He said it was good experience for me to get acquainted with representatives and learn how to lobby at the Capitol.

So the first thing I did was to learn about national parks. With the help of W. B. Acker, I quickly absorbed a vast fund of knowledge in this field. When I felt I was ready to tackle the Capitol, I spent long hours up there, meeting the proper congressmen, trying to interest them in this legislation. National parks didn't arouse much enthusiasm, and the Raker Bill died in both the 62d and 63d Congresses (March 1911–March 1915).

Sometimes when Secretary Lane's private secretary was sick or away, I had to fill in there. Once I almost got into a real pickle. Lane called me into his office. He was furious over some editorial in a California newspaper that had blasted him. He said to me, "Get a notebook and take a letter." I hesitated and stammered out that I could type quite well, but I wasn't much of a stenographer. He said he didn't care—just write down what he said.

So he reeled off this letter to the editor, and it was a real tirade. When I got to typing it up that night, I found my notes were a complete jumble. From what I could remember and what I could pick up in my shorthand, I felt the letter was just no good, too nasty. I used as much as possible and substituted a few thoughts. In the morning I typed it up on his letterhead and presented it to him. He read it over.

Scowling, he said, "Albright, I don't think this is the way I dictated this letter."

I replied, "Well, it isn't exactly, Mr. Secretary. I did the best I could, but I told you I wasn't much of a stenographer. I couldn't make all of it out from my notes." He kept looking at the letter, frowning and muttering to himself, apparently puzzled about what he had really said. I stood there, trembling all over. At last he put me out of my misery by reaching for a pen and signing it without another word.

Washington summers were close to unbearable. While the civil servants labored on through the hot and humid days, the high officials fled to cooler climes. Knowing little about areas over which they had jurisdiction, Secretary Lane, Adolph Miller, and their wives went west to inspect national parks, reclamation projects, and Indian reservations. At a parade in California, Lane suffered a severe attack of angina and had to remain there for some time. Miller returned alone. I always thought that Lane never seemed really well after that experience.

Actually, the summer was a blessing for me. It gave me a breather. On Sundays, my one day off from work, I did a great deal of sightseeing. Being a nut on history, I toured the Civil War forts and all the museums and famous buildings around Washington. Then I walked the Chesapeake and Ohio Canal. It took me three Sundays to complete the whole route. Then I tramped over the battlefields of Manassas and other nearby Virginia and Maryland scenes of the 1812 and Civil War fighting. I took the overnight cruise to Mount Vernon. I used my pass to the Library of Congress to read and read and read. With everything I did, I found new interests, so I needed more books to find information about them.

Although the weather was close to unbearable, I religiously followed the daily routine I imposed on myself shortly after arriving in Washington. I rarely got to bed before midnight, but I was up around 6:00 A.M. With my friend Neil Judd, an archaeologist at the Smithsonian, I ran down to the tennis courts, played tennis for an hour, ran back to the YMCA, had a shower, and breakfasted at Mrs. Travis's rooming house. Afterward I walked a mile from Twentieth and G Streets to Seventh and F and was in my office promptly at 9:00 A.M. At lunch I walked to Fifteenth and F for a glass of milk and a piece of pie.

Usually I had time to spare during my lunch hour, so one of my favorite things was to stop at the Geological Survey in the Iron Front Building to chat with some old explorer. As there was no retirement age in those days, I could usually find some wonderful characters of eighty or so still working. I learned an enormous amount of history and geography from their tales of nineteenth-century days.

With all my busy schedule, I never forgot Grace Noble. I got a letter off to her nearly every day telling her of my exciting experiences. We were corresponding regularly now. Once I dared ask if she were engaged. She replied: "I'm not engaged, have never been engaged, and don't know that I ever will be engaged!" She later told me that when she wrote that, she practically proposed to me. Her words certainly gave me hope that maybe I had a chance to win her myself.

The one drawback in leaving Berkeley was giving up on law school. During the summer, I decided I had a firm enough grip on my job at the Interior Department to go back to law school. I investigated all my local options and found that Georgetown University fit my needs. It did not have the new Harvard case book system as did the University of California, but it had the advantage of instruction by some of the finest lawyers and judges in the Washington area. Classes were held five nights a week until about 9:00 or 9:30 P.M. I could take the courses only a few blocks from the office. And thank goodness, for many times my work would keep me until a few minutes before class. Then I would sprint that short distance, sink into my seat, and listen to my stomach growl. No dinner again. Although I knew I had my work cut out for me, I believed it was worth it to get that degree, so I signed up for the winter term.

Between work at the office and increased time spent at the Capitol on the national park problem, law school at night, and extra duties Miller requested, I found my six hours (or less) of sleep a night was my only respite. That first year in Washington I had practically no social life. There simply wasn't time for it, although some had to be squeezed into the twenty-four hours. The Millers were a very social couple and entertained a great deal. Often they found they had an extra lady on their hands and knew exactly where to find a spare bachelor to be her partner at dinner. Miller had given me his old formal dress outfit, so I didn't even have that excuse. But fine cuisine was served and the guests were interesting and many times proved useful in the future.

One man whom I saw several times there was Franklin D. Roosevelt, the assistant secretary of the navy. He always escorted a beautiful woman, not his wife. She was never really identified. Seventy years later I read an article in *American Heritage* about the great love of his life, Lucy Rutherford. And sure enough, there was a picture of this lovely lady of long ago.

Once Roosevelt came into the office to call on Lane. I was temporary secretary to Lane that day, and while Roosevelt waited to see him, we had a nice conversation. He told me that he had come to see Lane about the "Franklin Club," which was composed of men named Franklin—Franklin Houston, the secretary of agriculture; Franklin Lane; himself; and another man whose name I have forgotten. They got together to play poker or other card games.

Shortly after Adolph Miller returned from the West in the fall of 1913, President Wilson called on him to help formulate the Federal Reserve system. During most of the time until the bill creating the Federal Reserve Board was passed in December 1913, Miller was away from our office, and the burden of extra work for me was difficult to handle.

However, I learned a great deal in a very short time, and it was invaluable to me a year hence.

When Miller was appointed to the new board in June 1914, he resigned from the Interior Department and asked me to come with him. I truly did not like finances and banking, and anyway I was planning to return to California to practice law as soon as I graduated from Georgetown.

Of course, with Miller's exit, I was most uncertain about my own job. I had a frank talk with the secretary and found him to be very warm and concerned about me. He suggested that I continue all my normal work, and, with my law school training, I could now start working along with the solicitor of the Interior Department. It was a big boost for me, and I found I had more and more work in both old and new fields.

The year 1914 was eventful and confusing. There was always interesting work at the Interior Department. There were tempting offers to join prestigious law firms in San Francisco as soon as I received my law degree. Best of all, Secretary Lane promised me a long-awaited vacation to California. Before leaving on that, I graduated from Georgetown University and passed my Washington bar exams. I also took and passed the California bar in Los Angeles and then headed for San Francisco, where my primary objective was to convince Grace Noble that she should marry me.

After a visit with my dad in Bishop, I arrived in Berkeley on July 26. Knowing that Grace would be at church on this Sunday morning, I went to visit my mother, who wasn't too pleased that I was anxious to see a special girl she had not chosen.

Many sly questions and some delicate probing by my mother followed every one of my futile phone calls to Grace. Early on, she had picked out brides for each of her sons. Obviously, I was totally unconcerned about Bessie Fish, her choice for me. A few years hence Leslie also slid past her to pick Marie Bradford, a college classmate. Dewey actually did get engaged to her choice but managed to get that called off while in the army. He married a different girl too.

When one of my calls to Grace was suddenly answered, all I could say was, "Hello, I'm here."

She laughingly replied, "And I'm here—why don't you come here, too!" Of course, I was out the door in minutes. Grace was everything and more that I had been dreaming about for a year. Her beauty, her gaiety, her intelligence—everything about her was enchanting. We were spontaneously glad to see each other, and it seemed as though we had known each other for years instead of one single evening. Our correspondence had opened up gates of friendship and rapport.

From that time until August 9, we spent every moment together except when Grace had to teach school. I used these hours to investigate job opportunities and visit my family as well as Will Colby and other friends. Together, Grace and I went to the theater, had long talks over dinners, and enjoyed an incredibly wonderful day at Muir Woods.

At Muir Woods, the beautiful stand of redwood *Sequoia sempervirans* was saved from being flooded for a proposed reservoir by Congressman William Kent. He bought the three hundred acres and donated it to the federal government in 1907. President Theodore Roosevelt proclaimed it a national monument the next year. In my efforts at the Capitol regarding the park service, I had gotten to know Kent very well. He was an ardent conservationist and had several times been a sponsor of bills to create the park service, all up to now unsuccessful. Looking back on that day, I knew I wanted to report to Kent that I had seen his gift, but I suppose I was also unconsciously testing Grace, wanting to see what sort of an outdoor girl she was. She passed the test with flying colors.

I called for her very early in the morning and discovered another plus. She was right on time and waiting for me, dressed for the day's outing in a nice suit and sturdy walking shoes. She had a superfluous fancy hat on, but that only added to her charming appearance. We took the ferry across San Francisco Bay to Marin County and then the Mount Tamalpais and Muir Woods Railroad to the monument. This took about two hours altogether. The monument was nestled in a sheltered canyon on the lower western flank of Mount Tamalpais. We wandered through the magnificent grove of trees, and Grace got her first experience of Horace Albright on a sightseeing expedition. In other words, we had to see the *whole area* while I read her excerpts from my guidebook. She seemed engrossed in my words, the flora, and the trees.

I was having such a marvelous time that I quite forgot about time. Around noon it was getting warm, and she gently hinted that she could use something to drink. So we went back to a little food stand where I bought some sandwiches, pickles, and milk and walked back to a bench under the trees to eat our picnic. It was a complete failure, for the sandwiches were dry and rather smelly, the milk was sour, and Grace didn't like pickles.

That ended the Muir Woods part of the day, and we returned to Berkeley the way we had come. We were rather silent coming back on the ferry. I, of course, thought I had made a mess of things and was sure I had at least one strike against me. Grace told me later that her silence was simply starvation and sore feet.

On August 6, seeing my time in California drawing to a close, I suddenly realized that, before I left, I must ask Grace to marry me. I had to have her consent. So I went over to Alameda, brought Grace back to Berkeley, and took her to a lovely little restaurant for dinner. There was a full moon as we walked up to the campus and strolled along talking for quite some time. When the path led us to the western edge of the campus near the eucalyptus grove, we stood on the little bridge over a stream that flowed along through the trees. I was so nervous I was shaking with the fear that when I proposed she would procrastinate and not reply or worse still turn me down. I don't even remember this, but Grace said that I began quoting poetry, starting with Longfellow's "The Bridge" ("I stood on the bridge at midnight," etc.) and continuing with "Horatio at the Bridge," and a few more.

Finally I simply blurted out that I adored her and asked her to be my wife. She hesitated momentarily (an eternity for me, for I guess I was holding my breath), and then she accepted and threw her arms around my neck and I got my *first* kiss! After we were married, I asked her why she had hesitated. She said, "I guess it flashed through my mind—do I want this man to be the father of my children?"

On August 9 the weather was foggy and bleak and so were Grace and I. She skipped church, and we spent the whole day together. We tried to discuss our future, but it was terribly uncertain. We knew we had a long engagement ahead of us. The primary reason was financial, because I had no money to support a wife. In fact, I didn't know what sort of a position I would have when I left the Interior Department, which I meant to do in the not too distant future. I planned to practice law, but I didn't know where. Behind all this was my growing concern that a war would intervene.

While I was on this vacation, World War I had broken out in Europe. The Archduke Franz Ferdinand had been assassinated in Sarajevo on June 28. Armies mobilized, ultimatums were exchanged, the world held its breath, and finally on August 4 Germany invaded Belgium, which precipitated declarations of war by England, France, and other nations. Although President Wilson immediately tried to reassure Americans that we would not get into a European conflict, I had a dreadful feeling we might end up in it too. With my military background, I'd surely be in the forefront of those to be called into the army. Of course, I never mentioned this to Grace. So we left it that she would continue teaching school, and I'd stay in Washington until I decided on my future.

Then it was a difficult good-bye, with many "I love you"s and promises to write every day (and we rarely missed). I took a taxi to the station and boarded the Western Pacific train at 8:10 P.M.

Leaving my lovely new fiancee was terrible, and it was quite a letdown to get back to Washington. I found my responsibilities and workload had doubled. Although my title and salary remained the same, Secretary Lane, knowing of my admission to both the District of Columbia and California bars, extended my "clerking" to features involving the law and legislation. Of course, I always had the responsibility of Miller's work, as the assistant to the secretary position had not been filled and it seemed that it probably never would be.

One of the first things I did, in a personal way, was to borrow money. I had never done this before, but I had to get Grace an engagement ring. Not only did she need one before she could announce our engagement, but I guess I was always afraid someone would come along and steal her away from me while I was in Washington. It wasn't easy to acquire this loan. Most of my friends were every bit as poor as I, but someone, not I, told Huston Thompson about my problem. He assured me that he was good for whatever I needed and urged me to get "as beautiful a ring as your Grace is beautiful." I couldn't have found one like that, but I bought a lovely plain gold ring with one reasonably sized diamond in a so-called Tiffany setting. I must add that I repaid the entire amount of $275 before Christmas to Thompson, a real friend. But when you add in her October 23 birthday present, a small gold pendant and chain, you will see why I didn't eat very often.

As to my work at the Interior Department, there was a new authority in the national parks section. Early in 1914 Miller decided to set up an office with a small staff in the West to inspect the parks, plan for their development, make estimates of costs for improvements, and purchase supplies. He selected Mark Daniels to head it.

Daniels was a University of California graduate in landscape engineering, 1905. He had later taken some graduate work in landscape architecture at Harvard. Miller was very interested in this subject, and, faced with the need for professional help with his new home and grounds at

2320 S Street in Washington, he inquired about a landscape architect. A friend suggested Daniels. Miller asked him to come to Washington. He not only arrived promptly, but he made an instant and profound impression on Miller. Daniels was a very smooth and personable young man, a fine speaker, a wealthy man-about-town type who had his own lucrative architectural firm of Daniels & Wilhelm in San Francisco.

The cost of the new parks office was to be prorated against the appropriations for the various parks. Each park received a separate appropriation from Congress rather than a single one for the Interior Department to dole out. Daniels, as general superintendent and landscape engineer of national parks, went back to San Francisco, set up his field office in the Mondnock Building on Market Street, hired a competent assistant, R. R. Young, and a staff of clerks. With these men, among whom was a part-time employee, Dan Hull, he planned needed buildings, gateways, and other facilities. Hull later proved a very valuable engineer in the National Park Service.

The only real contribution Daniels made was the design of the Park Service uniform. He started with the basic Forest Service outfit, threw in a little feeling of the military uniform, changed a little bit of this and that to jazz it up, and added new decorative features. He forgot about the hat, so everyone wore about what he pleased.

However, Daniels's failings were many. He alienated powerful men like Louis Hill of the Great Northern Railway, and he instituted the most complicated accounting system anyone had ever devised. Even trained government accountants shook their head in puzzlement and disbelief as they tried to understand the value assigned to stacks of pipes for possible use in the future, trees that might or might not be cut to construct a building, etc.

Actually, I had little or no contact with Daniels until Mather arrived. The truth was that no one person was exclusively concerned with the business of national parks until much later.

Knowing the time I had allocated myself to remain at the Interior Department, I now had to give serious thought to my next career move. My main objective was always to return to California to get into mining and water rights law, but I chafed at the idea of joining a firm such as Lindley's. One night, on the spur of the moment, I wrote Beverly Clendenin, a classmate, and suggested that when he finished law school, we should form a partnership to practice together in California. His instant reply was yes.

On January 14, 1915, I wrote back:

You don't know what a world of good it did me to receive your letter during the holidays, just when I was about as blue and homesick as it is possible for a man to get and still endure the agonies of it all. . . . I am delighted to know that you have given my proposition to form a partnership favorable consideration. Now, Clen, it seems to me that we should decide definitely, in the very near future, just when we will begin our practice. . . . I think I can arrange to be there August 1, but I may go through the national parks with Assistant Secretary Stephen T. Mather, '87, who has just been appointed to fill Professor Miller's old position. He has requested me to act as his private secretary for a time, and I think I will go with him. . . . It will be a relief to work with Secretary Mather, and if I can get a trip through the Northwest and back home again, it will be worth my while to take up my old duties again as he wants me to do. The Secretary has told Mr. Mather that he is agreeable to my leaving here, inasmuch as I am determined to leave the whole Department in a short while anyway. . . . In case I do go with Mr. Mather, I shall not be able to reach Berkeley much before August 1st, and, of course, I could not go right on to the southland immediately. Someone in Berkeley will demand a week or two at least . . . but I will be ready on September 1st for sure.

Of course, these plans for the future were derailed forever by the second most important event in my life (naturally Grace was the first). If you believed in astrology, it could be said that the stars ordained that the paths of Stephen Tyng Mather and Horace Marden Albright were destined to cross.

Enter Stephen Tyng Mather
1914–15

I never referred to Stephen Mather as Steve or even Stephen. He was always "Mr. Mather." That summed up the love and respect I had for the man. He altered my life forever and made me a better man for it. There was an old saying: "These fellas remind me of each other—they're so different." That fit Mr. Mather and me. And yet the longer we were together, the more we melded into one team, an indivisible unit. The relationship we formed in 1914 not only deeply enriched my life, but I believe proved of great significance for our beloved country.

It all began in December 1914. By now I was handling most of the work assigned to Adolph Miller's vacated office as well as tasks in Secretary Lane's office on a regular basis, various interbureau problems, and congressional matters. I also was forming plans to leave Washington permanently when the winter was over.

Unknown to me, Lane was investigating a new man to fill Miller's position. It came about in this way. There were always hundreds of letters to Lane with complaints of one sort or another. He was a diligent worker and actually read scores of these and, what's more, paid attention to some. He even answered a few in longhand. One day in the late fall of 1914, a particularly critical but very interesting letter came to his attention. It was written by a Stephen T. Mather of Chicago. It seems he was a native Californian, had become a millionaire with a borax business he had out there, was a member of the Sierra Club, made frequent vacation trips, climbed mountains, and took an active interest in the national parks of the region—and happened to be a graduate of the University of California.

Mather's letter was an angry protest against the exploitation of the parks, the conspiracy of private businessmen to steal land on which the giant sequoias grew, and the attitude of the government—the Department of the Interior in particular—in ignoring, actually abandoning, its sacred trust to protect them. The letter was long and contained specifics as to his complaints.

Lane was intrigued by this letter. A short time later he visited Chicago, talked to a friend named John Wigmore, dean of the Law School at Northwestern University, and inquired whether he knew a Stephen Mather. Wigmore did, and he later told of his relationship with Mather:

Somewhere around 1900, a young friend of mine, an instructor in chemistry in the University of Chicago, used to do the analysis of samples of borax for Stephen Mather's company. Mather was just succeeding in his independent struggle against the so-called borax trust and his industry was headquartered in Chicago. It must have been through this young chemist, Frank Burnett Dains, that I first made the acquaintance of Stephen Mather. Mather being a patriotic Californian had organized in Chicago a California Club, and was President of it, and, as I was born and brought up in California, Mather was always urging me to be faithful in my attendance of the California Club. This accounts for my personal acquaintance with him. In the meantime, another chapter of acquaintance was going on with Franklin Lane. When I left Harvard College in 1883 and went back to San Francisco, a group of young men organized a Municipal Reform League. Frank Lane and myself were two of the active members. The League broke up when the young men were separated by fate in different directions, but Lane and I had kept up our acquaintance and mutual respect and affection. So in 1912 Woodrow Wilson was elected President and Frank Lane, in 1913, after having been Interstate Commerce Commissioner, was selected as Secretary of the Interior, and one day in 1914, when he was passing through Chicago, he had this interview at the Blackstone Hotel. The name of Stephen Mather had been mentioned to him, but I have no recollection how he had learned of the name. But he did *not* know Mather personally. So I arranged a luncheon in order that he and Mather could become acquainted, and he could make up his mind whether Mather was his man to take up the administration of the

National Park System. Mather's company by that time was very prosperous, and Mather was a highly patriotic admirer of the possibilities of California. I suppose that this was the reason why I thought that he would be a good man to take up the question of improving the National Park administration—that we need more good citizens who are able and willing to relinquish the pursuit of the dollar and undertake public service. At any rate, you may take it as certain that this meeting at the Blackstone Hotel was the reason why Frank Lane selected Stephen Mather to be the Director of the National Park System. I do not remember who was the third person at the Blackstone meeting.*

[Signature]

* In fact, I was the third person.

The story of Lane and Mather has been recorded in history quite differently. I myself probably cemented it into fact, as I think it was the story circulating around the Interior Department before Mather actually came to work there. The tale went that Lane and Mather were old friends from the University of California and that when Mather complained about the state of the national parks, Lane wrote him: "Dear Steve: If you don't like the way the national parks are run, why don't you come down to Washington and run them yourself?"

In reality, they didn't know each other. Mather had graduated from the University of California with a Bachelor of Letters degree in 1887. Although registered in the class of 1889, Lane never did graduate. Adolph Miller, who knew both men quite well, graduated in Mather's class and affirmed that the two were not personally acquainted until 1914. So let's go back and straighten out the history of Stephen Mather's trail from borax executive to assistant to the secretary of the interior.

The Sierra Club had been organized in 1892 with John Muir as its president. In 1904 Stephen Mather had become a member when his attention had been caught by the twin crises in which that organization was embroiled—the proposal to dam the beautiful Hetch Hetchy Valley of Yosemite and the recession of a huge section of that park, including the Minarets and Devils Postpile, at the insistence of mining and logging interests.

The following year Mather joined the annual mountain outing of the Sierra Club, this one at Mount Rainier in Washington. During this climb, he became good friends with Will Colby, Joseph Le Conte, and others with like interests in the Sierra Club, as well as members of the Mazamas, a similar organization of the Northwest. Through discussions around the campfire at night, the faith, devotion, and philosophy of these associates of John Muir made a deep impression on him.

A few years later, in 1912, Mather made the first of his own mountain trips in the Sierra. Again he met Colby and other Sierra Club members. One of the highlights of Mather's life was the opportunity to have a long talk with the legendary Muir, whose whole life at this time was devoted to fighting the Hetch Hetchy dam. To save this twin of the Yosemite Valley from flooding simply to provide a never-ending source of water for the city of San Francisco was the flame of Muir's passion, which caught fire in Mather. Muir had also interested him in another of his vital concerns—the addition of vast majestic Sierra areas to Sequoia National Park or, better still, the creation of a new park between Yosemite and Sequoia. Mather picked up that banner too.

Also in 1912, Mather came to Washington and attended the congressional hearings on the Hetch Hetchy proposal. Little is known of his involvement, if any, in these hearings. However, he must have made an impression there, because in June 1913 Robert Bradford Marshall, chief geographer of the U.S. Geological Survey, answering a letter from Mather, stated: "Yes, indeed, I well remember, and still appreciate the pleasure of having met you at the memorable Hetch Hetchy Hearing in Washington last Fall, and I feel quite positive that your presence had considerable to do with the powerful decision of the Department in answer to the San Francisco question."

In 1913 Mather was back in California. He learned that his friend from college days, Adolph Miller, was about to leave for Washington to become assistant to Secretary of the Interior Lane and would be in charge of national parks. Mather quickly arranged a meeting and discussed the proposed extension of Sequoia with him. He obtained from Miller the latest maps of the region, sent to him from the Geological Survey by Robert Marshall. Then he contacted Marshall, writing that he had been "out in God's country" and had been involved with Colby, Miller, and others concerning the Sequoia project and offered to help in any way possible.

Marshall picked up on this overture, for he saw an opening to offer his ideas on national parks to Miller. As Marshall wrote to Will Colby:

> I should be glad to know Prof. Miller as intimately as he would allow, but solely for the good of the national park question as a whole, as you know one of my greatest delights is to help the cause in any way possible. Secretary Lane, of course, is busy beyond reason, and it is a human impossibility for any man to grasp all of the details of the propositions that come before the Department of the Interior. He must, therefore, of necessity, rely upon others to advise him before final action, and if I can be of use in any way in that line, either direct to Secretary Lane or through his assistant, Mr. Miller, I shall be more than glad to do so.

The same day Marshall wrote to Mather, advising him that Hetch Hetchy would eventually go to San Francisco, but that the ones who had fought for Hetch Hetchy should now use their influence to work on a new concept for the Sierras. It would be a park that contained "what might be called three Yosemites—the Tehipite, Kings River Canyon, and Kern River Canyon." He closed his letter by writing: "I am grateful for your remarks to Mr. Miller regarding my knowledge of parks in general, and I shall be very glad indeed to give him any information I possess on the subject, and hope that he may have the time in the near future, to pump me dry."

Mather jumped on Marshall's suggestion about working for a Sequoia extension or creation of a new park. From then on, he kept in close touch with Marshall, receiving new maps of the Sierra from him, arranging for possible publication of his articles on the parks, and finally setting a date at the Prairie Club of Chicago for him to lecture on the national parks.

In August 1913 Marshall, in Washington, wrote Mather about the California situation, saying that "Muir and the Sierra Club are doing all they can for the cause at long distance, but it needs some real live man on the ground here to handle the matter personally. I wish it were possible for you to shoulder the task."

Was this the first seed to be planted in Mather's brain?

In March 1914 Mather proposed a "Tahoe to Mt. Whitney" trip. Marshall enthusiastically agreed to join the party if official duties didn't get in the way, but he would at least provide information, maps, and suggestions on other people to accompany Mather. Deeply affected by the back country of the Sierra Nevada and intense discussions with his companions, Mather came out of that trip not only a devotee of the area and concerned about its future but also an emerging supporter of the concept of a national park service.

And so it would have been perfectly logical to assume that Mather talked these matters over with his friend Miller—and possibly Marshall—and then wrote the letter described in history. No one I knew had ever actually seen the legendary letters to and from Lane, but the factual background fits the picture.

Now back to events after the luncheon meeting of Lane and Mather at the Blackstone Hotel in Chicago. Lane was obviously impressed by Mather's personality, energy, and knowledge. But he had another reason for considering him to fill Miller's position. Lane was ever alert to get men of the Miller-Mather type, for he himself had never had an adequate income. He had always been dependent on his small salary, and these men were in a position to do things with and for him that he couldn't do himself.

One day Miller called to alert me that Lane was considering a man to fill his former job, and this fellow was coming to Washington to discuss the possibility. He didn't give me a name, but I soon learned it was Mather when, a few days after this conversation, I was summoned to Lane's office to meet him.

Mather and Lane had been closeted for some time, having a long discussion in the secretary's spacious office. Lane had outlined the work Miller had been brought to Washington to do and what had been accomplished, in particular about the federally owned parks. He stressed the fact that they were orphans. They were split among three departments—War, Agriculture, and Interior. They were anybody's business and therefore nobody's business. The time was ripe for some person who really cared to wade into the problem, get them united in a strong, separate bureau, and get Americans acquainted with their own scenic and historic sites instead of spending their time and money in foreign countries. Lane made it clear that Mather's job would mainly be to lobby Congress for a national parks bureau. Lane pointed out that he was hog-tied on that score for he was a "marked man" because of leading the fight for Hetch Hetchy.

Mather had seemed to be extremely interested as long as the conversation stayed on parks. Then Lane added divisions that Mather would be responsible for overseeing—the hospital for the insane, territorial problems, the Bureau of Education, and others. Mather blanched and protested that he just couldn't work with all the government red tape, policy differences, and situations he knew nothing about.

Lane hurriedly assured Mather that he wouldn't be concerned with much of anything except parks, that he'd be practically a free agent. "Just get out in the country, size up the park problems, and do a broad public relations job, so that you can convince the Congress of establishing an independent park service bureau. Besides that, this is a real opportunity for you to do a great public service." Not knowing the man, he probably didn't realize the final bit of persuasion was the type of thing that got through to Mather.

But Mather still had lingering doubts. "This is all so new to me. I have never been under restrictions or a lot of regulations and I'm just not temperamentally fitted for this type of work in Washington. I'll probably get into trouble before the job is an hour old."

Lane replied: "I'll give you a young fellow who knows the ropes and who'll handle the legal and other hurdles you'll run into. He's the man to keep you out of trouble, someone who knows the department, can handle the routine administrative work, and—wonder of wonders—a fellow graduate of the University of California whom Miller brought with him last year."

It was at this point that Lane sent for me.

From the moment I walked into the room and met Stephen Mather, I was struck by his appearance and personality, and, oddly enough, I have always said that I instantly felt a strong kinship with him. He was old enough to be my father, a bit taller than my six feet, with prematurely white hair, piercing blue eyes, and a smile that radiated friendliness, gentleness, and kindness.

Lane told Mather and me to go sit down over at the north end of the room beside an open hearth where a fire was burning brightly. "Talk it over," he said. "Let Albright explain the work already done, the problems ahead, and the situation for the future. He's been on this thing for some time, knows the roadblocks."

Mather and I settled down together on the brown leather couch. He immediately threw the ball to me by asking about my background in California. Where had I come from? When had I been at Berkeley? Why had I come to Washington with Miller, and what did I intend to do with my life in the future? He riveted his attention on my answers, interrupting frequently to pose new questions, jabbing his finger to make a point, restlessly moving head, body, and hands as he talked. His was a lightning fast brain with an electric nervous energy to go with it.

When he seemed satisfied that he had learned enough about me (for the time being), he switched to interrogation about the position he had been asked to fill. He listened to my summary of St. Elizabeth's Hospital and other fringe matters with which he would be dealing. Then impatiently he cut me off and said he wanted to hear about the *real subject* at hand, the national parks. What was the situation with them? What had Miller and I done so far? What was the outlook for the bill to create a park service that was before the Congress? These and a dozen more rapid-fire questions were hurled at me.

I replied slowly, carefully, and as completely as I could. My main emphasis was on the fact that no one person was exclusively concerned with the national parks and monuments. Acker was grossly overworked as it was. Miller had been involved in too many extra activities. I tried to paint a clear picture of why he could make a real difference. My detailed resumé of the progress of legislation through Congress, impressions of individual members, and thoughts on future action seemed to interest and impress him. His deep blue eyes bored into me as he became very quiet and thoughtful, questioning me on every point.

Then he abruptly switched topics by telling me why he thought he didn't want to take the position offered, repeating the reasons he had just presented to Lane. Naturally, I didn't give him any arguments, but he had so interested and excited me with his personality and energy that I found I was trying to make it easier for him to accept the job.

This conversation went on for several hours with no interruption. At last Mather put it to me that if I stayed with him, he'd go along for a year. I protested that I had been about to leave Washington, that I was engaged to a California girl, that I had to make some money to get married, and that I had a legal career waiting for me in San Francisco with Will Colby or with some other firm. As Mather knew Colby quite well, he understood and nodded agreement with my reasoning. But the longer we talked, the more our minds were in harmony. Mather's doubts gradually melted into enthusiasm, and his enthusiasm whetted my interest.

Finally, as it was getting late and Lane was obviously getting anxious to quit for the day, Mather and I rose to leave. Putting his arm around my shoulders as though we were old and fast friends, he said, "Albright, you and I would do well together. Keep your mind open. Let's think about it for a while. This isn't the time for promises, but if you'll stay with me for a year, I'll consider coming down to Washington to run the parks for a year. Think it over. We'll get together after the holidays." And, turning to Lane, he added, "I don't want to make any decisions today. I want to go home and think about all this. I have a family. I have a thriving business to consider. But if we agree on the action to be taken, it's a real possibility that I'll take a shot at running the parks for one year. And I really mean, *just one year.*"

After the Christmas holidays, in early January 1915, Mather returned to Washington. He told Lane that he would accept the offer, but with conditions. He would do everything possible to accomplish the goal of a national park bureau, *but* he would only stay one year. He also stated that he wanted Albright as his assistant "to keep me out of jail."

So Lane summoned me once more. Mather told me directly what his conditions were, and, although I had agonized over the thought of remaining much longer in the Interior Department, now I didn't hesitate a minute. "Yes, Mr. Mather, if you want me to help you for a year, I'll do it." There: I'd said it. I really hadn't asked for time to consider the proposal or even ask Grace. That was the power of the man.

I would be less than honest if I didn't add that Mather made my acceptance a lot happier by promising me an extra one thousand dollars a year to augment my government salary of sixteen hundred. This would be paid out of his own pocket. However, at the time I agreed to remain in Washington, I was unaware of this offer. It was made after I read him a letter from Grace in which she approved of my staying on in Washington, but gently reminded me that she would like to be a part of my life there. This extra pay from a private source was perfectly legal at the time. Within six months he raised his payment to me to two hundred dollars a month. Incidentally Mather himself only received a salary of $2,750 per year. Fortunately, he was already a millionaire, so he didn't care.

Mather moved to Washington immediately and took his oath of office on January 21, 1915. As he was not bringing his wife and daughter to Washington, I located a nice suite of rooms for him at the Powhatan Hotel at Eighteenth and Pennsylvania. This was close to the office and also to the place where I was living. It was very convenient because we were both workaholics. He frequently had me come along to dinner with him and then spend the evening in his suite working on departmental problems.

After he assumed his position as assistant to the secretary, Lane showed him around the office he was to occupy—one adjoining his own with a separate room for myself in between. I had taken the liberty of inviting several high officials of the department to attend the ceremony. When everyone had left except Lane, Mather, and me, Lane shook hands and left us. A moment after he had shut the door, his big, round, smiling face reappeared, and he said, "Hey, Steve, I forgot to ask your politics." Before Mather could answer, the door closed once more. Lane did not ask his politics, then or ever, although he surely knew that Mather was a Bull Moose Roosevelt Progressive. After lunch in the department dining hall, Mather and I toured the building, stopping in to visit with various people on the way. When Mather had seen enough of his new surroundings, we walked six blocks to the U.S. Geological Survey offices so that I could introduce him to George Otis Smith, the director, one of my mentors, and a great friend of national parks.

The next day of Stephen Mather's education was when I took him to the Capitol. The first office we visited was that of Representative John E. Raker, the co-sponsor of the bill to create a national park service. The two men hit it off as though they had known each other for years. They had many mutual friends and experiences in the Sierra Nevada. Most interesting of all, their ideas for this future park bureau were almost identical. Raker grew more cordial as they talked and was obviously excited that the Interior Department now had a man who had the authority to act decisively on behalf of the national park legislation he had introduced. Raker rushed to a closet in his room and brought back a stack of copies of his bill for us to pass around to people who might help us. On the spot we made plans for strategy at the hearings before the Public Lands Committee. Raker then hurried us down the hall to an office to meet another member of that committee and, after getting his approval, swept us along to meet more strategic congressmen. As I saw time and again through the years with Mather, his personality and enthusiastic energy carried everything before him as he charmed one important person after another.

The late afternoon forced us to call a halt to this frenetic activity. We settled on a visit to the Library of Congress, where Mather obtained a Congressional Directory to bone up on the members of the Senate and House committees we would face in our hearings.

When I got into bed that night, I finally had a chance to think. I came to the conclusion that Stephen Mather and I would make quite a combination. He was an experienced public relations man, created instant rapport with strangers, had a personality that radiated poise, friendliness, and charm, could talk easily with anyone he met, confidently instilling perfect strangers with his enthusiasm. It was hard for me to dig up reasons for my being a help to Mather except that I was knowledgeable about Washington, the Interior Department, and the Congress, was quite good at detail and administrative work, which he obviously hated, could help with legal problems, and, above all, was loyal and conscientious. And, at twenty-four years old, I was as healthy as an ox, able to work half the night as well as Sundays and holidays for him. Most of all, I so admired him that I found I was imitating him right from the beginning.

CHAPTER
5

Personnel and Personalities
1915

One of the first things the new partnership of Mather and Albright faced was park administration. A lot of Mather's criticism to Lane had been about the miserable conditions in the national parks he had visited, not just the rundown physical aspects, but the dirty, unhealthy conditions of lodging, food, and sanitary facilities. He blamed most of these on the men in charge of the parks.

Mather learned there was a general superintendent, Mark Daniels. Without even knowing Daniels, he disapproved of him and his whole setup. Mather questioned me very closely about the period during which Daniels had held the position of general superintendent and landscape engineer. I tried very hard to be diplomatic, as I personally liked Daniels. So instead of giving out much information, I simply handed over the department file. One of the first things Mather read was an account of the Louis Hill episode.

Hill, president of the Great Northern Railroad, was vitally interested in Glacier National Park. His railroad had built the hotels and chalets, even many of the roads, in the park. He welcomed the opportunity to meet with Mark Daniels. Hill had a private car waiting in St. Paul when Daniels joined him. Attached to the train were special cars that contained Hill's private limousine and his favorite horses. Fine food and plenty of "wet goods" smoothed the long trip to Glacier Park.

As Daniels and Hill were enjoying a leisurely horseback ride out in the park, Hill idly wondered why Mount Henry was bald, with trees growing only partway up the sides. Daniels instantly pulled out his little information notebook to see how much money there was in the congressional appropriations for Glacier. The sum was three thousand dollars—the entire appropriation for Glacier's administration, protection, and construction. Everything! Daniels made the grand gesture. "Mr. Hill, I have three thousand dollars with which I will reforest Mount Henry. There will be trees all the way to the top." Hill, who knew a lot more than Daniels about Mount Henry, was horrified. Instead of pleasing Hill, it threw him into a rage. He thought Daniels was absolutely crazy, tore up plans for the rest of the trip, and, returning to St. Paul, called in his lawyers and ordered them to file charges against Daniels. Nothing ever came of it though.

One day Mather called me in and said he had to make a decision about Daniels. Although he had done some good things in the way of designing park structures, they had turned out to be vastly too elaborate and costly. In short, any good points were counterbalanced by his odd bookkeeping system and his abrasive treatment of people he considered beneath his social level.

I was thrilled when, for the first time, Mr. Mather asked for my evaluation. I spun this around for a moment. Does a twenty-five-year-old "clerk" speak up with an honest assessment that might be at odds with his boss, or does he slip smoothly out of any definitive answer? Instantly I decided I could never be anything but totally honest with this man for whom I was developing such respect. I gave my opinion of Daniels in a few words: intelligent, artistic, clever, good conservationist, erratic, poor administrator, no financial sense.

Mather was always a very fair man and listened carefully. Then he quietly tore up his chart on Daniels and decided to do nothing until he got to know him personally. It was a method of decision-making that I saw repeated many times through the years of our partnership.

Next Mather turned to the problem of personnel running the individual parks. Most of them were political appointees. Many positions were filled when political power changed in a state or in Washington.

Mather decided he would hold a conference of park supervisors to meet and evaluate them in person and lay before them his ideas, plans, and principles. He decided to hold this meeting in San Francisco. He had come to the conclusion that the two great expositions to be held in San Diego and San Francisco in 1915 afforded the opportunity to publicize the national parks and encourage waves of visitors to Yosemite and Sequoia. Through the increased interest and visitation to the parks and the attendant publicity generated from this, he could focus congressional attention on a bill to create a national park service. So he called a conference of supervisors to be held in Berkeley in March 1915.

This was the first time I witnessed Stephen Mather in action. It was something to see.

Mather had one more idea to put into motion before we left for California. He was at heart a public-relations man and wanted the country to be aware of the national parks. He felt that he needed a full-time publicity man and contacted an old friend from his reporting days in New York—in fact, the best man at his wedding. At this time Robert Sterling Yard was the Sunday editor of the *New York Herald*. Yard was enticed into giving up his job and moving to Washington, where he would be in charge of publicity for Mather. As there was no money available from the government, Mather guaranteed him five thousand dollars a year out of his own pocket. Yard would join him immediately to make the trip to California with us. Thus was born a gifted and brilliant public-relations team of Mather and Yard.

With plans and ideas popping from Mather's head every minute, I was frantically busy trying to carry them out and, at the same time, perform all my usual duties and a good many of Mather's routine ones. From the very beginning, he said that he hated office work, administrative minutiae, what he called *chores*. With his nervous energy, he simply couldn't sit still at a desk and handle details. He preferred to conduct business with people he felt were important to his plans over long lunches or at elegant dinner and theater parties. He felt he could accomplish more this way than with the normal business methods. And in many respects he was right. Mather of Chicago made himself a known, well-liked, and admired personage in Washington in a very short time.

While we were working on plans for the conference in San Francisco, Mather was faced with a more serious matter—*money*. The chairman of the House Appropriations Committee was a rough, tough Irishman from Brooklyn, John J. Fitzgerald. He was the original penny pincher, suspicious of any new monetary proposal and ruthless in questioning witnesses. Mather was advised by everyone in the Interior Department to pad his proposed budget because Fitzgerald would chop it with a meat ax. He disregarded this and stated firmly that he would handle government finance as he had handled his business finance—honestly.

He could do nothing about the current appropriations bill before the Congress, estimates for the fiscal year beginning June 1, 1915. But he was prepared with a list of projects for the 1916 bill. One of the first proposals he made before the committee was to allow the government to accept donations of money or land for national parks.

Fitzgerald took an instant dislike to Mather because he had never heard of anybody wanting to donate expensive territory to the government. Even with help from William Kent and other newfound friends in the Congress, Mather didn't fare very well, and he temporarily put appropriations on hold. He concentrated on happier thoughts—his San Francisco conference.

Rounding up his personal party for the trip to California, Mather chose seven men. Robert S. Yard went to keep pumping out publicity during the trip. W. B. Acker, assistant attorney in the Interior Department, was included not because he was the only person who had a comprehensive grasp on operations in the parks, but because he had fought hard against invasion of the parks, especially Hetch Hetchy, and was also a formidable exponent of maintaining parks in their natural state with as little development as possible. Guy E. Mitchell, chief of the Executive Division of the U.S. Geological Survey, was knowledgeable about parks in general and a fierce adherent of them. Robert Marshall of the Geological Survey was already in Mather's mind to head a national parks bureau when it was established. Colonel Lloyd Brett, an army officer, was superintendent of Yellowstone National Park. California's Congressman Denver E. Church was an important adherent of Sierra parks near his Fresno district. And finally, Horace Albright went as private secretary, man Friday, and handler of all details.

Mather had gone on ahead of us to Chicago, but the complete party assembled there and on March 3 boarded a unique private Pullman car from the Santa Fe Railroad, named Calzona. It was most luxurious, with drawing rooms and bedrooms on each end and a spacious midsection, furnished beautifully with club chairs and tables for our conferences. Little touches for our comfort and pleasure were added, such as a writing desk equipped with engraved railroad stationery, cigar stands and spittoons (the latter fortunately unused), a table with glasses, pitchers of ice water, and, if requested, something stronger to drink, and a small phonograph with a rack of records ranging from Caruso to Victor Herbert's operettas and current dance music. As low man on the totem pole, I had the job of winding the phonograph up when someone felt like music. We thoroughly enjoyed this railroad car with all the comforts of a luxury hotel.

Mather held conferences most of the way across the country. This was a favorite diversion of his, for everyone to sit around and "jaw," as he put it. We discussed almost everything concerning parks, the upcoming conference in Berkeley, legislation, and personnel. But our conversation ranged far beyond that. One time the topic would be deadly serious— how to get the Grand Canyon made a national park while at the same time crossing swords with powerful mining men and the United States Forest Service. The next time it would be stories of Yard's and Mather's younger days as newspapermen in New York, the most memorable being the hilarious tales of Mather's scoops during the famous Blizzard of '88. And on and on.

Through an interesting coincidence, we added another man to our party as far as Trinidad, Colorado. This was Major General Hugh L. Scott, chief of staff of the U.S. Army. He was in civilian clothes on a mission to the Ute Indians, for he was one of only a few white men who were experts in the use of Indian sign language. Our acquaintance with him paid off later because of his agreement with us to remove troops from Yellowstone Park. He and Colonel Brett mapped out how this might be accomplished.

So every minute on Calzona was an interesting and educational experience for us all. In those few days, we got to know each other well. The camaraderie made us real friends.

The party arrived at La Grande Station in Los Angeles at 6:20 P.M. on March 7. We were there only long enough for Calzona to be switched to the last section of the 6:30 regularly scheduled train bound for San Diego (held for an extra half hour while our car was being attached). We also left Congressman Church at the station.

In addition to Mather's innate curiosity to see new things, we were led to San Diego by his desire to meet some old friends and interest them in helping to promote a national park bureau. He also wanted to study the big exposition being staged there in conjunction with the one in San Francisco. He was interested from the architectural standpoint because he already had in mind the need for distinctive structures in the national parks.

We arrived in San Diego at 9:50 P.M. and were met by newspaper reporters and an array of dignitaries from the Chamber of Commerce. I learned for the first time that Mather reveled in this sort of thing. He always had a speech ready for the occasion. He didn't fail this time, and it duly showed up in the newspaper the next day.

In 1915–16 there were two expositions to be held in California, in San Diego and San Francisco. Both were to glorify the state and commemorate the opening of the Panama Canal. Additionally, San Francisco wanted to show the world how the city had risen like a phoenix from the ashes of the earthquake of 1906. So of course Mather's first order of business was to have an extensive tour of the exposition as well as the famous zoo in Balboa Park. At the latter, he insisted that one of his group feed some of the wild animals. This surely separated the men from the boys. Marshall proved the bravest, feeding a mother lion and cubs.

After one last coverage of the exposition, we boarded Calzona, were honored guests at a banquet in Los Angeles, and by 10:00 P.M. were headed north once more. After we settled into our berths, Mather took us all by surprise: "You can't go to bed now. We're making a stop at Lang to show you where some of my mining properties are located." It was the middle of the night in the middle of nowhere when we dutifully got out in the desert and stared into the darkness while Mather and his partner, Thomas Thorkildsen, by the light from the train windows, ruminated over a map and discussed mining. I could hardly believe this day was still March 8—or was it March 9?

As I lay in the darkness, listening to the rhythmic click-clack of the wheels, I shook my head in wonder. I was certainly learning a lot about Stephen Mather. I thanked my stars I was young, strong, and healthy. His energy would have killed someone who wasn't. Had I not been so exhausted, I would have been too excited to sleep, as tomorrow I'd be in San Francisco, only a few minutes and a bay away from my precious Grace.

On Monday, March 9, our train pulled into San Francisco early in the morning. It was a beautiful day. Well, was is the right word. Mr. Mather and I went up to the Palace Hotel, where I got him settled in a fine suite on the third floor. When I was ready to leave, I told him I'd be staying at my mother's home in Berkeley and gave him the telephone number. He looked surprised and asked: "Where are you going? We have many people to visit here in the city. It'll probably take all day. Then I have arranged for a dinner party tonight at the hotel for a group interested in Yosemite and the Tioga Road. Very important that you take notes on this."

Here was another decision to be made. Do I just quietly put my entire private life on hold or do I draw a line? Again I had to weigh the problem carefully because I would be working under Mather for a year. I liked and respected him and felt an honest relationship was the best policy, so I replied, "I'm sorry, Mr. Mather. You know I have a fiancee here in Berkeley who has been very patient and understanding about my work in Washington and my decision to remain with you for a year. We haven't seen each other in over six months. With the conference starting tomorrow, we'll be very busy, so I know I won't see much of her then. I'll work with you today until time to catch a boat for the East Bay to meet her when she's through teaching."

He obviously was not used to someone objecting to his instructions. Silently he gave me what I always called his "eagle-eye stare." Then abruptly he said, "I want to meet this girl. Go to Berkeley, see her and the family. But bring her back to the Palace for dinner at eight."

Emboldened by this, I added that I must have some other free time for her even if it was during the conference. He shrugged his shoulders, nodded, and told me I only had to attend important conferences and committee meetings. He'd see about evenings. We had forged another link of understanding and friendship.

I took the broadest interpretation of Mather's instructions and left the hotel immediately, caught the ferry for Berkeley, and went directly to my mother's home. She was surprised and delighted to see me, as were my two brothers when they came in. Dewey had graduated from Berkeley High School and was splitting his time between working and attending Wilmerding in San Francisco, learning both building trades and mortician techniques. When he received certificates in these, he could go home to Bishop and step into Dad's businesses. My older brother, Leslie, had graduated from the university in 1914 but had stayed on to work toward a master's degree in history. We had lunch together while I filled them in on all my doings and heard theirs. It was wonderful to see them again, busy and happy.

Even though I knew it was too early for Grace to be home from her teaching job, I walked over to the Nobles' home and ate another lunch with Mrs. Noble. Of course, Grace knew I was in the Bay area but had no idea I was in her kitchen. So when she came home, she banged the front door closed and dropped whatever she was carrying on the hall table, chattering all the time to her mother about some event at school. As she rounded the corner into the kitchen, she didn't see me for a minute. Then she did! With an Indian war whoop she flung herself on me, dancing up and down, kissing me and babbling happily. Really not knowing her too well, I was rather taken back—but totally delighted. Grace was twice as beautiful as I had even dreamed, so vivacious, with her big brown eyes dancing like stars in that lovely face.

Her mother quickly remembered that she had some marketing to do, which left the engaged couple to catch up on their six months apart as well as discuss the future. Actually we had only a few hours, but we did make one major decision. We would somehow get married this year. The addition Mr. Mather had made to my salary was now sufficient to support two of us. Grace also had saved a good deal of her small salary and was ready to throw that into our pool for transportation, furniture, or whatever. It was amazing that two people who had been together so little could have such a deep understanding and love for each other. I think our correspondence had plumbed the depths of our minds. We were best friends as well as sweethearts.

About six o'clock I called a taxi, and Grace and I went in style to the ferry, crossed over to San Francisco, and went to the Palace Hotel. I sent a bellboy to tell Mr. Mather we were in the lobby, and he came down right away. On meeting Grace, he was obviously stunned by her beauty. She certainly was a vision in a lovely peach silk gown, wearing her grandmother's gold earrings and the little pendant on a gold chain, my first gift to her. I was equally enchanted by her. Don't forget, I had never seen her dressed up in "Palace Hotel high fashion."

Mather led us to a quiet corner, ordered some refreshments, and excused himself, saying he had some business to take care of before his other guests arrived. I don't know where he went, but he was back in a short time. In one hand he had a corsage of roses and, in the other, a small box. He handed both to Grace and laughingly said, "I don't know how Horace could ever have been lucky enough to get you. I wasn't around at that time, but I wish you all the happiness in the world." Inside the little velvet box was a small Tiffany brooch, silver with a diamond in the center. Grace was overwhelmed, and, always spontaneous, she jumped up and gave him a bear hug and a kiss. He threw his head back and just roared with laughter, saying that was the finest reaction he'd had to a gift in years. They were dear, close friends from that day on.

The other guests appeared very soon: six of them, all males. The only problem that arose from eight men and one woman was that everyone tried to sit next to Grace. Mather, of course, got one side and A. B. C. Dohrmann the other. It was all right with me, as I could look directly across the round table at her. Mather ordered a delicious dinner and fine wine. And I learned something new about my fiancee. She refused the wine, stating very courteously but firmly that she did not drink alcohol.

Aside from a few polite remarks about the dinner and inquiries about our trip, the conversation was entirely on Yosemite and the Tioga Road. Mather explained that he had already had discussions about this with another group of friends, including Sierra Club officers, at lunch that day at the Bohemian Club. The more he talked, the more excited he got about his plans for the road.

Finally he bluntly said: "I got you all together to call for contributions to buy the Tioga Road toll rights. I already have an option on them which calls for payment of about fifteen thousand dollars. I've put up one thousand myself and held up my partner, Thorkildsen, for another thousand. The Sierra Club has pledged funds and the Modesto Chamber of Commerce made me a pledge, so I have about eight thousand raised or pledged. How about it? If each of you put in one thousand, the deal is closed."

Needless to say, he had his money right then and there. He went on to close the deal, acquired the Tioga Road, and thus opened a new entrance to Yosemite Park. He even got one of those men at our dinner, an attorney, to handle the legal work, free. This was my first real experience with Mather's mesmerizing power of enthusiasm and persuasion. It was not the last by a long shot.

Mather had arranged for his national park supervisors to meet at the Sigma Chi House on the University of California campus at Berkeley on March 10. This was merely to greet his twenty-four guests while I assigned rooms and straightened out any problems they might have. I settled on Bob Yard as my roommate. Mather had been a Sigma Chi here and had later donated money for this new house. He had arranged with the current members to evacuate it for a week. He paid them to go to a hotel or bunk up with friends in other fraternity houses. His excuse for using the fraternity house was that he wanted to bring his park people together in a convivial and fraternal atmosphere, the spirit he wished to instill in his organization. He felt the park personnel would gain a feeling of camaraderie, a unity of purpose to accomplish his ideas and plans.

At 10:00 A.M. on March 11 the conference opened in California Hall on the university campus. There were about seventy-five men: superintendents, supervisors, and custodians of national parks and monuments; representatives of concessioners, transportation, and railroad companies; officials from other governmental agencies such as the Forest Service and

Bureau of Entomology; officers of the Sierra Club; several congressmen; and just anyone interested in the future of the national parks and monuments. One was Enos Mills, the "Father of Rocky Mountain National Park." Arthur Arlett represented the governor of California, and Mrs. E. T. Parsons of Berkeley had simply read about the conference in the local paper and come to see what it was all about.

Although Stephen Mather was the titular head of the conference, he did little more than introduce speakers. He recognized his lack of knowledge about the parks and the people in charge of them and about those operating the concessions. Basically he turned it over to Mark Daniels, the general superintendent and landscape architect of national parks, who was not only quite knowledgeable about the parks but also a good public relations man, a fine speaker, and an engaging personality. Furthermore, he was young, handsome, and projected an image of a leader, forcefully presenting ideas and plans for the future.

One of Daniels's most interesting ideas was his "village" concept. Probably because he was primarily an architect, he visualized that when visitors to a park became numerous, five thousand or so, the visitors' area would resemble a small city and should be treated as such. As a "village," it must have all the amenities of a municipality—water, electricity, telephones, police, a sanitation system, and food and lodging accommodations of all types. Projections should be made for future growth of tourism and for additional "villages" as needed. This was a perfect example of the grandiose visions that Daniels advocated. Although Mather liked the idea of small "villages," he didn't want "cities" in his parks.

Mather had scheduled an interesting evening at the Sigma Chi House and had suggested that I bring Grace. The dinner was to be put on by the ladies of the Sierra Club, with Joseph N. ("Little Joe") Le Conte and Will Colby, president and secretary of the club, as hosts. I was bursting with pride as I introduced my fiancee to the gathering that night. We had a great time with tales of Sierra outings, entertaining stories from our park supervisors, and, with Grace at the piano, loud and enthusiastic singing. And I learned something new about my chief. He had a fine baritone voice and loved to belt out the songs.

On March 12 the conference opened an hour later, again in California Hall. Mather and I decided it was important that I attend both sessions because they featured the men who actually operated the parks. As we had known few of them before this meeting, Mather told me to take notes, sizing them up. We'd compare our impressions later. Among others, the speakers were Walter Fry, supervisor of Sequoia National Park and the leading authority on forest fires; Gabriel Sovulewski and David Sherfey, supervisor and resident engineer from Yosemite; Samuel F. Ralston, supervisor of Glacier; Dr. W. P. Parks in charge of Hot Springs; and Colonel R. A. Sneed and Charles Ziebach of Platt and Sullys Hill National Parks. It really tested my concentration to stay awake when the latter two gave interminable talks on areas that were far below standards for national parks.

I came back to reality when I suddenly realized that W. B. Acker was at the lectern. He gave a fine talk on the history of the national parks and was followed by Roe Emery and David Curry, both fiery concessioners. No one could have slept through their speeches. When the conference broke up, I made it a point to speak to both of these men as well as other concessioners like Ford Harvey and Enos Mills, sensing they would be extremely important in the future.

Later, when we were back at the Sigma Chi House, I singled out the only two men who represented national monuments, Chester Campbell of Petrified Forest and John Otto of Colorado.

Mr. Mather was rather indifferent toward national monuments for two reasons. In his opinion, they were substandard to national parks, and most weren't "natural scenic wonders," although there were exceptions like Muir Woods. Obviously everyone, including Congress, ignored them financially. From the information I had read in Washington as a history buff, I had found most of them fascinating, especially those in the Indian country, such as Rainbow Bridge, Chaco Canyon, and Navajo.

It was shocking to me to learn that Campbell and Otto received only one dollar a month compensation for overseeing their monuments. Worse still, they actually were expected to pay their own way for the trip to Berkeley. That showed how little Mather and I really knew about our park system. I told Mather about this, and he felt equally badly. Before we left, he sent his personal checks for their expenses, an advance of $150.

This awakened us to take a closer look at the welfare of our twenty-three orphan monuments. Actually, they stayed ignored by Congress for a long time, so there was little we could do for them. The general public rarely knew they existed, or they were too far off the beaten track to visit. With no tourist traffic, there was no money from the Appropriations Committee.

I'll tell a little bit more about John Otto to illustrate the sad condition these monuments were in and the even sadder condition their custodians faced. I had instructed Campbell and Otto when they returned to their monuments to send me an expense account detailing the advance Mather had given them. I also told them that if there was any money left over, they were to return it to Mr. Mather. Well, Campbell's came in immediately with his check for about fifty dollars, but I didn't hear a thing from Otto. Finally on May 5 I wrote him a letter reminding him of my orders and also said I was "disappointed" in him.

Well, poor fellow, I guess he was really wounded, for back came not one but two separate letters as well as his New York bank draft for forty-six dollars. He apologized and said he'd put the money owed Mather in the bank thinking that "Mr. Mather may come through our way some other trip soon," and he'd give it to him then.

Needless to say, I felt terrible about the "Hermit of Monument Canyon," as he was called locally, who spent most of his life single-handedly improving and taking care of his monument—all for twelve dollars a year. I immediately wrote him, praising his work and assuring him that "I am not feeling at all unfriendly to you. Both Mr. Mather and myself are very much interested in your work, and ever since hearing your description of the Colorado National Monument, we have been looking forward to some time of meeting you in Grand Junction and going through the Monument with you."

As Mather was going to have a cozy dinner at the Sigma Chi House with his park personnel only, I decided I could slip away for a short time. I had gotten intrigued with these men and wanted to know them better, so I explained to Grace that we could go out to dinner, but that I felt I should join the group at the fraternity house afterward. As always, she was quiet and understanding. We ate at a little Chinese restaurant in Berkeley and walked back across the campus, just as we did on the night we got engaged, and I left her house by nine o'clock.

Then I joined the gang at the Sigma Chi house. It was a real rouser, for Mather was a great mixer and had broken the reserve of his guests, who were pretty much his age or older. It was quite an opportunity for both Mather and me to get to know these experienced men—and learn a great deal from them, I must add.

The next morning our conference changed locale. We all assembled at the Fillmore Street entrance to the Panama-Pacific International Exposition in San Francisco at 10:00 A.M. Few conference participants except national park people appeared. We were met by a full-fledged band, a group of officials in high silk hats from the Southern Pacific

Railroad, and Arthur Arlett, who greeted us on behalf of "my illustrious chief, Governor Hiram Johnson, and through him, our Commonwealth."

We were escorted by the band, blaring out martial music as well as University of California fight songs, to the Union Pacific exhibition pavilion. We must have been a rare sight for exposition visitors. Who on earth were these peculiar-looking fellows who warranted a brass band? There was no standard uniform yet for national park people, so every man was dressed differently: odd pants, boots, shirts, and hats—a pretty scraggly lot. Only a few of us "dudes" from the East were in suits, ties, and city hats.

The members of our party were to be the luncheon guests of the Union Pacific at its replica of the Old Faithful Inn, outside of which was a scaled-down version of a geyser with hourly eruptions, just like the real thing in Yellowstone. About midway to the inn, we happened to pass a bathing beauty concession. Here people could pay to go inside to see lovely girls swim around in a pool and then lie out on a sundeck to dry and show their forms in, for those days, shockingly abbreviated bathing suits.

Mather and his small Washington contingent kept marching to the Old Faithful Inn without noticing that most of his park personnel had dropped off. So when he looked around and found the majority missing, he ordered me to go find them. I did, but they flatly refused to come to the inn for lunch. I was too young and had no authority, so I gave up, went back, but didn't dare tell Mather where they were. He fussed and fumed, but our remnants, being honored guests, ate lunch and then walked to the afternoon session of the conference in the Southern Pacific Hall.

Again Mather told me to find "those bastards," strong language for him. Of course, I knew where they'd probably be. Sure enough, they were still looking at the bathing beauties two hours later. This time a few men listened to me, but most never budged until I rounded them up to go back to Berkeley late in the afternoon. I never did tell Mather that I had known where they were all the time.

Back at the Sigma Chi House that evening, Mather let bygones be bygones. He had invited a group of the evicted Sigma Chis for dinner with his men. During the evening he asked the fraternity boys to render some college songs and cheers. Now most of the national park men were past middle age, hard-bitten outdoorsmen, and few had been near a college prior to this conference. They stoically sat through the entertainment until the Sigma Chis suddenly gave the University of California's rousing fight cheer, "Oskie Wow Wow, Whiskie Wee Wee." With that one old fellow loudly exclaimed, "Thank God, it's finally time for a drink!"

The next morning the Sigma Chi House was vacated, when most of the conferees left for their homes. Only Mather, Yard, Marshall, and I stayed on. Yard wanted to delve into information at Daniels's office. Mather had another project in mind.

When I had moved Mather back to the Palace Hotel in San Francisco, he suggested we talk over an idea he had. I had already learned that "talking over" an idea meant listening while he restlessly paced around the room, gesturing to make his points, his words barely keeping up with his mile-a-minute brain.

He had decided that he would pick a park as a model for others in the system. Yosemite, of course, was his favorite. He would build or expand all necessary facilities, such as sewage disposal and a power plant. He would renovate lodging where possible, construct new hotels and eating establishments if necessary. And he had already decided that the latter things were necessary.

He kept using Mark Daniels's word "village." I finally spoke up and asked, "Does this mean stores, hotels, restaurants—like a village or town has?"

Everyone had gotten a good laugh out of Mather's statement at the conference a few days before: "Scenery is a splendid thing when it is viewed by a man who is in a contented frame of mind. Give him a poor breakfast after he has had a bad night's sleep, and he will not care how fine your scenery is. He is not going to enjoy it." Now he ignored my question and instead asked, "Horace, what do you think about my idea?"

Another fork in the road, another decision for honesty, agreement, or ducking the question. I replied, trying not to cross him but to downplay the whole thing, "I really didn't like Daniels's idea from the start. This sort of thing could get out of hand, grow into a nightmare that could overpower the natural scene. Maybe if you were always there to check on it, but someone like Daniels, who thinks in rather grandiose terms, could allow the growth of the 'village' as tourist traffic increases. Well, a veritable city could spread across the floor of the valley. Why don't you go slow, investigate the situation for a while?"

He sank into a chair, nodded thoughtfully, and remained silent for some time. Then he suddenly jumped up and said, "I don't like David Curry. If we follow Harvey's idea, we could eliminate him from the Yosemite."

As yet I wasn't used to Mather's sudden mental leaps and tried to figure out where his "village" idea and David Curry fit in. Mather had been deeply impressed by Ford Harvey's talk at the conference, in which he strongly advocated single concessions in national parks. Harvey, of course, was the son of the founder of the Fred Harvey Company, which ran the hotels, restaurants, and dining cars for the Santa Fe Railroad, including El Tovar Hotel at Grand Canyon. Not that Harvey felt all concessions should be under the same company, but all of one type should be, such as one lodging concession and one transportation concession.

"Hotels in each national park should be in one man's hands," Harvey had said; "he should not be there simply with a license to get as much money as possible, but should have a definite obligation and responsibility in the way of satisfactory service. . . . I firmly believe that this service must be a regulated monopoly." Mather loved those last two words and used them frequently when he spoke on this topic.

David Curry, who operated a large camp company in Yosemite, had spoken up vigorously against Harvey, saying that the idea was all right for a hotel monopoly but should not include all overnight accommodations; there should be different levels of concessions based on the tourists' ability or desire to pay. There would be competition, not between concessions of the same class, but between different classes. Harvey had agreed and said that was what he had meant too. But Mather had unconditionally accepted the concept of monopoly and clashed with Curry accordingly.

Pacing back and forth in his suite, Mather now began to spell out his thoughts. He expanded on the idea of more and bigger accommodations and services in Yosemite to lure thousands of additional tourists to the park. He grew more and more excited as he talked, and suddenly he jabbed his finger at me and said, "We've got to get going on this whole thing right away. Set up a luncheon or dinner party as soon as possible. I'll give you a list of men to invite to it."

Mather's list for his impromptu dinner party was impressive, some of the wealthiest men in both northern and southern California. I do not know exactly what transpired when they got together, for I was spending my last hours with my Grace. We had a candlelight dinner in San Francisco and *three trips* back and forth across the bay. It was worse than I imagined to kiss her good night—and good-bye. But I had learned through being with Grace that she was always the brave one, the chin-up girl, the smiling Pollyanna, as she was this last night before I had to go back to Washington.

PERSONNEL AND PERSONALITIES

When I returned to the hotel, Mr. Mather was waiting for me. A note in my key box said to come to his room whenever I happened to get in, no matter what the hour. He answered my knock immediately, saying, "Come in, come in. I must tell you what I did tonight." He was elated, as his dinner party in a private room of the hotel had gone well, and apparently his goals had been reached.

He had emphasized to his guests that all California would benefit by travel to the national parks in the state, but new and finer facilities would have to be built to encourage visitation. Together that night they formed the Desmond Park Service Company and agreed to put up $250,000 to get it going, to buy out the Lost Arrow and Yosemite Park Company, and to construct more accommodations. Of course, Mather agreed to invest in it too. Joseph Desmond, a supplier to construction camps (including Hetch Hetchy), was chosen to operate the new company, which would be in direct competition with Curry's camps. To help it get started on a good financial footing, Mather went so far as to promise a long lease for the company, to allow it to install bars and sell liquor in the park, and even to turn over army buildings for immediate extra accommodations. Laurence Harris (owner of a tent and outdoor equipment firm) and A. B. C. Dohrmann (a hotel supply company owner), and probably others as well, would be in a position to make quite a profit for their companies too, so they were chosen to sell stock in the new company.

I remained silent during this jubilant report until he finished with, "Well, Horace, what do you think of all this?" Frankly I felt a little sick, but didn't let on except to point out that there were several elements that would have to be checked out with the Interior Department solicitor. Actually, from a legal standpoint, I was concerned about Mather's ability to give out twenty-year leases, turn over army property, and sell liquor in a national park. Most of all, could he, in his official position, invest in a profit-making company to quash competition?

Nothing dampened his enthusiasm, and I said no more that night. He was so delighted that his conference had turned out successfully, that his Tioga Road was assured, and that his plans for the future of Yosemite seemed in good shape. He was raring to get back to Washington and carry them out.

CHAPTER
6

First Steps toward a National Park Service
1915

On the morning of March 15, the Mather party entrained for the East. It consisted of Enos Mills, Robert Marshall, Mather, and me. At the last minute, Mark Daniels was added. He had heard nothing about participating in the trip until Mather called to tell him when the train would leave. He didn't even have time to shave, and later, in Chicago, he had to buy more clothes because Mather decided to take him on to Washington.

After a brief stop in Salt Lake City, we spent several days in Denver. Mather took every opportunity to publicize the parks. I began to notice an odd thing: that when he spoke, improvement of roads, concessions, and increased tourist travel were his primary concerns. A drive for a national park bureau either came in second or not at all. Most of our time was spent with individuals and business groups interested in Rocky Mountain National Park, which had been created on January 26, 1915, and questions Enos Mills brought up concerning it.

Besides Enos Mills's persistent pushing for extensions to Rocky Mountain National Park, there were delegations urging Mather to promote other new parks in Colorado, particularly a Denver National Park (the Mount Evans region) and a Pikes Peak National Park. He flatly stated that he would not consider anything outside the jurisdiction of the present Rocky Mountain National Park, that he was not interested in "proliferating" new parks when the established ones required so much to bring them up to his standards. But he lavishly praised the areas being promoted and assured their backers that he would keep them in mind.

He did make one bad slip that was to haunt him in the future. Talking about his upcoming meeting with Governor George A. Carlson, he told the *Denver Post* that "there are many matters in which the Department of the Interior will need the cooperation of the state government. We expect to grant concessions for hotels within the park area and *for summer homes as well.*" It was a real slip, for Mather did not approve of inholdings in parks and surely didn't want to add any new ones.

This was an example of how his oratory could carry him away. At the time I thought it would be drowned out in his enthusiastic pep talk on travel: "What we want to do is to get the people coming to this new park. It is not a local park. The people of Chicago are interested almost as keenly in having it created as are the people of Denver and Colorado. It is the nation's park, and what we will seek to do will be to bring as many as possible of the people of the nation here to enjoy its delights." He added that he had arranged for the National Geographic Society to publish an article by Enos Mills about the new park and would have national publicity when the park had its formal dedication in September 1915.

On the March 20, while Mather and I were in conferences, Mark Daniels made a tour of the Denver mountain parks with Frederick Steinhauer, the park engineer, and came back most impressed. He gave an interview to the *Denver Post* and discussed national park rangers for the first time, I believe:

> I expect to be back here in May to begin the organization of your Rocky Mountain National Park as a national tourist and health resort. I will, first of all, have to select two men of Colorado for duty in the park as members of the national parks ranger service. That is a great body of men. It is a service that we are working on now to get it quite clear of all politics and of all political influence. We want to make it as great and as fine a service as the Canadian Northwest police; we want to make it as devoted to the public welfare and as proud of its work, even prouder. The men who get into the national park rangers service must be competent horsemen. They must be skilled in woodcraft. They must know about animals and birds and trees. They must be capable of caring for a lost baby or giving first aid to the wounded tourist. They must be sober men, absolutely healthy. They must be courteous and good tempered. The national park rangers service must be their ambition and their life. The national parks are the playgrounds of the people

of the United States, and the rangers must be men of the kind who can be depended upon and trusted and honored by everybody.

I cut that article out of the paper and saved it as one of the finest statements ever made about rangers.

Our visit to Denver concluded with a dinner in our honor given by the Colorado Mountain Club at the University Club. The president of the club, James Grafton Rogers, had been a fellow journalist on the *New York Sun* with Yard and Mather some years before. We had a lot fun listening to the adventures of the three fellow journalists in the old days in New York.

As we were about to board the train for Chicago the next day, Mather delivered these soaring words to the assembled reporters: "Bring the whole world to Colorado to admire and wonder at your matchless mountain scenery, to enjoy your splendid climate and to make the best possible use of your new national playground, the Rocky Mountain National Park."

As soon as Mr. Mather was back in Washington, he directed all his attention to ways and means of getting the national parks more widely known. He felt he had to get people to use the parks before he could get legislation and appropriations. Too few people knew about them. He believed that Congress had the cart before the horse, that it wouldn't appropriate money until proof was furnished that the parks were being used. Yet with no roads, trails, or other facilities, the parks couldn't be used. The only way to get ahead was to show that people were actually using their parks. So Mather put Yard to work on a giant publicity campaign.

There was quite a problem with Yard. We had no bureau, no money separate from the individual parks, no one to help us unless we "borrowed" people from other Interior departments. Although Mather was paying Yard five thousand dollars a year (about double Mather's own salary), he was not a government employee and therefore not entitled to an office or secretary. Mather got him put on the Geological Survey payroll at one dollar a month so he would have franking privileges and could travel at government expense. He then had me find office space for him. Only rooms under the jurisdiction of the Interior Department could be obtained, so I looked around and dug up two in the Bureau of Mines, which was located in a different building, a block away on E Street. I 'borrowed" a secretary from the Biological Survey for a while until Yard could hire one from the outside. Mather paid for the secretary too.

Mather and Yard turned all their attention to their publicity campaign. They whipped up support by waves of articles in newspapers and other publications across the country. Mather personally contacted writers he knew to pump out stories about the national parks and invitations to tourists to come to them.

At the same time, Yard began a dynamic publication, *The National Parks Portfolio*. It had two forms. One was a buckram folder in which were put pamphlets on the various parks. Grand Canyon was included although it had yet to be created a park and wasn't even under the jurisdiction of the Interior Department. The other edition was bound in a dark green hard cover. When the publications were sold to the public, the prices were thirty-five cents for the buckram, fifty-five cents for the hard cover. They came out in early 1916. They were written by Yard, with fine pictures donated by many sources—individuals, government, railroads, and others. Mather even prevailed on the Reclamation Service to detail its photographer to tour many of the parks and take both motion pictures and still views. He used many of the latter in the portfolio.

Mather himself put up more than five thousand dollars for the plates or cuts of the pictures, and he persuaded twenty-one western railroads to pay for the printing, about forty thousand dollars. The contract to publish the book was awarded to Scribner's, probably by the railroads. More than 350,000 portfolios were issued and mailed out to libraries, travel offices, editors, and others by the Interior Department from lists made up by the General Federation of Women's Clubs.

Later in 1916 a smaller edition was published, called *Glimpses of Our National Parks*, with an edition of 2.7 million copies, which were sold in the parks and in bookstores. This was a simple, all-in-one cheap paperbound booklet, but the text was by Yard and contained a great many of the fine photographs found in the portfolio.

One of my jobs was to supervise the clerks handling this distribution. However, the publication and mailing didn't go smoothly. One day when Mather was out of town, I was called in by Secretary Lane. He said he'd just returned from a cabinet meeting at which Postmaster General Albert Sidney Burleson had informed him that publications were going into the mails not properly mailable under franking laws. He had demanded an immediate report.

Lane smiled wryly at me and said, "Horace, It looks like some of my associates are going to jail." I immediately contended that the book was government property and had been accepted as a gift from Mather just as the Tioga Road had been. Lane passed this on to Burleson, who promptly rejected it. Lane called me back again and said, "You've got to think of something better. This fellow doesn't like me and doesn't like my department. And Wilson likes him a lot better than he does me."

Well, I decided to be like the Greeks and bear gifts, so I took one of our few leather-bound copies of the portfolio, had it wrapped at a gift store, and made an appointment with Burleson. I took the precaution of bringing along a number of our green hard-bound copies for his aides. Burleson was delighted with his gift, and we heard no more about the franking problem. Of course, when he was about to visit Yellowstone the next year, he called me up and gave it to me pretty straight that he expected somewhat of a free ride at hotels and other facilities. I told him politely that the army was in charge of Yellowstone, and I could do nothing.

The publicity radiated by Yard almost immediately produced results. Along with the public's heightened awareness of their "pleasuring grounds" came real progress for the parks in a general sense. As one example, a provision in the Civil Sundry Bill of March 3, 1915, authorized the secretary of the interior to accept land donated for park purposes. This made possible the donation of the Tioga Road and the Giant Forest in Sequoia to the government.

Mather delegated to me the everyday operation and problems in his office as they arose, as well as liaison with congressmen regarding the park service bill to be presented at the next session of Congress. He paid little attention to anything except public relations. He traveled constantly. He made an extended trip to the West Coast in May 1915. Part of it was on the Desmond hotel business in Yosemite, and another was a visit to Mount Rainier.

At the supervisors' conference in March, Mather had decided to let the matter of replacing worthless managers drift until he could find replacements. He had to make a change in Mount Rainier, however. When Lane became secretary of the interior, he fired the Rainier supervisor, Edward Hall, and replaced him with a real hack politician named John J. Sheehan. He was old and incompetent, and complaints to Mather said he was skimming off government money into his own pocket.

Mather found Sheehan worse than reported and promptly fired him, replacing him with Dewitt Reaburn. This was Mather's first "field" change and first experienced supervisor, a former topographical engineer from the Geological Survey. Before Mather even got back to Washington, however, the situation erupted, and I was summoned to Lane's office. He had received a tearful letter from Mrs. Sheehan, pleading with him to reinstate her husband. It seems that Lane had been in love with Mrs. Sheehan before either had married. Lane was very upset and asked me, as a lawyer for the department, what he could do. I in turn went to our department solicitor, who dug up a commissioner's job in Tacoma for Sheehan. Sheehan ended up with a better job at a higher salary.

Mather again returned to California the next month by way of Grand Canyon. Secretary Lane had directed him to see about a memorial to John Wesley Powell. A fund of ten thousand dollars had been appropriated for the Interior Department to erect a fitting memorial to the intrepid explorer of the Colorado River. He had been the first man to travel the length of the Colorado and go through the Grand Canyon by boat, in 1869 and 1872.

Mark Daniels had designed a bronze memorial plaque, and Mather seized on the opportunity to dedicate it by letting forth a stream of publicity to raise the interest in and awareness of the Grand Canyon. "Make this unbelievable wonder your next national park," he proclaimed to the press. But he found himself stymied about the plaque because a crafty Arizonan by the name of Ralph Cameron had filed mining claims on Sentinel Point, where the plaque was to rest. This just made Mather more angry and determined to safeguard this great chasm by creating it a national park, and he left the problem of placing the plaque to me when I was to come to California later in the summer.

In between cross-country trips, Mather raced around the East Coast cities, involved in publicity efforts. Sometimes he had me accompany him. I made my first trips to Boston and New York. In the latter we stayed at the Chemists Club, where Mather kept a permanent suite. One night we went to the Ziegfeld Follies, where Will Rogers performed his roping tricks. Another time Mather took me up to his ancestral home in Darien, Connecticut. Belonging to him now, it had been in the family since the 1600s, a beautiful white colonial home on a large wooded estate.

Sometimes I could slip away to enjoy the interesting events of our capital city. Around this time, there was to be a reenactment of the Grand Army of the Republic victory parade of May 23–24, 1865, to promote further "healing of the wounds." All Union and Confederate veterans were invited to participate. I was a member of the Interior Department's planning group and found ways to have two veterans I knew be brought to Washington to march in the parade: John W. Meldrum, U.S. commissioner (judge) for Yellowstone Park, and R. A. Sneed, superintendent of Platt National Park. Coincidentally, although in opposing armies, they were both wounded at Fredericksburg. It was a memorable sight to see hundreds of these proud soldiers marching to the stirring band music of "Dixie" and "The Battle Hymn of the Republic" while their battle-scarred flags waved above them. Like thousands of others lining the avenue, I had tears in my eyes, realizing the horrors they had suffered in the war of brother fighting brother.

Because the tourist season of 1915 was almost on us, there was an urgency to ready the parks for the anticipated increase in travel. Mather appointed a committee to investigate whether automobiles should be allowed into Yellowstone. Colonel Brett, the superintendent of Yellowstone, was to be the chairman.

However, Mather was too impatient to wait for Colonel Brett's evaluation. He heard that the House Appropriations Committee was to tour western reclamation projects, so he got himself attached to it. He simply couldn't sit still in the office. He felt he had to run the parks out in the field. If he could get key men into the parks and they could sit on a rock and talk things out, they could settle problems in a hurry.

He was back on the Pacific coast in June, where he rented a large house at 2231 Piedmont Avenue in Berkeley and set his wife and daughter up there for the summer. He spent some time in Los Angeles with his partner, Thorkildsen, on their Sterling Borax Company business as well as continuing problems with the Tioga Road.

Mather caught up with the Appropriations Committee and steered them through Yosemite, where he arranged to bunk with the irascible chairman, John Fitzgerald. He trailed along with them to other parks. Wherever they went, Mather showed them the terrible conditions in the parks—roads, sanitary facilities, transportation, food and lodging. He also pointed out what they (and their appropriations) could do to rectify the problems. In Yosemite he outlined his "master plan" for roads, the "village," and new accommodations.

In Yellowstone Mather showed the committee the problem of these roads and the conflict between automobiles and stagecoaches and let them in on the decision to allow cars to enter on August 1, 1915. Almost one thousand tourists enthusiastically drove their autos around the Loop in Yellowstone in that one month before snows closed the park.

While on the trip out west, Mather saw what effect this person-to-person approach had produced. He had gained enormous influence and personal friendship through firsthand experiences. So why not get a group of influential people from various fields of expertise together, take them out in a national park, and gain their enthusiastic support for Congress to pass a bill creating a park service? Why not dramatize the parks by getting editors, congressmen, publishers, and businessmen to go? After all, they couldn't write or drum up interest in the parks unless they knew about them firsthand.

Mather excitedly laid the plan out to me, and I was just as enthusiastic. "There's no time like the present," he said. "We'll make the trip this summer."

He chose Sequoia as the park to visit, for he felt the Sierra Nevada was the most spectacular scenic area we had in the system. Also, he was deeply interested in the enlargement of Sequoia with the addition of the spectacular Kings and Kern River canyons. By letting his party experience this area, he hoped to emphasize the need to add it to the existing park.

Out of his own pocket Mather would pay for everything for everybody—transportation to and from California, the latest camping equipment, all expenses of the pack trip including food and cooks. The trip would be for several weeks and would include twenty or thirty people. It was a grandiose scheme, but by now I knew him well enough to realize that the expedition would be a once-in-a-lifetime experience and exactly in his style. After Secretary Lane had given his wholehearted approval, we went to work on it immediately.

Mather drew up a long list of prospects, and I contacted them either by letter or in person. The original selection of thirty-one was pared down to twenty, as many had previous commitments. Robert Marshall of the Geological Survey was put in charge of the "Mather Mountain Party," as it was quickly dubbed. He had spent many years in the Sierra, had explored every part of it, and was eager to help, for he loved the parks and had an ambition to head a park service once it was created. He went to California immediately and began to organize the expedition.

• • •

As mentioned before, Ralph Cameron of Arizona had made a great deal of trouble for Mather because of his mining claims in Grand Canyon. (He made a great deal more trouble when elected United States senator in 1920.) This had resulted in Mather's inability to get the John Wesley Powell plaque situated. Mather directed me to go to the Grand Canyon on my way from Washington to California. He wrote from the park when he was there in June: "You will find the Powell bronze panel reposing on the front porch of the hotel. I got it out of the box myself yesterday and put it up there. Thanks to Mr. Cameron, we are held up in the location of the monument, owing to the fact that he has plastered a claim all over Sentinel Point."

My stay at Grand Canyon was brief, as I could do nothing about the Powell plaque except find a better place to store it than on the porch of El Tovar Hotel. As a matter of fact, it wasn't permanently placed and dedicated until some seven or eight years later.

From Grand Canyon I hurried on to Visalia, California, to join the other Mather Mountain Party members, who gathered on the night of July 14, 1915.

Now let me get back to the Tioga problem. Earlier I related that Mather had put down one thousand dollars of his own money and had gotten commitments of almost another fourteen thousand from others for the toll rights to the Tioga Road. Many had reneged on their promises, however, and other problems arose to prevent getting this abandoned road into condition for tourist use in the summer of 1915.

Mather had a one-track mind about Tioga. It was going to be opened for entrance to Yosemite from the east while the San Francisco and San Diego expositions were drawing the tourists. So he kept pouring in his own money. I don't know how much. Finally he decided he'd get others to chip in to pay him back.

I never did know how he arrived at the exact amount he said the parties could "subscribe" for the Tioga Road, but I do know that he ordered me to try to collect. I wasn't the only one, for I know Thorkildsen, Dohrmann, and several other San Franciscans had lists of "subscribers" too. Mather said I was to get a subscription of five thousand dollars from the Inyo Good Road Club, an organization based in my hometown of Bishop. For a long time Bishop had been pushing for a trans-Sierra highway, so I guess Mather felt they would be ripe to ante up for the Tioga project.

There was only one stumbling block. No one in the Inyo Good Road Club had the faintest idea about who had "subscribed" for them and how on earth their poor little organization could ever dig up five thousand dollars. I questioned Mather, but he just brusquely told me, "Get the money."

I immediately wrote an old friend of the family, Will Chalfant, who was the editor of the Bishop newspaper. He replied, "We cannot learn that anyone on behalf of Inyo has ever pledged this county for such an amount; in fact, we are informed that the suggestion was made by a representative of the Southern California Automobile Club, while his own organization promised nothing."

When I relayed the gist of the letter to Mather in California, he was furious, saying that Inyo and Mono Counties should be grateful for all the publicity and tourist travel they would receive because of the Tioga Road. And he let me understand in no uncertain terms that he held me responsible for delivering the money. It didn't matter how.

I was simply miserable and really had no idea what to do next. When you are only twenty-five years old and regarded as scarcely dry behind the ears by your old neighbors, how do you handle them? And if you don't obey your superior, what will he do? Well, I wrote Chalfant and got some sage advice from the old man (mainly telling me to calm down).

I never mentioned the subscription again to anyone. When asked by Mather about the Inyo Good Road Club, I simply said they had no money to donate. Fortunately, the money needed was somehow "subscribed"—almost all coming from San Franciscans. I never knew of any record that was kept of the total cost and total subscribed. Mather rounded most of it up himself, and if enough was not raised I suppose he just wrote another check. Also, when the legal procedures for turning the road over to the United States were completed, the government stepped in to clean up and regrade the road, so that it was passable for the tourists by midsummer of 1915. The whole episode was a rough learning experience for me, but it did work out all right in the end.

CHAPTER
7

The Mather Mountain Party
1915

The Mather Mountain Party was one of the greatest adventures of my life and one that had an enormous impact on the history of the National Park Service. Members had been arriving for several days by automobile as well as by the private railway car of E. O. McCormick of the Southern Pacific Railroad. The group gathered for the first time on July 14, 1915, in Visalia, California, at the Palace Hotel, for a dinner party hosted by local businessmen. It was a Mexican dinner, not for the weak-hearted, but probably designed to see who would be capable of enduring the exigencies of the mountain party. Later someone reported that "the coolest condition was the Tabasco sauce."

The mountain party was a fascinating mixture of occupations and personalities. The Interior Department contingent, besides Mather and Albright, included Mark Daniels and Robert Marshall. Others were Burton Holmes, renowned lecturer, world traveler, and author, and his cameraman, Frank Depew; Emerson Hough, popular novelist and magazine writer, an ardent conservationist; Gilbert S. Grosvenor, director of the National Geographic Society and editor of its magazine; Peter C. Macfarlane, novelist and writer for such magazines as the *Saturday Evening Post*; Congressman Frederick H. Gillett of Massachusetts, ranking Republican on the House Appropriations Committee and at sixty-five the oldest member of the party; Ernest O. McCormick, vice-president of the Southern Pacific Railroad, a forceful business promoter and leader in the development of Crater Lake National Park; Henry Fairfield Osborn, president of the American Museum of Natural History and the New York Zoological Society, paleontologist for the Canadian and U.S. Geological Surveys; Ben M. Maddox, owner and publisher of the *Visalia Daily Times*, general manager of the Mount Whitney Power Co., and leader in the development of Sequoia National Park; Wilbur F. McClure, California state engineer, the man responsible for construction of the John Muir Trail to connect Yosemite Valley with Mount Whitney; George W. Stewart, Visalia attorney and newspaper editor who had organized the publicity campaign to create the Sequoia and General Grant National Parks; Clyde L. Seavey, member of the California State Board of Control (state finances); Henry Floy, electrical engineer from New York City, Mather's brother-in-law; F. Bruce Johnstone, Chicago attorney and close friend of Mather's; and Samuel E. Simmons, Sacramento physician and brother-in-law of Robert Marshall. Lending critical support were Sequoia National Park Ranger Frank Ewing as chief packer and the Chinese cooks for the Geological Survey, Ty Sing and his assistant Eugene.

The next morning, Thursday, July 15, we were up bright and early, had a good breakfast, and climbed into cars provided by Mather and various Visalia businessmen. The route to be traveled to Sequoia National Park, up sixty miles and six thousand feet, was the narrow, rut-filled, steep, and torturous Colony Mill Road. It was a terrible road, so bad that the passengers often had to pile out of the cars and push to get them over the worst places.

At Cedar Creek camp, halfway up the mountain, we came on an awful mess. There were papers, tin cans, and parts of lunches scattered all over on the ground. Mather stopped the cars and got Gillett and McCormick to help him pick up the debris. When it was spotless, Mather left a sign warning, "We have cleaned your camp. Keep it clean."

The weary travelers felt that the long, trying ride to Sequoia Park was well worth the pain as we gawked at the giant redwoods. A camp was laid out on the floor of the Giant Forest.

A word about the equipment for the outing: earlier Mather had written his guests that he would provide transportation, food, bedding (newfangled air mattresses and sleeping bags), and services. They only had to be responsible for their personal needs. "Our suitcases and city clothes will be left behind when we leave Visalia," he told them, "to be expressed around the point from which we leave the mountains, so that they will be available when we come out." Even so, although there were levis, boots, and western hats present, everyone wore a shirt and tie up the mountain.

That night, after we had changed to "great outdoors" clothing, dinner was served—a sumptuous one prepared by Ty Sing, who was to be the camp cook for the next two weeks. He had been handpicked by Marshall, who knew him from Geological Survey expeditions as the finest gourmet "chef" available. Ty Sing had worked for the survey for twenty-eight years, and for this trip he had brought Eugene, another USGS veteran, as his assistant.

A famous picture was taken by Gilbert Grosvenor to commemorate the "dinner under the redwoods," as Mather called it. It was served on a long table, covered with a white linen tablecloth, but our seating was on logs and, where they ended, wooden boxes. Although we had had little knowledge of each other just the day before, we seemed like old friends by the end of the first evening in Sequoia. Nicknames even emerged: "Chief" Marshall, "Tenderfoot" Grosvenor.

After the fine repast, sleeping bags and air mattresses were laid on the pine-needled floor under the giant trees. Mather warned everyone to stay away from areas where debris might fall, but Grosvenor, unafraid, laid out his bed against a mighty redwood trunk. I felt Grosvenor was so important that I said I'd join him and even offered to inflate his air mattress, thinking how difficult it would be for an eastern "greenhorn" to do this at six thousand feet. I had to show off a little by scorning the use of a pump. Instead I just used my lungs to blow it up. What's more, I stood on the mattress while inflating it. Emerson Hough tried to do the same for Maddox, but had to use a bicycle pump.

This first quiet night in the woods came to an early and abrupt end when Johnstone and a fellow member of the Sierra Club introduced their new comrades to the fine points of mountain reveille. The rousing Sierra Club yell not only woke everyone up but jolted a few nerves to boot.

After breakfast the wranglers brought around horses and mules to be assigned to members of the party. Most picked mules; a few elected horses. Before we left, a famous photo was snapped by Grosvenor that later appeared in the *National Geographic Magazine*. It showed thirty men, arms outstretched, encircling the General Sherman Tree, the largest in the world. Of course, it took the addition of two horses, hidden by the trunk, to complete the circle.

Back in the saddle, we set off through the Giant Forest, led by Walter Fry, supervisor of Sequoia National Park, who, along with a park ranger or a visiting scientist, explained the natural features to us as we rode along.

Arriving at Moro Rock, Mather insisted that everyone, old and young, out-of-shape or not, make the tough climb to the top of this giant outcropping. What little breath we had left after scaling the dome was sucked in when we silently gazed at the awesome panorama of the Sierra Nevada through which we were about to travel.

The following morning, after another ear-jarring Sierra Club yell shook the Mather party out of their sleeping bags, Ty Sing served an enormous breakfast of fresh fruit, cereal, steak, potatoes, hot cakes and maple syrup, sausage, eggs, hot rolls, and coffee.

Horses and mules stood by to be packed and mounted. Ty Sing selected the two most gifted-appearing mules and, from this morning on, would not let another person touch them. One mule carried linens, silver, dishes, washtubs, and Japanese lanterns. The other had two sheet-metal stoves along with Ty's pots, pans, utensils, and special sourdough starter. Each morning Ty would fix a new batch of dough from this venerable starter and pack it next to the mule's warm body. In his own words, this is how it worked: "We late. No time raise biscuit beside hot coals. We got to hustle. Mule get hot on all day trail and raise dough under stove and pots he carry on back. So we got hot biscuit for dinner all right. See?" "Major Domo" Sing rode next to these two mules but never took his eyes off the animals that carried the fresh fruit, eggs, meat wrapped in layers of wet newspapers, and other food.

The weather was perfect, warm and sunny with a soft breeze stirring the high branches of the sequoias, as the Mather Mountain Party slowly wound its way out of the Giant Forest. The saddled riders, followed by the pack outfit, numbered about thirty men and fifty horses and mules. Macfarlane and Stewart had dropped out at Giant Forest.

All day we enjoyed the beauty of the country except for the incessant photography of Frank Depew, who filmed us with both still and motion picture cameras. Of course, everything we did had to be repeated endless times until he was satisfied with his artistic achievements. Over and over, Depew ordered the party to halt as he arranged his scenes. Emerson Hough finally snarled at Holmes, "Look, if I'm going to be a movie star, I want to get paid."

After crossing 8,600-foot-high Panther Gap, the party descended into the mile-deep canyon of the Middle Fork of the Kaweah River, then stopped for lunch at Buck Canyon. Ty Sing would cook deluxe meals at breakfast and dinner but couldn't spare the time to unpack the mules for lunch, so in the morning he made up individual lunchbox meals.

After our midday meal, Mather suddenly jumped up, stripped, and leaped into the icy waters of a nearby stream. Challenging the party as "chickens" and caroling out some appropriate "Buc, Buc, Bucs," he lured in a few brave souls, including McClure and Seavey. Suddenly he spotted me and yelled, "Albright, come on in! This is your native Inyo County water."

Alas, I had never learned to swim because the waters in Bishop were icy Sierra streams, so I shouted back, "I can't swim here. This is Tulare County water."

In the early afternoon we reached our destination for the day, Redwood Meadow, a beautiful area on private land, outside Sequoia National Park. It contained one of the loveliest groves of sequoias in the Sierra. Mather later bought it with his own funds and donated it to the United States government. Arriving at the meadow, we found our pack train unloaded and dinner being prepared.

"Roughing it" was not a term to be used for our dining. As it was every night on our trip, the table was set with a snowy white linen tablecloth and napkins, silverware, and china. Ty Sing and Eugene somehow managed to wash and iron the linen each day in addition to packing, traveling, unpacking, baking, and cooking meals.

Another routine was set up when darkness fell and the air became crisp. Frank Ewing, the head packer, built a roaring fire, and we gathered around it, discussing the events of the day and the wonder of our surroundings.

Sunday, July 18, was a bad day for Ty Sing. One of his mules had been packed early, then let out to graze. When the time came to leave, the mule could not be found. Everyone frantically searched. No mule. Mather impatiently said to forget it, that time was more valuable than the mule. Well, that was all right for Mather, but poor Ty was nearly in tears. This particular mule carried the "delicacies," so no more cantaloupe, fresh lemonade, or sardines and crackers.

The late start affected the party's timetable, and a change of plans had to be made: abandon the route through Farewell Gap and go only as far as Mineral King. We arrived at the Johnson camp in Mineral King about noon, so we had a wonderfully free afternoon, resting, fishing, and exploring. Osborn and Grosvenor set off with cameras and binoculars. Maddox scribbled notes for the *Visalia Times*. Emerson Hough was fascinated with the intricacies of packing and spent his afternoon with the men who handled this chore. From then on, he more often rode with the pack train than with the saddle group. Naturally, Depew was out taking photos. The energetic ones followed Mather in scrambling around the woods and eventually finding some more cold water for a swim. I'd been afraid this would happen, so I had sneaked off into the woods before Mather could catch me.

As if to prove that the tragedy of a lost mule could be overcome, Ty Sing and Eugene spent the whole afternoon whipping up a fabulous dinner of soup, salad, fried chicken, venison and gravy, potatoes, hot rolls, apple pie, cheese, and coffee. Some smart aleck asked where was the vanilla ice cream for his apple pie.

A question arose about the route for Monday. Marshall and McClure, the most knowledgeable about the Sierra, suggested the party cross the Great Western Divide via Franklin Pass rather than Farewell Gap. It would be shorter, faster, and easier. Mather agreed to that and then added, "We don't want to leave any bones behind us." Well, someone immediately asked what was this about bones. Mather solemnly described the hazardous terrain, the steep trail, sudden violent storms, rock avalanches, rattlesnakes, fierce mountain lions, and ferocious bears. And bones? Well, you saw them along the trail. Here and there. Animal and human. Just ignore them. They were just a fact of life in the hazardous Sierra!

Two of the hardy mountaineers slept on Mather's words. Or maybe didn't sleep, for in the morning Burton Holmes proclaimed that he had an ulcerated tooth. Although Dr. Simmons examined him and found nothing wrong, Holmes was adamant that he and Depew would wait at Mineral King for the scheduled stagecoach, although it wouldn't be there for several days. Mather felt pretty bad about the results of his kidding, but later admitted that he had wanted to see how the "fearless world traveler" Holmes would react. Of course, he got more than he bargained for.

Due to this unexpected event, another late start was inevitable. To speed up the journey, the Inyo County boys, McClure and Albright, along with Johnstone, volunteered to hike the steep, grueling trail with the pack train. It was slippery granite sand rising almost four thousand feet in just five miles. The crossing of the Great Western Divide, the approach to barren Franklin Pass, was particularly hard, weaving between the uptilted slabs and the mounds of old snow. At the summit of 11,600 feet, we silently gazed across the lesser granite peaks of the Sierra to the first sight of Mount Whitney, the highest mountain in the continental United States. Hough summed up the scene when he wrote: "North, south, east and west are mountains, and again mountains—and such mountains! A sort of delirium seizes one in surroundings such as these. The world seems very far away, and one seems put back into some primordial state of being in which civilization has not yet dawned."

In the afternoon, there was a steep descent into the gorge of the Kern River via Rattlesnake Creek. It was a magnificent experience except for the trail, which wound down in endless switchbacks. Sometimes seven or eight layers of horses and mules were in view, some heading one way and others seeming to be going the opposite direction. Off and on there were lush meadows, but many were gnawed flat by grazing cattle, which badly disturbed Mather. Once we came across the evidence of a snow slide a few years before with hundreds of trees uprooted or broken off above ground.

Halfway down, Johnstone dared everyone to plunge into an icy pool scooped out of a tangle of rocks. "Here we go again," I said to myself. And sure enough, Steve Mather was the first to drop his clothes and wade in, flapping his arms and making chicken noises to the others. Only four brave men got wet. And I can assure you I was not one of them.

Near the floor of the Kern River Valley, the trail suddenly dropped off about two thousand feet. This last precipitous descent had all but the hardiest gasping and worn out. Even after we reached the level floor of the steep-walled canyon, we still had four miles to ride before reaching camp at Upper Funston Meadow.

While we were fording the Big Arroyo, a major tributary of the Kern River, Johnstone's horse was swept off its feet. Gillett was next and refused to ride across, taking the foot log instead. He proved correct in that his animal was upset in midstream, rescued, but then mired in a bog along with almost every other horse and mule. It was a time-consuming and exhausting job to rescue the animals and ford the river, so when the group finally staggered into camp at 6:00 P.M. they were stunned to see that the pack train hadn't arrived.

Ty Sing with the food had gone along with McClure and me while we hiked on foot. Then McClure said he'd hurry along with one mule and take a "shortcut," leaving Ty and me to follow the regular trail. We joined the main party, but McClure never did appear until late at night, giving the excuse that the supply mule had somehow disappeared on him.

Now that wasn't the only bad news. Earlier in the day, while plodding along the trail, a mule carrying the cook's "essentials" fell sound asleep and quietly walked off a 300-foot cliff. McClure and I, who had been hiking along below, were astonished to see a mule come rolling over and over down the rocks, spraying knives, grapefruit, and assorted items. The mule landed on all fours and promptly climbed back up the cliff. Except for a skinned nose, he was unhurt and, said Hough, "probably never woke up through the whole episode." Poor Ty Sing frantically picked up the spilled items, cussing the mule in every language he knew. That evening Ty discovered his indispensable sourdough starter was missing, so there were to be no more delicious bread and rolls for the rest of the trip.

The dinner, although served at 10:00 P.M., was as delicious as ever, especially the applesauce made from the fruit damaged in the roll down the cliff. Ty Sing dressed up the dinner table with hanging Japanese paper lanterns, and some witty soul commented that we should have had electric lights when dinner was so late.

To compensate for the previous day, the usual siren call of the Sierra Club did not sound this beautiful morning of July 20. Mather and Marshall had decided the night before that their charges were exhausted and so let them sleep until 9:00 A.M.

Breakfast was late, but of course gourmet. Most of us consumed two grapefruit, several trout, two tenderloin steaks with potatoes, a stack of biscuits and honey, and a couple of cups of coffee.

Today was to be relaxation day: fishing, swimming in the Kern River, washing clothes. A few truly lazy souls did absolutely nothing but sunbathe and paid Eugene to do their laundry.

The next morning, Mather had us all back to normal and up at dawn. Before mounting our trusty steeds, he allowed time for a very solemn ceremony. The previous day Congressman Gillett had discovered a wonderful hot spring. Here a suitable-size bathtub had been dug out of the ooze, allowing Gillett to soak for hours while the 115-degree water bubbled over him. Now it seemed appropriate for Mather to anoint this spot by sprinkling "holy water" on it and solemnly christening it "Gillett Hot Spring."

About a mile north of the hot spring the walls of the canyon became almost vertical. It was an impressive sight, especially where beautiful waterfalls cascaded down the granite precipices. The ride this day wasn't difficult, and the party reached the destination at Junction Meadow far ahead of schedule. Here we found a lovely grassy field that seemed right in every way until it was discovered that mosquitoes and ants liked the area too. In the cool of the evening the pests disappeared except in McCormick's thirty feet of territory. To rid himself of them, he had carefully burned off the grass, but didn't realize that by doing so he had warmed the earth. The ants found this so cozy that they stayed around all night.

Most of the party relaxed at camp during what was left of the afternoon, but Mather was always unable to sit still for an hour. He coerced Grosvenor and me into climbing up into the Kern-Kaweah Canyon. It was a perfect afternoon. We reached the notch where the Kaweah Peaks lay spread out before us, with the Rockslide Lakes far below.

I will always remember that day, that place, and the discussion we had. This part of the Sierra presented a whole new world to us—even to me, a person never far from it until I was a grown man. We were silent and awestruck by the bold majesty of the vista. Then, almost in unison of thought and speech, we began an earnest discussion of what could be done to enclose the Kern, Kings, and Whitney regions into an enlarged Sequoia or an entirely new park.

Mather was all for an enlarged Sequoia, just one park, the present one plus General Grant and these other new areas. Grosvenor and I felt that Sequoia and General Grant Parks were "Big Tree" parks, whereas these wild, majestic canyons and awesome mountains projected a different image. Maybe someone had thought of the name before, but I always felt Grosvenor deserved the credit for the perfect name: "The Sierra Wilderness Park." Eventually, when our dream park was finally created many years later, the name "General Grant" was dropped and the new park was named Kings Canyon National Park.

Resting on that rocky ground with our eyes on the distant mountains and discussing our vision for the future, as though we had the power to make it come true, we took for granted that our immediate goal of a national park bureau was already accomplished. That was why this day was so memorable, for each of us contributed ideas, but also the practical avenues to reach these goals. We three remembered what was said that glorious afternoon when we returned to Washington.

Grosvenor vowed that the National Geographic Society would "march in step" to attain these goals. He fulfilled his promise by publishing, in April 1916, an entire issue on the national parks entitled "The Land of the Best," a glowing tribute to the "crown jewels of America." It greatly influenced the Congress when the time came to vote for the establishment of a National Park Service.

As for Mather and myself, Mather put it this way: "the spirit was riding high." I believe it might have been at this time that he began to see that the creation of a National Park Service was his highest priority, that the improvement of the parks and publicizing them would amount to little without the power of a formal, organized bureau in the Interior Department.

On July 22, after two comparatively easy days, it was time to energize the party. Marshall and McClure decided to break away to inspect Harrison Pass, an area through which the John Muir Trail might pass. The California Legislature had just appropriated ten thousand dollars for this project and had charged McClure, the state engineer, with its design and construction. He had asked Marshall, with his vast experience in the Sierra, to share his knowledge of the prospective route.

Mark Daniels instantly stated that he would go along. Marshall, shoving his flat-fronted hat back, took a deep breath and almost too politely suggested that Daniels remain with Mather. Looking belligerent and raising his voice so that the whole group could not avoid overhearing him, Daniels replied: "You'd like to get rid of me here and with the parks, too, wouldn't you?" Before Marshall could answer, Mather quickly stepped in and said he'd like a word with Daniels. He signaled Marshall and McClure to get on their mounts and leave. It was the end of a tense scene, the only unpleasant moment the party experienced. Later that year Mather forced Daniels to step down as general superintendent of national parks and replaced him, using a different title, with Marshall.

After the departure of Marshall and McClure, the remainder of the party climbed the east wall of the Kern Canyon. It was extremely steep and very slow going. Suddenly, at about 10,800 feet, the sight of Mount Whitney and its satellite peaks burst on the horizon to the east. Actually, Whitney is not easy to pick out from its neighbors: just one more granite spike along the saw-toothed backbone of the Sierra. "It's a sight fit for the Olympian gods!" Hough shouted.

When the main group reached the campsite at Crabtree Meadows, the pack train was missing again. Seavey rode around and located it a few miles ahead, but not in an idyllic meadow of lush green grass and wild flowers. The cattle had already stripped this meadow. Frank Ewing had led the pack train up Whitney Creek to another spot but found it had also been cleaned out by cattle. Then a heavy rainstorm rolled in, and Ewing decided to quit the search for an untouched campsite. "Mighta kept going to Lone Pine before we shed all the cows," he said later.

That evening we devoted most of the time to the mountain, the route to the top, and certain safety features concerning the climb of Mount Whitney. As Alaska was still a territory in 1915, Mount McKinley at

20,320 feet was rated as the highest in the union. Hough commented, "Mountains in Alaska make Whitney look like a bent nickel." Suddenly Gillett stated that he was not going to go with the assault party. He would stay in camp and wash his clothes.

Then Dr. Simmons declared that Emerson Hough really shouldn't go either. Hough exploded, "Why the hell not?"

He was told that his heart wasn't strong enough and that he might die if he exerted himself at that altitude. Simmons concluded with, "If you go up there, you do so at your own risk, but you'd better arrange to have a decent human burial because somewhere on that rocky slope you will find your last resting place."

"Well," said Hough, "I can't think of a better place to die." And he promptly bribed Frank Ewing with a ten-dollar bill to get him to the top.

Ewing assured Hough that "for ten dollars I'll take you apart and carry you up on the installment plan."

Although Bob Marshall had scheduled an early wake-up call and departure on July 23, it wasn't until 8:30 A.M. that the mountain climbers were in their saddles and off to Mount Whitney. It took about two hours to cover the four miles to the high meadow where the horses were to be left to graze while the men set off on foot to reach the summit at 14,502 feet. That was 1915. Now it is measured at only 14,495 feet.

Whitney is relatively easy to climb. It is said that anyone in fairly good shape, even a child, can make it. And the western or Crabtree approach, the original route climbed in 1873, was easier than the one up from the Owens Valley two miles below. The Mather party, with the possible exception of Hough, seemed to be in good climbing condition. However, it turned out that Maddox had to stop at thirteen thousand feet. Ewing dragged Hough all the way to the top. Everyone enjoyed the climb, often stopping to rest, take pictures, and examine rocks and plants. Moving slowly across jumbled, flat rocks at a gentle angle, we were almost surprised when we found we had run out of mountain. Twelve of the Mather Mountain Party had reached the summit, a two-acre surface, rocky but nearly flat, even sporting a stone rest house built in 1909. Grosvenor got there first by running the last hundred feet or so.

The view from the top was incredible. Waves of majestic peaks fanned out in all directions: the Kaweahs of the Great Western Divide to the west; the main spine of the Sierra from north to south; its eastern ramparts dropping off abruptly to the low Alabama hills and the Owens Valley. Across the flatlands were the dimly seen Panamint and Funeral Mountains enclosing Death Valley, the lowest point in the United States, 262 feet below sea level.

There was much awed comment on the panorama, especially as the party was standing on the highest point in the United States and, at the same time, gazing at the lowest point. I was so proud of Mount Tom (at 13,652 feet), which towered over my birthplace, Bishop, that I wanted to show it off to the party. But I was stunned to discover that I couldn't find it in the maze of towering peaks to the north. It was impossible to locate. With gales of laughter at my muttered frustration, my companions immediately nicknamed me "Bishop." Everyone who had a camera snapped photos while Osborn and Grosvenor took notes. Proudly crowing about his accomplishment in not dying, Hough strode around so energetically that the others began to fear he might yet make Simmons's prediction come true.

With the sudden appearance of black clouds, thunder, and lightning, the horseplay ceased. Marshall urged us to pick up our gear and get off the mountain fast, as Sierra storms moved rapidly and were ferocious. How right he was! Soon waves of snow nearly wiped out our vision. We started down the mountain, tacitly recognizing McClure as the leader. As a safety precaution, he spaced the experienced Sierra men—himself, Marshall, and Ewing—between groups of us novices.

The fury of the snow and sleet changed to a driving rain as we descended. The trail was treacherously slippery and uneven, sometimes invisible. Even for men who wouldn't acknowledge fear, it was a nerve-wracking experience. Suddenly Johnstone began to sing "It's A Long Way to Tipperary." He followed that with more rousing songs, and other voices joined in. Down the mountain came the soaked, half-frozen, fearful climbers, singing over the noise of the storm everything from "Onward Christian Soldiers" to Huhn's "Invictus" and saloon songs about "the goddamn Dutch."

Horses were waiting when we finally got off the mountain, and a fast ride back to camp was made. Here the weary climbers were met with roaring fires and dry clothes. Ty Sing's dinner surpassed his previous wonders. He even had concocted an English plum pudding with brandy sauce for dessert. Warm, and with a full stomach, the bone-weary mountaineers headed for the sleeping bags, which had miraculously been kept dry.

There were no wake-up calls the next morning. The only sounds were groans from partially disabled veterans of the Mount Whitney climb.

Osborn fared the worst, for he was one of the oldest. His muscles were not accustomed to the Sierras, and he had also scraped his leg rather badly. He was still in his bedroll when Dr. Simmons came along. Somehow he mistook Osborn for Hough. He shouted gleefully to the camp, "Hey, look at this! I said the climb would kill Hough, but I didn't say when. For proof, here's the body!"

And then Hough leaped forward, fully clad, wildly exhilarated, shouting with glee, "Hey, look at this! Though dead, he has arisen!"

Everything moved so slowly this morning that it was close to 9:00 A.M. when the party hit the trail. For the first time our leader, Steve Mather, rode at the head on his trusty white mule, "Tobe." It wasn't long, however, before Bob Marshall had to take over because yesterday's storm had obliterated part of the trail. The party wound its way slowly by Mount Guyot to Siberian Pass, where we stopped for lunch. The morning had been another sensory experience, with the glow of sunshine alternating with the flashes of lightning and furious black thunder heads. Grosvenor later wrote glowingly of "the divine dignity of the Great Siberian plateau, nearly 13,000 feet above the sea and bordered by bleak peaks towering 3,000 feet higher, and yet carpeted from end to end with blue lupine and a tiny yellow flower I did not recognize." When the storm finally broke on us, the overhanging trees and rocks along the South Fork of Rock Creek offered enough shelter to keep us moderately dry.

On reaching Whitney Meadows in the early afternoon, we found 350 cows occupying the intended campsite. Everyone was getting a little exasperated with these domestic beasts on federal land, leveling the grazing and leaving an unsanitary mess behind. Marshall bitterly observed that the government received the ridiculous sum of thirty cents per cow for the privilege of destroying what God had created to sustain the flora and fauna of the region. It was a learning experience for Mather and me. We fought grazing in national parks the rest of our lives.

As Sunday was supposed to be a day of rest, the Mather Mountain Party was content to stay at Big Whitney Meadow. We set up camp here, just a short distance from Golden Trout Creek. Hough was gleeful at the sight of so much life in it. "If you aim right, you can hook the fish, land it in the frying pan, and let Ty do the rest." It seemed like paradise to the weary travelers.

The most active—usually the same gang of Mather, McClure, Albright, Marshall, and Grosvenor—today were joined by Seavey and McCormick. Off we went, exploring, hiking, and photographing. In camp Johnstone, fulfilling a promise to Maddox, was writing a chronicle of the trip. Osborn puttered around collecting specimens. Simmons tried to find a use for all the medical equipment he'd brought but could only dig up a few scratches and insect bites. As usual, Gillett and Floy, saying and doing little, were quietly lapping up the beauty of the Sierra.

Hough was making a conclusive study of the Golden Trout. The minute he had spotted them in the crystal waters a few yards from camp, he had been enchanted. Their color was a miracle to him, and he had to know why they sparkled and glowed. He ran up and down the banks of the stream. He caught some, studied them, and threw them back. He furiously scribbled in his little notebook. Later he wrote for *Forest and Stream* magazine: "There you are in Golden Trout country. There are several streams here each of which has a yellowish bottom and which hence raises Golden Trout. It is considered the correct thing to have a species of these named after you. There were eighteen in our party, and each of us had a new species named after him. When you are in the business of getting famous there is no use drawing a line too soon."

Monday, July 26, started a new week with everyone rested and refreshed, but hanging around camp there was a certain air of sadness. It was to be the last full day on the trail, but an unforgettable one, traveling from Whitney Meadows through Cottonwood Pass to Horseshoe Meadows. At the summit Floy and McClure felt playful and stood up on their saddles to get their pictures taken. Of course, Mather had to copy them and insisted I do the same. At the strategic moment, Hough shouted to Johnstone, "Hey, now's the time to give that goddamn Sierra yell."

Then it was all downhill to the lovely grassy meadow where we made camp early in the afternoon. McClure, Marshall, and I broke away from the main group and headed for Cottonwood Lakes. The remainder of the party spent a lazy afternoon around camp. Fishing held the attention of most men, as the trout-filled stream was only fifteen feet from Ty Sing's stove.

Because we would be returning to civilization the next day, there was a lot of scrubbing of clothes and bodies. Sadly, the razors had to end the competition for best facial hair of the expedition. Gillett and McCormick had been bearded at the start, with McClure, Hough, Osborn, Floy, and Grosvenor sporting mustaches. By July 26 everyone in the party looked like a caveman. Mather shaved everything but his mustache and preened around with this fluffy, silver bush until the next morning. I hated beards and had only grown one because of my imitation of Mather. After I scraped my face clean that day, I never again had an extra day's growth.

Our farewell dinner was late but festive. Ty and Eugene had outdone themselves. Japanese paper lanterns were again strung between the trees. Small "bouquets" of cones and green boughs were at each place on the freshly washed linen tablecloth. Dinner was superb—more than usually superb. Along with trout, venison, and the last of the treasured "tasties," as Ty called them, was a special dessert—the pastry that enclosed a "future fortune" for each of the Mountain Party. Ty Sing had personally written his notes in Chinese and English. They showed that this man could be counted not only as the "gourmet chef of the Sierra" but as the "philosopher of the Sierra."

Unfortunately, not all of Ty's wise messages are known, but a few were recorded. To Marshall: "Chief, long may you search the mountains." To McClure: "Long may you build the paths through the mountains." To Mather: "The sound of your laughter will fill the mountains when you are in the sky." Mine said: "You are the spirit and soul of your leader." And to Hough: "Where but in the mountains would such a man be spirit with the mountains."

As our final bonfire burned brightly and the last round of fine Havana cigars was lit, Mather stood up to say a few words of farewell. Apparently they were very inspiring, as several of us recorded almost the same message. Paraphrasing, it went something like this:

> Well, men, we've had a glorious ten days together, and we'll have a few more before we part in Yosemite. I think the time has come, though, that I should confess why I wanted you to come along with me on this adventure. Not only for your interesting company, but to hope you'd see the significance of these mountains in the whole picture of what we are trying to do. Hopefully you will take this message and spread it throughout the land in your own avenue and style. These valleys and heights of the Sierra Nevada are just one small part of the majesty of America. Although Sequoia, Yellowstone, Glacier, Crater Lake, and others are already set aside, just think of the vast areas of our land that should be preserved for the future. Think of the Grand Canyon of the Colorado, the wonders in our territories in Alaska and Hawaii.
>
> But unless we can protect the areas currently held with a separate government agency we may lose them to selfish interests. And we need this bureau to enhance and enlarge our public lands, to preserve

infinitely more "for the benefit and enjoyment of the people," as the Yellowstone act stated.

So I ask you writers to go back and spread the message to your readers. You businessmen to contact your clubs, organizations, and friends interested in the outdoors. Tell them to help financially and use their influence on members of Congress. To you, Gillett, as our only congressman present, go after your colleagues for a national park bureau. You employees of the state, urge cooperation between state and federal governments. To each of you, to all of you, remember that God has given us these beautiful lands. Try to save them for, and share them with, future generations. Go out and spread the gospel!

Stephen Mather could always inspire and excite people, and this time was no exception. To a man the Mather Mountain Party of 1915 took his words to heart and contributed far beyond his expectations.

On July 27 our party separated, with Ty Sing, Eugene, and the pack train turning back toward the Giant Forest while the Mather group headed six thousand feet down the sheer east wall of the Sierra to Lone Pine. Mather gave cash to everyone in the pack train, and the cooks received spontaneous gifts from the grateful men they had cared for so lovingly—silver dollars and gold pieces, linen handkerchiefs, a pipe, innumerable cigars, varied fishing tackle, a gold watch chain, Simmons's box of medical supplies, and Hough's favorite red shirt for Ty, who had taken a fancy to it, a shirt so old and worn that everyone said it wouldn't last Ty back to Giant Forest.

After a night in Bishop, where the Mather party was welcomed in various local homes with hot baths, dinner, and real beds, we reassembled in Little Round Valley for a trout breakfast and then were chauffeured across the Tioga Road, an almost perpendicular climb on a barely improved surface. Fifty-six miles long, it had been built by Chinese labor in 1882–83 for a mining company. Mather and associates had purchased it, and the United States government had improved it for use by the summer of 1915.

The car I was in was an old open Studebaker, driven by Bishop grocery man Will L. Smith. McCormick sat in the front seat and Hough behind the driver on the outside overlooking the 2,000-foot gorge. I sat beside Hough, door ajar, with one foot on the running board. Smith assured us that he knew every twist, and we prayed he was right. When he wanted to point out the sights, he would stand up and gesture with one or both hands off the wheel. Whenever he did this, I froze at the open door, ready to leap if the car started to plunge over. Hough was ready to follow and sobbed hoarsely in my ear, "Goddamn this scenery-loving sonofabitch!" McCormick was frozen in his seat, later confessing he had given up hope for his life.

With the gods watching over us, our party somehow reached the summit of Tioga Pass, where Mather, Will Colby, and a delegation from the Sierra Club ceremoniously cut a ribbon and dedicated the Tioga Road. Then the whole crowd moved in unison down to Soda Springs at Tuolumne Meadows, where the Sierra Club hosted a dinner and endless speeches around a campfire too small for so many people. Colby was the real hero of the evening, for he had a supply of Old Crow bourbon available behind his tent.

The next morning, the last remnants of the Mather Mountain Party split up. As it would be my first opportunity to see Yosemite Valley, I chose to go with rangers on horseback. The others went by car with Mather down the Oak Flat Road to Yosemite Valley.

The immediate effects of the mountain party were local: elimination of toll roads; publicity creating strong support in the San Joaquin Valley for extension of Sequoia or the creation of a new park to encompass the Kings and Kern canyons; purchase of the Giant Forest, the heart of Sequoia; fifty thousand dollars from the federal government; twenty thousand from Grosvenor and the National Geographic Society; precedent for private parties to purchase lands and donate them to the government (with Gillett in Congress paving the way); and impetus for the U.S. government to aid in the completion of the John Muir Trail.

Then, of course, the ideas brought forth in our daily discussions during the trip produced national results as well. The publicity about the mountain party, through newspapers and magazines, focused attention on the parks and the need for a national park service. The newly found belief in conservation and the concept of "wilderness" was generated from influential men in our group.

But, above all else, I think that every one of us who lived together, ate together, rode together, talked and thought together, and experienced the camaraderie of those two weeks provided a bond of friendship and blood-brotherhood that turned dreams into reality in the future. There was never a time when Gilbert Grosvenor did not use the force of his influential publication behind a national park project on which we needed help. Gillett fought political pressure any number of times to help us in the Congress, especially when he became head of the powerful Appropriations Committee. Hough, Macfarlane, and fellow writers and publishers poured out support through the years whenever we needed them.

For myself, I believe that what I learned on that memorable Sierra trip lingered throughout my life, echoing back to me in formulating policy, standards, and philosophy for the National Park Service and in my conservation and preservation endeavors after leaving the service.

Exploring the Parks, North by Northwest
1915

From Tuolumne Meadows, several park rangers joined me to mount our horses and descend into the valley of the Merced Yosemite. With all the grandiose descriptions I had heard and all the pictures I had seen, I still wasn't prepared for the majestic beauty of this land. The high country was bleak and primordial, whereas the valley radiated grandeur with its sheer cliffs, airy waterfalls, clear lakes and streams, soft meadows, and stately trees. It had taken us three days of horseback riding to arrive at the Sentinel Hotel, where Mather, Marshall, and a few others were resting from their strenuous outing.

No rest for me though. Mather instantly assigned me to talk with David Curry, to relay Mather's intentions of strengthening his rival, the Desmond Company, and warning him to be quiet and take orders or find his lease nonrenewable.

I found the Curry situation a mixed one. Curry was as combative and difficult as everyone had said, but from the first moment I met her I loved his wife, Mary Curry, fondly called "Mother" Curry by all who knew her. I was sure no man was worthless who had a wife like her, and through the years her intelligence, good humor, and great common sense kept me from allowing anyone to do real harm to the Curry Company.

Mather was immersed in Desmond Company matters. He kept me out of them except for a bare sketch of his decisions. I felt he really didn't want me to be involved or even to know too much of the inner workings of that outfit. This was probably because he knew I was concerned and suspicious about the whole concession plan he and Dohrmann and the others had set up. Actually, I was more worried about his own financial involvement in that company.

I managed to see almost everything in the valley in my spare time. I hiked up to Vernal and Nevada Falls and walked the circumference of Mirror Lake, taking dozens of pictures. Tourists were camped along the Merced River. Their makeshift tents of bed sheets angled off their flimsy cars, while the children floated in tire inner tubes on the water. And it was quite a sight to see everyone getting a liberal shower of dust whenever an auto passed by.

Without Mather's knowledge, I made a careful inspection of the trails, roads, sewage disposal, ramshackle power plant, hotels, and Camp Curry—the latter both by day and by night. One evening I went incognito to the camp to enjoy the singing. I was sort of sorry there was no Curry Firefall anymore, when buckets of flaming coals were poured over the cliff from Glacier Point to the valley.

The firefalls were ended in this way. Only a month or so after Adolph Miller and I came to Washington in 1913, David Curry came into the office making all kinds of demands. Miller listened impassively, although I knew his famous temper was beginning to boil at Curry's dictatorial ranting. When quiet reigned once more, Miller spoke softly but murderously: "Mr. Curry, I am not going to give you anything you demand. In fact, as a lesson to you, I am going to take away something in which you have great pride. You no longer can produce your firefall." It was a terrible blow to Curry and also to his scores of summer visitors.

Of course, there were things that upset the perfection of the natural scene, the signs of man's presence: cows grazing in meadows, barns, stables, piles of manure along the road, ugly fences, many of them broken down. But even these didn't spoil my first visit to Yosemite. I loved every minute, as it was really my first experience as a tourist to a national park and my first experience as an "inspector" for the Interior Department. I took copious notes and gave them to Mather when we returned to Washington. Contrary to what I had anticipated about my being secretive, he wasn't angry at all. In fact, he was rather pleased at all the information I had gathered.

After two or three days in Yosemite, Mather was itching to get on the move again. He had his private car and chauffeur come up from Berkeley to drive him back to the Bay area. I was supposed to go with him, but he suddenly detailed me to go to Wawona to inspect the hotel there and meet the owner. Then he waved good-bye, shouted, "Have a good time and behave yourself," and went off to join his family in Berkeley, where he intended to follow up on his Giant Forest plan, spend some time at the exposition with his daughter, and have a rousing few days at the national convention of Sigma Chis.

At last I hopped the train to Berkeley and arrived on August 7. And I was in seventh heaven. When I had left Grace the summer before, I hadn't expected to see her for at least a year, and now here was the second visit in about four months.

Our time together was quite limited. Mather, notwithstanding his promise to let me have some free days, was ready to get back to national park business. So Grace and I sandwiched in several trips to the exposition, one movie, and a few hours of making plans for our future.

Mather had seen enough of expositions and cities and decided we'd get out and inspect some national parks. He had only brushed Mount Rainier with the Appropriations Committee and hadn't really seen the park since he had climbed there with the Sierra Club ten years before. E. O. McCormick of the Southern Pacific Railroad had enjoyed himself so much on the mountain trip that he suggested we all go along together to Oregon and Washington. He assured us that he always had some legitimate company business to attend to, so we could travel in his private car, Sunset.

Mather asked Robert Marshall to join us. He did not ask Mark Daniels. He had grown to admire Marshall immensely, and it seemed apparent to me that he was grooming him to take Daniels's place as head of the parks when a bureau was set up.

So here we were again, some of the mountain party, aboard this beautiful private rail car. We left San Francisco on the night of August 18. In the morning we were met in Klamath Falls and driven up to Crater Lake National Park, about fifty miles of the worst road I had ever been on. Probably an animal track would have been better than that deep-rutted dust bin. We had left McCormick with his railroad car to meet us when we came out of the park at Medford.

At the headquarters of Crater Lake, we were met by William G. Steel, the supervisor. We had gotten to know him at the superintendents' conference, although he had been very retiring and not easy to talk to. The lake had been discovered in 1853, but it took the vision and determination of Steel to make it a national park. From 1885 until 1902, he had devoted his life to this cause and had accomplished wonders almost single-handedly. A political appointee had been the park's first supervisor, but in 1913 Steel had replaced him.

Because of a short tourist season due to inclement weather, difficult access, and poor accommodations, few people attempted to make the trip up to the park. Consequently, it received scant attention and miserly appropriations. It was in terrible shape, and something drastic had to be done.

Mather had requested that George Goodwin be "loaned" to him from the Army Corps of Engineers, and he met us at park headquarters. Steel had managed to get a road started that would encircle the lake, but the rest of what passed for roads were impossible. It took Goodwin to straighten out these problems. While working on this, Goodwin, Mather, Marshall, Steel, and I traveled for two days around the rim, studying where vista points should be located as well as making decisions on campsites, trails, and lodgings for future tourists.

Accommodations were a real problem. Steel and an old friend, Alfred L. Parkhurst, had been running the only concession in the park, the Crater Lake Company. They were too poor to build the thing up and couldn't be thrown out because they had the only accommodations. On the other hand, Mather determined they couldn't stay.

On the August 22 our party climbed into open touring cars to drive down to Medford. If we thought the trip up was bad, it was a dream compared to this one. Those seventy-five miles will live in memory. It was a boiling morning to start out with and got hotter by the minute as we bounced and crashed over something someone had the nerve to call a road—much worse than the one from Klamath Falls. For the first time ever, Mather gave up trying to talk. He just held onto his hat with one hand and a handkerchief over his face to ward off the dust with the other. When we staggered out of the car in Medford at the University Club, lodged over a grocery store, we were tired, hungry, thirsty, and parboiled.

We were met by two delegations—a group of Reclamation Service people and a group interested in national parks, Crater Lake in particular. So after we had scraped off a few inches of dirt, we joined these men as well as E. O. McCormick, who had made his way around to Medford. We still hadn't eaten and we were still parched.

Mather had two bridge tables set up in the meeting room and told me to take the Reclamation group while he would talk to the men interested in national parks. Someone brought in trays of deliciously cool pastel drinks, which looked and tasted like fruit punch. On empty stomachs, we sipped these while talking to our visitors. Every time my glass seemed to be nearly empty, it was miraculously refilled or replaced by a new one.

When night was coming on, someone said we had to get to the station to board McCormick's railroad car. None of us who had spent the afternoon in the University Club—McCormick, Mather, Marshall, and myself—were able to tell for sure what had occurred, to whom we had talked, or how we got back to the train. Somehow I got to the station and even deposited all our bags safely on the private car. The only thing I vaguely remember of the lost afternoon was that some Medford men were singing, to the tune of "You're a Grand Old Flag," "You're a grand old town, You're a fine business town, And forever advancement you'll make, You're the center of a land renown, The gateway to fair Crater Lake," etc. We later found out that our innocuous beverages, called "Rogue River Rhapsodies," were mostly aged applejack. It was probably one of the few times in our lives that any of us got drunk.

We went on to Portland, where we had a series of meetings concerning the problems we had found at Crater Lake. Mather talked to a group of businessmen as well as representatives of a mountaineering club in Portland, the Mazamas, whom he had been with in Mount Rainier in 1904. His enthusiasm paid off as usual. He raved over the lake, saying, "When I was a boy, I used to take sticks of blueing and see how deep a shade I could color a tub of water. I never achieved any blue as profound or as deep as that you see in the Crater Lake water."

Then he exhorted them: "All you people from Medford and Portland had better get together or Klamath Falls will take business away from your end of the state. There is every advantage in having Medford and Klamath Falls cooperate, as no one wants to go to any park and return over the same ground."

Local newsmen promised informative and enticing articles about the park. The Mazamas entered wholeheartedly into Mather's idea to apply political pressure to improve the roads on the state level while he obtained appropriations on the national level.

Mather persuaded R. W. Price, the manager of the Multnomah Hotel in Portland, to buy out Parkhurst, form the Crater Lake National Park Company, and get busy on suitable food and lodging. Changes were made almost immediately, and eventually a large, rustic hotel emerged from the old shell. It opened in 1928.

Lastly, McCormick got up to announce that the Southern Pacific would add a new rail spur for an east entrance to the park, starting at

Weed in California and extending to Eugene in Oregon. This would be known as the Crater Lake Cutoff.

Many people from Seattle to Portland were urging us to make national parks out of every volcanic mountain from Mount Baker to the California border. Mather and I agreed we couldn't make every peak a park and didn't have time to inspect them. We already had Mount Lassen, which had been erupting and was quite the sensation. It had been made a national monument and in 1916 was upgraded to a national park.

Maybe this is the place to tell a little story about the hearings on Lassen. Right after the park was created, I had to go up to the Capitol with a deficiency estimate to take care of the operation of the park until the next regular appropriation bill was passed. A member of the committee before which I had to appear was old Uncle Joe Cannon, who had been Speaker of the House for years before the present Democratic Congress took over.

When it was too hot for him, Cannon would take off his coat and take down his suspenders so that his pants seemed likely to fall off. On this day the committee chairman, who was from South Carolina, went on and on about our estimates. I recognized that he was thinking in terms of city parks like those in Charleston when he asked, "Are you going to plant some lawns and grow some roses and other flowers up there in this Lassen?"

Before I could tell him this was a huge volcano with a great forest around it, thousands of acres of wilderness, Uncle Joe, blowing smoke like a furnace from his black cigar and with trousers about to drop on the floor, jumped to his feet and barked out: "They don't plant roses and grow flowers in these areas. It's a big place. Big place. Pretty near as big as your whole dern state."

Well, you see, you had to educate these congressmen. You'd have to be careful that you didn't let them know that you knew they didn't know what you were talking about. You had to work around it, pretending that they did know.

When a new park was created, usually by pressures from their areas, congressmen inclined to get the cart before the horse. An amendment would get tacked on limiting annual expenditures to tiny amounts. Of course, we'd have to go back and ask for more. Then the standard saying from them would be, "Well, let's see some people in the park. Let's see what the use of the place is. Give us some people. We'll give you some money." And our quandary was: if we can't get anybody in because of no roads, no development, no accommodations, how can we get any money? And vice versa.

We arrived in Tacoma on August 27 and went to the hotel. We were met by two groups of Mount Rainier supporters, men from Tacoma and Seattle. One reason we had come to visit the park was the rivalry between these two cities over whether the park should be called Mount Rainier or Mount Tacoma.

Aside from that, their interest in the park had forced them to work together, and they had accomplished a great deal under an organization called the Seattle-Tacoma Rainier National Park Committee. Mather found he could work with all of them, as they were mainly interested in money, and he had a lot of ideas about how money could be made if only the park could be improved to lure more tourists. More tourists meant that more appropriations could be squeezed from Congress for better roads and perhaps even an enlargement of the boundaries. That meant more tourists. A perfect circle.

We were entertained at dinner that night, and Mather, as usual, soothed their apprehensions, asked for their suggestions, and enlisted their support for his plans. He made a point that first-class facilities should be set up in the park, financed by private capital, and when they were completed the backers should be given long-term, monopolistic contracts. He played the same game that he had in Oregon, warning that if local Washington state people didn't come up with this type of concession company, he'd have to look elsewhere. Shortly thereafter, the Rainier National Park Company was organized and went into operation, with the former concessioners selling out to the new monopoly. By 1917 a beautiful new hotel was opened at Paradise, replacing the crude old camp.

There was one thing I remember about that evening in Tacoma. Some man, whose name I never did get and who seemed to be an expert on animal and plant life, propounded in detail that boundaries of a park should not be made along geometric lines. They should be drawn to protect the flora and fauna, the flow of streams, the interworking of nature. He suggested that here in Rainier the west and south boundaries should be irregularly extended to accommodate natural forces. Everyone was fascinated, and Mather asked him to write up his ideas for us to study when we returned to Washington. Unfortunately, he never did, and we never found him again. But I for one never forgot what he said, especially a few years later when it applied to the Greater Yellowstone situation.

At Tacoma we were joined by Asahel Curtis, who would be leading our party in Mount Rainier. He was a famous photographer, the brother of the even more famous Indian photographer Edward Curtis. The brothers fought like cats and dogs and hadn't spoken to each other in years. When the Seattle and Tacoma men organized their committee, they chose Curtis as chairman and T. H. Martin as secretary. Another interesting addition to this committee was Richard Ballinger, who had been secretary of the interior under President Taft and a longtime national park advocate.

Mather intended to inspect every inch of the park and decided to do it via pack trip. In cars provided by the Tacoma-Seattle Committee, we drove to the park. A new road from Longmire to Paradise Valley had opened in June. Designed by Hiram Chittenden, who had engineered the roads in Yellowstone, it was a marvel. Climbing a perilous 3,000-foot grade, up a narrow canyon road, it was nearly as heart-stopping as the Tioga but even more gloriously scenic and very much safer.

At Paradise, Mather inspected the "Camp in the Clouds," owned by John Reese. There were two hotels at Longmire, outside the park, but this was the only accommodation for tourists within Mount Rainier. Reese's camp was a filthy mess of floorless tents and greasy food, but amazingly enough, sparkling clean linen. To replace it, Mark Daniels had designed a spacious resort hotel, but Mather made an instant decision to exchange Daniels's ideas for a rustic-type building to nestle in the hills. And that's what was built.

Shortly before we arrived, a 93-mile Wonderland Trail, which encircled Mount Rainier, had been completed for hikers. Mather planned his pack trip to get a good inspection of it, but time did not permit us to complete this circle.

The pack train consisted of Mather, park supervisor Dewitt Reaburn, Robert Marshall, Chief Forest Ranger T. E. O'Farrell, Asahel Curtis, myself, and ten horses. Mather was on the Reese inspection for so long that we weren't "horse-borne" until 3:00 P.M. We crossed over the lower Nisqually Glacier, started on the wagon highway at Tahoma fork, and branched off on to the pony trail around the west side of the mountain. It was slow going, as the trail was very narrow and rocky.

Here we had some real excitement. Mather was leading when he plowed into some nests of yellowjackets. Our horses reared and would have flown in all directions had there been any place to fly. All we could do was to keep our horses' heads down and circle them out of the buzzing inferno. Mather rode directly through it all and was the only one, I think, who wasn't even stung. We didn't get very far and made camp early on the north fork of the Puyallup River.

The next day dawned brilliant and clear. Mather excitedly roused everyone out and started saddling his horse. Curtis politely suggested that we all might like to eat something before setting off on a tough ride. Mather seemed a little startled. I really don't think he thought about food when his mind was racing to the adventures ahead. We did sandwich in some breakfast before we were mounted and crossing over to the Fairfax–Spray Park trail.

It was a glorious day for me, as every minute was a fresh experience, with new glimpses of this fascinating wooded and iced park around every bend in the trail. Curtis had his camera on the ready and snapped innumerable pictures of us and the majestic mountain that always formed a backdrop.

Again we made camp early at Spray Park. We had just gotten off our horses when we heard a great rumbling roar that lasted for almost five minutes. Curtis explained that it was a giant avalanche over Willis Wall, a sheer 4,000-foot drop on the north face of the mountain, not far from us to the east. Most of us newcomers to Rainier were scared stiff, but Mather was all for going to see it. Stubbornly, Curtis absolutely refused to show him the way.

After dinner, lounging around the campfire, we talked until nearly midnight. It was a magical night with a full moon and the camp enclosed between the brilliant glaciers. A memorable interlude was when Asahel Curtis recited a few poems about the mountains, the spirit of nature, and the wildness of the outdoors. I especially recall his rendition of Robert W. Service's "The Spell of the Yukon." It was an evening reminiscent of the Mather Mountain Party, the camaraderie, and the spiritual closeness of the group.

The next day was Sunday. Mather decided we'd leave our horses at Spray Park and set off on foot. We hiked twelve miles through the Spray, Mist, and Seattle sections of the park to the west bank of the Carbon glacier. We crossed the glacier for one and a half miles above its terminus at an elevation of more than six thousand feet. From here we emerged in Moraine Park and descended to Glacier cabin (3,100 feet) at the junction of the Spray and Moraine trails. Our horses had been returned to headquarters, so we rode on what Curtis called a "gasoline speeder" down a logging company's road to Cardonado, quite a distance outside the remote northwest park boundary.

Gratefully, we saw some automobiles waiting for us here. T. H. Martin of the Inter-City Committee and J. F. Hickey of Tacoma had thoughtfully decided our party probably had enough saddlesores by 6:00 P.M. We sank into the soft seats with paper cups of lemonade while they drove us back to the hotel in Tacoma. We had covered about eighty-five miles on horseback and foot. It was a most memorable trip in all respects.

We stayed over in Tacoma for part of the day, as Mather had agreed to give a talk on the national parks at noon at the Commercial Club. He opened this with: "I visited Rainier National Park ten years ago and climbed to the top of the mountain. I have been interested in national parks ever since. The great view gave me an inspiration, a love for the open." Then he compared the last few days with this first trip, complimenting everyone who had helped improve the trails and other conditions, saying they were much better than before. He also said that he would recommend to Secretary Lane that the road projects be speeded up, so that visitors could see more of the magnificent park. And he certainly would get the concessions improved because he found them most deplorable.

He never once used the name "Tacoma" or "Rainier." Before he spoke, I had warned him to remember the story about Grover Cleveland's vice-president, Adlai E. Stevenson. It seems he had made a visit to Mount Rainier, come back to Tacoma, and made a speech about the glories of the mountain without calling it by name. He concluded with, "Ladies and gentlemen, there is no doubt in my mind what that mountain should be called." There was great applause because the audience thought he meant Tacoma. He then went on the Seattle and made the identical speech, word for word, with the same ending, and got the same applause because, of course, they thought he meant Rainier.

Well, we also went on to Seattle the next morning. We met with a number of people in connection with launching the Rainier Development Program. Mather wanted to be sure no noses were out of joint because we had spent quite a bit of time with Tacoma men.

Marshall, Mather, and I did sneak away to make a quick trip across the Olympic Peninsula to get a glimpse of Mount Olympus National Monument, which was held by the Forest Service in the Department of Agriculture. We all thought it spectacular and greedily eyed it as potential national park material (which didn't come about until I got it in 1933).

We were supposed to be driven by some local enthusiasts out of Seattle toward Mount Baker, but we deliberately got back too late. We didn't want to get into any discussions about making this area a national park. That left only an hour or so until we had to catch our train for Denver.

It was a relief just to rest and do little for a couple of days on the train. When we arrived in Denver on September 2, however, the frantic pace began again. Bob Yard was waiting for us at the hotel. He had been in Rocky Mountain National Park for a month, gathering information for the *National Parks Portfolio*. Yard and Mather spent the time before dinner talking over plans for their publicity campaign.

That night we attended a dinner given at the Brown Palace Hotel to honor Mather, who gave his usual pep talk. His ideas were getting bigger and bigger. Speaking of Rocky Mountain National Park, he said: "Some system that might be designated as an 'Americanized-Swiss' plan might be adopted with profit. We can adapt the Swiss idea of inns, chalets, and campsites at intervals of nine or twelve miles over a complete system of roads and trails covering all of the areas of scenic interest and combine these with some of the up-to-date American ideas and methods and make the great new park one of the greatest assets in the world."

The whole next day was spent with Mather while he consulted various individuals or groups. There was a delegation from Ouray, Telluride, and Silverton that pressed for a national park in their San Juan area. There were several others promoting Longs Peak, Pikes Peak, and numerous others of the great Rocky Mountains of Colorado. Mather hated to discourage anyone, so I was left to deliver his standard rejection: "At present, we have too much to do in existing parks. No more peaks for parks at this time."

While I was meeting with these groups, Mather had struck up an acquaintance with another delegation who called themselves the Park-to-Park Highway Association. Their goal was to promote a system of good roads to link the national parks of the Rocky Mountain area, a paved highway (few were paved at this time) from Rocky Mountain National Park to Yellowstone, 564 miles, and perhaps, then, on to Glacier. They had already organized a caravan to publicize the idea. The leader was Finlay MacFarland, a Packard dealer from Denver. A former mayor of the city, F. R. Mills, other Denverites, and a group from Wyoming led by Gus Holm of Cody were to leave the next day for Yellowstone.

Mather was delighted with the idea and volunteered all the help he could give. He went even further to inform the local papers that he had organized the caravan through the *Rocky Mountain News* and the Denver Chamber of Commerce. He would take the train and meet the auto party in Cody. They, in the meantime, would take notes of current road conditions, scenic points of interest, and other features, which he would compile into information the government would then publish.

September 4, 1915, was dedication day for Rocky Mountain National Park. At 7:30 A.M. a great throng of dignitaries and common folk assembled in their autos at the Majestic Building, Broadway and Sixteenth. Governor George A. Carlson, Congressmen Charles Timberlake and Edward Taylor, Mather's party, and delegations from the Denver Chamber of Commerce, Motor Club, and others were provided shiny new Packards by Finlay MacFarland to make the drive up to Horseshoe Park. As they pulled out, a grand procession of anything on wheels, estimated at about three hundred cars, followed the leaders 105 miles to Horseshoe Park. Bank president Leroy Bennett personally drove the Packard containing Mather, Governor Carlson, Congressman Taylor, and Horace Albright. Our driver knew every inch of the road, was a fascinating storyteller, and gave us a good grounding about this new park that none of us had ever seen—including the governor and congressman.

We arrived about noon and found that the local Women's Club of Estes Park had provided a lavish picnic-style lunch and hot coffee for all. The stirring music of the Loveland band boomed above the crowds of visitors until it was time for the formal ceremonies to begin. At 2:00 P.M. the twenty-five–piece band from Fort Collins called everyone toward the speakers' stand with a rousing rendition of "The Battle Hymn of the Republic." As Enos Mills of Estes Park, chairman of the park dedication, rose to address the crowd, the band struck up "America," and a group of schoolchildren sang. The patriotic spirit seemed to grip the audience, which lustily joined in for the second and third verses.

Mills then began to extol the beauties of the region he had worked all his life to make a national park. He was quite an orator and had everyone enthralled with the sentiments that rolled out. All of a sudden thunder, lightning, and a deluge of rain also rolled out. Mather was the next speaker. He labored through his speech, praising the beauty of the new park, while an absolute downpour washed over his bared, silver hair, tanned face, and almost worthless raincoat. Governor Carlson then launched into his sonorous oration. No one could hear a word for the thunderous roar of the storm. He cut his speech short and graciously backed up to his seat in a hastily contrived canvas shelter.

The next day the *Rocky Mountain News* reported: "As Governor Carlson concluded, the clouds parted as if by the action of some mighty, unseen hand, and the sun of Colorado broke forth in rain-tinged splendor from across the newly laid snow on Longs Peak and made a new fairy land of the dazzling land of bewilderment."

Our party escaped to tour as much of the park as we could before dinner. We returned to the Longs Peak Inn for a fine steak dinner. Afterward Mather, Yard, Trowbridge, the park's supervisor, and Enos Mills had a long conference—how long I don't know, because I wasn't asked to join them, so I gladly hurried off to bed.

Wonderland and Beyond
1915

Early the next morning, after the dedication of Rocky Mountain National Park, we ate a quick breakfast, drove to Loveland, and climbed on a train bound for Cody, Wyoming. I had never been to Yellowstone and was terribly excited about seeing "Wonderland," as the magazines called it. Although Mather had made his first trip earlier in the year with the House Appropriations Committee, he had not come in through the eastern entrance. At that time, though, he had met with men from Cody and had organized the Cody Sylvan Pass Motor Company to carry visitors from Cody to the Lake Hotel in Yellowstone.

Now Mather decided we would travel from Cody by stagecoach even though cars had been permitted in the park since August 1. The purpose of this trip was to see how the mix of car and stagecoach was working out. Well, we were traveling right along, bumpy and uncomfortable but moving at a pretty good clip, when we came on a string of autos. They were having a terrible time, trying to get up a steep grade; the road was just one big muddy mass of ruts. Our stagecoach was passing them neatly when Mather suddenly shouted to the driver to stop. He had recognized our friends from the Park-to-Park Highway Association, the ones who had driven all the way from Denver.

We in the stagecoach were bent over laughing at the situation, but when Mather got back in and we were on our way again, he gave us quite a lecture on the humiliating mess. He fretted and stewed over it, taking it all personally that he had pushed for autos to be allowed into Yellowstone, that he had encouraged the Denver group to come to the park, and just think of it, the roads were absolutely impassable—or impossible.

When we got into the park itself, we found conditions vastly better. Mather perked up and slipped back to his usual cheerful frame of mind. An excellent road system had been laid out many years before by army engineer Hiram Chittenden, the same one as at Mount Rainier. Colonel Lloyd Brett and his road man, Major Amos Fries, had been doing a wonderful job of maintaining them. We also found that the rigid schedule set for autos and stagecoaches was working well. Stagecoaches left early and proceeded about ten miles; then the automobiles were allowed to go and the coaches were drawn off to the side of the road.

We stayed in Yellowstone for only a few days, but it was long enough to make a thorough inspection. We covered the so-called Grand Loop, now traveling by automobile, as one day on the stagecoach had been quite enough. Mather was in and out of the car at every hotel, geyser, camp, cascade, garbage dump, and ranger station. I was right beside him with my ever-present notebook and pen, taking dictation.

I certainly did remember that magnificent park. This year of first experiencing Grand Canyon, Yosemite, Sequoia, Crater Lake, Mount Rainier, and Rocky Mountain had not prepared me for the kaleidoscopic wonders of Yellowstone. It had most of the sights the other parks had, plus extra marvels.

We left from the north entrance of Yellowstone at Gardiner to go to Glacier National Park, on the Montana-Canada border. We arrived on September 11 at Belton, on the western side of the park.

Right away Mather became agitated and unusually upset when he inspected the park headquarters, which was at the end of a terrible road up Fish Creek, not far from Lake McDonald. He stamped his feet and shouted that this situation would never do. Poor Samuel Ralston, the supervisor of Glacier, tried to explain that all the land between the railroad and the lake, about three miles plus the shoreline, with a good road running through it, was privately owned.

Mather instantly quieted down and said, "Well, if that's the only problem, I'll buy it myself." It was not for sale. As luck would have it, however, another tract nearby was to be sold on foreclosure. Through Ferris White, a brother of his attorney in Chicago, Mather bought that tract for eight thousand dollars. But there was one hitch. It was subject to redemption. A year later, when the man who had the right to redeem was going up the courthouse steps to exercise that right, he dropped dead. So Mather's luck held. Eventually he acquired the property and later gave it to the government.

This discussion took most of the day, so we weren't ready to leave on the trip across the mountains to the east side of the park until about 3:00 P.M. We crossed Lake McDonald to the John H. Lewis Hotel on the east shore, where our horses and pack outfit were waiting. It was already snowing very hard and piling up fast. Ralston, several rangers, and the packers all protested our attempt to start the trip.

Mather had just about been persuaded to call it off when Ralston mentioned that he was deeply concerned about a party that had started over the pass that morning, a Mr. Frederic A. Delano, vice-governor of the Federal Reserve Board, and his two young daughters. Well, Mather knew him in Chicago and was afraid he'd be ridiculed if it became known that he was too afraid to tackle a snowstorm that hadn't stopped Delano and the girls.

In ten minutes we were on our horses and off for the Continental Divide and East Glacier. As we began to climb up toward Gunsight Pass, the intensity of the storm was frightening. We could barely see a trace of a trail, and we were numbed by the slash of the snow and the biting wind. Frankly, I was scared to death, but we made it. When we reached Sperry Chalets, it seemed unbelievable that we had only traveled seven miles from the hotel. It was pitch black, the blizzard continued unabated, and everyone, even Mather, was ready to call it quits.

The Great Northern Railroad, under Louis Hill, had been the most powerful force behind the creation of Glacier National Park in 1910. The following year the company began an explosion of visitor accommodations in the park. By the time we made our first trip there in 1915, they had built two huge, luxurious hotels, Glacier Park and Many Glacier, as well as nine chalets, at Sperry, Gunsight, Going-to-the-Sun, St. Mary, Many Glacier, Granite Park, Belton, Two Medicine, and Cut Bank. Hill had been impatient about government appropriations for roads, so he had road construction begun to link the hotels.

When I awoke on the morning of September 12, I was almost afraid to open my eyes. Another day like yesterday was almost too much to contemplate. But, lo and behold, the sun was smiling out from a blue sky. The storm had worn itself out. I found my clothes had been dried out and even ironed, so I rushed outside. What a dazzling sight! It seemed impossible that every new national park appeared more spectacular than the last—or at least more unusual.

Sperry Chalets consisted of a lounge-dining chalet and a large three-storied dormitory chalet for fifty to seventy-five overnight guests. The buildings were constructed of local rock in the Swiss chalet style. They were perched on the wall of Sperry Glacier Basin at nearly seven thousand feet, surrounded by towering Mount Brown, Edwards Mountain, and Gunsight Mountain.

As I stood gaping at the awesome beauty, Mather joined me. Neither of us spoke for some time. Then I heard him say, "Horace, what God-given opportunity has come our way to preserve wonders like these before us? We must never forget or abandon our gift." One in spirit, we never did.

After a hearty breakfast, our packers had us ready to tackle Gunsight Pass. Working our way upward through snow and ice three feet deep on the dangerous, narrow, rocky trail, we reached the pass around noontime. From this notch in the Continental Divide between Mount Jackson (10,023 feet) and Gunsight Mountain (6,900 feet), we surveyed an incredible panorama—waves of peaks to the east and the valley of the St. Mary, whose waters flowed to Hudson's Bay. To the west could be seen the Lincoln Divide country and Lake Ellen Wilson, whose waters ran to the Pacific Ocean.

From here the descent to Gunsight Chalets was particularly treacherous, a series of switchbacks along sheer cliffs and over tilting snow fields. No one spoke. Our hands gripped the reins more from tension than from necessity. When Gunsight Chalets finally came into view, lying far below us at the base of Mount Jackson, someone let out with a lusty cheer. We all war-whooped along with him.

We reached these lodgings, resembling the other rocky Swiss-style chalets, around 2:00 P.M. Hugging the shore of Gunsight Lake, deep in the shadow of Mount Jackson, was a large, rambling, one-story lounge and dining chalet and a two-story dormitory that could accommodate fifty guests. Part of one chalet was being restored, as a grizzly bear had practically torn it apart the winter before. During the following winter the chalet units were wiped out by an avalanche and never rebuilt.

It had been a rugged day, but magnificent. The Sierra Nevada, the Cascades, the Absarokas, and now the Rockies of Glacier—all so breathtaking, so different. Though not as high in general as some of the other ranges, Glacier's peaks somehow seemed especially awesome. Whether it was the unusual tilt of the layers of rock, the giant flowing glaciers, or the deep valleys filled with dark blue lakes, I didn't know. But Glacier always remained one of my favorite national parks.

The following morning we rode the nine miles out to the Going-to-the-Sun Chalets at the head of Upper Lake St. Mary. It was a beautiful, restful boat trip ten miles down to the foot of the lake at St. Mary Chalets. The glimmering lake was enclosed by towering mountains, rocky promontories, and fingers of glaciers, its waters a brilliant emerald green.

One of Louis Hill's big touring cars waited here to drive us the thirty-two miles south to Glacier Park Station. The road was not finished yet, but the views of the Two Medicine and Cut Bank valleys were marvelous. Two or three times our car got bogged down, and the driver had a hard time extricating it from the mud. Finally, about eight miles from our destination, it got hopelessly stuck. Fortunately, some Blackfeet Indians came along on horseback. They hitched us to their horses and dragged us to where it was possible to drive once more.

While being pulled along, we came on another car equally mired in mud, with just one man in it. Mather went over to the gentleman and said: "My name is Stephen Mather. I'm assistant to the secretary of the interior and in charge of the park. Could I be of service?"

The gentleman came up snarling: "Just the man I'd been waiting to find, the one who has the responsibility for this horrible mess passing itself off as a road. My name is Burton K. Wheeler and I am United States district attorney for Montana." (He was later U.S. senator from Montana and candidate for vice-president in 1924.)

Well, of course, Mather soothed him down immediately by explaining about the lack of a central park management as well as bare bones appropriations. Being a politician, Wheeler caught on fast and apologized—though somewhat grudgingly. The Indians hauled him out too, and his lighter car could get along by itself while we followed, horse-drawn. What a mess. Typical national park roads!

We spent the night at the Glacier Park Hotel, completed only a few years before. How does one even describe the "Great Trees Lodge," so called by the local Blackfeet Indians? First, there was a lobby four stories high with twenty-four giant fir-tree pillars ringing it, huge Indian-design carpets, a buffalo skin tipi, great Japanese lanterns, shops, and other wonders. Then came a dining room to seat two hundred hungry people at a time, waitresses in Swiss costumes, not to mention a swimming pool, a sun parlor with afternoon tea, outbuildings with laundry, a power plant, a fire station, and an eighteen-hole golf course (yet to be constructed). It was a thousand feet from the railroad station, with real Blackfeet tipis nearby and real Blackfeet Indians who greeted the trains, danced on the lawn at regular intervals, and posed for endless picture-taking by the tourists (for a few pieces of silver, of course).

Mather was fascinated. Here was the perfect hotel for a national park. And he loved the chalets too. He would contact Louis Hill right away to get plans and specifications for the Glacier hotels and chalets. He'd have Daniels get to work adapting them to specific national parks: a luxurious one for Yosemite, one at the rim of Crater Lake, etc.

"Wouldn't these resort hotels be just right, Horace?" he enthused. I didn't say much, just admitted it was all pretty awesome, but somehow this particular one seemed awfully big, too ostentatious for the lovely natural setting. We agreed, though, that Glacier certainly had the jump on the other parks in accommodating the tourists, but its roads, trails, and personnel were just as woefully inadequate.

On September 14 Mather and I parted company. He went west to California and I headed east to Washington. Leaving Glacier in the ice, snow, and subfreezing temperatures, I hit Chicago two days later on the hottest day of the year.

Back at the office on Friday, September 17, I found my desk completely covered with paperwork that had piled up during the nearly three months away in the West. Furthermore, there were four telegrams from Mather: problems and instructions on Daniels, the Desmond Company, the Powell memorial at Grand Canyon, and other issues.

Late Monday afternoon my appointment with Secretary Lane lasted two hours while I related our trip in detail and presented problems, evaluations, actions taken or proposals for urgent consideration. He was quiet, thoughtful, and extremely interested.

It also turned out he was not all that pleased. He questioned me minutely on the Yosemite concession situation and Mark Daniels. Even though I skirted Mather's personal financial involvement with the new Yosemite company, Lane was uneasy about the other actions Mather had taken and agreed that top legal men in the Interior Department should review them immediately. In the meantime, until Mather returned to Washington to confer on the entire Yosemite problem, Lane felt that Desmond should be allowed to operate a monopoly. Curry and the other Yosemite concessioners would give half their net profit to the Desmond

Company, and in turn Desmond would give fifty percent of its net to the government. It wasn't my place to argue, but, knowing Curry, I felt the secretary would have an explosion on his hands.

This turned out to be true. A few days later I received a letter from Mather in California: "Curry is acting up very badly, trying to make as much trouble for Desmond as he can and the situation is somewhat complicated in view of the fact that the Secretary had taken it up."

I replied to him: "The Secretary believes that all hotel and camp concessions should be under one management ultimately, but Desmond has not gone about his end of the proposition properly . . . and has been directly the cause of Curry's determination to carry his case to Washington. He is dubious about your being able to get Curry in with Desmond under any circumstances."

In the same letter I pointed out that Lane was almost more disturbed about Mark Daniels. "The Secretary is pretty sore at Daniels," I wrote. There were two immediate headaches. First, Daniels had gotten an architect, Mr. Multgart, to work up plans for Desmond's new accommodations in Yosemite. Second, apparently while Daniels was in Denver, he solicited work for his own architectural firm to do a lucrative job for the Park Commission, a real conflict of interest.

I was relieved to be able to tell Lane that both of these had been settled. Mather had written me: "Multgart had prepared a perfectly impossible lot of plans for Desmond involving an expense of $300,000 and looking more like a fine piece of architecture in the Court of Abundance than a mountain hotel. I told Daniels I would not even submit it to the Secretary and was surprised that Multgart had been working along those lines. It is such an ornate scheme that it would not harmonize with Daniels's plan for a village. It's finished."

And I contacted the people in Denver, informing them of Daniels's conflict of interest. They assured me that the San Francisco firm would be given no further consideration for their work. Lane was relieved but said: "Why the fellow has no conscience, has he? Anyway, no conception of the relation between his private and official positions."

At this point Mrs. Lane, who had come into the room during our conversation, spoke up: "Frank, I have for a long time thought you should get rid of Daniels."

As it turned out, Lane decided to leave the entire matter to Mather when he returned. I wrote my boss: "I am sure that whatever you suggest about getting Mr. Daniels out, he will act upon your advice. However, I am not away from my opinion that it is going to be a little difficult to work the 'Chief' [Robert Marshall] in."

The two problems of Yosemite concessions and Daniels consumed an inordinate amount of time for the next few months for Mather and me. Fortunately, both were settled, Daniels permanently and Desmond-Curry temporarily.

Mark Daniels was young, handsome, intelligent, a fine architect, a good conservationist, a great storyteller and after-dinner speaker. But he couldn't establish authority over the tough, independent supervisors of the parks. Next, his bookkeeping system was driving everyone crazy, as it was impossibly complicated. As pleasant a fellow as he was, he somehow kept putting his foot in his mouth and making enemies of important people. Lastly, this matter of carrying on his Daniels & Wilhelm architectural firm in San Francisco and at the same time conducting all kinds of government business—sometimes in conflict—well, it was borderline at best.

Finally, Mather had decided Daniels just wasn't the kind of a man he wanted to become director of a park service once it was officially created. He had become very fond of Robert Marshall and felt he was the sort who could run it once Mather and Albright had pulled out. So Mather began to look for ways to slip Daniels out and Marshall in.

Knowing that Daniels and Marshall didn't like each other and had broken out into open rivalry on the mountain party in the summer, Mather planned to make things just a little difficult for Daniels and at the same time hand out important work to Marshall. When Mather asked me to set up some assignments for Marshall, I offered an alternative. Being afraid that jealousy and open warfare between the two men would be harmful, I suggested that Mather speak openly and honestly to Daniels: give him a chance to leave quietly, letting him tender his resignation.

It happened just that way. Mark Daniels, with utmost goodwill, resigned as of the end of 1915. He was really relieved to give up parks and return to his lucrative architectural work. Afterward he remained a fine friend, often rendering good advice and unpaid work. His San Francisco park office was closed.

Mather organized a new office in the Interior Department, a miniature model for his future park service, with Bob "The Chief" Marshall as general superintendent of national parks. From the Geological Survey, Marshall brought along his secretary, Isabelle Story, and his chief draftsman, Arthur Demaray, both of whom became real stalwarts of the Park Service for the rest of their lives.

Now, as to our other problem: Yosemite concessions. Things went from bad to worse. Curry went to Desmond's San Francisco office, where the two men got into hand-to-hand combat. The newspaper account said Curry got the worst of it all with, among other things, a black eye. Secretary Lane swore he had had enough of these fellows and telegraphed all concessioners in Yosemite to attend a meeting in his office on October 15. Before going to Washington, Curry launched an intensive advertising campaign against the "Desmondizing" of Yosemite, advising people to write or telegraph Lane to get rid of Desmond. Of course, this only infuriated Lane more.

Along with Mather, Albright, and the secretary, David and Mary Curry, Daniel Joseph Desmond, and representatives of other hotels, stables, and the meat market were present in Lane's office on the morning of October 15. Mather explained his desire for improved facilities and his belief in a monopoly to handle all services. For two days the discussions went on, with most of the concessioners agreeing to sell out to the Desmond Company. Harry Best's photography studio and a couple of others were exempt, as Mather didn't think them important enough. Both Curry and his wife absolutely refused to sell and said they'd see everyone present, as well as the rich San Francisco backers of Desmond, in hell before they'd change their minds.

Actually, Lane had come around to feeling a great deal of sympathy for the Currys and was toying with the idea of giving them the monopoly. That is, until he lost his patience with David Curry's ranting. Then he cut them off and arbitrarily granted Desmond a twenty-year franchise. However, out of respect for Mary Curry or because of the numerous letters and telegrams resulting from Curry's ads, Lane held off on a monopoly for Desmond. He granted the Currys a single year lease. Nothing was really settled, as a barrage of events the following year demonstrated.

When Mather had returned from California, after taking his wife and daughter home to Chicago, he gave up his suite at the Powhatan Hotel. Marshall and Secretary Lane had jointly sponsored Mather for membership in the prestigious Cosmos Club on Lafayette Square, and he was duly elected during the summer. This gave him the opportunity to move over there. Members, chosen for distinguished professional and business accomplishments, formed a sort of fraternal organization and a gentlemen's club. Mather thoroughly enjoyed this convivial atmosphere and opportunity to find interesting (and usually helpful) people from many walks of life.

Without women in our lives, Mather and I would often eat dinner together, usually at the Cosmos Club. At the end of one long November day, he said: "Let's have dinner at the club. We need to have a long talk. We have our futures to think about."

We had a leisurely dinner in the Cosmos dining room, known for its fine food, spacious view of Lafayette Square, and, I might add, the lack of women, who were not allowed inside the sacred compound. Afterward we went up to Mather's rooms and talked until nearly 2:00 A.M. He took his shoes off, sank into a comfortable chair, and put his stockinged feet on a low table, waving his hand to me to settle into the matching chair opposite him.

He began by saying: "Well, Horace, we said we'd give it one year to straighten out the parks and get a bill through Congress authorizing a bureau for them. That year is almost up. Get a piece of stationery over on the desk and let's make a list of what we think we have accomplished." I still have the list I made that night.

1. STM is satisfied that we have covered a vast area of the country (he about thirty-five thousand miles), accomplished some worthwhile things, and learned many important lessons from our travels and the people we got to know. He feels that our inspections of most of the larger national parks have taught us both a great deal. He added that he hadn't caught up with me yet in knowledge of the Interior Department and the Congress, but what difference did it make as long as I attended to these matters! (He laughed at that.)

2. STM recognizes that his principal task was to obtain authority for a park bureau in the national government and find a director to lead such a bureau. "I bow to you on this score, Horace," he said. "You always put this first, and I've been putting the condition of the parks first. The focus was off just a bit as I was genuinely so appalled at their condition. So much worse than I had thought when I took this job. But by working on the problems of the individual parks, I think we've gotten them ready to be put into a unified system. So that's a plus."

3. STM thinks we have appreciated the problems arising from the advent of the automobile and have begun taking steps to accommodate them—improving and adding roads, etc.

4. STM feels his greatest accomplishment was in the field of concessions, instituting the idea of monopolies, planning new

construction, and interesting people in investing in accommodations, transportation, etc.

5. STM says we can't take much credit for the superb job of publicity. Yard has accomplished miracles in that field and made Americans very conscious of their national parks.

6. Most of all, STM says that we have made a marvelous team! And I did keep him out of jail! (More laughs at me.) I add my agreement. He's the dynamo, the enthusiast, the public relations man, I the detailer, analyzer, pragmatist, and suspicious lawyer!

"Read your list back to me now and let's see if we've used our year well or whether we'd better high-tail it out of Washington," he jokingly said. So I read it all.

Suddenly he switched topics and moods as he was prone to do. "Now what are we going to do in the future? I've pretty well decided we'll have to extend our stay for another year, as we didn't reach the primary goal of getting the park legislation through. That will now have to take precedence over all other matters. Now we'll . . . "

I interrupted him at this point: "Mr. Mather, you're using the word 'we' when you should not be including me. I am adamant in holding to my promise to my fiancee and even to Secretary Lane that I would not stay longer than one year. I'm almost twenty-six years old and have got to get going on my legal career. It's my chosen field of work, although I have loved every minute of this past year and the national park work. We can discuss the future of the parks, but please leave me out of it."

Mather remained quiet, staring straight into my eyes and obviously doing a lot of thinking. I met his gaze. This lasted maybe three or four minutes. Then he spoke softly and told me that he couldn't take exception to anything I had said, that he understood my feelings. Especially about "your most charming Grace."

But he gave me to understand that if I wouldn't stay, neither would he, that I was that essential to his making a success of setting up this National Park Service. I don't believe I had ever been so proud, but I reiterated that I had to leave at the end of this year.

More silence. He suddenly, vehemently, barked out: "I simply must stay and finish up this job—and you can't leave me. Now I've been bitten by an idea. Here's my proposition to you. Go out to California for the Christmas season, see your family, marry your lovely girl, have a nice honeymoon, and then bring her back with you to Washington and stay with me for another year, or until we get the park service created and organized. Of course, I'll keep up your supplemental income of two hundred dollars a month. How's that sound to you?"

I thought about it for only a few minutes and then told him I'd contact Grace and give him an answer as soon as possible.

Again came the mercurial switch in mood as he jumped to his feet and said, "Now here's another thing. You know, we'd hoped to inspect Hot Springs Reservation and never made it. Let's go down there right away for a few days, take the baths, rest up and work all this out."

That was fine with me, and as soon as I agreed to this Mather typically ordered, "Get another piece of paper, Horace, and let's make a list of what we have to do in the future." I inwardly groaned, feeling he hadn't taken me seriously, that he was already assured of getting his own way. Actually, of course, he understood me well enough to know I'd already capitulated. But out came paper and pen once more, and here is the second list, which I also saved:

1. STM says the national park service, a bureau to administer the affairs of the parks and monuments as a system and under uniform policies, must be created from the Smoot and Raker bills then pending before the Congress. An interim organization must be set up in Washington to take the place of Daniels's field office, which is to be discontinued. This would be headed by Marshall, giving him the authority and responsibility to test him for a possible future directorship as well as relieving both of us from some of the detail work. Also, a program for the permanent bureau, when created, must be set up which would include policies for development and protection of the parks, improvement of roads, encouragement of business enterprise for public accommodation, and for rounding out our existing parks—internal private holdings as well as exterior boundaries—and securing worthy additions to the system.

2. STM thinks we should only ask for modest increases in appropriations to take care of needed improvements in roads, mainly widening them and eliminating hazardous curves, etc., for automobile safety.

3. As to improvement and extension of facilities in the parks—not to be just roads and trails, but telephone lines and power and sewage

installations. Use the authority given the Secretary of the Interior in 1883 to grant concessions. STM says that, from his experience in the City Club of Chicago, he learned about the public responsibility of utilities and service companies and what controls they should have and what they should pay. Above all, we should find men who would consider making investments in park enterprises.

4. STM says that, aside from the Sequoia extension of the Kings and Kern Canyons, the restoration of the Minaret and Devils Postpile areas to Yosemite, the addition of the large southern area eliminated from the Rocky Mountain organic act at the last minute on objections of cattlemen and miners, and the Grand Canyon of Arizona, we should temporarily forget additions to the park system.

Here we came to a halt on the list. Perhaps because I thought I might not be involved in future operations or maybe because I felt I could always speak freely to him, I openly disagreed with Mather on this last proposal. I said that I honestly thought we shouldn't limit the acquisitions. Lassen, Hawaii, and the great Alaska park should be pushed in the Congress too.

I also thought we shouldn't overlook the East. I told him I had become acquainted with a Mr. Dorr, who was trying to create a national park along the coast of Maine at Mount Desert Island. Eastern parks seemed a very practical idea to me, for most of the American people lived east of the Mississippi, so they were represented by most of the Congress. Therefore, if these constituents had some parks too, it would mean more consideration for the national park idea and more appropriations for the whole system. And anyway, didn't the people in the East deserve some parks without having to travel thousands of miles to get to the great western ones?

Mather gave me a steely eyed look and sharply said, "Nonsense! The wonderlands are in the West. Once people hear about them and more roads are improved, they'll make the trip."

Nothing more was said at this time, but it was one of only a few basic policies that we never really agreed on, although he never stood in my way.

I wasn't able to write Grace the next day, as Mather and I went to Baltimore for an all-day conference with some railroad people and then to a dinner party that night. I decided to say nothing further to Mather until I had consulted with Grace. But time was getting short and, as frugal as I was, I splurged and telegraphed her on November 24—a night letter, of course.

It must have been a real shock to her because I had never suggested that I might stay more than the year with Mather. I'm afraid I simply hadn't much experience with my fiancée—or for that matter, any experience with any women. I just didn't think past my own plans.

Imagine, as a young bride-to-be, receiving the following telegram with no prior consultation: "Will remain with Secretary M. Can you set date at Christmas or few days afterwards. Can be away from Washington December 12th to about January 5th. Reply tomorrow night. Am leaving Friday afternoon for Arkansas. Address letters Arlington Hotel, Hot Springs. Serves you right for paying attention to a whirlwind. Lovingly, Horace."

Back came her telegram—not stingy. It was a day letter. "Telegram received. Everything satisfactory. How about December 23rd and remain in vicinity for X'mas. Otherwise 27th but prefer 23rd. Both of us wanted for big family dinner X'mas day in San Francisco. Will write to Arkansas. Lovingly, Grace."

Her telegram gives the whole picture of this remarkably thoughtful girl: agreeing to my wishes with no questions asked, no protests, no complaints, and thinking of our families at Christmas.

We didn't get away to Arkansas as fast as we thought we would. Lane had already told me to assemble all the national park data for the annual report of the Department of the Interior. Now he had me coordinate the reports of all the bureaus in the department as well as extraneous information and assemble them for the finished product. I'm sure it would have been impossible without the knowledge and help of W. B. Acker. He stayed long hours many a night with me, getting that report in shape.

At the same time, Lane instructed Mather and me to learn how to estimate appropriations and other routine obligations. Again Acker did most of the teaching. He was always patient, good-humored, and endlessly knowledgeable. We used to say the whole Interior Department could be run with Acker and a few secretaries.

Another reason we stayed around in Washington was a banquet in honor of Stephen Mather. Gilbert Grosvenor and the National Geographic Society were the hosts. It was given on November 17 at the Cosmos Club. The Mather Mountain Party was the focus of the evening, and most members of it were present. We had a great time reminiscing, singing songs from the campfire evenings, and best of all watching a few movies taken on the trip. They were marvelous and brought forth more laughter and storytelling.

When the evening drew to a close, Grosvenor presented Mather with a special enlarged photo of the three of us when we hiked up to the notch where we could see the Kaweah Peaks spread out ahead and Rockslide Lake below. Everyone in the Sierra party was given an envelope of Grosvenor's pictures of the trip, a marvelous memento, for he was a superb photographer.

Hot Springs, Battlefields, and a Wedding
1915–16

Finally, at the end of November 1915, Mather and I were able to get away from Washington for the long-planned inspection of Hot Springs Reservation in Arkansas. Included in the party that finally reached Hot Springs were Mather, his wife, and various friends and business associates.

I was part of the welcoming committee from the Business Men's League when they met the Mather party as their train pulled into the Missouri Pacific Station in Hot Springs on a warm, cloudless November 29. From the station the party was taken to the Arlington Hotel in old-fashioned, open horse-drawn carriages.

The Arlington Hotel was on Central Avenue, the main thoroughfare of the city, a broad, shaded street lined with elaborate bath houses on one side and imposing hotels everywhere else. The Arlington was the largest and most luxurious of these. It was a magnificent multistoried, Italianate-style conglomeration of soaring twin towers with an arched portico around the base and a roof garden on top. Inside, it sported every luxury imaginable—various dining areas, a swimming pool, massage parlors, and a ballroom. All was marble with stained glass, intricate iron works, and tiled floors. A few years after our visit, it burned down, only to be replaced by an even larger and more grandiose Arlington.

After refreshing ourselves in our rooms, everyone gathered for a lovely luncheon. Then the ladies excused themselves while Mather's male group, plus local park officials and businessmen, went on a tour of Hot

Springs. It took six carriages to accommodate us all. This was the first visit for both Mather and me, and we were quite impressed. In fact, it became one of Mather's favorite spots, to which he retreated when things got too stressful.

Hot Springs had been the first *reservation* area set aside by the federal government, in 1832, thirty-two years before Yosemite and forty years before Yellowstone. It did not actually become a *national park* until 1921, and somehow it never seemed like a national park. In 1915 it was a small city of about twelve thousand people nestled in a narrow valley surrounded by heavily forested hills of the Ozark Mountains. About fifty miles away, but still hovering over it, was Hot Springs Mountain, from whose sides the hot mineral waters flowed down into town. These radium, silicon, and other mineral-laden waters poured forth from forty-six springs at an average temperature of 135 degrees. They were channeled into bath houses and other facilities, all of which were under the supervision of the Department of the Interior, which performed inspections and set rates. There was additional land in the reservation outside the city—mountainous country, a lake, and some streams for fishing.

Mather was eagerly looking forward to experiencing the full treatment at one of the marble palaces on "Bathhouse Row." We were informed that we had to have a physician check us out before we could go. Again the federal government was omnipresent, as all physicians had to be passed by a local federal board. When we appeared at the appointed physician's office, we were handed a circular, which stated:

> Relief may be reasonably expected at the Hot Springs in the following conditions: In various forms of gout and rheumatism; neuralgia, especially when depending on gout; metallic or malarial poisoning, paralysis not of organic origin, the earlier stages of locomotor ataxia, chronic Bright's disease and other diseases of the urinary organs, functional diseases of the liver, gastric dyspepsia not of organic origin, chronic diarrhea, catarrhal affections of the digestive and respiratory tracts, chronic skin diseases, especially the squamous varieties, and chronic conditions due to malarial infection.

This was signed by the surgeon-general of the U.S. Army and the secretary of war.

Furthermore, we were informed that the Interior Department had employed the world-renowned authority on radium Professor Bertram B. Boltwood of Yale University to make exhaustive tests on the water. He reported, among other things, that "the waters of the Arkansas Hot Springs are radio-active to a marked degree. And the radiation from radium and its disintegration products produces an ionization of the atoms of whatever substance the rays penetrate. Chemical effects follow the ionization."

Well, Mather and I felt we were not only going to see the wonders of the bath house but to experience a fountain of youth. So off we went to the finest one in town, the Fordyce Bath House, adjoining the "Grand Entrance to the Government Reservation," a gateway of stone pillars topped by eagles.

We were stunned by the splendor. According to its brochure, Fordyce was a spectacular three-story "Spanish Renaissance building of soft, ivory-glazed terra cotta, combined with tapestry brick." Inside, the walls were of veined marble with pink marble staircases, mosaic tile floors, flowing fountains (one of Hernando De Soto receiving a drink from an Indian girl), and an art nouveau dome made of eight thousand pieces of glass depicting Neptune's daughter and playmates.

We were stripped, wrapped in robes, and escorted to the thermo room for a hot "bake" on a porcelain cot. After that, I'm not sure in what order we were "treated." There was a Turkish hot room, a needle and shower room, a pack room with rows of porcelain cots to recuperate on, and a cooling room. There was a hydro-therapeutic room, where they tried to tempt us to use the sun-ray cabinets, frigid cabinets, spray machines, and Sitzbaths (later I found these were mainly for visitors who had syphilis).

We thought we were through when we completed the tour of the first floor, but we had hardly started. We went up the marble staircase to the second floor and a very short stay in the mechano-therapy department, where we tried out some of what the brochure called "scientific wonders, every conceivable mechanical device and ingenious 'Zander-gymnastic' equipment—artificial rowing & horseback, vibrators, etc."

On the third floor we gave only a passing glance to one of the twenty-two "private staterooms" (eight by twelve feet with maid and valet service), the gymnasium (punching bags, vaulting horses, trapeze), the luxurious assembly hall spanning the entire front of the building, with the gentlemen's parlor and billiard room at one end, the ladies' parlor, beauty shop, and music room at the opposite end. A magnificent lighted roof garden topped the building, where tables, benches, and couches were profusely scattered, so that a visitor could enjoy refreshments and the panorama of the city and the Ozarks, day or night.

Mather and I were almost worn out from all this inspection. Not just from trying all the waters and sports activities but from laughing so much. Every new bath or drink of that awful mineral water set us both off into gales of laughter. Staggering out of the great pool onto a wide marble bench, he gasped, "Horace, how much more of this can we take?" Before I could answer, our tour guide suggested that we follow him and try the "vapor experience," so down to the first-floor bath rooms we went. Here were deep tubs with very hot water—a very pleasant and relaxing experience. Then up to the massage room for the highlight of our visit—a long, remarkable rubdown and, for me at least, a short catnap.

The rest of our time in Hot Springs was most enjoyable. There was a lavish banquet in honor of Mr. Mather at the Arlington Hotel on the night of November 30, hosted by the Business Men's League. Someone had rounded up three of the finest chefs in town to prepare an elaborate menu. Not wanting to appear stupid or ignorant, I ate every exotic bite, even the Rockaways and Snowbird, without knowing what either was. I still don't know.

In between social activities and department business, everyone enjoyed hours of rest and more adventures in the bath houses. Mather became almost addicted to them. Several times when no one could find him, I went to Bath House Row and checked each place until I located him. Usually he turned up at his favorite, the Fordyce, always in the waters or getting a massage. I had the last page from the Fordyce brochure framed and sent it to Mather for Christmas. It was a drawing of an old wheelchair covered with cobwebs and underneath was printed "Permanently Interred." I pasted a picture of Mather on it as though he was the one in the wheelchair.

Up at dawn on December 3, Mather and I joined some local people for a horseback trip to Ozark-Lithia Springs. We had breakfast there and exchanged horses for automobiles to visit Mountain Valley. It was a beautiful ride up and back through the lush forests. Returning to Ozark, we mounted our horses once more and rode back to Hot Springs.

I barely had time to wash up, change clothes, grab my suitcase and my typewriter, and race off to the depot, as my train for Washington left at 2:30 P.M. Mr. and Mrs. Mather and their party didn't leave for Chicago until 5:50 P.M. Naturally a full contingent of the local press heard and reported Mather's farewell comments. But imagine my surprise when the *Hot Springs New Era* included a few pearls of wisdom from "Mr. Mather's Secretary, Harry M. Albright."

I took the long way around to get back to Washington, traveling via Memphis and Chattanooga. With my love of history, I couldn't pass up the first War Department battlefield park. As soon as I got off the train in Chattanooga, I spent twenty-five cents for *Book of Battles: Chickamauga, Chattanooga, Lookout Mountain and Missionary Ridge*. It stands out as the most complete guidebook I ever had.

It was early in the morning, so I spent the entire day following that guidebook, riding streetcars along the flatlands and a horse-drawn buggy to the top of Lookout Mountain, but mainly on foot. Twice self-appointed guides, both Confederate veterans, showed me around. Neither had been in these battles, but they were very knowledgeable because they had put in long years of fighting. One had served with Lee's Army of Northern Virginia and had been at Appomattox. The other was in Joseph Johnston's army when Sherman was marching through Georgia.

It was a fascinating experience. I never forgot that day, as I'm sure it marked the germination of my plan to get battlefields and other historic places into the future national park system. When I was traveling toward Washington that night, I got out my typewriter, wrote Mr. Mather about my visit to Chattanooga, and told him my thoughts about getting these battlefields away from the War Department. I didn't say too much, but I did mention that I felt other types of historic areas should also be included under our projected bureau.

It seemed rather revolutionary, but I was really fired up. Just one quote from this shows my youth and inexperience, but also my determination when I set out to do something. "Why should a military department be in charge of lands which are predominantly an attraction for all the people? It seems to me that our new bureau ought to be concerned with all areas the Federal Government wishes to preserve and protect for the education, interest and enjoyment of the population. I guess you think I am grasping at too large a concept, but I have real determination to plunge into this thing with the War Department if you are in agreement and I have some spare time in Washington."

Back at the Interior Department for about ten days, I quickly cleared up all correspondence and minor problems that had accumulated while I was in Arkansas. The only thing of real importance was assuring that all loose ends were tied up regarding the completion of Mark Daniels's work. He was officially out of the Interior Department on December 10, 1915.

Then my only other concern was to find a nice but inexpensive jewelry store and buy a wedding ring. The night before I was to leave, the

Adolph Millers had me over for dinner and gave me a beautiful cut-glass lemonade pitcher and glasses as a wedding gift to take to Grace.

Washington was almost deserted for the holidays, so I managed to get away to California on December 15. In Chicago Mather's chauffeur met me at the train and took me to the Prairie Club, where Mather and I had lunch and spent a few hours discussing the latest news. I brought him all the paperwork that seemed important, my twenty-one–page report on our trip to Hot Springs, as well as a summation of recommendations for its improvement.

Then on across the country for the third time this year. And quite a trip it was—a raging blizzard most of the way. At Cheyenne I remember our Pacific Limited was covered with ice, and the Pullman doors had to be chopped free to let passengers get off.

But at 8:40 A.M. on December 19 the California sun was shining brilliantly as I arrived in Oakland and saw my Grace running down the platform and into my arms. Three days of fun, excitement, partying, and opening gifts concluded with the happiest day of my life—my wedding to Grace Marian Elizabeth Noble.

We were married at the First Presbyterian Church in Berkeley on the bleak, foggy night of December 23, 1915. The bride was late because the dressmaker bringing her veil crashed into a fire hydrant in the dense fog and Grace's mother suddenly decided her wedding dress wasn't "modest" enough. So a lace insert had to be added at the neckline. Minister Lapsley McAfee concluded the lovely ceremony with words we always obeyed: "Be lovers always." A party at the Noble home on Ellsworth Street followed the ceremony. My old granddad was late, as he got lost in the fog, drove off the road, and plowed through a fence into a barn. This wasn't the only catastrophe for the evening. When Grace and I were ready to leave on our honeymoon, my dad tripped on the leg of a table loaded with food and upended it all over my new father-in-law.

We newlyweds took a taxi to the Hotel Oakland for our wedding night. Grace always loved to tell the story that, when I locked the door of our room, she took one horrified look at me, panicked, fled to the bathroom crying, and threw up. As she said, "When he turned that bolt, my stomach turned with it." She added that she sat in the bathroom wondering who this man was that she had married, having only seen him a few dozen times in her life. Well, all ended well, as she said she never felt that way again. And years later, on our sixty-third wedding anniversary, I was taped as saying, "When the Golden Anniversary arrives, it's the husband who cries."

The festive Christmas season united Albrights and Nobles but ended all too soon. A telegram from Mather summoned me back to Washington, instructing me to return by way of Grand Canyon. On December 31, 1915, we newlyweds boarded a train for Los Angeles, then headed east on the Santa Fe Railroad's Navajo. This was Grace's first trip across the country, a wondrous experience. At Williams, Arizona, we transferred to another train for the run to the park and late in the morning of January 2, 1916, checked into El Tovar.

El Tovar was a low, rambling, rustic-style building, built of local rock and pine logs, and perched on the very edge of the great canyon. It was owned and operated by the Santa Fe Railroad and Fred Harvey Company. Three hundred visitors could enjoy steam heat and electric lights, a solarium, lounges upstairs and down, a beautiful dining room serving the renowned Harvey food, and luxurious rooms looking out over the canyon.

We were met by the only official of the federal government, Forest Service Ranger Claude Way. Grand Canyon Forest Reserve had been established in 1893 and made a national monument in 1908, but was kept in the Department of Agriculture until made a national park in 1919. So I had no jurisdiction or even a right to make an inspection of the area. But Mather and I already regarded Grand Canyon as ours.

Mrs. Way was waiting for us at El Tovar, reserving the best table in the dining room. She was a fascinating person, beautiful, with a vivacious personality, and full of entertaining stories of the times she had spent as a trick rider with Buffalo Bill's Wild West show.

After we had enjoyed a fine breakfast, I was anxious to get on with my appointed job of inspection, as we were only going to be here a short time. Mrs. Way had thoughtfully brought along all the winter equipment the Albrights might need to hike to the Way cabin. It was a beautiful, clear day, sharply cold, but not unpleasant. We four took our time walking along the canyon rim to let Grace get her first view of its splendor.

For Way and myself, it was a careful examination of mining claims along some of the choice sections of the rim. I was angry and depressed at the problem, knowing that these inholdings were damaging our attempts to have the Grand Canyon changed to a national park. The mining situation also didn't help with our scheme to "rob" the Forest Service, not only of the canyon but also of Kaibab lands on the north rim to enlarge our future park. Although Way was in the Forest Service, he was our kind of park conservationist, sympathized with our plans, and asked me outright to consider him as park supervisor if the service was created and, eventually, the Grand Canyon was brought under it.

The ladies had been patient through all this, but were now beginning to freeze, so we cut back through the forest toward the Way cabin, three miles of difficult terrain. By the time we reached it, dark clouds and a rising wind had sprung up. Soon it was snowing heavily. We were forced to stay indoors and even spend the night, for it was impossible to return to the hotel. That was sad, for Ford Harvey had left instructions for us to be extended complimentary accommodations and meals.

The next morning we woke to a brilliant blue sky and mounds of new snow. Grace was dressed and outside playing in it before I could even shave. When I joined her, she was like a child, laughing and shouting while we had a great snowball fight and a duel with three-foot-long icicles. There was much picture taking. A horse and an outfit (Mrs. Way's fancy showgirl clothes) were produced for her to climb aboard for her first picture as a western cowgirl.

Our day was spent with the Ways on a sightseeing and inspection trip by sleigh around the "Rim Drive." We stopped over at Hermit's Rest, a remarkable building designed by Mary Colter. It appeared to be an almost haphazard pile of rocks, merging into the landscape, with a stone deck extending to the very edge of the canyon. Inside, the building was a large open area with a vaulted ceiling and glass windows facing the canyon. We sat before the immense, arched rock fireplace, with the huge blazing logs quickly thawing us out while we had tea and cakes and drank in the splendor of the view. Grace was fascinated by the place and had the Ways take pictures of us inside by the hearth and outside seated on furniture made of tree stumps.

We had a hard time pulling ourselves away from this beautiful and charming place, but time was getting short. At last we were able to enjoy our lovely room at El Tovar, overlooking the canyon, while we washed and changed clothes. Then we again joined the Ways and had a notable dinner, but unfortunately we couldn't even sample all the delicious food. Our train was about to pull out for Williams at 7:45 P.M. There the Pullman connected to the eastbound California Limited, the most deluxe of the Santa Fe line.

As nice as the Navajo had been, this California Limited was positively elegant. This was a through-travel-only train. Local passengers were not carried. It was strictly first-class. Green upholstery was used with koko, mahogany, and satinwood interior finish. Dining was not the same on all Santa Fe Railroad trains. Most lesser-fare trains were served with dining cars east of Kansas City, dining rooms west. The latter were usually in splendid hotels along the way at Albuquerque, Gallup, and other stops. Our sumptuous dining car was a through car and had linen, silver, and cut glass, ferns, and ceiling fans (to remove all kitchen odors). There was a whole car devoted to the gentlemen—a smoking and reading room, a barbershop, a porter to press clothes, and daily papers to keep up with the stock market. Of course, the ladies were unable to enjoy it—no women allowed.

Now comes the tale my beloved wife told about me for years to come. After breakfast the next morning, I bundled my bride in the warmest clothes she had, wrapped her in a train blanket, and seated her on a carpet-covered wicker camp chair on the rear platform of the observation car. As we headed across Arizona and New Mexico, it began to snow again. Besides the snow and soot from the coal-burning engine, there was a wind chill factor about forty degrees below zero.

From Bob Marshall I had acquired a fine United States Geological Survey guidebook, a description of the rail trip from Chicago to California. There were some problems about the book. It was written for someone going from east to west, and the Albrights were going from west to east. And another thing: it was written by geologists for geologists. Information other than about rocks was rather limited. While my bride almost froze to death, I stood up and read the book aloud, on and on, from back to front. There were endless pages like: "About 4 miles west of Newton is an area of sand and gravels which fill a broad, moderately deep underground valley in shale, excavated by a large stream that long ago flowed across the region from the north and finally deposited the gravel and sand."

As usual, Grace was a real trooper and never complained. Not then, at least. Recalling this honeymoon ride sixty-three years later, she remarked: "It was my first lesson in sightseeing with Horace Albright. He never missed one detail, and he's never missed one since."

The Albrights arrived in Chicago at 11:15 A.M. on Thursday the sixth. I guess Grace was never so glad in her life to reach civilization and distance herself from my little red book. It was my twenty-sixth birthday, so we celebrated with lunch in the Tea Room on the seventh floor of Marshall Field's elegant department store. The Choralcelo (Celestial Choir) performed every day from noon to 2:30 P.M.

On January 7 at 11:40 A.M., we boarded the Chesapeake and Ohio train for Washington, arriving there about 5:00 P.M. the next day. Somehow I had forgotten that, being married, I would have to find a new place to live. All-male quarters would no longer do. It was too late in the day to do anything about it, but the Robert Marshalls came to our rescue and kindly took us in until the twelfth. We began apartment-hunting immediately.

Grace and I rented rooms and ate our meals at a boarding house, but Grace and the landlady took a dislike to each other at once. The woman was a "deep southerner," and Grace overheard a reference to the new boarders as "damn Yankees." Grace then started singing "Marching through Georgia" and other offensive Civil War songs. On March 13, however, we moved to an apartment of our own, the Lonsdale, at 238 California Street.

These early months of 1916 were exciting for both of us. As Mrs. Mather lived in Chicago and only visited occasionally in Washington, Mr. Mather lived alone at the Cosmos Club. He loved to have people around him all the time, so he had us accompany him to elegant dinners, to the theater, and to some of his official functions. Grace acted as his hostess. He paid for everything, wouldn't let us spend a nickel. We truly enjoyed his company and his choice of entertainment. Of course, many an evening after dinner I took Grace home and went back to the Cosmos Club, where Mather and I worked until after midnight.

If we weren't with Mather, we were being entertained elsewhere. It was a real social whirl with the Yards, Marshalls, and other acquaintances from the Interior Department and friends from the University of California. There were dinners, the theater, and dancing at the Willard. Delightful, memorable events.

One in particular stands out. On Tuesday, March 7, 1916, the National Geographic Society gave its annual banquet on the tenth floor of the Willard Hotel. It honored Alexander Graham Bell, the inventor of the telephone and the father-in-law of Gilbert Grosvenor.

As Grace and I entered the ballroom, crowded with hundreds of people, we were greeted by a choral group loudly singing "Here Comes the Bride." The chorus consisted of Gilbert Grosvenor, Alexander Graham Bell, Stephen Mather, and Secretary of the Interior Franklin K. Lane. Then came thunderous clapping and cheers from the assembled guests. Grace smiled radiantly and graciously bowed her head while I choked up with pride, thinking, "She is the most beautiful woman in the room and everyone knows it."

Western Adventures and Washington Maneuvers

1916

The whirling social life with Mather stopped when he left on his travels. There were short trips to New York, Boston, and Chicago, but then he was out west most of the remaining time until September, drumming up publicity or working on concession problems.

Toward the end of 1915, Mather had let Daniels go and closed his office. Then, on December 11, 1915, he appointed Bob Marshall as superintendent of national parks and Joe Cotter, who had been Lane's secretary, assistant general superintendent. Not knowing how Marshall would work out, Mather had him merely take a leave of absence from the Geological Survey.

Marshall knew parks well and was intensely anxious to be the director of the Park Service should it be created. So Mather had him oversee the *field* operations of the parks and monuments. His work sent him on the road in the spring, and he too remained out west for most of 1916.

Lane found Cotter almost indispensable and used him in his office most of the time. Mather told me that I was to concentrate on getting the bill to establish a national park service through the Congress. This was to be my main goal. "Don't let a lot of little things get in your way and take up your time," he said.

In recognition of my expanded work load, on May 16, 1916, Lane elevated me to assistant attorney for the Department of the Interior and raised my salary to two thousand dollars per year. With all this, I still had a secretary only when I could beg, borrow, or steal one from some office, or Bob Yard would lend me his secretary, the one Mather paid for. When I was desperate, I occasionally had help from the people Marshall "borrowed" from the Geological Survey, Arthur Demaray and Isabelle Story. Even so, I had to answer a good portion of the correspondence or write reports on my own typewriter at night, or whenever I had a free moment.

Here is where my best friend and companion came in, for Grace began to spend long hours at the office with me, filing, pasting material in scrapbooks, just about anything to keep my head above water. No pay, of course. She even wrote a college thesis–type paper on the history of the Interior Department for Secretary Lane but signed it H. M. Albright. She gave up most of her social life and even more gladly gave up sightseeing and lectures. Her only break was when her mother and sister came for a six-week visit. They also made a trip to New York, Grace's first.

Many people had believed in and promoted a separate administration of the national park system ever since the artist George Catlin had first uttered the words "national park" far back in the nineteenth century. Legislation had been introduced time and again in the early years of the twentieth century. President William Howard Taft and his two able interior secretaries, Richard Ballinger and Walter Fisher, were active promoters of a national park service.

The president stated firmly in a special message to the Congress on February 2, 1912: "I earnestly recommend the establishment of a Bureau of National Parks. Such legislation is essential to the proper management of those wondrous manifestations of nature, so startling and so beautiful that everyone recognizes the obligations of the Government to preserve them for the edification and recreation of the people." Fisher strenuously followed this up and almost succeeded in getting a bill passed.

Although this bill failed, I recalled Fisher's words time and again when we were in conference on our 1916 bill: "Our whole park system has been more or less an accident. . . . There has been no coordination between parks. Congress each year makes appropriations for each particular park as it comes along. The local pressure, the pressure of the particular individuals or organizations that are interested in it, determines in each case what amount of money shall be appropriated. . . . If we worked out a problem with one park, it was always a mere chance if the results benefited any other."

We couldn't openly state it, but we felt that the perpetual defeat of a park service was due to the unrelenting pressure of Gifford Pinchot and his influence on the Forest Service. Pinchot always believed the Forest Service should take over the national park areas.

Superintendent conferences had been convened in 1911 and 1912 in which a variety of interested individuals and organizations had promoted a park service. One of the most prominent was the American Civic Association and its president, J. Horace McFarland. He was knowledgeable, articulate, energetic, and like a bulldog in his tenacity to make "*1916 the year to win*," the slogan he wrote on notes to me. In Washington he was my main contact outside the members of the congressional committees.

The atmosphere seemed different when the Sixty-fourth Congress convened in December 1915. Although John Raker had introduced park bills in 1912 and 1913, which had died in committee, he was ready to try again. But James R. Mann, House Republican minority leader from Mather's own district in Illinois, couldn't swallow Raker, thoroughly disliked the California Democrat, and stated openly he would never support any bill Raker introduced.

Raker presented his bill, H.R. 434, anyway, partly because of Mann but partly because his name was smeared with Hetch Hetchy. He always felt badly about his part in promoting Hetch Hetchy and hoped he could redeem himself by pushing through a national park service bill with his name attached. All Mann and others thought was: "What was this? A fellow who helped destroy part of Yosemite is now mothering a national parks bureau?"

In the meantime, McFarland and the American Civic Association had approached Representative William Kent, a Progressive Republican from California, to introduce a bill. Kent was the man who had donated Muir Woods to the government for a national monument. Coming back from California, late for the opening of the congressional session, he introduced his own park bill, H.R. 8668, not knowing Raker had already done the same. As it later turned out, this gave us the opportunity to rewrite the bills to remove some provisions that had led to defeat in the past. Our co-sponsor in the Senate was Reed Smoot of Utah.

Hearings on the two bills, Raker's H.R. 434 and Kent's H.R. 8668, were held in April 1916 by the twenty-one–member House Committee on Public Lands, chaired by Representative Scott Ferris of Oklahoma. Fortunately, we had a fair number of supporters: Edward Taylor of Colorado, Carl Hayden of Arizona, Louis Cramton of Michigan, and of course the triumvirate from California—Raker, Church, and Kent. American Civic Association officials McFarland and Richard B. Watrous gave powerful testimony and were followed by Mather, Marshall, and Yard. Marshall was questioned mainly on the cost of the parks and what appropriations would be involved if the new system came about.

One committee member, Irvine Lenroot of Wisconsin, was deeply opposed to more bureaucracy. Since Wilson had become president, whole new sectors of government had been created to deal with the Sixteenth Amendment and the income tax, the Federal Reserve System, and tougher antitrust laws. Fortunately, Raker sort of sidetracked that sticky problem by making a statement of his own to close that particular session.

There were other hearings, of course, in both the House and Senate. The latter were short and pleasant. The chairman, Henry Myers of Montana, was very pro-parks. To iron out some of the language problems and strike out items that seemed potentially troublesome, an important change took place. With the approval of Raker and Kent, a substitute bill, H.R. 15522, was introduced to replace the original bills.

During these months, there were numerous meetings with a fluctuating group of men: Mather, Kent, Raker, Yard, Marshall, McFarland, Watrous, Grosvenor, various other members of Congress, and people who came to Washington on visits or offered suggestions by mail, such as Mills, Colby, and Osborn. I don't think I missed a meeting, since I was "keeper of the stacks of papers," as someone called me. Our meetings were held at various places: Kent's or Yard's home, a congressman's office, the Cosmos Club, the National Geographic Society offices.

From the beginning, the general outline for the legislation was known to all, a pickup from former bills. When we had the chance to write a new bill from the Raker and Kent bills, however, there was a split over how specific to be. Some favored carefully spelling everything out in detail. Most, though, felt the bill should be somewhat vague. Congressmen have a tendency to nail down ideas with carefully worded clauses, their own or those favored by their constituents or vested interests. We didn't want endless specifics. Specifics are too hard to reach agreement on. Also, knowing Mather and I would at least start up the organization before leaving the government to go our separate ways, the majority expressed the hope that we could institute the ideals and plans we all had discussed and agreed on. These might not be adopted if the organic act was too narrow and specific.

There has been a persistent question through the years about whether we were aware of and discussed the paradox of use and enjoyment of the parks by the people versus their preservation "unimpaired." Of course, we knew there was this paradox, but the organic acts creating Yellowstone, Yosemite, and other parks always contained these opposite tenets. We felt it was understood to be the standing policy.

The same is true of wilderness: we didn't specifically state policy about wilderness at this time because we concluded it was understood. Every previous act demanded that the parks be preserved in their natural state. Their natural state was wilderness. That was why the 1916 act made no provision for roads, trails, buildings, or anything else—only that concessions could be granted.

The general philosophy of the time was "use." Resources were to be used. There'd always be more. Men like Theodore Roosevelt and Gifford Pinchot were for "preservation with use." Hence the national forest idea. Our group and followers were conservationists and preservationists. No use of resources, no change in the general state of national park areas. But roads to enjoy the outstanding, easy-to-visit features of a park while leaving most areas in wilderness, accommodations for the people of all incomes in a wide price range, conveniences for health and safety.

We recognized that the introduction of automobiles would vastly increase the visitation to the parks and their use. However, we also knew the Congress would count tourist visitation to decide how much money our bureau would get to operate the park system. Dollars would be doled out according to the number of visitors.

Knowing we couldn't read the future was another reason for a nonspecific organic act. Obviously we could never foresee the future population of our country or the rabid demand for recreation. The belief in 1916 was that education and passive enjoyment were the foremost reasons for the parks. We realized that time could and would change conditions, so we didn't want ourselves or future park officials to be stymied by tight restrictions.

In May 1916 H.R. 15522 was reported favorably out of the House committee, although Lenroot stuck to his guns about bureaucracy, and much to our surprise our friend Edward Taylor joined Lenroot in voting against it. Taylor explained: "The great stumbling block is that the members of Congress fear you are building up another bureau here that will start in a small way and soon get up to a big appropriation."

That's the way matters stood when the infamous Washington heat and humidity set in. Grace and I worked together a good portion of the days. Then we would walk home after work and climb the four flights of stairs to our suffocating little apartment. It was often so hot that my bride simply couldn't, or wouldn't, cook, so we went out for dinner to a place called Wallis's. Later, when the temperature soared to around the hundred-degree mark, we switched to the more expensive restaurant in the Hotel Occidental, which charged $1.25 for a complete meal and even had ceiling fans. Many times our older and more affluent friends had us over for dinner, obviously feeling sorry for us. Aside from these little dinners, our social activities almost came to a halt. There was little time for anything besides work.

At last the park service bill proceeded to the House for a full vote. There was more debate than we had counted on. The two sticky points were Lenroot's bureaucracy and a last-minute add-on by Kent to allow grazing in the national parks. Lenroot's Wisconsin colleague, William Henry Stafford, hated almost everything, but he hated red tape, paper-work, and bureaucracy the worst. We heard plenty about these at the time, but even more later. Now a simple amendment severely restricted the amount of money for the bureau headquarters and personnel in Washington.

As for grazing, Mather himself had a lot to do with this problem. During his appearance before the committee, he had been ambiguous. One time he intimated he was against grazing, but at other times he spoke clearly for it. Nicholas Sinnott of Oregon had proposed an amendment that stated: "The Secretary of the Interior may grant the privilege to graze live-stock within any national park, monument, or reservation when, in his judgement, such business is not detrimental to the primary purpose for which the reservations were created, namely for the enjoyment of the people and the preservation of the vegetable life and other national features." When asked about this, Mather replied: "We feel that in certain portions of the present parks and in other parks, which may be later created, that the opportunity to graze under such restrictions should be allowed."

Yard, McFarland, and I were sitting together at the hearing when Mather uttered these words and then went on replying to more questions in the same vein. He even stated about Sequoia: "The greater part of the [new proposed] park area is being used for grazing and could continue to be used by stockmen. It would be our idea, say in a beautiful meadow, to fence off certain portions that the campers could use. We can provide for the campers and increase the facilities for campers as they come in larger numbers, at the same time taking care to protect the interest of the stockmen."

Frankly, we were stunned, for we thought grazing was anathema to everyone in our conservationist group. Later, when we asked Mather why he took that stand, he answered that he felt that grazing had to be in the bill to get it passed; that he had already sanctioned, or rather hadn't changed, the existing policy of allowing grazing in Mesa Verde, Yosemite, and Sequoia; and that ideals had to be stretched sometimes to reach an immediate goal. He had been afraid that Kent would be angered if opposed and that Raker would turn on him if he came out forcefully against certain other practices in the parks. Raker was pushing to change Lassen National Monument to a national park, but leaving in clauses to allow a railroad, grazing, and other adverse uses. Mather let it become a park on August 9, 1916, under those conditions. It seemed bad enough at the time to have a pro-grazing stand attached to the not-yet-created park service, but later it became a real nightmare for me during the war.

One more thing we thought had been settled in the committee hearings was the transfer of national monuments in the Department of Agriculture to the Department of the Interior when a national park bureau was created. There were national monuments in three departments— War, Agriculture, and Interior. The War Department had the military areas, but there was a fine line as to others. They had all been in the Interior Department until 1905, when the Forest Service was created and placed in the Department of Agriculture on Gifford Pinchot's demand. As Mather commented before the committee: "If a monument comes from public lands, it's Interior; if it comes from Forests, it's Agriculture."

But what about the Grand Canyon or Mount Olympus, superb natural-wonder Forest Service monuments? It was obvious that Grand Canyon had to be a national park, but Mount Olympus was something else, for President Wilson had carved it in half to accommodate mining interests. This had so angered Raker that, in his H.R. 434, there had been specific language to transfer these areas, and a hint of others, to the park service.

Well, the chief forester, Henry Graves, stated: "We are heartily in favor of the establishment of a National Park Service," and he admitted that those two monuments should go under the jurisdiction of Interior when they became parks. However, he insisted that language even hinting that all Forest Service monuments might go to the park service be stricken from the bill.

Earlier Mather had been almost indifferent to the monuments and had told the committee: "There has been very little done to the national monuments. Under the law little or nothing can be done with them; they are simply set aside, presumably, until such time as Congress decides to develop them." Now, in his most soothing and ingratiating manner, Mather tossed the monument issue to one side by assuring everyone that he wasn't concerned with monuments. "We focus our attention continually on the parks and don't eye any of the Forest Service monuments except those mentioned." He later laughed to us, "Well, at least, not right now."

Much as we would have enjoyed taking all the monuments, we kept quiet and let the members of Congress squash this. And they did.

On July 1, 1916, the House of Representatives passed our bill with only Lenroot's frugal amendment and Kent's grazing proposal appearing to pose some problems. The Senate followed suit on August 5. The two bills had to be reconciled by a joint conference. Now the real work was to begin.

In the midst of all the Washington work and conferences on the national park service bill, I received a telegram from Mather, followed by a long letter. He had again become vitally concerned with the Park-to-Park Highway and planned a trip to Yellowstone to go over the route from Thermopolis to Cody and thence around the park. He was intensely interested in how the traffic pattern of cars and stages was working out. He wanted to take a party of friends along and instructed me to precede him, arrange transportation, and be on call to take care of his guests. Incidentally, I was also to make a thorough inspection of the park and write a full report to Marshall on the conditions.

I wrote back suggesting that as long as Marshall was already out west, why didn't he just come to Yellowstone and make the inspection himself. An instant telegram came back: "No, Horace, you do it."

So I went west on July 16, leaving my bride behind to fend for herself for the first time. Passing through Denver, I arranged for two touring cars to come to Thermopolis, Wyoming, to carry the Mather party through Yellowstone. But I went ahead, arriving in Thermopolis on the morning of July 19.

Except for the one thousand inhabitants of Thermopolis, the average person could have zipped through town and never known it existed—that is, except for Mather and the Park-to-Park Highway Commission. It was important to them because this highway was to pass through the town on its way from Denver to Yellowstone, and Mather thought the hot springs here could be developed into a northern version of the Arkansas Hot Springs.

My two-day inspection of the roads and natural phenomena in the area was a varied experience. It was most assuredly no Hot Springs. It had no fancy Fordyce Bath House or other trappings of wealth seen in that Arkansas city. But I was surprised to see the brightly colored hot mineral terraces and streams of boiling water that serviced the highly touted bathing area. They were so like Yellowstone's Mammoth.

Then there was the amazing sight of the Bighorn River serenely flowing through town, after suddenly carving out the awesome chasm through the Owl Creek Mountains. This area became known as the Wedding of the Waters, for it was the same river with only a name change from the Wind to the Bighorn.

That was the good news. There was also the bad news: the odd wildlife "zoo" (with aroma rising from a handful of moth-eaten elk, deer, bison, a mother bear, and two cubs); the raw, hot, dust-laden wind that blew incessantly; and the bug-ridden hotel.

On July 21 Mather's party, including his wife and a number of personal and official friends, arrived on the Chicago, Burlington and Quincy Railroad. The chauffeur-driven, seven-passenger White touring cars I had ordered from Denver were brought around, and off we went to Cody for the night at Buffalo Bill Cody's Irma Hotel.

At Mather's instructions the party split up. The route I was to take was the Grass Creek oil field road via Meeteetse, while Mather and the main party would take the one recommended by his Denver Park-to-Park-Highway friends. Our road was passable but had few directional signs, some of which pointed in the wrong direction. Mather's road turned out to be simply terrible, full of ruts, dusty enough to strangle a person, and forty miles longer.

I was sitting in the Irma Hotel, at the famous bar given to Buffalo Bill by Queen Victoria, drinking a long cold lemonade, when my chief and his exhausted group staggered in about 7:00 P.M. We assembled for dinner at the Irma, mainly because it was apparently the only place to eat. It turned out to be a disaster, with bad food and terrible service.

Halfway through the meal, Mather told me to go out and check the kitchen. It was about the dirtiest, most unsanitary place I had ever seen. After I had reported in detail what I had observed, Mather summarily called in the manager, read the riot act to him, and told him a full report would be made to Wyoming congressmen as well as Secretary Lane of the Interior Department.

The rest of the evening turned out to be equally bad. First of all, Mrs. Mather insisted on sitting up all night in the lobby after she discovered "things crawling in the bed." Mather ordered a pillow and blankets for her, saw to her comfort, and then disappeared back to the lice, bedbugs, or whatever.

He didn't last long there because when he opened the door to his room he found two men asleep in his bed. Downstairs at the desk, he demanded another room. "There is no other room," said the clerk. "You'll just have to make your bedfellows move over."

Thoroughly enraged, Mather went to locate me. He found me rolled up in a blanket on the floor. About eleven o'clock I had been awakened by some strange man crawling into my bed, falling asleep immediately, and giving off the loudest snores I'd ever heard. Lying there awake, I had become aware of various bugs that had missed Mrs. Mather, so I had chosen the floor over the bed.

Now Mather and I together attacked the surly clerk. He finally disposed of us in "The Annex," a dilapidated building a block or so from the Irma, on cots without sheets, but also without bugs.

The Irma hadn't improved very much by morning. I was up at 5:30 A.M. to see how the tourists were handled when they came in by train from Billings, Montana. I rode the bus with them from the depot to the Irma. Arriving at the hotel, a lady asked where she could wash up before having breakfast. The desk clerk gave her a jerk of the thumb and a curt reply, "Head of the stairs." The lady picked up her heavy suitcase and was halfway up the long flight of stairs when a bellboy offered to help her. He escorted her to the second floor and down a long hall to the end of the building. Here he discovered he had taken her down the wrong hall. The washroom was at the end of the opposite hall. Though my first, this was certainly not the last of my unfortunate jousts with the Irma.

Our party breakfasted and was ready to go at 9:45 A.M. The road to Yellowstone was amazingly good compared to 1915. When we stopped to look at the Shoshone Dam, "The Sensation of the Cody Road," we found the gate locked. So we helped the ladies climb under some pipe bars while the men went over the gate to get to the steps leading down to the top of the dam.

Mather was furious about the situation. "It's dangerous. People could get killed. Break this whole thing open," he ordered. The chauffeur produced a hammer and began to break the padlock. Suddenly a caretaker appeared. Mather lectured him on the dangers of people circumventing the locks and had him finish destroying them. "And leave this gate open. No more locks, do you understand?" The poor fellow was quaking and never even questioned the authority of this distinguished-looking fellow who was ordering him around. As a parting shot, Mather called over his shoulder, "And get rid of those unsightly, dilapidated wooden buildings over there."

"Yes, sir, yes, sir, right away, sir" echoed after us.

Just before we reached the entrance to Yellowstone, Mather had us stop at the Pahaska Lodge, also owned and operated by Buffalo Bill Cody. It turned out to be just as bad as the Irma, if not worse. Lunch was one dollar, far too much for the horrible, greasy, inedible food served by loud, boisterous, grimy, but glitzy waitresses. Mather muttered to me, "Could Cody be operating a combination eating place and brothel?" After studying the situation, he ordered us not to eat a bite. He threw cash on the table (fifty cents per person) and stalked out, vowing to make the place change or he'd close it.

Of course, he had no more jurisdiction over the Pahaska than he had over the Shoshone Dam, but if he decided to do something, it got done. I had learned that much about Stephen Mather in the year and a half I'd been around him.

Leaving Pahaska, we drove to the Lake Hotel and thence through the Hayden Valley to the Canyon Hotel, where we were to spend the night. We "easterners" were very much excited to see large herds of elk in the Hayden Valley, deer grazing like tame sheep on the grassy slopes around the Canyon Hotel, and best of all roaming bears waiting for the nightly handout of carefully picked-over scraps of dining room food.

It was hard to imagine such ferocious animals as bears being so tame and so photogenic. But there were tourists outside the hotel snapping pictures right and left while bears sat up and acted like trained dogs. That is, I suppose, as long as the photographers were throwing pieces of candy bars and cookies to them. They looked mighty unreliable to me.

I always thought the Canyon Hotel one of the most beautiful in the world. Built during the fearful winter of 1910–11, it hugged the contour of the hill above and beyond the grand canyon of the Yellowstone River, though too far away to see the canyon itself. It was huge, a mile around, and yet it blended as one into the landscape. The architect, Robert Reamer, who also designed the Lake and Old Faithful hotels, commented on this, his masterpiece: "I built it in keeping with the place where it stands. To be in discord with the landscape would be almost a crime." Inside it was equally breathtaking, especially the lounge, projecting forward from the main hotel two hundred by one hundred feet, with a grand staircase descending to lounge areas and, at night, a ballroom with soft, discreet lights and a dance orchestra.

What a relief it was that night to be in this beautiful, luxurious hotel, to eat in the lovely dining room with windows framing the vista toward the canyon, to luxuriate in clean bathrooms with large tubs of hot water, to sleep in comfortable beds with fresh sheets and Hudson Bay blankets, and with not a crawling thing in sight.

In Yellowstone our party covered all the roads on the so-called belt line, the circular route around the park. Mather led his party on the sight-seeing tour. Although I was with them most of the time, I traveled in another car, with Major Amos Fries, the army engineer officer in charge of road-building in the park. He poured out a flood of valuable information, from which I made copious notes and recommendations, such as signs that should be erected to locate and explain attractions to tourists, parapets that should be built at dangerous curves or precipices, hiking trails that must be constructed to scenic spots. Completely discontinue all stage traffic and institute bus transportation for tourists without their own cars. Move the administration building at Mammoth to where tourists can find it to get information or talk to officials. These notes were later incorporated in a full-scale report for Marshall.

John A. Hill, one of the Interior Department inspectors, had just completed a tour of the Yellowstone concessions, so Mather told me not to bother with them. However, my innate nose for details forced me to inspect every inch of the camps, hotels, boats, and public campgrounds anyway and enter it all into my final report.

Mather read my notes and found them most helpful when he cornered the concessioners in Mammoth just before we left the park. He weeded out some of them and came to a final conclusion that all lodging had to be consolidated under Harry Child and his Yellowstone Park Company. It didn't happen all at once, but it got underway at this time. Although most of the report dealt with roads and concessions, I also listed all the game I had seen and commented on birds, wild flowers, and trees.

On the morning of July 23 we set off from the hotel to tour the east side of the park. It was a glorious day, brilliant and a little cool, actually more than a little cool as we wound our way up the steep road to the top of Mount Washburn. On the north side of the mountain we had great difficulty getting around a huge snow bank just below the summit. Reaching the summit, everyone was awed by the view and had to have numerous pictures taken to prove we had made it. Then we came down the mountain and drove north through the lush Lamar Valley to the Buffalo Farm.

Here were kept a small herd of bison, around 280 nonnative transplants. The native species of bison, the last remnants of the millions that had once covered the Great Plains, were deliberately separated from the Buffalo Farm animals and roamed far off in the hills to the east. We all enjoyed seeing the great, shaggy beasts up close, no matter what the variety. And on the way back to the Canyon Hotel, driving through Dunraven Pass, we watched an enormous herd of elk slowly trail across a hillside.

On the twenty-fourth we again climbed into our White touring cars and took the so-called cutoff from Canyon to Old Faithful. Everything went smoothly until we arrived at Fountain. Now there had to be a decision on which of two roads we would follow to the Old Faithful Inn. Fries couldn't help in the decision, as he hadn't tried the one road himself. So Mather decided to have us take that unknown road while he and his group took the other.

Fries, Alexander Vogelsang (Interior Department solicitor), and I set off on the road to Upper Geyser Basin by way of Firehole Lake and the Fountain Geyser. There were no signs warning people not to use it, but there should have been. It was almost impassable. Sometimes high centers compelled us to run out in the woods instead of on the road. Then chuck holes, deep mud holes, and streams running across the road threatened to delay our progress almost every second. I was so battered, shaken up, and bad-tempered from the experience that I told Fries I would see to it that this road was closed immediately to automobiles and probably to all other transportation too, although sometime it ought to be constructed properly, as there were so many wonderful geyser formations and hot springs along the way.

Fortunately, Mather and party had taken the direct route through the forest and found that road in fine condition. We arrived at the wonderful, rustic Old Faithful Inn long after their group had enjoyed lunch. They were now out on a tour of Upper Geyser Basin with a young army officer. Fries and I grabbed a bite to eat, inspected the camps and kitchens, watched Old Faithful erupt, and walked out to meet Mather's group when we saw them strolling across the basin toward the hotel.

Mrs. Mather and another lady vowed they couldn't go any farther without tea and nourishment. Giving them time to have tea, though, was a bad idea. We had to drive rather fast back to the Canyon Hotel, and no road in Yellowstone was really good enough for speeding. The rush was because Mather and I had to attend a meeting of the National Park-to-Park Highway Association that evening, and Mather was to be the principal speaker.

For a later generation used to interstates and superhighways, it's hard to imagine the excitement of transcontinental or even regional systems of roads. But in 1916 every automobile association, chamber of commerce, and tourist-oriented area was planning a "yellow brick road" to untapped riches of the suddenly motorized American. Numerous motorist magazines, whole sections of newspapers, and gorgeously colored ads in national magazines from auto manufacturers lured the public to buy a car and "See America First." Within a few years the Lincoln Highway, the Ocean-to-Ocean Highway, the Pacific Highway, and dozens of other famous roadways appeared.

Among the most popular and most promoted in the West was the Park-to-Park Highway, dreamed up the year before in Denver, established to connect all the national parks of the Rocky Mountain region and the Pacific slope. And here this association was convened at the Canyon Hotel with one of its biggest boosters, Stephen Mather, ready to give them a pep talk.

And that he did. I used to be perpetually amazed at how Mr. Mather would gradually get so wound up, so excited, as he talked. His voice would rise in pitch. He'd talk faster and faster. And then his ideas would grow, or new ones would even pop up, until they would exceed what he had started out to say.

This particular evening he was rather tired after all the sightseeing and gave a circumspect, short speech, the main theme being "don't count on the government."

I must make it clear that I regard this highway as a project to be handled by the various national park states, and by counties and municipalities therein. . . . Our work is still in the parks themselves, yours in connecting the parks; ours to encourage travel to the parks by publicity and other methods, yours to thoughtfully assist the tourist and keep him in the right frame of mind as he goes from park to park. . . . May we all succeed, and in succeeding prove that the "See America First" movement is, from the point of view of health, recreation and wealth, the most important propaganda in the nation today.

The next day Mather decided that they hadn't spent enough time at Old Faithful and had seen too few eruptions of various famous geysers, so we would go back there. Everyone except Fries and me set off with Mather's checklist of geysers and a schedule for their displays. We could have thought of many better things to do, but we despondently trudged off to finish inspecting the concessions.

It's a good thing we did, for we uncovered a veritable cesspool. Fries had told me about the O. W. & W. N. Hefferlin Old Faithful Camping Company and how Inspector Hill had decided to close them down for the 1917 season. Fries suggested I see a few of them, for he was nervous that next year might be too late for some poor, unsuspecting tourists. After all, the year before a man had suffered from more than the normal ptomaine-laden meal and had shot at the cook, although fortunately his aim was thrown off, no doubt by the wormy venison about which he was complaining.

We first looked over the Old Faithful camp, which was bad enough. But Fries said, "You haven't seen the worst. Let's go back to Canyon." We did, and he was right. The camps consisted of some old tents without walls or floors, old tables, stoves, and sleeping equipment. The preparation, cooking, and serving of meals were all in one tent with no partitions between. Cooking went on near the dining tables, with provisions lying around on small tables or on the ground. Flies were abundant, and some of them were reposing on a large piece of ham. In the rear of the tent two large buckets of refuse were found uncovered, and it was evident that greasy dishwater had been carelessly thrown out of the tent on the shore of the Yellowstone River. The river apparently was also used as a latrine.

The following day was much the same for the sightseers and much the same for Amos Fries and myself. We checked out various roads, bridges, where parapets ought to be built, where trails ought to be laid out, and where and what sort of signs ought to be put up for tourist information.

We saw several interesting things along our way from Upper Geyser Basin to Thumb. First were the army engineer road gangs. I don't recall now whether the men were being punished or hired and paid for this tough work. In any case, as it had rained hard the night before, they were in the process of "dragging" the road to smooth out the damage.

The other encounter on this road was a marvelous mother bear and her two cubs. Mama was an exceptionally large black bear, astride the center of the road, so we were forced to stop the car. She advanced on us and almost seemed to say, "Hey, I've been here since dawn. What have you got for breakfast?" Fries, who was used to this particular bear at this particular spot, yelled at her, "Don't try to hog it all. Go get your babies and then we'll give you something." She obviously understood, for she lumbered over to the edge of the lodgepole forest and immediately two cubs emerged to join her. It was a great experience for me to see the antics these three went through for the stale crackers Fries kept in the car just for an occasion like this. He had to keep warning me, though, that they might look and act cute but were, in reality, vicious wild animals.

July 27 was a date that would stick in my memory forever. When Mather and I had been in Yellowstone the year before, we had looked down at Jackson's Hole from Shoshone Point, at the south end of Yellowstone. We had been fascinated by the brief glimpse but had no time to get down there. Now I suggested we pay a visit to the area, but Mather felt it wasn't in our jurisdiction, time was short, and it would be hard on the ladies.

However, my nagging and his curiosity eventually led us to make a detour from Thumb to the Teton Valley. The road to the south gateway of Yellowstone and even to the Snake River bridge was passable, but from there on down into Jackson's Hole was terrible, absolutely impossible had it rained.

When we reached the south boundary line of Yellowstone, Mather shouted to the driver to stop. He got out of the car and studied the only sign there, put up by the Forest Service: "NORTH BOUNDARY OF THE TETON NATIONAL FOREST." Mather called to me: "Horace, make a note of this. I want a sign, right away, in front of this one, and bigger: 'SOUTH BOUNDARY OF YELLOWSTONE NATIONAL PARK.'" He added that an imposing gateway to the park should be built as soon as possible.

Everything was forgotten as we slowly, very slowly, picked the right ruts to drive around Jackson's Hole. On the east side of Jackson Lake the road was worthless. It was really no road at all, simply a makeshift built by the Reclamation Service to replace one from Lizard Creek to the dam. I wrote Marshall that the Reclamation Service was to blame: tell them to fix it and charge the promoters of the dam for the cost. It was very important for us to have a decent road so that our tourists could see this magnificent area as a side trip from their visit to Yellowstone. On his return to Washington, Mather went directly to Secretary Lane about the condition of the road. Lane ordered Reclamation Director Davis to allot ten thousand dollars to build a new road. It was done. And that was how we first got our foot in the Jackson's Hole door.

Even these terrible roads were forgotten in the splendor of the lush valley, the sparkling lake, and the backdrop of the magnificent, snow-capped Teton Range. It left us all speechless. I'll never know what the others in our party were thinking, but I know I had never been more thrilled and excited. There was something about this awesome Rocky Mountain area, something about the jagged Tetons rising abruptly from this valley, that struck a deep chord in my mind and spirit. All I could think of was, "Now this is a national park!"

The journey down to Ben Sheffield's lodge near Moran was very slow. The road had been flooded out by work on the new concrete dam, after the old wooden one had been swept away. This forced us to wind our way on a trail through trees and sometimes underbrush, probably an old elk path. Finally we dropped down to the spread of log buildings and tents along the edge of Jackson Lake adjacent to the new dam. It was quite an establishment. We later learned that Sheffield had expanded tremendously since the new dam had gone in. Besides the growth of his little hunting and fishing lodge, there now were other buildings and even a post office in the great town of Moran.

We arrived just in time for a marvelous lunch in his tent dining room. His log dining room had burned down a short time before. Sheffield came in carrying a platter on which T-bone steaks were piled high, with rich juice cascading from one steak to another. While we ate, he gave a lively history and pep talk about the region and then took us out on Jackson Lake for a panoramic view of forest-clad foothills and the Tetons towering above.

We came back in time to freshen up and enjoy another delicious meal. Afterward we sat outside, almost silent, in awe of the twilight creeping over the mountains, shutting out all but the sharp, jagged edges of that magnificent horizon of peaks.

A good night's sleep and a hearty "cowboy" breakfast readied us for the struggle back to Yellowstone. Reaching Thumb, we left our cars and rode back across the lake on the steamboat *Jean D*. It was a most enjoyable cruise with about forty passengers on board. Mather loved it so much that he instantly envisioned building a beautiful boathouse below the Lake Hotel and running larger boats back and forth on a stepped-up schedule. Along with this idea he thought that transportation could be arranged to pick up tourists at the south end and detour them down to the Jackson Hole for a night at Sheffield's. As soon as he got to Mammoth, he summoned the officials of the boat company to organize his plans, which turned out to be vastly too expensive unless tourist travel increased enormously.

Our whole trip went wonderfully well until near the end. Solicitor Vogelsang hadn't been feeling too well, had forgone the Teton trip, and blamed his troubles on the high altitude of Yellowstone. At Mammoth Mather didn't like his continuing problem and asked Colonel Brett to call in the army doctor. After a thorough examination, the doctor reported that Vogelsang was experiencing a heart attack and should get away from Yellowstone as rapidly as possible. Mather immediately packed him up and took him to a hospital in Ogden. The prompt action probably saved his life, made possible his swift recovery, and gave him those extra years as first assistant secretary of the interior (1916–21), during which he lent us such a helping hand.

Mather stayed in Ogden only long enough to see Vogelsang out of the woods. Then he went on to San Francisco. With Mather gone and the Thompsons off to Denver, I gathered up the Purdys and Mrs. Mather and took them back home to Chicago, then went on alone to Washington. As the train pulled into Union Station on August 3 at 4:40 P.M., my first sight was my lovely Grace waiting for me on the platform.

Aside from having to leave my wife alone again, the trip to Yellowstone had been a wonderful interlude. Not only had it been a tension-breaker, but it also was a marvelous learning experience. For the first time, I had been able to see exactly how a national park functioned under reasonable management, how poorly concessions were handled, how much improvement was needed in ordinary facilities such as roads, how transportation operated, how average American tourists used a park, and how they managed to survive the pitfalls of a system without central organization. Yosemite had only been an example of everything going wrong. Now I felt I had an insight into how a national park service could take hold of the helter-skelter conglomeration and turn it into a finely honed system. I also recognized that the hardest work was still ahead.

With all this knowledge, there was absolutely no time, no organization, no money to do anything about it. It would have to wait until our bureau was created. And Mather had laid it directly on my shoulders to see that the Smoot-Kent bill could be passed and signed into law this year. He was not very hopeful and decided to stay in the West until fall. I was determined not to be waylaid on other matters, just somehow to force that bill through the Congress.

A National Park Service Is Born
1916

The summer of 1916 was one of the hottest on record in Washington. It seemed to drag on endlessly. Our office still had no permanent personnel. Grace put in more and more hours on my work, as I had less and less time to do it myself. We worked together, often during regular hours, usually on Sundays too. She did routine clerical work and the never-ending scrapbook pasting while I typed reports, kept Mather up to date on Washington affairs, and devoted myself to the park service bill.

Unfortunately, I also had to wrangle with problems in various national parks because Marshall was not holding up his end and was proving to be a poor administrator. Once more my savior was W. B. Acker. Although badly overworked himself, he was always ready to help.

Getting the national park bill through Congress was a thankless job, for 1916 was an election year. More importantly, it was a presidential election year. To the incumbents, getting reelected was the only thing that counted, so they were frequently back home campaigning. This was the problem when trying to get the House and Senate bills reconciled for a final version. To round up all six conference members at one time to discuss compromise was close to impossible. This one was away in California this week while another was back home the next.

Before and during the hearings and on into summer, the friends and adherents of Stephen Mather and national parks let loose a torrent of publicity for the parks and for the bill. George Horace Lorimer and his

Saturday Evening Post, featuring Herbert Quick, Emerson Hough, and other writers, kept up a running commentary. Railroads issued their summer timetables and brochures filled with national park propaganda. Automobile and highway associations, chambers of commerce, and newspapers (especially those near a park area) kept up the good word. Bob Yard diligently pumped out information to all these organizations as well as working on his own *Parks Portfolio II.*

Probably the single most important publication to influence the members of Congress was the April 1916 issue of *National Geographic.* Gilbert "Tenderfoot" Grosvenor had come through for Stephen Mather and the ideas he expressed around the Sierra campfires. This issue of the magazine was titled "The Land of the Best—Tribute to the Scenic Grandeur and Unsurpassed Natural Resources of Our Own Country." There were even some pages in full color and a foldout panorama of the General Sherman Tree at Sequoia. The entire issue focused on the wonders of America, with a heavy emphasis on national parks. Grosvenor left nothing to chance. In case some dull-witted congressman failed to see the magazine, he had a copy delivered by messenger to each one of them.

During this summer of controversy, Mather remained in the West. After being assured that Vogelsang was out of danger, he had gone on to San Francisco. The Desmond Yosemite Company was a constant worry. Desmond was not a diplomatic person, not a manager of any kind. He had constant trouble with workmen, with the financial men overseeing the company, and with the ordinary tourist. The accommodations and food produced a chorus of complaints. The company was losing money as fast as the Curry Company was making it.

More trouble for Mather arose when serious complaints about Robert Marshall began to arrive on Secretary Lane's desk. Although Marshall was a brilliant geographer and engineer and knew the parks better than anyone, he was also tactless, stubborn, and quick to argue. He alienated half the people he met. He seemed to have little knowledge of expenses, with frequent overruns on estimates, especially for the Yosemite power plant.

Lane talked the problem over with me and suggested that while out on the coast with Marshall Mather should just fire him. Knowing how tired and stressed-out Mather was, I politely disagreed with Lane. I said I'd write Mather, say nothing about the complaints Lane had received, and suggest that he have Marshall travel with him for a while. Mather was a superb judge of people. He would catch onto the situation fast enough and decide what to do. Under my breath I muttered, "Please, God, keep Bob at least until we get that park bill passed."

As it turned out, Mather was so happy and so eager to escape to the Sierra Nevada with his second mountain party that he never bothered to reply about Marshall. He temporarily ignored the problem and even asked Bob again to organize a Sierra mountain trip for him. But he didn't invite him to go along.

The second Mather Mountain Party was as memorable as the first. Mather's original list of companions was almost twice the size of the 1915 list, but only seven men ended up accompanying him: Harold F. White and F. W. Grimwood, friends from Chicago, Bob Yard, famous photographer Edward S. Curtis, George Davis of the Geological Survey, and E. O. McCormick and Wilbur McClure, who had been on the earlier trip. Ty Sing was there again to cater the meals. The group traveled along the new John Muir Trail from Yosemite through Evolution Basin and the middle and south forks of the Kings River to Sequoia National Park. Mather was on top of the world, ecstatic, with all his cares temporarily banished.

Meanwhile, our park bill awaited a House-Senate conference to agree on the final version. On the face of it, that sounds simple. However, President Wilson's popularity had dropped severely by 1916. Democrats were frightened not only of losing the White House but, worse, of losing their own congressional seats. Republicans thought they smelled victory and eagerly looked forward to Charles Evans Hughes as president and to a powerful Republican Congress. So rules were set up that skipped the normal adjournment of the Congress and substituted recesses. They would meet one day and then recess for up to three days or more.

I almost ripped my hair out when I realized how much harder it would be to corral the conferees, as now more than ever they would be home campaigning. It was a losing battle. I'd get two or three together, but some pivotal person would be campaigning. I'd get a different group, only to get some written instructions from a representative or senator telling me he would never accept this or that.

Time was getting shorter and shorter before the elections. I was getting more and more worried that if this bill couldn't be passed in this Congress, we'd have to start all over. What if the administration changed from Democratic to Republican? What about a new batch of congressmen, a new president, a new secretary of the interior? All would have to be courted and placated. It was too gruesome to dwell on. A decision for action had to be made now.

I talked to the heads of the Public Lands committees, Representative Scott Ferris and Senator Henry Myers, the chief conferees. The latter I caught at Union Station as he was about to leave for New York. I pleaded for help to arrange a meeting to work out a compromise on the bills. Both congressmen felt it was impossible to get the whole committee together. Fortunately, however, the two men were close friends, saw my point, and, as they were now real park boosters, suggested that just the three of us make a settlement and then present it to the other conferees.

That sounds simple, but it was not. One fiery hot day Ferris arranged a meeting in his office in the Capitol. Just Myers, Ferris, and I were present. Even with four electric fans blowing on us, it was like a Turkish bath. We hammered out a general agreement between the House and Senate bills. Whether it was the heat or the long day, we decided we'd had enough and would set up another meeting to finalize it word by word.

Three or four days later, Billy Kent called to tell me to be at his home on F Street to finish the compromise bill. The three of us from the first meeting were there, but this time we were joined by McFarland and Watrous from the American Civic Association, Frederick Law Olmsted, Jr., Raker, and Kent.

I remember that at one point Olmsted wanted to change a few words in the famous paragraph he had written for an earlier park bill, the one example of lofty English in our organic act: "The fundamental purpose of the said parks, monuments, and reservations . . . is to conserve the scenery and the natural and historic objects and the wild life therein and to provide for the enjoyment of the same in such manner and by such means as will leave them unimpaired for the enjoyment of future generations."

Poor man. Everyone jumped on him at once. McFarland said: "Don't you dare change a thing, Olmsted. Your one paragraph sells the whole bill."

The important differences had been the Senate's elimination of the grazing allowance and the dispute over monetary allocations for the Washington office. Myers allowed the grazing (except in Yellowstone), and a compromise amount was fixed for our Interior Department office. It took several more sessions with several other people to write the final compromise bill, but these dealt mainly with unimportant words and phrases.

But that wasn't the end of it. Now Ferris and Myers said that it was up to me to get the other conferees to agree. It wasn't just getting them to agree. It was trying to find and catch them. And that's what I did for several weeks. Up and down to Capitol Hill on the streetcar, find a representative at his home, find a senator at his club. If any one of them wanted to change even a word, I had to go back to all the rest for approval.

I never knew I could be so persuasive, pragmatic, and controlled in temper. Grace used to laugh so hard at home at night when I'd blow off steam, call some of our noble legislators every name I could use in front of a lady, and then sit down and fuss over my little black notebook. It listed each conferee on a separate page with information on where he spent his leisure time, what hours he could be found at the Capitol, and when he was away.

On August 15 the Senate accepted the compromise bill and passed it with flying colors. A few days later it came before the House of Representatives, and trouble loomed. Ferris called to tell me that Irvine Lenroot had assured him he wouldn't get in our way, but that his Wisconsin colleague, our old enemy William Henry Stafford, was still there with all his hatred of any new bureaucracy and would fight us.

Ferris made a suggestion. He said that Stafford was a golf nut and played every chance he got. We could include him in an interesting foursome and have him safely out on the course at the time the vote was taken on the bill. It was a great idea, but before we did anything about it Ferris called back to say he had more than enough votes for us. Forget Stafford. On August 22 the House also passed the bill. Senator Smoot called and gave me the good news.

All that was needed now was to get the bill engrossed, printed, and signed by President Wilson. It was early afternoon. Grace had come to work with me in the morning, for she flatly refused to stay in our apartment to suffer another blistering day. She had actually slept on the fire escape a few nights. We were trying to play catchup with the accumulated paperwork and newspaper clippings.

We were wildly excited about the passage of the bill. We hugged each other and danced up and down the office. A couple of people ran in to see what all the commotion was about and then joined in the celebration.

Suddenly I had an idea. I told Grace to stay at Interior under the electric fan while I went up to the Capitol. Here I found the enrolling clerk and inquired when the bill would be sent to the president for his signature. He didn't know. Just then the telephone on his desk rang. I didn't mean to eavesdrop, but my antenna must have been up because I heard him repeat: "Yes, sir. The president wants the army appropriation bill right away for his signature. I'll get it ready and send it down immediately."

I pounced on the words "president" and "sign." Quickly I asked if the clerk would please put the national park bill in the same envelope, so Wilson would sign it too. He shrugged his shoulders, found our bill, inserted it with the army bill, and gave it to a clerk to take to the White House.

I don't know what transportation the clerk used, but I raced out of the Capitol and jumped on the first streetcar heading west. I had to get off at the Willard Hotel, so I ran the rest of the way to the White House, arriving with no breath and my shirt wet through.

The Capitol messenger hadn't arrived yet. I had met Maurice Latta, the White House legislative clerk, several times at the Cosmos Club. I used all the persuasiveness and smooth talk I had to convince him that he should be sure President Wilson signed the park bill when he signed the army bill. I went further and requested that he save the pen used to sign the bill, explaining about Mather being away in California and wanting to give him that as a gift. Latta knew and liked Mather and agreed.

Just as I was leaving, I also asked if he would please call me when Wilson had actually signed our organic act creating the National Park Service. He said he would, and I gave him our phone number. Well, it wasn't ours. We couldn't afford one. A public phone was in the hall inside the front door of our apartment building.

Now I rushed back to the Interior Department, told Secretary Lane what I had done, and suggested that he call Latta and repeat my requests. He kindly followed up on that and was assured by Latta that he'd personally take care of everything. As I was leaving, Lane put his arm around my shoulders and said: "This a real milestone for the department. I'm proud of you boys. I knew you and Steve would do it." Well, it certainly was one of the greatest moments in my life.

It was dinner time when I sagged into a chair in my office, too exhilarated and exhausted to move. Grace was still excited, hugged me, and said: "Come on. Let's go to the Willard or some other really expensive place, have dinner, and celebrate." She rarely asked for anything special, so I usually did what she wanted, but I was wrung out. "How about a nice quiet meal at the Occidental instead?" I asked. And, of course, she readily agreed. That's what we did: ate a rather quick meal and walked home.

Before we went upstairs, I called the White House, but there was no word on the signing. We climbed the four flights of stairs to our devilishly hot apartment. Grace got the couch cushions and adjourned to the fire escape, while I lay on the floor nearby, clad only in underwear.

A NATIONAL PARK SERVICE IS BORN

It wasn't very long before I heard, "Mr. Albright. Telephone." Grabbing my pants, I hobbled into them and ran down the four flights. It was Ray Gidney, calling to see if we would come to Jean's birthday party. Up the four flights again. This was repeated twice. How all these people suddenly had to call on the same evening—the wrong evening—I'll never know. But the fourth time was the charm. It was Maurice Latta. President Wilson had signed our bill about 9:00 P.M. Joseph Tumulty, Wilson's secretary, had the pen and would keep it for Mather. August 25, 1916, had been quite an incredible day.

The following morning I sent this telegram to Mather at the Palace Hotel in Visalia, California: "Park Service bill signed nine o'clock last night. Have pen President used in signing for you. Appear before members Senate Subcommittee on deficiency bill today. Also Chairman Fitzgerald of House Subcommittee. Wire instructions regarding matters you wish me handle before leaving. Horace."

The deficiency bill was a reminder to Mather about our precarious fiscal situation. With fear and trepidation, I appeared before the House and Senate committees to ask for additional appropriations. My point was that the Congress created the National Park Service but gave us no money to operate our Washington office. I was up at the Capitol, hat in hand, begging for some appropriations to see us through until money could be allocated in the spring for the full fiscal year of 1918.

The Senate committee was inquiring, polite, didn't ask for too many details, and seemed to pass on it. But now I was staring at House Committee Chairman John J. Fitzgerald. It was like facing a firing squad. He asked more impossible questions and probed into more matters than his committee was supposed to cover.

My worst concern was the need for more money for the power plant in Yosemite. Congress had looked over the design and costs proposed by Henry Floy, Mather's brother-in-law, and on the basis of these had appropriated $150,000 to build an entirely new plant. One of Marshall's main tasks in the summer had been to oversee this construction. Well, it had a long way to go for completion when the money ran out. Mather blamed Marshall. Marshall said the plans were too elaborate for the money allocated. I didn't know the ins and outs of the situation, but only that I had to try to get more money to complete the project.

Finishing the hearing, Fitzgerald glared at me and roared: "Albright, that power plant can stay rusting in that valley until Gabriel blows his horn, an everlasting monument to bureaucratic waste." I left town the next day without knowing what this fearful ogre would do and, frankly, not caring except to wish him a quick and horrible death. As I wrote William Colby, "I took a terrific punishment at the hands of Chairman Fitzgerald."

To get out of Washington was a real relief. Mather had instructed me to meet him in Glacier National Park and bring my "bride" for a real honeymoon. Not only had he been grateful for all that I had accomplished during that endless summer, but his conscience had also begun to bother to him. He confessed to me that he had been thoughtless about our original honeymoon and suggested that I take Grace out to Glacier National Park for a real honeymoon. Marshall wrote out my travel orders and assigned some work for me to take care of in Glacier. Mather would pay for everything over my four-dollar government per diem.

But now Mather tacked on a new twist. After returning from his Sierra mountain trip, he intended to go with E. O. McCormick to Yosemite. Then they would travel in Sunset, McCormick's private railroad car, to check on the roads and prospective railroad to Crater Lake and hotel construction at Paradise Valley in Mount Rainier. Afterward Mather would proceed alone and join us in Glacier.

Three on a honeymoon! Well, anything looked good if we could escape Washington, and as long as I was with Grace I could put up with Mather, too.

The "Glacier Mountain Party," like Mather's Sierra mountain parties, was created to indoctrinate the group with the fundamental ideas of the newly formed Park Service and enlist their help, financially and otherwise. Mather insisted that Grace go along. My bride, who had never been on a horse, must now join twelve men to cross the mountains from Lake McDonald to the eastern side of the park.

On September 6 our pack train set off for East Glacier, following almost the same route Mather and I had taken in 1915: Sperry Chalets, then across Gunsight Pass to Going-to-the-Sun Chalets on Lake St. Mary. The next day the weather turned vicious, so Supervisor Ralston advised going by launch to St. Mary Chalets and driving by car to Many Glacier. But Mather laughed and shouted: "On your horses! We need a little adventure!" Obediently we climbed into our saddles and started for Many Glacier Hotel, twenty-six miles away over some of the most rugged terrain in the park. The weather was merciless, a mixture of sleet, hail, and snow, hard-driven by a brutal wind. Eventually we reached Many Glacier Hotel and spent several days inspecting this region. Mather's plans called for us to continue by horseback to Glacier Park Hotel, but when Roe Emery offered comfortable cars instead, most jumped at the chance—including Stephen Mather.

A few days later Mather left for Washington while Grace and I went on to Yellowstone. Arriving on September 13, we stayed at the home of the superinten- dent, Colonel Lloyd Brett. After a few days of sightseeing, Grace's first, I had to get down to business with Colonel Brett.

During the trip to California in March 1915, Mather and I had made a verbal agreement with General Hugh Scott, chief of staff of the army, for the withdrawal of the troops charged with protecting Yellowstone. During the winter of 1915–16, Mather and Scott had several meetings to solidify arrangements. The transfer from military to civilian control was to become effective on October 1, 1916.

Brett and I had a myriad of details to work out: the transfer of Fort Yellowstone and the army stations in other parts of the park, horses, huge amounts of equipment, the discharge of certain soldiers who would become National Park Service rangers and maintenance personnel, the consolidation or elimination of concessioners and new agreements with the remaining ones. So Saturday the sixteenth saw the two of us off on inspection tours around the park.

When we returned to Mammoth, Brett assembled the men who would soon be discharged from the army to become rangers in the National Park Service. Some were scouts, others regular army troopers. Brett had gone over the men very carefully, turning down those he did not consider fit timber for the new force. However, he didn't hesitate to let his own finest, most exceptional men leave his command to join us.

I spent a good deal of time talking to each man individually. They were quite a group, tough as nails, but experienced, honest, and excited about their future work. I was very impressed. I always felt they set the standard for our future corps of rangers.

Sunday was a quiet day for the ladies while I put in most of my time working at the colonel's office with Chester Lindsley. He was Brett's right-hand man, a civilian who was designated to become supervisor of Yellowstone when the army relinquished control to the Park Service on October 1, 1916. He was a very capable, knowledgeable fellow, and I had every confidence that he would carry out the instructions I was leaving with him and would manage the park efficiently.

At this time it seemed that Lindsley would be totally responsible for the Park Service takeover, to see that scouts were transformed into rangers, that army property was completely accounted for and turned over in good shape, and that approved construction would be carried out. However, Mather persuaded General Scott to allow Colonel Brett to remain to aid Lindsley until all the troops left Yellowstone. This turned out to be near the end of October.

But right now I also needed Lindsley's advice about the concessions, for I was apprehensive about Mather's plans. They were perhaps too radical and too fast to initiate at the same time the revolutionary change in management of the park was taking place. It turned out this meeting of ours was most valuable, giving me a new slant on some of Yellowstone's problems.

Ten of us enjoyed another festive dinner at the Bretts. The army men got off on various entertaining tales of their adventures. Lloyd Brett was a great raconteur. He gave us a wonderful picture of the Indian wars in which he was engaged after he graduated from West Point in 1879. We later learned that he had received the Congressional Medal of Honor for bravery in a battle with the Sioux.

On Monday, September 18, the Albrights were driven to Gardiner and entrained for the East. We arrived in Washington on September 21 at 4:40 P.M., dumped our baggage at home, ate dinner downtown, and with a sigh of relief sank into our own bed at last. It had been an exciting and fascinating learning experience, but when would the Albrights get a real honeymoon? (In Hawaii in 1920. But that is another story.)

Mather returned to Washington in early October to meet with General Hugh Scott. In Scott's office the three of us checked out all the details of the National Park Service assuming control of Yellowstone. I was asked to fill them in on my trip to Yellowstone and observations there.

Scott suddenly changed the subject. "Mr. Albright, I'm curious about how you fared with your testimony before John Fitzgerald." That startled me, but I gave a full and truthful account of Fitzgerald's tirade about the Yellowstone changeover and his warning that he hadn't given up. He swore he'd have the army back in the park some day.

The attention focused on Yellowstone did accomplish some important things. The concession problem was basically solved. All the credit goes to Mather. While we were in the park in the summer, he made a decision on the boat franchise and cleaned up part of the accommodation tangle. Ever since Ford Harvey had introduced him to the idea of extended monopoly, Mather had been solidifying his future strategy. He would try out his ideas in Yellowstone. If they worked, he would extend them to all the other parks.

Mather called a conference of Yellowstone concessioners in Washington on December 10, 1916. There was not much give and take with the issue. Mather simply dictated that Harry Child got all the hotels in the park under the Yellowstone Park Hotel Company. His Yellowstone Transportation Company consolidated all the transportation lines. This was because the hotels were a losing business and transportation a money-maker and also because Child was heavily backed by the powerful Northern Pacific Railroad. As part of the deal, Child was ordered to get rid of all horses, stagecoaches, and other equipment and have his operation completely motorized by 1917. This is where the railroad company came in. It helped out financially when Child disposed of stage-line equipment and bought 116 new White buses for more than four hundred thousand dollars.

Frank J. Haynes had owned one of the transportation companies Child acquired. He was paid off by Child and then given the monopoly for photographic stores. The camping companies were also consolidated and eventually ended up with Child too. Someone said, "Harry owned everything in Yellowstone except the rattlesnakes."

February 1902. "Perhaps more than to either of my parents, I looked to my maternal grandfather, Horace Marden, as a model." He is seen here with his wife, Lizzie; their two daughters (the only survivors of nine children) and their husbands, Wils Yandell and George Albright; and their grandchildren. Horace Marden Albright is farthest on the right.

Horace M. Albright graduated from Georgetown Law School on June 16, 1914.

Grace Marian Noble, 1914. At Christmas I received my first portrait of my "beautiful brown eyes," as I called Grace.

Arriving on the private Pullman car Calzona for the National Park Conference, which opened in Berkeley, California, on March 11, 1915, were (left to right) Oliver Mitchell, Stephen Mather, Horace Albright, Congressman Denver Church, Robert B. Marshall, W. B. Acker, Robert Yard, and Colonel Lloyd Brett.

Three Blackfeet chiefs visited Mather (seated at desk) in April 1915 to protest the use of white men's names in Glacier Park. In their hands were small steel hatchets, not Indian tomahawks. Standing left to right: Bird Rattlers, Curly Bear, Wolf Plume, an Indian interpreter, H. M. Albright, another interpreter, and R. B. Marshall. Photo by Scherer Studio, Washington, D.C.

Albright with the Mather Mountain Party in the Sierra Nevada, California, July 14–29, 1915. "By July 26 everyone in the party looked like a caveman."

"Moving slowly across jumbled, flat rocks at a gentle angle, we were almost surprised when we found we had run out of mountain." Twelve of the Mather Mountain Party reached the summit of Mount Whitney, the highest mountain in the continental United States. Horace Albright stands third from the right and Mather to his left. National Geographic *photo by Gilbert Grosvenor.*

On the following pages:
August 27, 1915, Nisqually Glacier, Mount Ranier National Park. "It was a glorious day for me, as every minute was a fresh experience, with new glimpses of this fascinating wooded and iced park around every bend in the trail." Photographed by Asahel Curtis are Mather, Albright, and Marshall (in center of group). Washington State Historical Society.

July 11, 1915, my first visit to the Grand Canyon. Later I remarked: "I hate to have a Grand Canyon Park where one has to walk along the rim, hopping on one foot and keep the other out over the canyon."

"September 4, 1915, was dedication day for Rocky Mountain National Park." Among those gathered were Acting Supervisor Charles Trowbridge, Stephen Mather, and Horace Albright.

Albright at Mammoth Hot Springs, September 1915. "I had never been to Yellowstone and was terribly excited about seeing 'Wonderland,' as the magazines called it."

December 3, 1915. Mather (above) and Albright joined some local people for a horse-back trip to Ozark-Lithia Springs, Arkansas.

Honeymoon at Grand Canyon, Hermit's Rest, January 1916. "We sat before the immense, arched rock fireplace, with the huge blazing logs quickly thawing us out while we had tea and cakes."

August 1916. "The second Mather Mountain Party was as memorable as the first." Standing: F. B. McClure, Harold White, Robert Yard, George Davis. Seated: Stephen Mather, E. O. McCormick, F.W. Grimwood, and Edward Curtis, who served as photographer for the pack trip along the John Muir Trail in the Sierra Nevada.

August 1, 1917, on top of Cadillac Mountain, Sieur de Monts National Monument, Maine. Secretary of the Interior Franklin K. Lane (right), seen here with Custodian George Dorr, became a true champion of the monument, later known as Acadia National Park.

August 17, 1917. As "Personal Representative of the Secretary of the Interior" I met Viscount Kikujino Ishii, his party of fifty, and innumerable San Francisco dignitaries and State Department bureaucrats when they visited Yosemite. Albright is seated in the middle seat with James Rolph mayor of San Francisco.

September 12, 1917, Mesa Verde National Park. "The sun spotlighted the ancient complex called Spruce Tree House with what the locals called a 'colorado' glow—the Spanish word for red. It was ethereal."

"At about 14,260 feet, Mount Evans was the most prominent peak seen from Denver." Albright and fellow mountaineers on the summit, October 5, 1918.

December 1918. Mather traveled with a party of friends through the Northwest and had an especially great time at Mount Rainier.

July 15, 1919. Horace Albright, on his first day as superintendent of Yellowstone National Park.

Troubling Signs
1916

Although Mather had cleaned up the Yellowstone concession problem, he certainly had not solved the concession problem in Yosemite. It was in worse shape than it had been the year before. His old enemy David Curry had slammed his foot in the door of a car and, because of diabetes, had contracted gangrene and died in April 1916. He had a bad apple of a son, and soon Mather and Foster Curry were locking horns. The whole mess was simply too much for Mather, so he tossed the Curry problem to me.

To solve this, I went to Secretary Lane, knowing he shared my fondness for Mrs. Curry and my sympathy for her difficulty in operating the company and reining in her son. After some discussion, we decided to let Curry matters drift, giving the company a decent franchise of five years and Mrs. Curry an opportunity to plan the future. Lane's only stipulation was that this was his plan, his plan alone, in case Mather got upset by the solution and turned on me.

Lane had been frank with me in questioning Mather's volatile mood changes. I assured him that Mather was fine, that it was only stress. He had so much on his mind, especially Yosemite.

Desmond had resigned and left a financial disaster behind him. Two of his hotels burned down under suspicious circumstances. Then there were two huge hotels in the works, one at Glacier Point, and another, the Grizzly, on which construction hadn't gotten beyond some foundations. The service, food, accommodations, and bookkeeping were in their usual mess. Creditors were howling like wolves at the door. The San Francisco backers paid a cash advance of seventeen thousand dollars and then were forced into a voluntary sixty-percent assessment on their shares.

Of course, Mather was financially involved in all this. I never asked and I never knew the exact details. His Chicago attorney handled it all. From a legal standpoint, though, this scared me as it had earlier. Should Mather's involvement become common knowledge, he would probably be dismissed from the Interior Department, and the high regard in which he was held might be permanently damaged—and the National Park Service with it.

I delicately tried to talk to Mather about it, but he just clamped his mouth shut and would not say a word. Fortunately, once more, by telling me nothing, he kept me out of the situation, but I knew he was deeply concerned and worried about his favorite park and his favorite project.

To get his mind off his problems, Mather did two things. First, he engaged in a frenetic social whirl. Mrs. Mather lived in Chicago. He lived at the Cosmos Club in Washington. He hated being alone. He rarely was. He loved entertaining friends and did so with a lavish hand. There were luncheons for congressmen, writers, and anyone else whose company he enjoyed, dinner parties at the Cosmos Club for men only, and lovely suppers at the finest hotels, with theater parties afterward, for mixed groups.

One of the most beautiful evenings was a large party he gave in honor of Grace's twenty-sixth birthday on October 23, 1916. It was at the Willard Hotel. At her place at the table was her birthday present, twenty-six pink roses in a magnificent Dresden china bowl. After dinner we all went to the Belasco Theater to see *The Boomerang*, then to a supper club for a midnight repast and dancing. Mather was one of the most thoughtful, kindly, and generous men I ever knew.

His many friends entertained him too. Fortunately for Grace and me, we were included in most of the larger parties. I remember a particularly great evening. General Scott was an intimate friend of Buffalo Bill Cody. Cody was in Washington with his 101 Ranch Show, so Scott had a dinner party in his honor: just Scott, Mather, the Albrights, Buffalo Bill, and several of the latter's friends from the show.

Buffalo Bill was as picturesque as you'd imagine, alert physically and mentally, marvelously entertaining. He was especially pleased that so much attention was being given to his namesake town. Turning to Mather, he said: "I particularly want to thank you for your part in this publicity about

Cody and for honoring my Irma Hotel and Pahaska Lodge with your visits."

That was the wrong thing to say. I mentally cringed, and for good reason too. Mather always spoke up when he had something on his mind. He smiled sweetly and, in a cool tone of voice, replied: "Mr. Cody, I did indeed visit your hostelries, but I assure you I will not again unless you take steps to rectify the sad conditions they are in."

To my great surprise, Buffalo Bill roared with laughter. "Send me a list of sad conditions. We'll see they're corrected." And with that Buffalo Bill Cody rounded up the party and swept us off to enjoy his dazzling 101 Ranch Show.

Another thing Mather loved was to throw plans and ideas around among groups of men, so he instituted all kinds of meetings. "Let's see how they play," he'd say. He arranged several in New York and Philadelphia. Then he rounded up Lane and some friends from outside the government and paid for them to come to Atlantic City to discuss plans for improvement of the parks and methods of protecting them better.

It turned out to be a rather disturbing meeting. As time passed, Mather grew excitable and wildly extravagant. It was quite unlike him. His ideas were not very realistic and were fearfully expensive, especially as we had no guarantee of funds. He had told me right from the start of our relationship: "I've got a lot of ideas, some good, some bad, some terrible. Now it's going to be your job to sort out these ideas, and, when you think there's a bad one, throw it out—or throw me out." Fortunately, there was no necessity for me to try, for everyone politely ignored the situation. However, this meeting eventually produced some fine ideas on when and in what amount appropriations might be doled out to our service. Only later did I recall Mather's unusual behavior.

Mather sent me off on some short trips during the next month. There were several meetings in New York with government officials and the American Game Association concerning the care of wild animals in Yellowstone during the winter season. There was deep concern that some animals, the bison and the antelope in particular, might die out as a species. Years later this problem would be called one of "endangered species." Back in 1916 there were two real, or imagined, threats.

One was how to protect animals against famine in the worst climatic years. In fierce winters, there was an incredible loss of life among the elk and other ungulates. Starvation took a heavy toll, and the question was, should the animals be fed artificially? Should hay be bought and brought to them? And if so, where was the money coming from to do it? Actually, fear was so great about the bison that grain was grown for them up in the Slough Creek area of Yellowstone. But what to do about the others? There was a sharp division of opinion on this question.

This led to the other problem, the matter of the predators. They were always waiting on the sidelines for the young and the weak. The predators had been very vigorously pursued by the army. By 1916 mountain lions appeared to have been wiped out, and only a handful of wolves were left in Yellowstone. Coyotes roamed in abundance even though hundreds were shot or poisoned each year. Rows of coyote skins were hung out in Gardiner for the taking.

I had gotten very interested in game protection and had been getting a crash course from my "tutor," Henry Fairfield Osborn, president of both the Museum of Natural History and the New York Zoological Society. I think he mailed me a package of books and brochures at least once a week and then quizzed me on them when I saw him. He was the first one to teach me about balance of nature, about allowing predators to exist as a balance for too great an increase in their natural prey. It took years before I was able to build on these ideas and put them into practice, but at least I was learning all the time.

The months from October to the end of 1916 were filled with odds and ends of national park business. We were so stymied by lack of funds that we could initiate practically nothing.

Mather was like a caged lion. He got into one controversy after another with Bob Marshall. It was frustrating for Mather, as he was very fond of Bob and had high hopes for him. Likewise, Bob was as devoted to Mather as all the rest of us were. He felt he was doing a good job and simply couldn't figure out why he wasn't pleasing Mather. It was a bitter, acrimonious situation.

Both had a deep love and interest in the parks, but Marshall had a more thorough knowledge. Mather visualized that Bob would become the director of the new bureau, that he and I could then quietly slip away to pursue our interests as originally planned. However, what had started as simple differences of opinion between the two men progressed to an irreparable break. Mather criticized Marshall's methods of accounting, his arrogant handling of people, and his quarrels with concessioners and superintendents. He overlooked his fine traits and any attempt to make peace.

Marshall also ran into trouble when Mather told him to write the National Park Service report for the 1916 Interior Department annual report. Mather disliked the results intensely and ordered me to write another one. I hated to do so, as I was fond of Marshall and didn't want to see a fight develop between Mather and him. So I went to Secretary Lane with the problem. His answer was for me to go ahead and obey Mather but take my time about it. He'd include Marshall's version in his annual report and get it to the Government Printing Office as fast as possible. He'd take the blame if there was any fallout. That's the way it went, except that Mather was furious that Marshall's was the official report, and he had mine printed separately at his own cost. I think only a few copies of mine ever surfaced, and I had to make my own peace with Bob Marshall without taking sides in their quarrel. During the two terrible years ahead, although he hated Mather and never forgave him, Marshall stayed a loyal and faithful friend to me, giving me help and advice.

Marshall's final misstep was when he rashly ordered an early closing of Yellowstone, believing that a threatened rail strike would cut off the stream of tourists. Besides infuriating Mather, it caused a furor with everyone in Montana and Wyoming who made a nickel off the park, and complaints poured into their representatives in Congress. Now these people in sparsely populated Montana might not have made any difference, but the Child family did. Immediate reaction came from the junior senator from Montana, Thomas J. Walsh.

Harry Child owned the hotels and transportation in Yellowstone. He was taken seriously ill and was supposed to be dying. His only son, Huntley, took over the business without his father's knowledge or permission. He was an arrogant, spiteful "whipper-snapper," as Mather called him. The dislike was mutual.

Huntley feared Mather's plans for concessioners, feared for his profits melting away. The soldiers stationed in Yellowstone, of course, were bored to death and spent most of their pay in the little rundown town of Gardiner, at the north entrance to the park. Here Child had interests in almost every store. Most of all, Harry Child's hotel interests were financially backed by the Northern Pacific Railroad, and he was half owner of the largest cattle ranch in Montana.

When Huntley Child raised cain with Senator Walsh, you can bet Walsh got busy. He immediately protested the park closure and then extended his quarrel to troops leaving Yellowstone. With few exceptions, Walsh was the meanest man with whom I ever crossed swords. And I crossed plenty with him until his death in 1933.

Marshall had accidentally stirred up a hornet's nest. This was the last straw for Mather. He removed Marshall as superintendent of national parks and returned him to the Geological Survey. Marshall was enraged and bitter, and he forever held a deep-seated grudge against Mather. In correspondence he complained to his friends throughout the country. In person he claimed to anyone he met—even in the sacred halls of the Cosmos Club—that Mather was a megalomaniac and was mentally unbalanced. He said he was "fired" (not transferred) because Mather wanted him out of the way so he could have the directorship himself.

In the course of time, a letter Marshall wrote to Secretary Lane surfaced and seemed to corroborate what he had been saying. On December 22, 1916, Marshall wrote Lane:

> Mr. Mather informed me last evening that he felt he should take the position of Director of the National Park Service when it was your privilege and pleasure to make the appointment, and that you desired him to do so. You no doubt know that I have had some reason for expecting that the honor and responsibility would come to me when the Service was organized. However, in view of Mr. Mather's statement of his and your wishes, it seems to me best to retire now, as I do not for a moment desire in any manner whatsoever to stand in the way of your wishes in the management and development of the national parks. Therefore, may I presume to ask you to allow me to return to my position in the Geological Survey at your earliest convenience?

Marshall felt he had been betrayed by his close friend, Stephen Mather, had been summarily put aside with apparently no warning. It was a messy business, especially when Secretary Lane let Mather know he was displeased and openly showed his affection for Marshall. All this had a very bad effect on Mather and weighed heavily on his mind.

In October Mather told me Secretary Lane wanted him to investigate an area of sand dunes in Indiana. Senator Thomas Taggart of Indiana had sponsored a resolution calling for hearings on the dunes in preparation for including them in a national park.

Mather growled that we had no money to improve existing parks and no money to develop new parks like Lassen and Hawaii. Interesting areas east of the Mississippi weren't in any future plans at the moment. Why did we have to waste our time considering sand dunes? I answered, "From a legal standpoint, if the Senate says we do, we do."

"All right, Horace," Mather replied, "if we do, you will go with me to investigate this sandpile." I tried to duck out by saying I thought there was too much work in Washington for me and even threw in the fact that Grace hated being alone so much and hadn't been feeling too well.

"Nonsense, Horace, we haven't much real work to do around here and we'll take Grace with us. Do her good. Tell you what. Bob Yard is coming, so we'll have him bring his Margaret. Then all of you come stay at my house in Chicago until after the election. You and Bob will be on government business. I'll treat the girls to the trip. How's that?"

What could I say? Grace and I left for Chicago at 7:30 P.M. October 28 on the Baltimore and Ohio train.

Mather and his daughter Betty met us at the Chicago station at 3:40 the next afternoon. In his elegant, chauffeur-driven limousine we returned to his equally elegant Dorchester Street home. We had a lovely dinner and spent the evening there, with Mather and myself in his study looking over maps of the dunes while Grace and Mrs. Mather got better acquainted. The latter was a tall, impressive lady, rather quiet and withdrawn but kindly, austere and aristocratic but gracious—quite different from her ebullient, gregarious husband.

About ten o'clock Mather took us over to an apartment he owned where we were to sleep; meals were to be at his home. When the Yards joined us several days later, they also stayed at the apartment.

The next day, October 30, Mather conducted a hearing as specified by Taggart's resolution. It was held in the federal building in Chicago. About four hundred people attended, and many from various fields of art, science, education, and business spoke on behalf of the dunes.

The next morning Grace, Mather, and I met a large contingent of professors from the University of Chicago, friends of Mather's from the Prairie Club, and a wide assortment of politicians, with a few women mixed in, about twenty in all. We rode in a private railroad car to Michigan City, Indiana, where we were met by the mayor and his group of fifteen or more people. He had plenty of cars lined up for the drive out to the sand dunes, which stretched for miles along the southern shore of Lake Michigan.

The scene was most impressive—towering dunes rising from the blue lake to the forested interior. As a matter of fact, a good portion of our party took one look at the formidable sand hills and decided to remain near the cars, later joining us for lunch. Led by Professor Henry C. Cowles of the University of Chicago, a renowned botanist, only about half the party trudged out across the dunes, had numerous photos snapped, and took a long, pleasant lunch break at the Prairie Club's Beach House. A lot more of the group decided the comfortable wicker chairs and pleasant view were preferable to hiking in sand, so we were down to about ten brave souls, including Mather, Grace, and me. We had a really interesting and fun time for another two hours, at one point sliding down the dunes as if they were snow hills. Then it was back to the cars and the train and a quiet evening at the Mather home.

However, there was a surprising change in Mather. Although he was always electrically energetic, I had rarely seen him so excitable. He couldn't sit still. He paced up and down, laughing and talking a mile a minute about what a marvelous national park these dunes would make.

I tried to throw cold water on his enthusiasm. "Mr. Mather, all the prospective land is privately held and would cost a couple of million dollars to purchase it. Where on earth could we get the money? Congress won't even give us enough to run the Washington office. At that price, why would they even consider these sand dunes, no matter how wonderful?"

He overrode every objection I brought up. This sudden about-face on creating parks baffled me. He had been so adamant about consolidating the system, improving it, but not trying to expand it except for Grand Canyon and existing park extensions. Now he was wildly excited about sand dunes. Not that the area wasn't interesting. It was, and in time it did become part of the park system. For now, I kept quizzing and discouraging him about it.

Suddenly he whirled around, glared at me, and, for the first time since we had met, barked out: "Horace, this is none of your business!" That hit me like a thunderbolt, and it hurt too. My face must have registered how badly I felt, for he came across the room, gripped my arm, and said: "It's all right. You didn't mean any harm and I forgive you." Forgive me? Here he had switched moods in two minutes and was all rosy and good-humored. These mood switches made me very uneasy. They were so unlike him.

The next day it seemed to be water over the dam. Mather appeared to be his usual self and wanted to get down to business. Yard had arrived in the meantime. We spent the remainder of our visit in Chicago,

TROUBLING SIGNS

November 1–8, on National Park Service affairs, meeting with railroad officials and concessioners like Ford Harvey. Mather also spent some time at Sterling Borax on affairs of his company, while I used his office and a secretary to write the official report of our sand dunes inspection for Secretary Lane. Mather detested writing and never had written more than personal letters since finding I enjoyed writing and did a reasonable job of it. Along with Bob Yard, I was also "allowed" to write his speeches.

Tuesday, November 7, was election day. Mather had become more and more nervous and worried as the day approached. It was infectious, for Yard and I were getting jittery too. This was quite unlike either of us. We three had talked ourselves into believing that if Woodrow Wilson and his Democrats weren't reelected, our beloved Park Service would be in mortal danger. A Republican administration was unknown to us and therefore feared. As a matter of fact, all three of us were so-called Progressive Republicans, although I was the only one who had voted for Wilson in 1912. Of course, I didn't admit this to my boss, for he probably would have fired me for not supporting Teddy Roosevelt.

Besides this, I was the only one of the three who was very concerned about the European war. This was mainly because I was of fighting age. America had been interested but not deeply concerned with that conflict until the election. Suddenly there was apprehension that a new administration might get our country involved in the war. Wilson's campaign was run on the slogan "He kept us out of war." Theodore Roosevelt bellowed about fighting the Germans, and the Democrats tagged his slogans on their opponent: "A vote for Hughes is a vote for war."

On election day Mather was the only one who could vote and did so as soon as the polls opened. Yard and I were residents of the District of Columbia, federal territory, so couldn't cast our votes. By nighttime, Mather was fit to be tied. We were all supposed to go to the theater, where he had reserved a box for the Franz Lehar musical *Alone at Last*. At dinner he suddenly decided he wouldn't go, but insisted that Mrs. Mather, Grace, and Margaret Yard attend anyway.

We three men adjourned to the Quadrangle Club to listen to election returns. Mather was a bundle of nerves, never sitting down, pacing around the room, talking incessantly. The returns coming in were not very hopeful for Wilson, and this only increased Mather's agitation. Men began to glower at him. A few made shushing noises. Yard whispered to me: "Horace, let's get him out of here. He's getting too upset. What'll he do if Wilson loses?" We convinced him that it was almost time for his limousine to pick up the ladies at the theater, so we'd better be taken home now.

When the three women walked in from the theater, they saw a sad and sorry group of husbands. Mather was slumped in a chair with his head in his hands, moaning about the American people being a bunch of idiots— that is, the easterners and midwesterners. The southerners were passable, but he had faith in what the dependable westerners would do. I was disconsolately sitting on the stairs silently watching Yard pacing up and down, figuring out what course we could take in the future, relying on the fact that we could dredge up Mather's connection with Teddy Roosevelt.

Then Yard suggested that we all pile into the limousine and drive around town checking on further election results, anything to get Mather's mind occupied. Mrs. Mather declined to go and excused herself. The rest of us drove around Chicago stopping at various nightspots, hotels, and clubs until we decided that Wilson had lost. Charles Evans Hughes was our new president.

Hughes thought so too, and he went to bed apparently not realizing that California's thirteen votes could reverse the outcome. When a reporter saw that California results were favoring Wilson, he came to the Hotel Astor to talk to Hughes. His valet said, "The president has already retired," and the reporter replied, "When he wakes up, tell him he is no longer president."

The next day, results proved that Hiram Johnson's vindictiveness had cost Hughes the election. By the slim margin of four thousand California votes, Woodrow Wilson was reelected. Mather was delighted, and, according to him, the National Park Service was saved. Grace and I returned to Washington the next day.

On November 17 I received a telephone call from Mr. Mather. It was most unusual, for we almost never incurred the expense of a phone call. His voice sounded odd to me, strained and anxious. He told me to get the first train and come to Chicago. When I asked the reason, he replied, "Horace, do as I ask."

I had to tell Secretary Lane where I was going, for I needed travel orders from the department. He questioned me rather thoroughly and then asked, "Why are you evasive, Mr. Albright? Is there something wrong?" I answered that everything was fine. It was probably just a matter of clearing up the Indiana Dunes report, which of course was already in my possession being polished. He wasn't particularly satisfied but gave me the proper papers, and I left at noon.

I hated like the dickens to leave Grace, for she was crying, said she didn't feel well, and as always was terrified of being alone. We had been married almost a year, and with all my short trips away she had managed either to have someone come stay with her or to go to a friend's home. Not knowing how long I'd be away, I phoned one of Grace's friends and arranged for her to stay there while I was in Chicago.

When I walked into Mather's study on the eighteenth, he looked up from his desk in surprise. "Why, Horace, what's the trouble? What are you doing here in Chicago?" I was stunned and hardly knew how to answer. I fumbled in my coat pocket and brought out Lane's orders, which of course had given no reason for going to Chicago.

"Didn't Lane give you any reason for these? What's his problem? Didn't he tell you anything?"

I gulped out, "He just told me to report to you."

"What's the matter with the man? There's nothing here for you. Better get on the first train and go home." But on second thought, he added, "Well, I was about to meet some people from the Great Northern Railroad. You'd better at least talk to them, so you can report you were doing Park Service business." This I did and then caught the night train back to Washington, totally perplexed and inwardly somewhat frightened. What on earth was the matter with my chief?

Mather returned to Washington sporadically for the remainder of the year. His sole interest was a conference of national park superintendents to be held in Washington in January 1917. Bob Marshall and I had initially been detailed to plan this meeting, but Mather now shut Marshall out, only a few weeks before the conference was to open. Mather's plans for the conference were to discuss ideas for the Park Service once money had been allocated, to interest congressmen in development of the service, and to bring in men from outside the government to add new ideas and recommendations to use in the future.

It was an ambitious undertaking. He cared about nothing but making a success of it, and I devoted every minute of my time to seeing his plans carried out. But suddenly my life seemed to be a toboggan going downhill fast.

Grace hadn't been feeling too well even before we went to Chicago. On December 7 she stated she was really sick, but because of her normal good health and strength we both passed it off as "just one of those things." A week later she had to confess she couldn't go on as she was and finally consented to see a doctor. He told her it was just a bad case of nervous indigestion.

The same day we received a telegram saying that my brother Leslie, who was in Europe, had contracted typhoid fever.

By the sixteenth Grace was so ill she couldn't eat a thing, could barely get out of bed. The next day the doctor finally came to the conclusion that she had a serious case of yellow jaundice (which today we know as hepatitis). I don't believe I had ever seen anyone so sick. I was frantic. There was no other person at the office, so I had to go to work, but I simply couldn't leave my girl alone. I ended up calling on Eva Larsen to take Grace to her home to nurse her properly.

The next day, Sunday the seventeenth, we received word that my dearest brother Leslie had died.

Aside from Bob Yard, there was absolutely no one to help with the conference. Mather remained in Chicago over the Christmas season, not returning until the day before it was to open. When Marshall and Acker heard of my predicament, they offered their help. What a blessing they were!

And none too soon. Yard had placed articles about the conference in newspapers all around the country, and interest in it exploded. We had dozens of requests for information or tickets to attend the sessions. We did not have enough help in answering letters, and we had no more room at the National Museum, where our conference was to be held. What more could go wrong?

A telegram arrived on December 30 saying that my beloved grand-dad Horace Marden had died in San Francisco of a heart attack. I was alone in the office when it was delivered. I put my head down on my desk and cried for the first time in years. All the recent events stacking up were suddenly too much for me. My granddad had been my inspiration, probably the one who had shaped my ambition and character more than anyone else. Now the second close relative was dead within two weeks.

I was more than ever filled with dread that the news of Leslie's death and her father's passing would cause my mother's death too. My inclination was to catch the first train for California, but the responsibility for Grace and for Mather's conference had to take precedence. Both were such a deep concern to me, especially with the way Mather had been acting recently.

TROUBLING SIGNS

The eventful year of 1916 ended with my Grace's first outing after her illness when we joined a small group at the Shoreham Hotel on New Year's Eve. Mr. and Mrs. Mather gave an elegant, festive dinner to celebrate the banner year we were just concluding. Champagne was in order. Mather was ebullient, laughing, and lighthearted as he proposed a toast: "Who would have thought a year ago tonight that 1916 would end in such a burst of glory? We have accomplished a miracle and will go on to reach higher pinnacles of success in 1917." We all rose, lifted our glasses, and drank to the glowing future of 1917.

CHAPTER
14

Collapse
1917

The morning after the gala celebration of New Year 1917, Mather said we had to have a serious talk before the conference on national parks opened. He was very secretive. Instead of using his office, we met in a small conference room rarely used by Lane or his other assistants, and he admonished me to tell no one of our meeting.

He started off the conversation in an extremely somber vein, mentioning past successes but dwelling almost entirely on failures or projects uncompleted. It was somewhat of a surprise to me, for Mather was usually all enthusiasm, bursting with ideas and optimistic plans. He wasn't one to look back. The more he talked, the more depressed he seemed.

He kept going over his disagreements with Bob Marshall, and repeatedly he said, "Horace, do you realize this is the day Bob's transfer from our outfit becomes effective?" He never got over Marshall's estrangement and enmity.

He also dwelled on the problems with various park concessions, particularly the Desmond Company in Yosemite. Making the Grand Canyon a national park, and the mining claims there, deeply disturbed him.

He even worried about Lane. With the election over, he felt Lane would probably be replaced by a new secretary, who would not be interested in national parks, or, worse, be antagonistic to them—"probably be some citified easterner who wouldn't care a tinker's damn about anything west of the Hudson unless it would be to develop the resources."

There was no use in arguing that some of the ideas seemed pretty pessimistic, so I remained silent and listened to these downbeat troubles.

For the first time, Mather told me in some detail about his financial involvement with the Desmond Company and the serious trouble it was in, especially since Desmond himself had disassociated himself from it. He confessed that he, along with a few others, was committed to bailing the company out. Of course, I had long known that the whole matter had been kept under wraps, but he seemed unaware that there were possible illegal elements involved. Apparently innocent of the law, the participants had gone along with their plans and agreements until circumstances had forced them into a box.

Alarmed and apprehensive, I asked if he would fill me in on details. After all, I was an attorney and had spent some time investigating the legal angles of their problem. I honored this man, and in his present condition I was fearful that he could bring disgrace on himself, his partners, and the new National Park Service. The more I turned it over in my mind, the more worried I became, and the more questions I asked.

He suddenly clammed up. He instructed me to forget our meeting and everything that we had talked about. Instead, my concern for him made me press for details, offering any help I could give him. He became very nervous, his voice rising. Suddenly he refused to discuss the matter any further, and he switched to the question of who would run the new service.

Mather knew that Lane wanted him to be confirmed as director, but he was indecisive. He seesawed back and forth. First he felt his job wasn't finished until the bureau was set up, with proper appropriations and an organization to provide smooth operations. Then he lapsed into this black hole of depression, talking about his inability to solve the vast assortment of problems.

"I'm not an organization man. I like to do things in the field, not fiddle-faddle around an office, pushing papers and digging around in details. When you leave, I would have nobody to take care of these things, and I simply cannot tackle them by myself."

Well, now we were getting down to the nuts and bolts of the conversation. He had to know whether I was going back to California, whether I was going to leave the service as planned after the superintendents' conference and appearing before congressional committees for appropriations to start up the Park Service. He probed and probed without coming directly to the point.

Although I had been offered opportunities in several fine San Francisco law firms and a teaching position at the University of California, I really had been too busy and concerned with national park affairs to think beyond the conference and the appropriation problems. Looking across the room at this worried, disturbed man, whom I had learned to admire so deeply, I made a fast decision.

"Mr. Mather, let's not concern ourselves with these problems today. You know I'm always with you and will not walk away until we have an opportunity to assess our future. We're like parents to this new National Park Service. We created it, we gave birth to it, and we'll always take its interests to heart. Let's just tackle one thing at a time. Let's make this superintendents' conference, into which you've put so much of yourself, a great success. That's the prime consideration right now."

Well, he instantly brightened up, jumped to his feet, and began his pacing, which always meant furious thinking, a problem of his feet keeping up with his mind. He switched moods completely as he began rattling off details and instructions about tomorrow's meeting. I left him with a feeling of relief.

Stephen Mather had a brilliant conception for this Fourth National Parks Conference. He hoped that the broad inclusion of people from a variety of fields would result in discussions leading to plans and policies for the organization and future direction of the new bureau. It was to be a teaching and a learning experience for all, designed to cover as many spheres of knowledge concerning the national parks as he could find learned speakers—economics, reclamation, roads, sciences from botany to biology, photography, art, education, and even religion. The concept was fascinating, and Bob Yard carried out his chief's ideas superbly. He contacted the participants and suggested the topics for their lectures, and if there was to be a slide show, he chose the pictures to be shown.

For my part, I had the management of the sessions, seeing that the speakers were lined up in proper order and obtaining any equipment they requested. I also saw to the refreshments, accommodations in hotels, and problems that arose for our guests.

It was a bright, sunny morning of Tuesday, January 2, 1917, when hundreds of people streamed into the auditorium of the New National Museum for the first session of the National Parks Conference. There were more interested applicants than we could handle here.

COLLAPSE

The morning session opened right on time, with Mather presiding over the theme of economics and the national parks. He filled the morning with fairly innocuous talks by Secretary Lane, Senator Reed Smoot, and Representatives Scott Ferris, Irvine Lenroot, and William Kent, leaders in the fight to pass the bill creating the National Park Service. It was most interesting to hear the divergent views of the congressmen.

Mather closed the morning session with an accolade for Robert Marshall. As he spoke, his voice began to tremble and his hands twisted his program into a knot. He abruptly stopped talking and simply stared at the audience. Bob Yard, who was near him, quickly shuffled just enough to jar him lightly. He seemed to waken from a trance and then finished with a fine announcement of the exhibition of paintings to be shown in the evening session. The meeting was adjourned. Only Yard and I seemed to notice the interruption. From the look on his face, I could see that he was as concerned and fearful as I, but we didn't discuss it.

After lunch Mather had scheduled a real eye-opener, someone to shake the audience awake after their encounter with much delicious food and drink. He also thought he needed a person who would keep the audience from drifting away in the afternoon as so often happens. So he scheduled as leadoff speaker the fireball Enos Mills, "Father of Rocky Mountain National Park," a famous writer and lecturer.

The topic of Mills's speech, as printed in the program, was "The National Parks for All the People." One interesting thought he reiterated several times was that it would never do to have public schools make money for their upkeep or public playgrounds make profits to operate them. So why should national parks become moneymakers to pay for themselves? Let the people's taxes take care of property they used and enjoyed.

As Mills had taken more than a lion's share of the afternoon, other speakers sympathetically shortened theirs. But it wasn't only Mills who rambled. Strangely, Mather interjected several unscheduled talks of his own during the afternoon—his thoughts or experiences in various parks. Speaking about concessions in Yosemite, he rambled about the Desmond Company. He explained that after paying interest on the investment and depreciation, the company would keep seventy-five percent and give twenty-five percent to the Park Service for the first five years. Then it would be fifty-fifty. Normally the government took a flat percentage of the gross receipts, so this was an odd arrangement.

My attention had kind of drifted off until I heard Mather say: "A group of public-spirited men of broad vision are working out a most comprehensive set of plans, etc." I came to with a jolt, my heart nearly flipping over for fear he was about to go on to explain his part in financing the Desmond Company. That would have been a catastrophe. While I was still holding my breath, he abruptly switched topics.

Later, when he was to introduce Assistant Attorney General Huston Thompson, Mather wandered off on Crater Lake. He told a long story about how sheep had grazed there and destroyed all the wild flowers, which had fragile roots due to volcanic ash in the soil. He added that it would take fifty years or more to see them again unless artificial means were used to reintroduce them.

At this point in his story, Mather's voice began to falter and he seemed about to cry. Hardly daring to move, I thought a diversion would have to be created immediately. But what? The chair: I'd let my chair crash on the floor. As quickly as the thought flashed into my head, Mather's voice strengthened and he quietly announced Huston Thompson as the next speaker.

Another puzzling moment was past, but with each my apprehension was growing. What on earth was the trouble with my beloved chief?

An evening session was held at 8:15 in the galleries on the second floor of the New National Museum to honor the opening of the First Annual Exhibition of National Parks Painting. Dr. William H. Holmes, curator of the National Gallery of Art, addressed the gathering.

During the festivities, Mather called me over and gave me a card with the name of James L. Smith engraved on it. He told me to get rid of Smith, who was being detained in a nearby corridor, apparently causing the guard some trouble. When I located Mr. Smith, I found him to be a pleasant, well-dressed man, hugging an enormous, paper-wrapped package. I dismissed the guard, telling him that I would handle the situation.

Introducing myself to the gentleman, I asked what I could do for him. Indicating the package under his arm, Smith replied that he had come to display his paintings of national parks. He added that he was very unhappy because the guard had refused to let him into the exhibit room. I carefully explained about the conference, that it was by invitation only, and that this exhibition was not open to the general public at this time.

"Well, Mr. Albright, that's not the point," said Smith. "My paintings of the national parks are the finest in the world, and I am the greatest painter in the world. So my paintings should be in the gallery, now." His voice echoed down the corridor, growing louder and louder as he began to unwrap his artwork and go into details of his greatness. I nervously looked around for the guard, but of course he had disappeared. It was only a question of time until this uproar would reach the guests, but what to do with this mad artist?

At this moment, around the corner came a total stranger. With no introduction, I hauled him to one side and briefed him on my problem. While Smith babbled on, pulling his paintings free of the paper, we quickly agreed on action to be taken. We each grabbed one of Smith's arms, lifted him off his feet, and hurried him to a guard, who carted him away. I returned to pick up his paintings and thus lost track of my helper.

Later I discovered who had helped me hoist Mr. Smith out of the National Gallery. It was Orville Wright. At the afternoon session of January 5, he spoke to the conference on "Air Routes to the National Parks." Most of the conferees shook their heads in disbelief at his futuristic ideas, and I decided I'd been dealing with two loonies instead of one that night at the National Gallery.

The second day of the conference, January 3, started off on a bad note. I was at the auditorium before seven o'clock again, but no one else was around. About half an hour later Bob Yard walked in and wanted to know where Mather was. He had to talk to him immediately about a switch in speakers. As he obviously wasn't here, Yard went off to call him at the Cosmos Club.

Mather had left the club about 6:30 A.M. That early? In the black of night? And where was he? I suggested maybe he'd gone to meet someone for breakfast, but Yard seemed terribly worried. "Bob," I said, "you seem to know something I don't about Mr. Mather's odd behavior. You've known him far longer than I have. I'd surely appreciate it if you'd tell me what is troubling him. Maybe together we could do something about it."

"Oh," replied Bob, "he's just tired, too much to do and think about. He'll be all right."

So we let it go at that. But as the ten o'clock starting time for the second session approached, I was really getting nervous. So was Yard. Before I had time to open my mouth, he said: "Horace, I've tried every place I can think of and I can't locate Steve. I'll have to take his place as presiding officer. But what will I tell them about Steve's absence?"

"Don't even mention it," I said. "Everybody will just think you are supposed to be there instead of Mather."

And so it went. Fortunately, it was a terrible, rainy day. The attendance was very poor. So few showed up that we moved from the auditorium to a smaller room in the museum. Yard explained to the audience that this second day was devoted to education: education of people to know their parks and to show how parks could be used to educate the people.

January 4 was a lost day. Stephen Mather never appeared. Yard was so exhausted by his concern and efforts to find Mather that he became ill and had to go home. I contacted Congressman Gillett to check the Capitol and Secretary Lane to advise him of the problem. Neither could find a clue to Mather's whereabouts, but Lane advised me to "keep a lid on the situation" until he could do more investigating. I kept up the announced schedule of "Recreational Use of the National Parks" and had Enos Mills preside over the sessions.

When I entered the auditorium the following morning, there, big as life and apparently fit as a fiddle, stood Stephen Mather. Well, you can imagine my astonishment. All the way to the museum I had been tossing around one idea after another about what would have to be said to the conference concerning Mather's prolonged absence. Now he greeted me very calmly, inquired how things had been going, and started reviewing the upcoming events of the conference.

Stunned into silence for some time, I finally blurted out: "Excuse me, Mr. Mather, but could I ask where you were recently? Yard and I needed some advice on a few issues and were unable to locate you at the Cosmos Club."

He looked at me in an odd manner and replied, "Well, of course you couldn't. I've been here at the museum most of the time running the show."

Now it was my turn to stare and mutter: "Well, we must have missed you with all the crowds. But where did you spend the night?"

With that he furiously turned on me: "I don't believe that is any of your business, Horace. What's wrong with you? What do you mean where was I at night? I was at my home. With my wife." Of course, his wife and home were in Chicago.

Well, I certainly wasn't going to argue. I was grateful that he was alive and well. So I changed the subject immediately, settling on the morning conference program. Mather pleasantly discussed this with me as though the previous conversation had never taken place. And he opened the session promptly at 9:30 A.M.

COLLAPSE

He told the assembled group, which was even smaller than before, that the meeting would be "more or less of a desultory nature," mainly confined to answering questions that had been placed in a box the day before. After several questions, Mather signaled to me to take his place and then quietly exited the auditorium. My first inclination was to run after him, but I didn't dare, as there was no one else to assume the chair of presiding officer. I spent the next hour or so running the show, but inwardly in a panic. Where had Mather gone? For how long? What was this disappearing act all about?

After several other speakers had finished their dissertations, I was suddenly asked a question about Hetch Hetchy. Right in the middle of my reply, Stephen Mather nonchalantly reappeared and assumed the role of presiding officer.

Fortunately, one of the questions was for Enos Mills, who could talk on anything for any length of time. It provided a much needed breather. The question was, "Would women make good guides in the national parks?" Yes! "The profession of a guide in a national park is that of a philosopher and a friend and an instructor. Hence I do not see why a woman could not do this as well and in many cases even better than a man." He added that guides should have equality of opportunity among the women as well as among the men. Of course, guides meant rangers, and this was heady stuff in those days.

When Mills stopped long enough to ask if anyone had a question, Mather quickly stepped in and added his own thoughts on the subject of guides—very clear, very rational, very thoughtful. Then Enos was back, lecturing again on his favorite subject, freedom of competition in national parks, allowing as many concessioners as wanted to compete, anathema to Mather. But he remained calm, simply letting Mills go on.

The morning session ended with Mather exhorting everyone to be back in the afternoon. "All those who are interested in the development of motor traffic to the parks should make a point of attending," he said. And, of course, who was more interested in motor travel to the parks than Stephen Mather? It was almost a phobia with him. Yet he was not seen again until the following morning.

Much later, various men who attended the conference told me that they had only given casual thought to Mather's absences up to this time. They imagined he was just terribly busy with details of the meeting. But his absence from a session devoted to his favorite topic (along with concessions) now seemed highly unusual, almost bizarre. Questions arose in many minds as to whether he was ill, upset, or angry at something. Frankly, as long as he appeared well and strong, I gave up trying to decide where he went or why. Just get us through one more day, I prayed.

The afternoon session passed quietly with a large audience and interesting speakers. Probably the most intriguing was my friend of opening night, Orville Wright. He made quite a prediction. "While it seems certain it [aerial navigation] can never compete with the railway train or the steamboat in carrying large bodies of people, it will be but a short time till parties now accommodated in automobiles will be safely and easily carried." He added that no matter how many people came to a park in airplanes, the only way to see parks was from the ground. Most of us thought he didn't have all his wheels on the track.

The evening session went smoothly, with not a sign of Mr. Mather. But there he was at the lectern the next morning, ready to preside over the last day of the conference. He could hardly be recognized as the gregarious, fun-loving, convivial man he usually was. Now he wore a somber visage, unsmiling and seldom mixing with conferees.

The morning session was devoted entirely to the Grand Canyon. Before the second speaker could follow the first, Mather suddenly told the audience he had been called to the Capitol for another committee meeting and walked out. Yard and I exchanged helpless looks, which meant, "Let the cards fall where they may."

When the lunch break came, Yard and I decided he'd have to take over once more if Mather didn't reappear. For the first time, Bob hesitantly gave me a hint of Mather's trouble, probably a nervous condition like the one he had experienced years before. He hastily reassured me that it wasn't anything serious, that Mather just had to get away sometimes to relax and calm himself when he felt too nervous and tired. With the conference over, he'd be free from stress, could leave Washington for a long rest, and then he'd be just fine again.

I questioned Yard to get some details about this former problem. When? Where? Under what circumstances? Most of all, what happened? He shrugged all my inquiries aside: "Ask Steve yourself someday when he's his old self. It's really not my place to discuss it." I could see his point and dropped the subject.

When the afternoon session began at 2:30, there was Stephen Mather at the podium once more, calm and unruffled. I was almost getting used to this. Mather remained until the session ended late in the afternoon.

COLLAPSE

Everyone heaped praises on Mather, the most memorable being Emerson Hough's: "In the short period of two and a half years, changes bordering on the miraculous have taken place in the entire administration of our system of parks ... and we all know very largely where the credit for that work should be placed."

I don't know much about the evening session, as I left when the afternoon session was finished. I checked with Mather to learn if he needed me for anything else, but he just looked at me dolefully and said, "There isn't anything else for you to do and there really isn't much use for me either." I tried to buck him up by reminding him of all the wonderful things that had been said about him, the praise everyone was heaping on him, how the conference had been such a marvelous success. He just stood there, sadly shaking his head and muttering, "I don't know, I just don't know."

Well, I didn't know either and was so concerned that I hunted up E. O. McCormick, our old friend from the Southern Pacific Railroad. I related the conversation and suggested he take Mather over to the Cosmos Club with some other friends to have a late supper and a convivial, relaxing evening. He'd already thought of the same thing and had corralled Hough, Congressman Gillett, and Ford Harvey. They'd cheer Steve up for sure.

I felt that I should probably go along with the conferees for the evening, especially the park superintendents and supervisors. I had banked on spending a good deal of time with them, discussing problems and getting their opinions and suggestions. And here the conference was over. Mather really hadn't talked to them at all, and I had seen so little of them, obviously missing a golden opportunity. Within minutes, I noticed that everyone had split up and gone in different directions.

Normally I guess I would have pursued my idea, but I was physically and mentally exhausted. Worry over Mr. Mather had taken a lot out of me. Then, too, it was my birthday, and I had barely laid eyes on Grace for a week. At home, she was waiting for me with my favorite chocolate cake aglow with twenty-seven candles. As I blew them out, I must have made a fervent wish that Mr. Mather would be back to his old self again.

• • •

I honestly don't recall whether it was the evening of January 7 or 8 that my world seemed to collapse. I suppose it's the old saying that we don't remember what we don't want to. My memory comes back in strong with a telephone call about ten o'clock on one of those two evenings. It was E. O. McCormick. He talked rapidly and with a sense of extreme urgency. "Horace, get over here to the Cosmos Club as fast as you can. Something terrible is going on with Steve. For God's sakes, *hurry*! Run!"

I raced up the stairs, repeated to Grace what McCormick had said, and then literally ran all the way to the club. Hough was waiting for me by the front door. "Steve has totally come apart. He's raving, absolutely insane." I didn't waste time, just told him to take me to Mather.

I wasn't prepared for what I saw a few minutes later. His friends had taken Mather into a small reception room and closed the door against curious onlookers. Though loosely held by McCormick, he was rocking back and forth, alternately crying, moaning, and hoarsely trying to get something said. I couldn't understand a thing. He was incoherent. His movements became more agitated while his voice rose. I feared he might possibly hurt himself. As I was younger and stronger, I replaced McCormick, holding him with both arms. Several of us talked quietly to him, trying to soothe his wild mood, but to no avail. Suddenly he broke out of my hold, rushed for the door, and, with an anguished cry, proclaimed he couldn't live any longer feeling as he did. We all understood what he said that time.

McCormick and I grabbed him and hustled him upstairs to a bedroom. Hough went to locate a doctor. Fortunately, there was one at the Cosmos Club, so he was at the room in a few minutes and efficiently got a sedative down Mather's throat. Within ten minutes, he had calmed down considerably, which gave us time to have a consultation with the doctor.

McCormick and Hough related the events of the evening at the Cosmos Club, where the group was having dinner in a private room. Apparently Mather had been getting more and more depressed since the conference had ended. When he should have been pleased, he felt that he had not measured up to his opportunity, that he had accomplished little or nothing, and that he should leave the government service at once. He kept referring to his inadequacy to meet the problems before him and saw no future for himself in this work, which he said he loved above every other activity in his whole life.

His friends were increasingly concerned about his behavior and kept trying to cheer him up. No use. As the meal progressed, Mather talked incessantly, more deeply depressed than ever. He was a failure. He would leave the Park Service. There really was nothing more in life for him. Then he lapsed into silence. He seemed to lose interest in the conversation

COLLAPSE

around him, grew silent, and when he did speak referred to little but his troubles. The other men nervously kept up a running conversation about trips they had made with Mather, praising him, laughing about the good times.

Suddenly Mather broke down completely, put his head on the table, and began to cry. His friends were completely in the dark, didn't know what had happened or what to do. They were simply appalled. I was called because they hoped I might know how to handle him.

Of course, I didn't. I proposed that we find Bob Yard immediately. I felt he had knowledge of some earlier problem Mather had experienced. But Yard and his family had gone away to New Jersey. Then I remembered that Mather had told me his wife might be visiting her mother in New Jersey. We agreed that I should call Jane Mather immediately, even though it was past midnight. Those three would stay with Mather, who was now huddled in a ball at the corner of the bed, muttering incoherently to himself.

Mrs. Mather answered the phone herself. She was quite calm and didn't seem alarmed as she listened quietly to my account. I gave her all the information I could recall since she had been here in Washington the week before. For the doctor's information, she told me, in minute detail, of the severe mental breakdown her husband had suffered in 1903. She thought his present state seemed very similar to that time, when he had collapsed from overwork and nervous tension. In 1903 he had tried a five-week vacation in the South and appeared to be much better. However, it didn't last.

In June 1903 he had spent four months in a sanitarium in Wisconsin and then a few more at the shore in Atlantic City. But every time he went back to work in Chicago, his trouble flared up. Finally the doctors made him give up all work and go to Europe for eight months. When he returned, recuperated and fired up to get back to his position as manager of sales in the Chicago office of Pacific Coast Borax Company, he found that Borax Smith had cut him off the payroll one month after he had gone to Europe. This was a terrible blow and almost set him off again.

Mrs. Mather said that he had been saved by a new interest and activity. In the fall of 1904 he had joined with an old friend, Tom Thorkildsen, in a new company, mining and refining borax, in direct competition with his former employer. Reorganized in 1908, it became Thorkildsen-Mather Company, then Sterling Borax. It was extremely successful and made Mather a millionaire. Although he had suffered short periods of nervousness or depression from time to time, he had seemed to control a more serious episode by avoiding business concerns and escaping to the West, to the wilderness areas, as in 1906, 1912, and 1914.

After Mrs. Mather had provided me with as much information as was necessary at the time, she gave me specific instructions to take Mr. Mather in the morning to Dr. T. H. Weisenburg in Philadelphia. She would contact him to make arrangements and to expect us before noon.

The doctor at the Cosmos Club listened to all this information and decided Mather was safe until morning as long as someone stayed with him. He gave him another sedative, which he said should put him to sleep. It didn't. McCormick insisted on staying with me, as Mather was so restless. We had the club bring in a cot for me. McCormick lay on the other twin bed next to Mather. It was a weird night, and we three got little rest. Mather would suddenly wake up, crying or calling out incoherently, extremely agitated and rolling around on top of the bed or, several times, leaping onto the floor.

At daybreak I went to Mather's lodging and packed his clothes and personal items, putting everything else in several boxes to store at the club. I could get them later. I took a taxi home to tell Grace what had happened and to pick up a few things for myself, not knowing how long I might have to be gone. She was dreadfully upset, for she so loved Mr. Mather. I made her promise to go stay at Eva Larsen's, as she really wasn't well enough to be alone. Then I returned to the Cosmos Club.

McCormick and I got Mather washed and dressed in clean clothes. Fortunately, he was almost somnolent, whether from depression or sedatives I don't know. It was a blessing, however, as we could get him to the train and manage the short ride to Philadelphia. McCormick's influence had gotten us a drawing room, so we could let Mather rest in a quiet atmosphere. McCormick and I were worn out and didn't say five words on the whole trip, so saddened and depressed ourselves that there was nothing to talk about.

In Philadelphia we took Mather in a taxi out to Dr. Weisenburg's office. An attendant gently led Mather away, so we could talk freely with the doctor. As we waited in a comfortable parlor, the door opened and Jane Mather appeared. We went over events of the last few weeks, and she recounted her painful experiences with Mather's nervous breakdown in 1903. It certainly looked to us like a similar mental illness.

About an hour later, Dr. Weisenburg joined us. We three reiterated all the facts we knew about both 1903 and the present. He listened carefully and asked quite a few questions, but was noncommittal, saying only that he would contact us as soon as he had made an evaluation.

Mrs. Mather asked if we could say good-bye to her husband. The doctor discouraged her. However, when she insisted, he left the room and shortly returned with Mather and the male nurse. Mrs. Mather attempted to talk to him, but he just stared blankly at us all. Mrs. Mather turned and left the room. McCormick and I were close to tears as we watched the attendant slowly lead our dear friend away down the hall. By this time, he had apparently sunk into a deep, silent abyss, not appearing to know people or his surroundings. He was to go to a sanitarium in Devon, Pennsylvania. He was not to see or talk to anyone until further notice.

Mrs. Mather and I had a quiet talk alone before we separated. We agreed that nothing should be said about Mr. Mather's condition to anyone except perhaps Secretary Lane. And even to those who had witnessed his breakdown that night at the Cosmos Club, I was to gloss over his condition, say that he was fine, just suffering from exhaustion. A little rest would have him back on the job in no time. She was very sensitive on this score. She requested that I take care of all government duties in which Mather was involved, as well as his financial concerns in Washington. She would have his attorney in Chicago handle Mather family matters as well as his borax business. We would coordinate our efforts and keep each other informed.

She felt she had never been involved in Mather's affairs and could now only advise, not take charge. I had never known Jane Mather well but was most impressed by her quiet acceptance of her husband's illness, by her ability to formulate plans under stress, and by her competence in arranging her life and her daughter's in the emergency. I reassured her, promising to take as much as possible off her shoulders. Young and inexperienced as I was, I didn't realize what this would entail.

On the way back to Washington, McCormick and I agreed we would keep everything to do with Mather's problems under our hats. If asked, we would give no explanation except that he was worn out and needed a rest, that he would be back soon. There would be absolutely no hint of mental problems, no leaking of details. He added: "Horace, we'll leave it at that. And I won't even expect any further details unless you wish to tell me. I understand." We parted at Union Station, the saddest men anyone would ever want to meet.

CHAPTER

15

On My Own
1917

The first thing next morning, I asked for an appointment to see Secretary Lane as soon as possible. I was standing before him about twenty minutes later.

Lane listened intently to me, only interrupting when he needed more information on some point I made. I told him everything I could remember, holding back nothing, dating back six months or so as I kept recalling Mr. Mather's unusual behavior from time to time.

When I fell silent at last, he seemed deeply sympathetic and moved by the sadness of the situation. He appeared to roll the facts around in his head and finally asked: "Albright, you know this man better than anyone. Do you think he will ever be well enough to assume his duties back here? Would the strain be too much even if he seems to recover? Should I think about replacing him now?"

I didn't hesitate a minute: "Mr. Secretary, there is no one else like Stephen Mather. I really believe he will recuperate, although no one knows exactly how rapidly, but no one else should take his place unless it is absolutely necessary. There really isn't anyone on earth like him."

He thought about this and said, "Do you think you can replace him?"

And I replied: "No, I just said there is only one Stephen Mather. I can certainly keep his place open, can surely do all that is necessary in the foreseeable future to try to obtain the necessary appropriations and to organize the National Park Service. That much I can promise you."

"But, Albright, you have told me repeatedly that you were going to leave the department as soon as a Park Service was created. Now what?"

"Well, that's just not in the cards," I said. "Not until the future of the service can be delineated, started up, and assured that plans Mr. Mather and I have formulated can be realized."

The secretary stood, put out his hand, and said: "We'll let it stand at that for the time being. It certainly isn't my choice to replace Steve, and I hope you will convey this to him until I can do it myself. Go ahead with whatever plans you and Steve have made, but just keep me informed. I'll keep everything you have told me today and what may come up in the future close to my chest."

In the future I assessed Franklin Lane in a different light because of his political intervention on conservation matters, but I always gave him credit for his decision at this time, and I was deeply grateful for his assurances. He could have called on any number of people, under political pressure, to replace Stephen Mather. But his friendship and trust fortunately made him give the right decision in 1917. It certainly gave me the needed boost of confidence.

Then the charade began of hiding Mather's true condition from the public eye. Dr. Weisenburg called to tell me that he had completed his studies of Mather. He said he was worn out, exceedingly nervous, and seriously depressed, which gave the most concern for his recovery.

The seriousness of his illness never got beyond the doctors, Mrs. Mather, Lane, and me. I was part of this conspiracy in 1917, and several other times through the years, to hide his mental problems. I always kept the papers concerning these at my home, in my own personal files. In later years, I often wondered whether I should destroy these records for the sake of his family, but was held back by the thought that, as a historian, I ought to save them. Was I right or not? Well, as I approach my century mark, it seems so far in the past that the whole story should now be related.

For the first few weeks, Mr. Mather's condition worsened. Twice his despondency caused him to attempt suicide. Once he broke away from his male nurse and tried to hurl himself down a flight of stairs. I don't know any details of this or the other attempt. It was not my policy to ask questions, just to wait until I was given the facts. However, by the end of January 1917, Mather was eating and sleeping normally, but was restless and constantly worrying. This was apparently the pattern of his former breakdown.

Mrs. Mather was optimistic. He had pulled out of that one. He could pull out of this one. One difference to her was the fact that he was more deeply immersed in the national parks than he had been in business in 1903. She felt strongly that he should be cut off from the Park Service forever.

Dr. Weisenburg totally disagreed. He felt Mather's salvation lay in healing him physically and then slowly reintroducing him to the only thing that seemed to interest him, national parks. He recommended that Mather be kept in isolation from everyone except his doctors and nurses until his depression had lifted. When that time arrived, he felt I was to be the first one allowed to visit. Mrs. Mather could see him afterward.

When Weisenburg told us this, I started to protest, but Mrs. Mather quickly agreed, saying, "Stephen always could be more at ease with men than with women."

The doctor replied: "It isn't men versus women. It's national parks versus anything you might bring up, Mrs. Mather. We have to go along with him, rivet his attention on the one thing that seems to be paramount in his mind at this time."

Back at the Interior Department, I consolidated Mather's and my work operations and tried to see any of our field personnel that were still in Washington. It was the only opportunity to discuss field problems, for there was no way I could get out of Washington in the foreseeable future.

I was lucky to find Washington B. Lewis, a popular fellow known as "Dusty," still sightseeing and roving around museums. Undoubtedly he was the most important superintendent to be brought into the park system, a superb engineer, another "steal" from the Geological Survey. He had taken over Yosemite in March 1916, had proved to be extremely capable, a master at dealing with the quarrelsome concessioners, and was already one of our trusted lieutenants. We had several long sessions together. I was so impressed with him that I decided to let him help me in the field and to try him on work outside of his own park.

One more thing I had to settle immediately was Bob Yard. The minute he learned that Mather had left Washington, he rightly guessed the truth of another breakdown and raced back from vacation, assuming that he would step into Mather's shoes. I had a long, careful talk with him, telling him that Lane had instructed me to take over Mather's job until further notice, that he was to continue his same work, that I would continue paying him from Mather's funds. Above all, he was to have no communication with Mather until Weisenburg gave permission.

Yard immediately circumvented me. He contacted Thorkildsen to try to see Mather and, failing that, attempted to write Mather. Fortunately, he sent the letter to Mrs. Mather to be forwarded. The letter was returned unopened. Next he wrote Mrs. Mather, pouring out a lot of tales about Washington affairs going badly and about how he was trying to fix them, but how he must talk with her husband. She was quite alarmed, sent me his letter, and appealed for help.

I sat Yard down and had another straightforward talk with him. "Bob, perhaps you didn't understand me the first time I told you Mr. Mather's situation. You went through his 1903 breakdown, and you know if doctor's orders aren't followed, it could be a disaster for our friend. Maybe a permanent disaster. Now I'm a lot younger than you, but I happen to be in charge here, and you will obey me or you will be released to go back to newspapering in New York. Believe me, and let's work together to accomplish what Mr. Mather would want us to do." I expected him to explode, but instead he quietly agreed.

By the middle of January every other problem had to be put aside as I was called to appear before the appropriations committees for our funds for fiscal year 1918. Mather's absence actually made it easier for me to testify, as the members knew and liked him. Then, too, I played on their sympathy for his tireless work and subsequent "exhaustion."

That was the Senate committee. The House committee was another matter. I had to spend nearly three days defending our estimates. The committee, as usual, handled me pretty roughly. Of course, the chairman was our old enemy, Fitzgerald the curmudgeon. He singled me out for a severe verbal beating because of unauthorized enterprises undertaken by both Mather and Marshall during 1916.

Fitzgerald regarded the removal of troops from Yellowstone under the plan worked out by Mather and General Hugh Scott, using the revenues of the park to cover the costs of the new ranger force, as unauthorized if not unlawful. He was determined to put the troops back in the park no matter what the cost in money and in men who might be needed for military service.

Furthermore, plans for the Yosemite power plant had been changed to such an extent that a large deficiency had been incurred. Fitzgerald blamed Marshall and Mather and was furious. As though it was all my fault, he roared at me in the same vein he had used the year before: "Albright, that power plant will remain in Yosemite forever, as is, and I hope it will always be there to rust as a monument to the incompetency of you men running the national parks."

The Sixty-fourth Congress adjourned on March 4, 1917, without taking any action on the appropriations. It was a real blow, as I thought I'd have to go through this whole thing again with the next Congress. Fortunately, I didn't have to give testimony again, and the bill passed in June pretty much as we had requested except for Fitzgerald's insistence that troops return to Yellowstone.

This wasn't the only financial ordeal. A more urgent problem was emergency appropriations in the Deficiency Bill, the only avenue to get money to operate the Park Service until regular appropriations were forthcoming for the fiscal year. Lane roared with laughter when I reported that I had "crawled on my knees in sack cloth and ashes," begging for the money. Ever after he would tease me, when I asked for anything, by calling me "Old Sack Cloth and Ashes."

The Deficiency Bill finally passed on April 17 and provided for deficiencies in appropriations for the fiscal year ending June 30, 1917. That is, it covered appropriations for the Washington office for the period April 15 to June 30, 1917. It certainly wasn't much to go on, but something was better than the nothing we'd been operating on since the Park Service was authorized in August 1916.

One bright spot occurred on February 26. Mount McKinley, in Alaska, was created a national park. We had been working on this for some time with the Boone and Crockett Club, which was trying to save the Dall sheep and other wildlife for which the region was famous.

Sadly, McKinley was treated like our other new parks, Lassen and Hawaii. No money was made available to staff, operate, or improve them. Not a red cent to hire a superintendent and rangers. Nothing for protection of the wild animals (and there was unlimited hunting of them by poachers). Nothing to make it possible for visitors to enjoy the wonders of volcanic activity and the magnificent Alaskan wilderness.

One of the problems in operating the bureau was my inability to get anything printed. I had learned a lot of bureaucratic tricks in my years around the government and decided to use one that other bureaus did. Whatever they wanted printed, they would get it introduced as a bill or have a congressman make a speech about their topic. Consequently, it was published in the *Congressional Record* and was printed in vast quantities.

On March 3, 1917, the day the Sixty-fourth Congress was to adjourn, I brought up a batch of things I wanted printed to Representative Billy Kent of California. I explained: "Billy, I'm in a real fix. Haven't a nickel to get these articles I wrote printed up. They're really important, especially the stuff I wrote urging the creation of the Grand Canyon National Park. I need to send them out all over the country to rally support for the project."

That's as far as I got. Billy was feeling very jolly, largely as a result of end-of-the-session liquid celebration. He quickly grasped what I had come for, gave me a healthy swat on the back that almost knocked me down, and roared: "You old coon, you know I'm always ready to do anything for the National Park Service. Let's make this Grand Canyon a national park. Hey, let's make the whole damn country a national park and introduce a bill to abolish Congress."

On February 27 I received a letter from Dr. Weisenburg that made my day. He wrote that Mr. Mather seemed well enough to allow me to visit him. With Congress adjourned and the Wilson inauguration hoopla concluded, there was an opening to slip away from Washington. I made plans to go to Philadelphia on March 7 and thence on to Devon to see Mr. Mather.

I had the blessing of Secretary Lane. He said, "I want this whole episode of Mather's illness kept under wraps." He made it clear that the position of director of the National Park Service was still open. Mather had not been appointed to it because of the seriousness of his illness. It followed that if his breakdown leaked out, there would be political pressure to fill the directorship with someone else. Lane concluded with, "Albright, this is just between the two of us, our secret to keep."

After spending the night at a hotel in Philadelphia, I met with Dr. Weisenburg at his office and had a long, fruitful discussion. He gave me a detailed report on Mather, going over every fact he knew from his birth to the present morning. He even made a phone call to Devon, before I had arrived, checking on Mather's immediate condition.

It was a tragic story of this brilliant, creative, and successful man who was burdened with a mental condition that could burst upon him, without warning, when fatigue and stress mounted. In the light of contemporary knowledge, his condition might be labeled manic depression. His energy and exuberance, which accomplished so many great things, could turn to deep, silent, suicidal depression with little warning. In 1917 treatment was a program of isolation from the outside world coupled with a regimen of plenty of sleep, a nourishing diet, and regular exercise. Above all, no excitement, no problems.

Weisenburg explained why I was the first one to be allowed to visit. Mather had requested me, not only because he said I was "the one he trusted above all others," but because his sole interest at this point was the national parks. Mrs. Mather endorsed this move, as she felt I would have the judgment to filter what Park Service news could be discussed and what should be withheld. Weisenburg grimly warned me, though, that I had a tremendous responsibility to maintain a balance between giving Mather news of the Park Service for which he hungered and yet not divulging anything controversial or upsetting.

Devon bore no resemblance to a hospital. It was a lovely, large home tucked into green lawns and lush forested land. When I arrived, I was immediately taken down a long carpeted hallway to Mr. Mather's suite of rooms. They consisted of a large, brilliantly sunny sitting room with a rather Spartan but warmly pleasant bedroom painted yellow and a bathroom with tub and massage table branching off to the side. The sitting room was furnished with comfortable chairs covered in pale green, a few side tables, and Mather's own small desk from his Chicago bedroom. The only decorations were two framed pictures of Yosemite, which I learned that Mrs. Mather had relayed to him as a gift from Dusty Lewis. I noticed immediately that the glass had been removed from the frames. I also checked and was relieved to see that there was no evidence of windows with bars. I had dreaded the thought that this free spirit could have been cooped up like an animal.

As I entered the room, Mather jumped to his feet, bounded forward, and gave me a bear hug. "Horace, how wonderful to see you," he said. As he stepped back, I saw tears on his cheeks, his hands shaking, how close to the surface were his emotions, how difficult it was for him to control himself. I guess I might have had tears in my eyes too, as I saw how incredibly better he looked, physically strong and healthy, with his old animated expression and shining blue eyes. It hardly seemed possible that the frightened, shaking, dispirited shade of a man two months ago had been replaced by a vigorous, smiling figure.

Weisenburg had warned me that physical appearance meant nothing. "Take special, gentle care of his fragile mental condition. He is not at all well yet."

Mather excitedly threw a barrage of questions at me. "Did McCormick get his OK on the rail line? How fares the Desmond Company? What about our appropriations? How did Fitzgerald act?" It was wonderful that he had such a recall of our problems, and yet I had been forbidden by Weisenburg to discuss anything controversial. Because of such a flow of questions, I had time to pick out one to answer, and I chose the good news, Mount McKinley National Park. I had brought the bill passed by the Congress as well as a stack of photos of the park and congratulatory letters to him from various sources across the country. It immediately diverted him. We kept up our conversation on one thing after another, all very light and inconclusive. Things were going perfectly.

Then I inadvertently mentioned Bob Marshall's help on some road and trail planning in Mount Rainier. Bob Marshall! From being a happy, talkative Mather, he erupted from his chair, pounding back and forth the length of the room, calling out Marshall's name and denouncing himself and his treatment of Marshall in the worst possible terms. Although totally alarmed, I fortunately didn't have to cope with the situation. The male nurse quickly signaled me to leave and gently but forcibly steered Mather toward the bedroom.

In a few minutes the nurse reappeared and suggested that I go to the kitchen to have something to eat, and he'd get back to me. He did very shortly, telling me he had administered a mild sedative to Mather, that I could go back now to say good-bye. Mather was quite calm once more though disinclined to talk. However, he sat quietly and listened to me for perhaps another fifteen minutes. I was nervous about his silence.

He loved jokes, so I quickly dredged one up. I still remember it was about Mesa Verde. It seems some woman tourist was walking around an old cliff dwelling there, listening to the guide explain what an incredible civilization the ancient Anasazi had built here. Suddenly she inquired, "Well, if these people were so marvelous, why did they build their towns so far from the railroad?" Mather loved it, slapped his knee, and roared with laughter. I left him on this high note, promising to come back very soon.

On March 17 I wrapped up my work and caught the train for Philadelphia once more, again spending the night at the hotel. The next day I spent over eight hours with Mr. Mather. I determinedly steered him away from current events and problems but had long talks about the future, such as what glorious things we would do when we got the Grand Canyon into the Park Service.

The most gratifying time came when Mather's nurse wheeled in a projector and screen. I had brought motion pictures of the 1915 Mather

Mountain Party. While it was shown, he laughed, recounted anecdotes, and pointed out scenic features. When it came to an end, he said, "Oh, this is wonderful. Show it again." We showed it again, and again, and I think a fourth again.

My joy didn't last long. I received a short note from Dr. Weisenburg telling me that my visit had been a little strenuous for Mather. He didn't blame me, saying that it was difficult to hold him down now that he was somewhat better. "Any sustained effort on his part tires him and then, of course, causes the consequent depression." I felt terrible, even if I apparently wasn't to blame.

• • •

WAR. It changed everything. For the nation, the National Park Service, and me personally. On April 6, 1917, President Woodrow Wilson asked Congress for a declaration of war against Germany and its allies. The majority of Americans had believed Wilson during the recent presidential campaign when he had promised to keep us out of the war. That had been the key to his defeat of Hughes. But now patriotic fervor swept the nation, and the United States was off to make the world safe for democracy.

For the National Park Service, the war held up many things Mather and I had in the works or had planned. However, in view of the fact that I was now alone and solely responsible for the bureau, it did enable me to slow down, contemplate, and quietly formulate policy and operations.

As for the immediate situation, my first order of business was to have a complete review of the national park war policy with Secretary Lane. I offered my resignation as acting director, a position to which he had just appointed me. I outlined my military background in college and my qualifications for an appointment as an officer in the army. At heart I loved the military, and in spirit I was perhaps overly patriotic. I really wanted to enlist as soon as possible and see service in France. Lane, listening passively as usual, let me pour out my emotional presentation.

When I had exhausted my rhetoric and oxygen, he quietly said: "No, Albright, you can't be spared to play soldier. You know the government of the United States not only has to be a white knight in armor and save the world, but we also have to operate and preserve the nation at home. A war can't be run without soldiers and a government can't be run without competent men. I'm sending in the proper papers to exempt you from wartime service."

I tried to change his mind. It was a dead end. He stopped me then and closed me off throughout the war. Gradually I came around to his thinking that with Mather incapacitated perhaps he had no replacement for me, and valuable men in the Park Service, like Dusty Lewis, were also irreplaceable. I ended up talking many men of this type out of enlisting or freezing them in their government positions.

I always regretted not serving my country in wartime, but my Grace certainly didn't. Philosophically, she bordered on being a pro–draft dodger if necessary to keep me safely home with her. However, she was the first to volunteer her service through the Interior Department and was soon appointed the head of its ladies' service division.

Although I was frantically busy in those first few weeks of war activity, I felt I had to respond to Dr. Weisenburg's urgent summons to see Mr. Mather. He reported that Mather was terribly upset by the advent of war, frightened, and worried over the national parks. "You must come quickly and reassure him," Dr. Weisenburg telegraphed, "or I am fearful for a serious setback in his condition."

So on April 15 I entrained for Philadelphia, had a few hours of consultation with Dr. Weisenburg, and spent a good portion of the sixteenth at Devon with Mather. Indeed, he was in a fearful state, pacing back and forth, wringing his hands, and deeply depressed. He fretted over what effect the war would have on the parks and our plans for them. I tried to let him talk it out, but he became more and more agitated. Finally, I linked arms with him, slowing his walking down, quietly explaining that our department was being virtually ignored, that if any problems arose in the future, Lane and I could handle them. Nothing to worry about.

The male nurse had slipped away and now returned with large iced glasses of lemonade, Mather's favorite beverage. Mather sat down, sipping his drink, quiet and subdued. It never ceased to astound me how he flipped from one mood to the other in a matter of minutes.

On May 9, 1917, Secretary Lane formalized Mather's and my positions. There were now funds from the Deficiency Bill to pay salaries and organize the bureau. Furthermore, Lane felt confident enough about Mather's future recovery to have him approved as director of the National Park Service and myself as assistant director. At the same time, I was officially designated acting director during Mather's absence. There was one slight hitch. Both the directorship and assistant directorship called for men in civil service, and Mather and I did not have civil service status. Secretary Lane simply went to President Wilson and asked him to waive the rules and appoint us directly because of our knowledge and experience in park affairs.

However, when I happily broke the good news to Mather, he rejected the position. He said he wasn't well enough to become director now and probably would never be strong enough in the future to take on the burdens of the office. Mrs. Mather agreed, feeling strongly that the job would kill him sooner or later.

Weisenburg felt that Mather had to accept the position, to have an interest that would bring him back to physical and mental health. I finally had to promise Mather I would remain as assistant director for a year or longer if necessary. Only then did he agree to let Lane go ahead with his appointment. My appointment was May 9, Mather's May 16.

There was one thing connected with my new appointment that I had to settle. Heretofore, Mather had been paying me two hundred dollars a month over my government salary. Then when I was promoted to assistant attorney in the Interior Department, with a salary of two thousand dollars, I asked Mather to dispense with his allowance, but instead he merely lowered it to one thousand dollars a year. Now I discussed the situation with him in light of my new position as assistant director. I insisted that he dispense with his monthly stipend, and he calmly agreed he would do so as soon as my new salary kicked in.

As it turned out, Mather secretly instructed his attorney, Oliver Mitchell, to keep me on at one thousand a year. When Mitchell sent me the usual check to handle Mather's financial affairs in Washington, he always included the monthly allowance for Yard and me. When I noticed that he was still doing this, I wrote him that Mather wanted mine stopped.

Back came the letter with Mather's instructions in it as well as the cryptic comment from Mitchell that I deserved the money far more than Yard. Mitchell added, "To what extent is Mr. Mather obligated to retain Mr. Yard?"

I answered: "So far as I know, Mr. Mather is not obligated to retain Mr. Yard at all. The obligation, as I understand it, was to employ him here for two years. Certainly there is no written obligation to retain Mr. Yard. Personally, I do not think he is doing work of a character that a man commanding a salary of $650 per month should do."

Liking Bob Yard personally, though, I suggested to Mitchell that we let the matter drift along until Mather was well enough to handle the situation himself. It was far too delicate for us when we had no real guidelines to follow. Mitchell replied that it might not be a good idea to leave the problem in Mather's hands. "I'm not sure if he will be in condition to undertake the unpleasant duty of tying a can to Mr. Yard. . . . Candidly I think we would be doing Mr. Mather the greatest kindness if we would dispose of the Yard matter."

I prevailed, insisting that Yard stay until Mather might be well enough to go over the situation quietly and thoroughly. After all, Yard was one of Mather's oldest friends, best man at his wedding, and a very volatile fellow too. Mather couldn't take any excitement of the type Yard conceivably could arouse.

As for my financial dilemma, Mather cleaned the situation up in a letter to me on May 6: "I want to continue to pay you $1,000 a year after you get your new government salary as assistant director."

"Hoofed Locusts"

CHAPTER
16

"Hoofed Locusts"
1917

The spring and summer of 1917 brought severe pressures. Finding qualified personnel to operate the parks was a continuing problem. Thanks to our congressional foes, the army had returned to Yellowstone. At Yosemite, Lewis had decided not to enlist in the army, and in a few parks good men were too old for the military. Elsewhere, however, we were painfully short of competent supervisors. When our supervisor in Glacier, Samuel Ralston, resigned, I quickly moved a new engineer, George Goodwin, over there. Once more, that incurred the wrath of Senator Thomas Walsh.

Mather continued his slow recovery and moved to a halfway house in Lakewood, New Jersey. Now my prime consideration was the war effort.

It was just as well that I could put my deep concern about Mather to the back of my mind, for I had to concentrate on Secretary Lane's desire to win the war through the Interior Department. Lane was a peculiar fellow. He could spend unlimited time on minor matters, study microscopic details, and still end up not making a decision, leaving it to a bureau chief or some other subordinate. He pretty much trusted his assistants and let them have their heads, which Mather and I deeply appreciated. On the other hand, in appearance, he rather resembled a bulldog, and that's what he became when he took hold of some idea or project dear to his heart.

The minute war was declared, he assumed his bulldog psyche and searched for ways he and Interior could contribute to winning the conflict. Most of us believed he was still feeling the effects of his pummeling by conservation groups and the western press over his championing of Hetch Hetchy and wanted to show he was a patriotic American. His first act was to have a complete survey made of his department to ascertain how and where each division could fit into the war plans. Acker and I immediately insisted that, under the law, the resources of the national parks could not be utilized.

The western cattlemen and sheepmen thought otherwise. They found the declaration of war a perfect opportunity to break into the national parks. Lane's inclination was to agree. But there was such an immediate outcry from conservation groups, interested congressmen, and powerful representatives of the press that he hesitated, then began to backtrack, and finally indicated that he would wait a bit and see how things went.

Then the newly appointed chairman of the National Defense Committee of California took a strong hand in the situation. He was none other than Dr. Benjamin Ide Wheeler, president of the University of California, an extremely vigorous and strong-willed man. Prior to our entry into the war, due to an old friendship with Kaiser Wilhelm, Wheeler had spoken favorably of the German cause. Now he felt he had to prove he was 100-percent American. As Lane, Mather, and I were all University of California men, it was an awkward situation.

At heart, Lane never was much of a conservationist or preservationist. Mather and I had gotten so much done not because of any strong convictions Lane held but because he had just left us alone to do as we wished.

Another sore point was that Wheeler's prime advisor was Court Dubois of the U.S. Forest Service. "Use" was the core of his bureau's tenets. For example, he happily offered statistics indicating that the carrying capacity of the Yosemite was ample for extensive grazing.

The upshot was that Lane drew up an order stating that sheep and cattle could be pastured in Yosemite and Sequoia. I was aghast and immediately sought an answer from the secretary as to his precipitous action without even consulting me. He hemmed and hawed and finally admitted it was a combination of Wheeler and Court Dubois. Why on earth was Interior paying any attention to the Forest Service, practically an enemy? Well, it seemed the Forest Service policies were far more patriotic than ours by allowing pasturing and other noble deeds in their forests. We had to prove ourselves too.

Lane casually added that Wheeler wanted fifty thousand sheep pastured on the floor of Yosemite valley and elsewhere in the park. That did it. For the first time I exploded. "Mr. Secretary, how could you possibly allow fifty thousand 'hoofed locusts' [a John Muir expression] in that beautiful park? It wouldn't recover from an onslaught like that until the next century."

He leaped from his chair, leaned across the desk, and bellowed right back at me: "Albright, you do as you are ordered. Wire Lewis and tell him to open the park to the sheep." I rarely lost my temper, but when I did, I knew how to rein it in. I did so now and reverted to being a lawyer trained to argue and persuade. No use. After a futile half-hour of presenting my case, Lane wouldn't budge.

I took a deep breath and said: "Then, Mr. Secretary, with deep regret, I tender my resignation. I simply couldn't oversee the ruination of park lands that belong to all the American people just for the simple greed of a few."

A dead silence reigned as Lane stared at me. I guess he was trying to decide whether I meant what I said. He apparently came to the conclusion that I wasn't bluffing, for he spoke in a very soft but deadly serious voice: "You are not to resign, but something must be done along this line. You send a telegram to Lewis to say that pasturing will be allowed in Yosemite. But you may work out a compromise for me. In the meantime, you are ordered not to discuss this matter with anyone. And I mean anyone."

With that menacing admonition, I went back to my office and closed the door. I remember sitting there staring at Mather's picture hanging over my bookcase and asking myself, "What would Stephen Mather do under these circumstances?" There are times in everyone's life when principle and necessity meet head on. The more I reviewed where Mather and I had been and what we wanted to do in the future, the more my decision was clarified. As in the case of so many other challenges in the past, I found I simply couldn't let my chief down. I couldn't resign and leave the Park Service. A lot worse things could happen to it without a guardian for Mather and the plans we had made. That was it. Our plans and dreams. I knew that our commitment to the service was deeper than some passing issue.

Well, I had one word of Lane's to cling to: compromise. This scheme had to be worked out carefully. First I wrote the telegram to Lewis as ordered and had Lane approve it. As I found out later, he never sent it. I next began to formulate a compromise, but never completed it, always procrastinating, telling Lane I had to get more facts.

I was sworn to silence, but I was sure, given some time, that Lane's decision about Yosemite would leak out and alert conservationists. I was correct. The Sierra Club learned of it from two or three sources, one of whom was an associate of Wheeler's. Colby immediately wired me for confirmation, but I didn't answer him. So the Sierra Club went ahead and got the California press to publish very anti-grazing stories. Then they pushed the California delegation in Congress on Lane, especially the newly elected Senator Hiram Johnson.

When I figured Lane had been pressured enough, I went to him with my compromise. Of course, he blamed me for the leak, swore I had gone against my word, and acted cool and distant. It was several years before Colby exonerated me. For now, Lane accepted the plan I presented to him. No sheep at all. Allow a few head of cattle in strategic, fairly worthless areas. Without consulting him further, I issued permits for grazing. Actually, Colby and his allies picked the cattlemen to place their animals in "just the right places," basically men they knew who would go along with conservation.

With all the publicity in the newspapers, I feared that Mather would somehow hear about the problem. I decided to write him a carefully discreet version: "I am in a dilemma as to how to handle the Yosemite grazing situation. The grazing demands are enormous on account of the short food supply and everybody except the Sierra Club, from the Governor down, including President Wheeler, is urging the opening of the park. I am afraid to go ahead, however, because I am not satisfied that it is absolutely necessary that the park be opened, and, furthermore, I think that a few of the old cattlemen like John Curtin are back of this move and are taking advantage of the existing conditions to open the old issues about grazing in the Yosemite." Mather absorbed the situation calmly and made no additional suggestions to me.

Spring brought a really exciting event for all of us in the Interior Department. A beautiful new building was completed for our department between Eighteenth and Nineteenth and E and F Streets, two blocks west of the White House. Interior had been quartered for more than sixty-five years in various structures in Washington, the latest being the eastern section of the old Patent Office Building overlooking Seventh Street. Even before its completion, there had been discussions about space, but no assignments had been made. Usually assignments were made by seniority of the bureau. The General Land Office, the Bureau of Indian

Affairs, and the Pension Office would take precedence over newer bureaus such as Reclamation and the Park Service.

On behalf of the National Park Service, I argued that we were entitled to an attractive view since we were concerned with scenery and natural sites. I requested that we have the fourth floor, just under the secretary on the sixth floor and the assistant secretary on the fifth floor. With this suite of rooms, our vista would be Potomac Park, the river, the Washington Monument, and the famous Octagon House. Because of seniority, the Bureau of Indian Affairs claimed the same space. Lane decided in our favor.

In June, when we moved, I was shocked to find the Bureau of Indian Affairs already dug in on the fourth floor. Judge Cato Sells, commissioner of Indian affairs, had usurped Mather's office space and also areas across the hall. He had ordered these remodeled according to his design. Temporarily foiled, I moved our bureau into all the space remaining on that floor. This forced some of Sells's group to descend to the third floor, separating them from their chief. It was soon a standard joke how Sells had outsmarted me—a painful joke, as the fat, walrus-mustached fellow was well disliked by all.

One day at lunch in the new office building restaurant, I decided I'd had enough of this joking and teasing. I jumped up on a table and loudly inquired: "Hey, where's the chief clerk? I'd like a crew at two o'clock this afternoon, for I want to proceed with a high-powered move."

Everyone, including the assistant secretaries, thought this looked like fun and wanted to watch it. However, when I fearlessly (or foolishly) stated I was going to move Sells out and Mather in, they ducked out with the advice to call it all off. I don't know if I'd have been so brazen except that I was outraged at Sells and knew he was away for a few days. Precisely at 2:00 P.M., when the crew arrived, I had Sells's furniture and all his other belongings evacuated into the hall and his Indian rugs thrown over them. The National Park Service moved in.

When Judge Sells returned, we all held our breath. Sells calmly went to his Indian Bureau on the third floor, ordered his belongings brought to the new locale, and never uttered a peep. I had gotten control of my floor as I had been promised, and my stock really rose with my fellow workers in the Interior Department.

Another incident made this insignificant official shine. Shortly after the Interior Department moved into its new building, we found few places to eat west of the White House. Consequently, employees organized an informal luncheon club in the basement. On stormy days I would simply take the elevator down there, but when the weather was pleasant, I liked to go outdoors and walk all the way around.

One day, as I was taking my time getting to the lunch room, an elderly gentleman hailed me to ask where there was a place to eat in the vicinity. He stated that he was a member of the president's War Industries Board, had been at a meeting in the Pan American Building, but now could find no restaurant in the area. I replied that there really wasn't any, but suggested that he come with me to lunch. He agreed if he could pay his own way. I offered my hand, saying, "My name is Albright. I'm with the National Park Service."

He shook my hand, replying, "My name is Edison."

I gasped. "Mr. Thomas Alva Edison?" He nodded, and we proceeded to lunch in our basement, where I proudly introduced him all around.

Several weeks later I once more saw Mr. Edison walking up Eighteenth Street and again asked him to join me for lunch. At first he refused, saying I hadn't let him pay the first time. However, I convinced him that the cost was a trivial amount, so he came along with me. When we reached the lunch room, it was unusually crowded. Even Secretary Lane was present. He usually ate in his own suite. We quickly found seats off in the corner. Secretary Lane got everyone's attention to tell us that we were to be the guests of Judge Sells, commissioner of Indian affairs. Three fine courses were then served: a delicious soup, a tasty steak, potatoes, and some vegetables, and finally a dessert.

When the last bite was swallowed, Judge Sells rose to give us a lengthy talk on the problem of wild horses on the Fort Peck Sioux Reservation in Montana. They were reproducing too rapidly and eating up all the forage for the Indians' horses and sheep. Consequently he had made a deal with a packing house to reduce the herds, process the meat, and distribute it to the Indians and any extra to war-stricken Europeans. Our delicious steaks had been part of the surplus horse meat.

When the luncheon was over, I sort of sheepishly glanced at Edison and apologetically said: "I didn't know anything about this horse meat. Really I didn't, Mr. Edison."

He laughed, clapped me on the back, and said: "Albright, I've wanted to taste horse meat all my life. And furthermore I really liked it."

With the Congress and President Wilson heading for their summer vacations, I felt that our office was operating well enough that I could get away from

Washington to attend to our problems out west in the field. Before I could leave, I had my own difficulties at home with Secretary Lane. When I suggested a fact-finding tour, he didn't like the idea and asked, "With no assistants, who will oversee the bureau while you are wandering out in the mountains three thousand miles away?" I assured him that the Washington office was doing nicely, that the summer doldrums wouldn't produce any problems, and that W. B. Acker could always be called on in an emergency.

Without making a decision, Lane cut off that conversation and swung into grazing in the parks. Not just Yosemite, but Mount Rainier, Glacier, and others. He told me he was going to go further in Yosemite. He'd decided to let everything but the valley be opened to grazing.

I yowled as if I was stuck with a pin and then fought back. "Mr. Secretary, if you let this thing get started, you'll never get rid of it, even with the Kaiser signing a peace treaty. If a wholesale grazing policy is instituted, we'll have it forever. Once approved, the precedent will be laid in concrete. Please, please, don't put your stamp of approval on it."

He ruminated over this outburst, scratched his nearly bald head, and then said, "What is your solution?"

I replied: "Well, of course, you know that my answer is no place, under no circumstances. But I realize, as I did before, that some adjustment has to be made." Lane and I finally hammered out an agreement. Only the extreme northwestern area of Yosemite would be opened. (Unknown to him, friends of the park would be given this franchise, so protection could be guaranteed.) Another decision Lane made was to let me settle the grazing problem in the various other parks when I arrived to visit them in the next few months.

One more thing we had a tussle over was whether Senator Walsh was to have the right to name the permanent supervisor in Glacier. I argued that we had to cease political appointments, that men had to be chosen by ability, for responsibility to the service, and to meet standards that we alone would set.

Lane basically agreed but didn't have the will or the ability to fight such a wild beast as Walsh. He stalled me along for a time, but finally caved in to Walsh and let him have his way. I really couldn't do anything, as our supervisors weren't covered by Civil Service. It was a sore point with me, and I determined to get them covered as soon as possible.

Then there was Bob Yard. He had been behaving pretty well since the last time I had laid down the law to him. Furthermore, he was keeping his nose out of national park affairs. I had been forced to make him bring me everything he wrote or was about to mail out. I hated to be so over-bearing with a friend, but Mather had to come first. Bob simply couldn't be trusted not to slip up. When he talked to people in person, he often sounded like Mather's oracle, expounding on policy with, "Steve and I have discussed this and we feel ..."

I closeted with him one more time and, in a friendly but firm way, let it be known that if I had another problem with him, I had the authority from Mather to cut him off from the Park Service along with his $650 per month.

There was also Yard's summer to be dealt with. He had grandiose plans not just to travel around our parks but to put in a lot of time and expense on Canadian parks. It was necessary to explain to him carefully that he did not work for the United States government, that the Park Service could not foot one cent of his travels. I suggested that he pick one park. How about Glacier? Spend his time doing a complete job on it, writing and taking photos for his next edition of the *Parks Portfolio*. He had already sold one book to Scribner's for a trade edition and a school edition of the same. Mather and I had discussed this aspect and felt he could probably make money writing a new book, his own book. With a good income, he could then be eased out of the Washington job.

I guess I was somewhat crafty in suggesting Glacier for the summer because I knew Yard had gotten to be a pal of many of the Great Northern Railroad people, mainly Howard Noble, the general manager of the Glacier Park Hotel Company. I thought they'd give him a break on his bills at the hotels and chalets. Although I never would permit an employee of the Park Service to do this, Yard was really outside a government position and could accept a break on room and board. Actually he ended up getting them practically free.

My affairs in Washington were in good shape. Dr. Weisenburg assured me that, although far from well, Mr. Mather had made a successful transition from Lakewood to his own home in Darien and would soon be able to spend the summer in the West. There seemed nothing to hold me any longer in Washington, so Grace and I boarded the train for Colorado, where we spent a week before she headed for California to remain with her folks while I continued my inspection trip. Our visit to Rocky Mountain National Park was a rewarding experience except for Enos Mills.

I should mention that Enos Mills was one of the meanest, most cantankerous, most fascinating men I ever knew. I'm pretty sure I never knew anyone who liked him—maybe admired him, maybe tolerated him.

But no one liked him. Even his brother Joe hadn't talked to him since childhood. Probably it was more that Enos hadn't talked to Joe. They both lived in Estes Park. Both owned hotels. Both wrote about nature. Both hated each other. Someone remarked that Enos Mills "used up friends like typewriter ribbons, a man unhappy without enemies." When Mills died on September 21, 1922, I received a telegram from Roe Emery, who had the transportation concession in Rocky Mountain: "Enos Mills died last night. Ain't nature grand?"

When I got to know Mills at the superintendents' conference in Berkeley in 1915, and later the same year at the dedication of Rocky Mountain National Park, I was rather in awe of him. He was already well known as the "Father of Rocky Mountain," a prodigious writer and promoter of national parks, a true conservationist.

In 1909 Mills had begun his advocacy of an Estes National Park. Then he met McFarland of the American Civic Association, and they associated themselves with Bob Marshall's 1912 report on the Colorado Rockies. Their work, plus the impetus of our drive from the Interior Department, was enough to get the park created in January 1915.

But there had to be some accommodation with the Forest Service, which had held the land prior to this time. This pragmatic compromise between the two departments poisoned Mills for the rest of his life. He never knew the word "compromise" was in the English dictionary. Ever after, he regarded the Forest Service as the devil incarnate, suspicious of its every move, rebellious against every decision, and venomously opposed to its every act.

Shortly after our bureau was created, Mills began to be suspicious of us and eventually spread his hatred to the National Park Service because he felt we knuckled under to the detested Forest Service. This reached a crescendo shortly before he died.

My relations with Mills had been most cordial after the 1915 conference and park dedication. I received a constant flow of letters from that time on. He frequently asked for maps and information on various parks and rewarded my quick responses with autographed copies of his books. He was a great friend of George Horace Lorimer, editor of the *Saturday Evening Post*, and was an influential conservation writer for that magazine as well as other periodicals. He pounded out books at quite a clip and loved to hear himself called "The John Muir of the Rockies."

So when I arrived in Rocky Mountain National Park on June 24, 1917, Mills was as nice as it was possible for him to be. On my last day in the park, I reluctantly had to face up to him. He didn't even let me get by the pleasantries when he roared, "Albright, what about this grazing situation?" Being of like mind with the rest of us conservationists, Mills had thrown a fit when he heard that grazing was going to be permitted in national parks. He had fired off a barrage of letters to me in Washington.

Now, in his office in the Long's Peak Inn, he accelerated his attack. The grazing program had been another example of Interior knuckling under to Forest Service. Forest Service was for "use," and now it seemed we were going to give in meekly to "use" ourselves. We were spineless, yellow-bellied slaves of the Forest Service.

I tried to explain that we were a new and tiny bureau with not much clout, whereas the Forest Service was older, larger, and had quite a following with the powers in Washington. The Forest Service already was leery of us stealing their lands (e.g., our push for the Grand Canyon). Although I tried to steer the conversation over to Mills's vital interest in Colorado parks, he kept interrupting me to talk more grazing.

Getting exasperated, I blurted out: "Look, Mills, this isn't the only park where I've been forced to allow grazing. Lane has instructed me to let down the barriers in back country Yosemite, a small section of Mount Rainier, and South Glacier along the railroad. Emergency war provisions. And don't forget that Congress has permitted grazing for years in places like Wind Cave, Mesa Verde, and Platt despite all our protests." That kept Mills quiet long enough for me to swing back to Colorado parks.

The city of Denver was an energetic promoter of parks—any and all kinds of parks. They had a fine system of city parks, and local mountain parks were being promoted. The Mountaineer Club as well as commercial interests were pushing for a single park, the Denver National Park, to cross the Continental Divide with a road to link it with Rocky Mountain Park.

Mills, of course, was in the forefront of the drive. And therein lay his current war with the Interior Department, represented by me. He started off by accusing us of working too closely with the Forest Service, complaining bitterly that we weren't fighting hard enough to get Longs Peak and other adjacent land out of its fiendish hands. Again I denied all his accusations, pointing out that his park plans were just too grandiose, that we were trying and would continue to push for a Mount Evans park, but that Congress simply wouldn't consider any more than a couple of major park projects per year. This year it was Grand Canyon and the possible additions of the Teton Valley to Yellowstone and the river canyons of the Sierra to Sequoia. Furthermore, all additions that would entail larger appropriations for the Park Service were probably pipe dreams in view of the vast war effort.

He became quite vitriolic, getting personal with his attacks. When I had enough of it, I cut him off with an icy: "Mills, you have no concept of government. One department does not come out openly fighting with another. Such things are just never done. Period."

CHAPTER
17

Summer in the Parks
1917

It was the beautiful, clear sunny morning of June 29 when my train slowly eased its way up the Yellowstone River Canyon to Gardiner, the northern entrance to Yellowstone National Park. I had to admit that it already had become my favorite park.

Chester Lindsley met me at the station and took me to headquarters at Mammoth. He had been acting supervisor of Yellowstone since the army had pulled out the preceding October. Now, with "Fitzgerald's Revenge," the army would return to power with 450 men of the Seventh Cavalry replacing our 50 civilian rangers on July 1. The troops remained until November 1, 1918, and they turned out to be a sorry lot. Most were new draftees, not the former fine disciplined men of the prewar army. They were rotated so often they never even got to know the park. Of course, a few rangers had been hired back by the army as scouts. But that didn't alleviate Lindsley's sorrow. As we climbed up the hill to Mammoth, I tried to cheer him by saying that the reason I was here was to ease this "strictly temporary" changeover.

First I directed that Lindsley and Interior Department personnel were to occupy what we considered the best buildings at Mammoth Hot Springs. As an attorney, I scrutinized every word of every federal law and every directive coming from the War Department. I found some nice loopholes. The Interior Department could keep title to all the buildings and objects within and without, the horses, and essential utility systems.

It appeared as though the troops were there at our convenience. We had to leave the upkeep of roads and the protection of the park to the commander of the Western Army Department.

With the tourist season opening and thousands of visitors pouring in, the government quickly heard a lot about valuable fighting men "frolicking" in a national park. The complaints contributed quite a bit to the eventual ouster of the troops by the rescinding clause of the Sundry Civil Bill of 1918.

One day a delegation from Montana and Wyoming came to the office to discuss the animal situation. The incredibly hard winters of the past few years had produced two results for the wild animals in Yellowstone. First, within the park there was a serious loss of elk, antelope, and deer to starvation. Second, as they drifted outside the park looking for forage, open season for hunting also resulted in a serious death toll. Their numbers were sharply reduced—antelope to the point of feared extinction.

In those days we really hadn't the time, money, or ability to make close scientific studies of the problem, but we did know that a few of the major predators somehow had survived despite the merciless hunting of mountain lions, wolves, and coyotes during the military occupation of Yellowstone.

This policy had been initiated at the behest of cattlemen and sheepmen during the administration of Theodore Roosevelt and carried out rather ruthlessly until shortly before we entered the picture. In fact, John Goff, the president's chief guide when he made western hunting trips, was given a four-year contract in 1905 to go to Yellowstone and "destroy the mountain lion, lynx, and bobcats that have been killing the deer and elk." He was allowed to keep all pelts (worth thousands of dollars), besides his pay as a forest ranger. Needless to say, there were few if any mountain lions or wolves left by 1916. It had been federal policy to placate the ranchers around the outskirts of the park as well as give the soldiers stationed there the opportunity to obtain hunting trophies and furs.

My sessions with the American Game Association, the lessons of Henry Fairfield Osborn and other scientists, the Boone and Crockett Club, and friends in the Biological Survey had taught me a great deal about keeping nature in balance, the necessity of maintaining all species of wildlife. It just plain went against my grain to wantonly slay animals in the wild.

However, Mather and I did not see eye to eye on this question. He felt the tourists loved to see wild animals, the more the merrier, and he envisaged herds of elk and antelope—the "gentle ones," as he called them.

He also loved bears for their entertainment qualities and somehow did not group them with the "vicious killers," as he called the predators.

It was an issue on which Mather finally let me have my way. Not too long after I became superintendent of Yellowstone, I stopped all killing except for coyotes when they became too numerous around antelope. Even then, I decided on a case-by-case basis, and few were eliminated.

I didn't put up a brick wall between myself and these men who came to see me in July 1917. I understood their fear of predators devastating their domestic animals, and I also understood the power of their representatives in Washington. My stand was that the army was once more the protective agent in Yellowstone. The Park Service had no power to enforce any policy on predators. That threw the ball to the army, and, knowing how long it took them to make a decision, I didn't worry.

But I added: "I have made our Park Service policy quite clear. The killing of wild animals, except predatory animals when absolutely necessary, is strictly forbidden. It is impracticable to kill off all predators. The balance of nature must be maintained." Later that year I made it a point to reiterate this policy in the National Park Service annual report.

In Yellowstone, with this group, my words were met with a hostile, stony silence, but nothing more was discussed. I was to have many a tussle over this issue when I had to face the problem on a daily basis as superintendent of Yellowstone after 1919.

Another serious problem was that there was no overall group responsible for management of the park; we had a real scarcity of responsible personnel. Lindsley was very upset by the fact that tourists were causing wholesale damage in the park, throwing objects into hot springs or geysers, breaking off chunks of algae-colored formations, and stealing blocks of obsidian from the famous cliff. I spoke to the military commander and asked him to instruct his men to arrest anyone caught in vandalism or theft. I also had Lindsley erect signs at every important point warning of fines or imprisonment for these criminal acts.

The concession agreement Mather had hammered out took effect in the summer of 1917. His idea of a "principal concessioner" providing a range of services under National Park Service regulations was proving to be sound. It worked out especially well when he combined Child's hotel company with a monopoly in transportation. The profit from the transportation would offset the hotel losses. Child had enthusiastically put out the capital to purchase first-class motor cars, replacing the defunct horse-and-carriage system.

In theory, Child's operational plans were perfect (as was proved later), but for now the war and the decrease in tourists wreaked havoc with his financial condition. The cost of his fleet of motor cars almost sank him, and he had to turn to the railroads serving Yellowstone for help. I urgently asked Child to hang on. Though difficult at times, he understood our aims and did a good job—we knew him and how to get along with him. For now he was preferable to new concessioners.

The only facet I had real doubts about was the boat concession on Yellowstone Lake. After Mather's initial enthusiasm, he later decided it was superfluous because of the motorized road transportation. I gradually came around to the thought that the boats were a marvelous scenic and exhilarating experience, although very expensive to operate. However, I never questioned Mather's decision, and they went the way of the dinosaur shortly after the general reorganization of the concessions.

The problem arising from the discontinuance of stage transportation was that everywhere you looked, there were piles of outmoded coaches, horse trappings, and other debris. As a side issue, there were abandoned camps, old stables, and disintegrating tent cities.

Mather had favored removing all old buildings that had housed tourists except for the modern hotels, and I went along with him until I received special instructions on July 3. In this letter he told me that he had reconsidered on the Fountain Hotel, found it "useless," and wanted it destroyed. The Fountain Hotel had been built in 1891 at a cost of more than $100,000 and could accommodate 350 guests per night. Only a little over twenty-five years old, it was considered "modern" in that it had hot water, electricity, and steam heat. Furthermore, it was nicely located and had the dubious honor of being known as "the bear hotel." It was here that all bears interested in gourmet garbage were fed the accumulation of the hotel leftovers before sundown. This was quite a tourist attraction and later spread to other "bear pit" lunch stations around the park. The problem of the Fountain had to wait, mainly because I wanted to talk Mather out of destroying it if I could. (I didn't.)

The present dilemma was: who was to clean up all the messy debris? The soldiers had little else to do, so they were put to work, but performed so poorly and half-heartedly that nothing much was accomplished until the National Park Service rangers in uniform were back.

The rangers were hard-working, knew what to do, and did it promptly and efficiently. People respected them and, for the most part, obeyed them. I have always thought that the competence, dedication, and pride of these early scouts-turned-rangers were the bedrock on which the esprit de corps of all future rangers was built and for which they are still famous.

Mather had always stated that his policy was to keep the Park Service small. That, plus the fact that our appropriations were minute, had led him to call on other agencies of government to do work for us. Now out in the park I met a fellow from the Bureau of Fisheries checking out the restocking of trout streams. He was a most interesting Norwegian scientist who gave me quite a lecture on stocking only native-type fish. He was upset that some officials in his department had been toying with the idea of taking fish alien to this environment (because of their size or other reason) and placing them in Yellowstone waters. It was known that early in the century Great Lakes fish had been introduced into Lewis Lake along with several other smaller lakes, with disastrous results.

The Fisheries man was perplexed as to why there were so few fish in the Yellowstone waters. I told him that the previous winter Emerson Hough, the *Saturday Evening Post* writer, had brought to my attention that fishermen outside the park were catching fish in enormous quantities from park waters and selling them to the hotel company at three cents a pound, really stripping various lakes and streams. I had immediately ordered that no Yellowstone fish could be used in any of the hotels, lodges, and camps, actually inserting this clause into the 1917 concession contracts. Even though I knew little or nothing about fish at this point—except how to catch them in Sierra mountain streams—I listened carefully to my friend from Norway, took notes on his ideas, and often used them in the future.

Once I had settled the most pressing problems, I had about one and a half days left to work on the idea of adding the Jackson Hole with its soaring Teton Mountains to Yellowstone or, if that was unacceptable, creating a Grand Teton National Park as a separate entity. I never got over my initial wonder at the unmatched beauty of that valley and its awesome, jagged peaks. It was just a natural to add to Yellowstone, a park lacking in this type of alpine beauty. However, the stubborn opposition of the Forest Service to giving up a foot of its territory, the skeptical attitude of the Hole's residents, and the lack of any Wyoming political power behind us temporarily doused the plan with cold water.

The ranching community didn't trust the new Park Service. They approved of their present situation with unlimited cattle grazing privileges on Forest Service land. They were aware of the new Park Service and its policy of "no use." Others feared losing tax-paying land to the federal government. In a sparsely settled state like Wyoming, the politicians fell in behind the opposition. It didn't look good.

My final official act in Yellowstone was to issue a directive designating Major E. M. Leary, commanding First Squadron, Seventh Cavalry, as superintendent of the park and Chester Lindsley as acting supervisor, National Park Service. I added that "nothing herein contained shall be construed to change the official status or duties of Mr. Chester A. Lindsley, the acting supervisor." I made sure we were firmly entrenched in Yellowstone affairs even though we no longer had full command.

The last thing I did in Yellowstone was to send a wire to Dr. Weisenburg. Before I got off into an area where I would be hard to reach, I wanted the latest medical update on Mr. Mather's health. The doctor reported back that he had talked to Mather in Darien that very day and found that all was going well. His lingering problems were suspicion, mainly of certain people, lack of self-confidence, and quick exhaustion. Mather still felt that he was incapable of handling the Park Service and was still very fearful of a recurrence of the mental, nervous, and physical breakdown he had suffered in January.

I again got the warning that nothing was to upset Mather. Under no circumstances was he to be presented with any problems or bad news. "Make Mather feel he has a finger in the pie but don't let him have a real taste of it." Weisenburg emphasized that although Mather was making slow improvement, his condition was like walking a tightrope. He could inch along to full recovery, or he could easily fall off into the dangerous suicidal depression if he began worrying and feeling stressful once more.

So I continued writing my chief short letters containing little tidbits of information, amusing incidents, touches of gossip about the locals, and suggestions and questions about plans for his western trip. My desire was to have him informed about each park as I moved around and yet never let on about a real problem—just let him feel that all was serene with the Park Service.

• • •

It was a rather subdued and lonely park that greeted me when I got off the train at Belton, headquarters for Glacier. The Great Northern Railway had bravely opened most of its fine hotels and chalets, knowing full well that the war and the government's discouragement of travel for pleasure would produce a serious loss in revenue. We in the Park Service took the approach that the war gave all of us, concessioners and administrators, a breathing spell to lay out plans for the future and shore up our operations. This sounds just fine except for two things. As usual we had the usual stingy appropriations to work with, and Senator Walsh's man, Walter W. Payne, had replaced our man, George Goodwin, as supervisor.

The two senators, Walsh and Henry L. Myers, appointed the men to operate the park, alternating first one and then the other. About this time Senator Myers told me: "Don't ask me to appoint or recommend any more people for rangers. Every time I recommend one, I make nine enemies. You do it yourself and make your own enemies."

Of course, Senator Walsh never did let go until 1920, when the Republicans took over the administration. Most of his choices were pretty awful. I remember one of Walsh's rangers had to be put on patrol along the railroad tracks to keep him from getting lost, and sometimes another ranger had to be sent to accompany him so he wouldn't get run over by a train.

As it turned out, Walsh's choice of Payne was really quite good. It truly surprised me to find a man who, although knowing little of national park operations, was very intelligent, attentive, and ready to do his best.

Well, Payne was the only good news from Walsh. I've said it before and I'll say it again. I thoroughly detested Walsh. Anyone could hate him on general principles, for he was ruthless, inconsiderate, and displayed no kindness to anyone about anything. I had any number of reasons for my feelings, not just because he was so indifferent or belligerent toward our conservation goals, but because I felt he had been a part of Mather's breakdown. He had thrown every monkey wrench he could into Mather's attempt to organize the concessions in Yellowstone. Mather felt Walsh somehow had a personal vendetta against him. Walsh had practically flung down the gauntlet with "any concessioner has a right to operate in Yellowstone." And Mather's passionate belief was one concession per operation.

As for myself, I found in Glacier that I was dogged at every turn by "Walsh wants this, Walsh wants that." This stubborn, cantankerous senator was like a red flag to the Albright bull. Roads were the most important projects that Mather and I had decided on for Glacier. And here I bumped head-on into Walsh. The most needed road was to hug the side of Lake McDonald to the Lewis Hotel and thence to the head of trails crossing to the east side. Even though the power of the Great Northern and Louie Hill was behind our plans, Walsh was stubbornly fighting us.

I was pretty sure the reason was that he owned a summer place on Lake McDonald. He had maneuvered a law (against general principles of the Park Service) to exempt from condemnation any private lands in the park. He simply wanted to be sure he didn't get evicted as well as insuring that the public would leave him in peace and privacy.

This was a general and long-running problem. My immediate problem was Walsh's connection with the Penwell Sheep Company. This was a rather sleazy outfit that wanted to run stock in Glacier for the patriotic reason of "helping feed our boys." Secretary Lane had so far been fairly noncommittal on details, but he had given Walsh the general nod of approval and had told me to work out a deal with the sheepmen. I had found these fellows arrogant and adamant. So it was funny how I accidentally found a solution to the problem.

I was in the lobby of the Glacier Park Hotel one night and overheard a couple of men praising the beauty of the park. The more I listened, the more I thought of the imminent destruction of the beautiful meadows and wildflowers over which they were rapturizing. Almost without thinking, I commented, "Well, it won't look like this after the sheep are allowed to eat it all up for a sack of silver."

I was surprised to find these two men immediately interested in my statement. They introduced themselves as Bruce Kramer of Butte, vice-chairman of the Democratic National Committee, and Walter Hansen, a powerful man in the Montana meat-packing business. They wanted to know what my grousing was all about. After a complete rundown on the problem, Hansen suggested that I grant him a permit for a small herd to graze on some isolated chunk of land of my choice, and thus all other applications for grazing could be denied.

Leasing was completed. It sounded tricky, especially as Kramer was a power in the Democratic Party and might go to Walsh with the whole plot. Not to mention a leak back to my boss, Lane. Kramer assured me that he "couldn't remember a thing that was said between Hansen and myself," and I felt I really had no choice but to gamble on his word. So that was the way the Glacier grazing situation was taken care of. Late in the summer of 1918, Hansen unloaded a carload or so of cattle in the southern end of the park. After the war ended a few months later, every head of Hansen's cattle was removed, leaving Glacier unharmed.

My four days in Glacier were insufficient, but I had to move on to other park areas.

One sparkling day in Seattle, after a morning meeting with civic officials and state engineers, I was entertained at a luncheon and then taken
on a tour of the city and environs. The new boulevards were proudly
displayed and, at one particularly lovely vista facing east, the car was
stopped. Silence reigned while we took in the beauty of Mount Baker on
the horizon. A gentleman broke our contemplation by asking: "Mr.
Albright, what might be your greatest wish for the state of Washington?
Another national park like Mount Baker?"

Without thinking, I quickly replied, "I want Mount Olympus
National Monument in the National Park Service." This was startling, as
these men obviously were Baker boosters, plus the fact that the national
monument was in the Forest Service. It had started out as a forest reserve
in 1897 by executive order of President Cleveland. It went through a
metamorphosis of sections being returned to the public domain for use
of lumbermen and land speculators. Then came a proposed national park
in 1904 and finally a proclamation of national monument status in 1909.
However, commercial interests never gave up, and with war in Europe
President Wilson was persuaded to reduce the monument by almost one-
half to aid mining and lumbering. Shortly afterward, this area was almost
totally stripped of timber. Someone called it "the rape of Olympus."

Later that afternoon, as we drove over toward Puget Sound, I saw a
portion of the damage and was horrified. I made a mental note to start a
push in the Congress to pry this area from the Forest Service, and I did
accomplish that aim in 1933.

However, on this day in 1917, I perhaps foolishly talked too much.
Several of my companions had fingers in the lumber pie in the Olympus
area, and unknowingly I made some future enemies. They came back to
haunt me as I pushed for Olympic to be made a national park. Naturally
my outspoken comment was relayed back to Forest Service officials. This
just made fodder for more suspicion, rivalry, and dislike by the "senior
service," already leery of us.

I'm the first to admit that Stephen Mather and I weren't overly
concerned about their attitude. We didn't dislike the Forest Service. We
didn't try to get into conflict, but we were free-thinking, pragmatic, and
aggressive. And most of all, we deeply believed that all their national
monuments plus a lot of other lands in their jurisdiction should be
released to our bureau because we were *conservationists* and *preservationists*.
They were users.

In Seattle and later in Tacoma there were numerous meetings with state, civic, commercial, concessioner, and recreational groups. Sometimes I was overwhelmed with the responsibility of handling these powerful groups without a single person with whom I could consult.

Some nights, when I was tired and confused over some problem, I'd sit in my hotel room and write fanciful letters to Mr. Mather. I'd pretend to discuss various matters with him. Then I'd read them back and try to imagine what his answers to me would be. It truly helped me to do what I felt Mather would approve of. I was learning, learning, learning all the time, with confidence and knowledge growing by standing on my own two feet and making decisions that I hoped were right.

Our meetings were all concerned with Mount Rainier National Park: proposed roads, concessions, grazing. I felt I'd have to go to the moon to get away from this last nasty problem, and Mount Rainier presented the worst one yet.

This was an absolutely pristine park. No domestic animals had ever grazed here. This was all the more reason the sheepmen felt their animals could be well fed. I was blunt and adamant. "No grazing in any Northwest park."

Then some fellow suddenly brought up the one point I had so far carefully avoided. The organic act creating the Park Service did not specifically exclude grazing. We had been forced to let this pass, for it was a demand of William Kent, one of the bill's prime backers. Only Yellowstone had been excluded.

Before I could answer this attack, another man added that President Wilson had a herd of sheep grazing on the White House lawn. If it was good enough for Wilson, it ought to be good enough for the Park Service. This was a sticky moment, and I brazened it out. "Listen, gentlemen, just because grazing was not specifically forbidden doesn't mean that grazing is going to be allowed. And furthermore, just because there has been grazing of domestic animals in the parks in the past doesn't mean we're ever going to allow grazing in the future. So I hope you clearly understand that there will be no grazing."

My words were met by stony silence. Don't think I wasn't doing some quaking inside, although Dewitt Reaburn, supervisor of Mount Rainier, told me I seemed as cold and immovable as an iceberg. I was thinking how my words would get back to Lane and what his reaction would be. Amazingly enough, the only repercussion I heard was a critical article in the *Tacoma News-Ledger* of November 4, 1917, stating that wild posies weren't as vital as mutton.

The pressure from State Agriculture Commissioner E. P. Benson to let sheep graze finally grew so enormous that members of the Mountaineers Club, real friends of the park, made a dramatic gesture. They offered golf clubs and lawns all over the Puget Sound area on which sheep and cattle could enjoy their meals instead of eating Rainier's wild flowers and mountain meadows. Even that didn't stop Benson. Along with the grazers and powerful local politicians, he kept pursuing the issue right up to Herbert Hoover, the national food director.

I spent July 14 and 15 roving around Mount Rainier with Supervisor Reaburn, a fine, knowledgeable fellow. We filled the days inspecting possible new trail sites, renovation of facilities at Longmire, and road work completed or projected, We then had a marvelous trip to the new Paradise Inn.

Almost 5,500 feet up the southern slopes of Mount Rainier lay this beautiful valley. The Indians knew it as Saghalie Illah, the Land of Peace. The white people called it Paradise. Where the old Camp of the Clouds had sprawled in the valley, there now stood a picturesque, rustic-style hotel, even in July half buried in snow up to ten feet deep in places. Inside, the stunning lobby rose to a mezzanine and reached heavenward to its pointed apex. Giant cedar logs, felled by a fire that burned the slopes of Rainier in 1885, were salvaged for the woodwork. The logs were hand-hewn by an old German carpenter working throughout the winter of 1915–16. In his spare time he created many pieces of furniture and a marvelous grandfather's clock that was placed near the great stone fireplace in the lobby. A few years later it was found necessary to add a wing of ninety-two rooms, and then the camp city disappeared.

After Reaburn and I had inspected the inn, the stables, and blueprints for some additional construction, he challenged me to a hike and the famous "Paradise sport of kings." I inquired in vain what that was, but he kept grinning and saying, "C'mon, Mr. Albright, change into these boots, weatherproof pants, and ski jacket, and I'll show you."

I did as directed, and off we hiked up the hill, plowing through the deep snow. After maybe twenty minutes, Reaburn suddenly stopped and proclaimed that we had reached the place. Here we stared down a rather steep couloir, long and sloping. "Now all you do to get back to the inn is sit down and slide."

"Slide? On what?"

"Well, you may have noticed that the seat of your pants is waxed. That's what you slide on. They're called 'tin britches,' and what you're going to do is called 'nature coasting.'"

Without giving any additional information, Reaburn sat down, shoved himself off, and whizzed away down the snowy slope. Afraid of being left alone on the mountain, I followed immediately. And what an experience! The snow here was more firm and produced a ride not far from a toboggan run. It was exhilarating, marvelous fun. Skimming along, I laughed and shouted, and then *pow*.

I guess I got overly exuberant and lost my balance, catapulting head first into the snow. I was still laughing so hard I couldn't get up and nearly scared poor Reaburn to death. He had pulled over to keep an eye on me, so when I tumbled, he came rushing up. He said later that he was afraid he'd killed his boss. With our "nature coasting" finished, we hiked slowly back to the inn.

My inspection schedule was interrupted by one incident after another. There was an emergency trip to Yosemite when Desmond abandoned his concessions and disappeared to Alaska. There was the crisis of replacing an incompetent supervisor in Crater Lake with Alex Sparrow. Then I attended the Bohemian Club's Hi-jinks at their Russian River camp. This led to invaluable contacts for the Park Service. It also resulted in my having to pass up a golden opportunity to accompany John C. Merriam and Madison Grant on an exploratory trip through the northern redwood country that resulted in the establishment of the Save-the-Redwoods League.

During this time, Mather was regaining his health and taking his first steps into the real world. Accompanied by friends and George McClain of our Washington office, who replaced a male nurse, he had a great time at Sieur de Monts National Monument in Maine and prepared for his trip to the West.

Ever since our mountain trip in 1915, Mather and I had been deeply committed to adding the magnificent back country of the Sierra Nevada to Sequoia. We envisaged combining Sequoia and General Grant National Parks with thousands of acres of wild, mountainous country, the canyons of the Kings and Kern Rivers, and the crest of the Sierra, including the summit of Mount Whitney, the highest mountain in the continental United States. This would create the largest national park outside Yellowstone. Then if we could regain the lost Yosemite region around the Minarets, the two great parks would almost meet. At least they'd be connected by the John Muir Trail across the crest of the Sierra.

We were knowledgeable enough to realize we had at least two strikes against us. First were the commercial interests: lumbering, power, grazing, and worst of all the city of Los Angeles and its eternal thirst for water. Second was the Forest Service. The latter was the most dangerous because it could use the former as allies in fighting the Park Service.

My days in Sequoia were divided between evaluation of our land extension, inholdings, roads, and the usual planning and financial problems that were rampant in every park. I returned to Yosemite on August 11. I knew I'd be stuck here for some time, so I wired Grace to catch a train and join me. The concession problem here was haunting me and had to be settled immediately, as I had received word from Mr. Mather that he was leaving for the West. I had already become a bit apprehensive about Mr. Mather, for his letters ceased after one from Chicago outlining his trip west. But happily he turned up in Glacier in fine spirits.

In Yosemite on August 15 Supervisor Lewis, several of his staff, and I made a horseback trip up to Tuolumne Meadows. As we rode off, I thanked my lucky stars that there were men like this for a park with so much trouble. After all, Yosemite was Stephen Mather's favorite and therefore needed the best. And the best the National Park Service had for a supervisor was Washington B. Lewis, better known as "Dusty" (probably because he was always covered with dust from his dried-up roads). He was an absolute gem, very intelligent, and a brilliant engineer. His main forte was his incisive knowledge of people and ability to get along with anyone. Fortunately he had agreed, at my insistence, not to enlist in the army. Yosemite needed him a great deal worse than the army needed one more uniformed body.

Another asset he had was his wife, Bernice. She resembled my tall, slim brunette wife, matching her in high spirits, laughter, and friendly charm. Bernice and Grace had taken to each other instantly, becoming great friends. The ladies had gladly stayed behind at the Lewis's home while their men set off for the high Sierra country.

The purpose of our visit to the Tuolumne was to check out the camping facilities, but of more importance was the opportunity to discuss plans for Yosemite and Sequoia with our allies in the Sierra Club. Prior to this, I had long discussions with Will Colby in San Francisco and also with a number of conservationists at a Bohemian Club gathering. They all had been enthusiastic and had given me assurance that they would help us carry out the ideas Mather and I had promoted. To our group at

Tuolumne, I reiterated the vision of a sweeping Sierra wilderness park extending northward well toward Yosemite.

A new bill was moving through the Congress, but without much hope of passage. Between the war and the opposition of local commercial interests and Congressman Denver Church, I inwardly felt there was little chance of success, but I kept up an optimistic front, enthusiastically preaching that our efforts should not be wasted at this time. Mather had tried to lure Church into the mountain party of 1915 to "educate" him to our views, but he refused the invitation. Now I urged that we strengthen our support in the San Joaquin Valley and formulate postwar battle plans to enlarge Sequoia and retrieve the section of Yosemite that had been removed back in 1905–6.

Looking back on that evening, it's hard to see how those dreams went down the drain for so many long years. Most of us were so young, so optimistic, so positive that we just couldn't lose. It's hard to realize that Kings Canyon National Park didn't come into being until 1940 and that the Minarets section of Yosemite remains to this day under Forest Service jurisdiction.

I then turned to the concession problem in Yosemite. The Desmond Company was a dangerous whirlpool of financial and administrative chaos.

Earlier in the summer, to avoid bankruptcy, I had ordered the closing of Desmond's upper park lodges and the cessation of many services in the valley. The company's reputation was ruined, so I even had the name changed to the Yosemite Park Company. The earlier loan of seventeen thousand dollars and the sixty-percent assessment on all stockholders had been of no use. It had only increased the stake that Mather had in this shady venture.

I had felt from the beginning that it was possibly illegal for him to be involved in a concession licensed by the government. If not, it was surely a conflict of interest. I was fearful of going to Interior's solicitor general to get a definitive legal opinion. Everything hinged on whether, or how soon, it might be dragged into the open. This now seemed not only possible, but inevitable. If a scandal erupted, it could be fatal to Mather's recovery and a terrible blot on the Park Service itself.

A short time later I met Mr. Mather in San Francisco. Although I was overjoyed to see him so physically healthy, his nervous condition appeared when we tried to discuss problems in Mount Rainier and Yosemite.

However, he also recognized the problem and cut our discussion short, saying: "Horace, I'm not up to these difficulties. You have been absorbing them for months and must solve them yourself or with your advisors. Give me a little more time. Then we can talk them over together for decisions. Carry on as you have been doing. Please don't feel I'm letting you down. I just need more time."

He was so magnificent in appreciation of his own difficulties that I was close to tears. All I could do was reassure him that everyone was pulling his oar, would carry on as he would wish us to do, that his Park Service was thriving according to his ideals.

Grace and I stayed in Yosemite until the end of August. I put in many hours with Mother Curry and son Foster, who was pushing his plan to buy out the Desmond Company. I was pretty sure he couldn't get the financial wherewithal. Just in case he could pull off this miracle, I wanted to make it clear beforehand that I couldn't approve of it without Mr. Mather's consent, and he was not well enough to make that decision at this time.

It wasn't all work and no play for the Albright and Lewis families. The girls had been having a great time together. One wonderful excursion for us all was a horseback trip to the Merced Wawona grove of sequoia trees to the south. It was a languid summer day, with easy riding through the beautiful forests, enjoying panoramic views and savoring the cool quiet of upland Wawona, some distance from the floor of the valley.

As usual, Dusty and I got to playing around. The party had dismounted to have refreshments and take a bit of rest. Our wives wandered off to a nearby stream to see if it ended as a waterfall to the valley. Dusty plucked some feathery stalks and stuffed them around his hat, totally covering it. He wrapped one of the extra saddle blankets around himself. Then he crept up on Grace and Bernice, suddenly letting out a wild Indian war whoop and scaring the very devil out of them. Bernice shrieked and promptly slid into the stream. My girl instantly swung with her leather bag, socked him full in the face, and was pulling out her long, venomous hat pin for a final thrust when she recognized her foe. While we husbands waited for a bawling out, our wives lay on the ground helplessly laughing. What a sight—Bernice wet and muddied, Dusty nursing a red and puffy cheek, and Grace still clutching her wicked weapon.

Then it was back to San Francisco early in September. I had several meetings with Will Colby about the Sequoia extension and the Yosemite recession and concession situations. I valued this man's intelligent, realistic analysis of our park problems and his readiness to help through his position with the Sierra Club. He and I came to the basic agreement that, although the enlargement of the parks should be kept before important members of Congress and bills introduced if possible, there probably was no way any major effort could be accomplished before the war ended.

A showdown with the Desmond Company was also avoided. I spent too many precious hours in San Francisco with Desmond Company officials. With A. B. C. Dohrmann I cajoled, pleaded, and finally played on his sympathies (Mather's illness) to wring a promise from him that he would try to clean up the operations in Yosemite, manage the finances, and keep the company on an even keel until Mather was well enough to make some decisions about it. I felt I had no right to do anything more than regulate the concession according to existing government policy. Surely I, on behalf of the Park Service, couldn't get myself mixed into the financial and operational end of it when Mather's possible conflict of interest was so deep. Again wait and see.

Before leaving San Francisco to join Douglas White for my first visit to Utah's national park areas, I wrote a long letter to Joe Cotter in Washington. It reveals my state of mind as I struggled with the many challenges of "laying the foundations."

I tell you, Joe, the thing that weighs the heaviest on me is policy making. Organizing this new Service, with few precedents to go by and no one but myself to make decisions is a terrible burden. I always try to think what Mr. Mather would want, but he's not around now and lord knows when he will be. So I'm on my own. I think of myself as an explorer in unknown territory. Each idea I have must be tested, each fork of the trail must be examined. Or maybe it's like constructing a house. I'm at the stage where I am laying the foundations. They are what everything else is built upon. I have no blueprints and no architect. Only the ideals and principles for which the Park Service was created—to preserve, intact, the heritage we were bequeathed. The devil of the thing is the conflicting principles in our organic act. How can we interpret the unrestricted use of the parks for the public and still retain them totally intact for the future? So it comes down to when I make a decision, I lay another brick for the foundation but must always be concerned that it does not impair the construction of the building as it rises. These bricks are setting the principles and precedents for the Service to follow in the years ahead.

Exploring a New World of Parks
1917

On September 4, 1917, I boarded a train for Los Angeles to meet Douglas White, a railroad official with whom I had agreed to visit Mukuntuweap National Monument in Utah. No Interior Department official had ever seen the place. I was deeply concerned about our national monuments, the forgotten orphans of the service. Only about $120 a year was allocated to each monument, $1 a month for most of their custodians.

The monuments were so fascinating, with such diversity. My love of both history and natural beauty made their varied characteristics especially interesting, and I wanted to learn more about them. Much as I hated leaving my Grace behind in Berkeley, Albright finances simply couldn't stretch to take her with me. We agreed she would join me in Denver for the return to Washington.

In Los Angeles White met me and rushed me over to a train already overdue to leave. He had been able to hold it, as he was the general passenger traffic manager of the Los Angeles and Salt Lake Railroad, in those days known simply as the Salt Lake Line. A few years later it was sold to the Union Pacific.

The next morning we alighted in Lund, Utah, and climbed into a vehicle that didn't look like it could even start, much less take us across to the monument. Fortunately, it didn't have to because at Cedar City we were met by two brothers, Gronway and Chauncey Parry, who operated an "auto service" to Mukuntuweap.

Word had preceded us that Horace Albright, "a special agent of Secretary of the Interior Franklin K. Lane," was to inspect the "scenic Mormon territories" and would address the population of Cedar City. No one had bothered to mention this to me until the Parry brothers tipped me off as we rode into the center of town and saw the waiting crowd. From the elevation of the back seat of the touring car, I gave them a rousing, impromptu speech about the National Park Service and the beauties of Utah (which I hadn't yet seen).

Joined by former state senator Henry Lunt and R. A. Thorley, we sped off toward the east in a fine eight-passenger car driven by Chauncey Parry. In Rockville Bishop David Herschi of the Mormon Church was added to our group, as I had been warned not to go into Mormon territory without a "native guide."

I had certainly picked marvelous companions for this trip to Mukuntuweap. Lunt and Thorley were veritable encyclopedias about the region. Douglas White was a clever storyteller, a great mimic, and something of a singer, and he kept us entertained every minute. Best of all, he had spent a lot of time at the monument and knew it well. And Herschi was wonderful, a joyful soul whose ebullient voice joined White in chorus after chorus of rousing Mormon hymns. Even my off-key baritone chimed when we came to "Oh, Come All Ye Saints."

It was just as well there was such diversion because the hundred or so miles to Mukuntuweap were a real test of physical fortitude. We spent the next uncounted hours bouncing and crashing over some of the worse roads I had ever experienced. The state of Utah obviously didn't give a tinker's dam about "Dixie," the southern part of the state, for convict labor had been used to make these so-called roads. Those men probably took out their hate and frustration on the projects. I fervently prayed that the pathetic appropriation of $10,000 that Utah's Senator Reed Smoot had wrung out of Congress for the monument's roads had been spent on a different set of workers.

We finally cruised into the little town of Springdale. Standing out in the boiling hot sun, waiting patiently to greet us, was Walter Ruesch. He was there to direct us to his home, where refreshments were waiting. I'll always remember the picture that greeted us at Ruesch's place. Framed in the doorway of this rude, rustic house was a serenely beautiful woman holding a small child, the epitome of pioneer grace. She was Marilla Ruesch, an unforgettable lady who was a key element in her husband's future success in the Park Service.

I guess you could call Ruesch somewhat of an employee of the National Park Service because he took care of some equipment the government had left here when the road work was finished. I questioned Bishop Herschi about him and suggested that I could hire him as a custodian of the monument, though I was only able to pay him a negligible salary.

The bishop replied: "Well, you wouldn't want this man. He has a terrible habit. You really couldn't have him around your tourists. Ever since he was a little boy, we have tried to do something with him, but we have never been able to break him of it, and, as the years pass, he gets worse."

Several times I asked him, "Why? What's the matter?" No answer.

Finally he gave in and answered: "I guess I'd better tell you what this poor man's problem is and why you just can't have him around people. The awful fact is that he swears. He just doesn't say one bad word. He just plain swears like it was the devil himself talking."

In the next few days I got to know this very pleasant, polite gentleman. He took me around to see the government equipment he was caring for, an old block and tackle. He told me the person from whom it had been rented had charged the government way too much for its use and voiced his opinion of the man. Although he spoke quietly, he not only used all the swear words I had ever heard, but he cooked up some of his own. He was certainly a full-flamed fellow if ever there was one. Actually he sounded a lot like my old grandfather, who proclaimed that it was all right to swear profusely and graphically because the English language was so darned inexpressive.

Later on Bishop Herschi confessed he'd overheard my conversation with Ruesch and said: "You see what I told you. The man is impossible."

But I liked Ruesch and admired his devotion to the monument. I went ahead and hired him on a day-to-day basis right then, later making him a full custodian and finally the superintendent of Zion National Park when it had evolved from Mukuntuweap National Monument.

There were a few difficulties with him, like the time the president of the Union Pacific Railroad and other dignitaries visited. They were a pretty high and mighty group, quite patronizing to Ruesch, but he retained a dignified, gentlemanly appearance throughout the three- or four-day visit. As they finally drove off, Ruesch turned to a ranger and proclaimed in a fine, bellowing voice, "Hell, the sons-of-bitches are gone, but I think the bastards enjoyed themselves."

Now beholding Mukuntuweap and the so-called Little Zion Canyon for the first time, I was surprised, excited, and thrilled. More than that, I was just plain stunned. I had no concept of the staggering beauty I beheld. Local Utah people said that Yosemite was a Zion without color. But this didn't faintly prepare me for the reality of the towering rock walls, splashed with brilliant hues of tans and reds interspersed with whites. The great towers, temples, spires, and peaks appeared unearthly as they encircled the narrow, lush gorge cut by the sparkling Virgin River. I remember exclaiming, "Oh, it is so like Yosemite."

Someone immediately corrected me: "No, Little Zion was not created by glaciers. It was created not too many millions of years ago by the water of this river carving out the soft sandstone."

Whatever created this marvel of natural splendor, it was love at first sight for me. Ever after, I claimed this national park (along with Grand Teton) as mine. From day one it was a personal crusade to mold it from a little national monument into a great national park.

I was excited and enthused by the grandeur of Little Zion, as I began to call it. I always preferred local names, especially native Indian ones, for natural wonders, but Mukuntuweap was a problem. It was an Indian name for the river. John Wesley Powell had translated the name as "straight river." I felt "Mukuntuweap" was too difficult to pronounce and really tough to spell.

I sounded out the local people and found they all used just the one word "Zion," which to Mormons meant "heaven" or a "heavenly place." That sounded about right to me, so I decided that when I returned to Washington and pressed for national park status, I would use that too. It also seemed to fit because the Mormons, who had settled here around 1860, had named many of the landmarks of the valley with religious themes, feeling they were like temples to God, such as Angels Landing, West Temple, and the Three Patriarchs.

During the few days I was at Zion, White and I covered an enormous amount of territory, often with Ruesch and other local men. We took horses to get to the top of the great cliffs, exploring the high country and studying the canyon from three thousand feet above to work out plans for extending the borders of the monument. We tramped on foot the full length of Little Zion Canyon to the very end of the Narrows. Here lay an incredible extension where outstretched arms can almost touch both sides of the overhanging cliffs and flowers drip down the walls with the seeping waters. We stood at dusk watching the last rays of the sun glow on the glistening walls of the Great White Throne. Truly a spiritual experience.

There were practical decisions to be made. Although few people except the locals visited here, I knew that as soon as publicity to create a national park was spread in newspapers and magazines, with accompanying pictures to show its beauty, tourists would begin to come, probably in droves. So the facilities in the area had to be taken into consideration.

It was incredible, but the government had actually spent ten thousand dollars on roads here. No complaints about that. Then there were the concessions. Up to this time, there had been no proper accommodations short of Cedar City, but White assured me he had a gentleman who was the answer to that problem. He introduced me to an old man, W. W. Wylie, who had constructed a tourist tent camp in Zion Canyon.

Well, I was amazed. I had never met him before but knew all about him, as he had originated the permanent camp system in Yellowstone, selling out there years before. His so-called Wylie Way was so efficient and popular that it was copied by the Currys in Yosemite. I knew of his integrity, honesty, and knowledge of national park standards. His camp here looked neat and clean. The Interior Department had already granted him a five-year lease for the camp and added the transportation franchise too.

I assured Wylie that I approved of his camp operations but asked him to submit future plans for these as well as how he was going to set up his system to bring visitors from the rail line. As there had been only three hundred tourists to the monument that season, there really hadn't been any test of how operations would go when large crowds poured in. However, I trusted Wylie's experience in Yellowstone and felt he would make a valuable contribution to solving concession problems.

I hated to leave Zion. I deeply regretted not being able to explore the other two canyons of the region and the ancient Indian cliff dwellings. I hadn't even known they existed until my visit. So again this fit my "perfect park," a combination of scenic wonders and historic sites.

But I had to push on with my inspection trip. Saying good-bye to the kindly Mormon people, I assured them that as soon as I got back to Washington I would go full steam ahead to enlarge this monument and have it made a national park. And so I did. President Wilson changed its status to Zion National Monument on March 18, 1918, and on November 19, 1919, it became a greatly enlarged national park.

In Salt Lake City Doug White and I were busy with a sightseeing tour for army draftees and then a meeting with Utah's Governor Simon

Bamberger concerning access roads to Zion. In his heavily accented voice, he shouted, "I build no more roads to rocks!"

On the night of September 1, 1917, I met Frank Wadleigh, passenger traffic manager of the Denver and Rio Grande Railroad, and climbed aboard a special car attached to a regular D & RG passenger train bound for Denver. It was the beginning of one of the most memorable trips I ever had, a complete tour of this railroad, narrow and broad gauge. The purpose was to explore Colorado, our present holdings, and possible future acquisitions for the park system.

We alighted from our train at Grand Junction, Colorado, in time to see the sun casting its first light over the lush valley watered by the Colorado and Gunnison Rivers. Wadleigh had a car and driver waiting for us, and after a hearty breakfast we drove to the west a few miles to Colorado National Monument to meet John Otto, the custodian.

Checking out this national monument had been one of the primary reasons for this trip. I was deeply interested in the condition of these orphans of the Park Service. I knew I didn't have time to hit the string in Utah and the Southwest, but I felt I could get a grip on the problems of the monuments if I inspected just one. This, of course, didn't count Mukuntuweap. In my mind it was already a national park.

To illustrate the difficult situation in the monuments, here is a quote from Robert Marshall's 1916 annual report to the secretary of the interior: "During the past session, Congress appropriated $3,500 for preservation, development, administration, and protection of the national monuments." In other words, the $3,500 had to be divided between the Interior Department's twenty-one monuments and had to cover everything, including salaries for the custodians.

Colorado National Monument was a fine example for me to study. I already knew John Otto from the Berkeley meeting. The area was visited by more tourists than most monuments and was kept in remarkable shape considering that only this one man was responsible for its total care. I was frankly astonished at the size of Colorado Monument, the height to which the plateau rose (nearly two thousand feet above the Grand Valley), the deep canyons, the colorful vertical cliffs and soaring monoliths, the comparison of sparse desert and lush areas at springs where water seeped through rocks to form gardens of brilliant flowers.

John Otto was a marvelous guide and knew every inch of his monument, which he tended like a personal kingdom. His pathetic pay of one dollar a month from the government couldn't even feed him, but somehow he had managed to fence in most of his twenty thousand acres to protect the deer, bighorn sheep, and birds. He had also constructed trails and a nice entranceway to the monument. He had inspired the local community to chip in to further his work. His first trail, the Corkscrew, started with $154 donated by subscribers to the local newspaper, just enough money to buy blasting powder and tools. Otto provided the labor. His devotion and magnificent work were most impressive, and I promised I'd somehow help him with supplies and future appropriations.

I told him there was one thing I would surely do when I got back to Washington. A township survey had showed that the monument did not include all the lofty monoliths intended by the original proclamation in 1911. In Washington I went to a great conservationist and friend of the parks, Congressman Edward Taylor of Colorado. He drew up a proposal to add these 3,500 acres adjacent to the south and west boundaries. It still took years before Otto's dream became reality, years after he had left his monument. That's the way things went for the national monuments, as Congress simply ignored them.

That morning in August 1917 at Colorado with John Otto was an experience and a lesson I never forgot. Otto's integrity, his love and self-less devotion to the land placed in his care, and his faith in our service and his country were a singular inspiration to me. The same held true for other custodians, such as Walter Ruesch, Evan Vogt, John Wetherill, Zeke Johnson, and others. They devoted their time and resources to the protection of their monuments, with little recompense, praise, or recognition.

Later, when I became director of the National Park Service, I was most aggressive on behalf of our existing monuments and the creation of new ones, as well as in obtaining the transfer to the National Park Service of all those held by the War Department and the Forest Service in the Agriculture Department.

Wadleigh kept nudging me until I woke up to the fact that our train would shortly be leaving Grand Junction. We boarded a magnificent private car tacked on to the end of a through train to Denver, the broad-gauge Royal Gorge Route. The car was quite a sight, with walls paneled in exotic grained woods, etched glass lighting, plush upholstered furniture, and touches of gilt glittering throughout. It was complete with a kitchen and several uniformed men to serve us. We lacked nothing that the nine-teenth-century nabobs enjoyed. Lounging in deeply comfortable swivel-ing armchairs and sipping iced lemonade, I was entertained by Wadleigh alternately reading from a stack of railroad booklets and telling marvelous anecdotes about the wild and wooly history of the line and the areas through which we were traveling.

I was awed by the spectacular mountain country unfolding along our route paralleling the Colorado River to Glenwood Springs, with its impressive resort hotels. The next eye-opener was the climb up famed Tennessee Pass through a towering mass of mountains to Leadville, still a booming mining town. Here we took a quick tour on foot in near blizzard conditions. Back on the train, we made a descent along the Arkansas River to Salida, where we were joined by John Steele of the Denver Tourist Bureau.

The next morning our party boarded another private car attached to a narrow-gauge train and headed west. At first it was a roller-coaster adventure, steep climbs up a pass and then down the other side on twisting tracks and muleshoe bends (narrow gauge for horseshoe). The last stretch to Montrose was one hundred miles of the Gunnison River Valley.

The day passed quickly as we chugged along through the Gunnison Valley, about one hundred miles from the west side of the pass at Sargent to Montrose. Shortly after leaving the town of Gunnison, several other narrow-gauge lines branched off to the north, and our line plunged into the Black Canyon of the Gunnison. Between Sapinero and Cimarron we rolled on a downward slope on the north side of the river through the depths of this awesome canyon. Our rails skirted the roaring torrent of the river, hugging the almost 4,000-foot perpendicular cliffs. The midnight-colored rocks above seemed dangerously insecure. The narrowness and depth of the canyon walls caused a shadowy twilight darkness at noon. The whole effect was eerie.

There was one startling sight along the walls of the canyon, a rock tower. It was named the Curecanti Needle, a solitary spear standing out like a finger pointing to the sky. It was the symbol or herald used by the D & RG as their logo for some time. Sadly, it has ended up half-submerged, a result of damming the Gunnison years later.

At Montrose, after a night in a hotel, Wadleigh had a car and driver waiting to take us out to see the Black Canyon of the Gunnison, from the top this time. The sorry dirt road from Montrose carried us about fifteen miles to near the rim of the canyon. We hiked out to the dizzy edge and then followed it along for miles.

What an amazingly different impression we had from the rim! The drop of a half a mile to the river was stupendous. The cliffs, which had seemed gray and threatening from below, now appeared striped and, in some places, quite colorful. The turgid, restless river was now a cool green ribbon.

Wadleigh and Steele talked excitedly about the tourist attraction this area could become. When they asked my opinion, all I could think of was a sentence in the Hayden Survey atlas of 1877: "There is nothing in America that equals the Grand Canyon of the Gunnison." Having seen the Grand Canyon of the Colorado, as well as other impressive clefts in the earth, I still was overwhelmed by the stark, prehistoric intensity of this one.

"By God, it'd make a magnificent national monument or even a national park," I said. Then I added, "And I swear it will be if I have anything to say about it." As director of the Park Service, one of the last things I asked President Herbert Hoover to do before he left office was to proclaim the Black Canyon of the Gunnison a national monument. It was created on March 2, 1933.

The following morning, we three again boarded Wadleigh's car on a different narrow gauge bound for Mesa Verde National Park. The country we passed through displayed deep valleys, steep passes, rushing rivers, railroad centers, and rough mining towns, including Ouray and Telluride. There was a peculiar remoteness to the land- scape, growing stronger as we headed south toward Mancos.

At Mancos we were met by Supervisor Thomas Rickner of Mesa Verde, who was waiting in a large touring car. After packing our bags on the running board racks, we climbed in and were off for the park.

Within minutes, I was disillusioned as we started up a misnomer called "the scenic highway to the park." Highway? This twenty-mile stretch was one of the most disreputable, dangerous, fearsome bits of slip- pery, rutted miseries I ever had the misfortune to travel. It scared me even to think that the United States government had the nerve to offer this as an approach to a national park. My imagination got the best of me as I visualized the publicity arising from tourists slipping off hairpin turns and plunging to their deaths from the cliffs. Despite doubts that I or anyone else could ever reach the mesa above, we actually did crawl onto the beau- tiful green tableland and proceed to our lodging near the overlook to Spruce Tree House.

I had met Rickner before but had never had much of a chance to talk to him, get to know how he ticked. That frightening ride up to the mesa gave me a pretty clear readout on the man. He had been a professor—of what I can't remember, but it certainly wasn't in the field in which he was associated at Mesa Verde. This man didn't know archaeology or anything else about his national park.

In the few days I was there, I found it was being robbed blind. Digging and stealing ancient artifacts was a common occurrence, almost unpoliced and unpunished. When I got back to Washington, I launched an investigation and later found out that Rickner's son-in-law was one of the worst offenders, a leader of a band of surreptitious "midnight diggers." However, the evidence appeared to clear Rickner and his daughter, who apparently had no knowledge of her husband's activities.

At Spruce Tree Camp we got out of the car to glimpse our first cliff dwelling. This first view of the ruins was worth all the white knuckles and gray hair of the approach ride. The sun spotlighted the ancient complex called Spruce Tree House with what the locals called a "colorado" glow—the Spanish word for red. It was ethereal. The size, complexity, and condition of Spruce Tree astonished me and so quickened my interest that I proposed we have a look all around the park.

"Not possible," snapped Rickner. "First of all it's entirely too late in the afternoon. Couldn't possibly see more than a glimpse of this huge layout. Secondly, you may not know that we have only one auto road; its destination is Chapin Mesa. Otherwise we walk or ride a horse." I felt chagrined, sheepishly admitting to myself that I not studied enough about this park before I opened my mouth and showed my ignorance.

So we piled back into the car and drove a few miles to the very southern edge of the park on what Rickner had called "a road." This was not just a matter of a surface for autos. When you saw ones like these in Mesa Verde, it came down to protection of life and limbs for tourists visiting our "wonderlands." I had my camera with me and took a few pictures of these ruts. Illustration was the best way to convince our budget-minded, usually stingy congressmen how desperately the Park Service needed appropriations.

When the road came to an end, we walked up to Sun Temple, excavated only two years before by the famous archaeologist Jesse Walter Fewkes. Although hundreds of cliff dwellings, hidden away in almost inaccessible alcoves, had been discovered and many explored, there had never been evidence of manmade structures on the surface top of the mesa. Fewkes became interested in a great mound of earth near the edge of Chapin Mesa almost directly across the canyon from Cliff Palace, the largest cliff dwelling in the park. It had a depressed, circular center covered by trees and shrubs. When it was excavated, he discovered a huge,

D-shaped building, undoubtedly a religious center, for it had no sign of living quarters. It was stunning. Even the ruins, located on the great promontory and imposing in size, over one thousand feet of walls, were awesome. Imagine what a sight it must have been to those living in the surrounding cliff villages when it was in pristine condition.

The panoramic view from about 8,500 feet elevation (or 2,000 above the Montezuma and Mancos Valleys) was breathtaking. You could see forever. To the southwest lay the Four Corners region, the only place in America where four states, Utah, Arizona, New Mexico, and Colorado, joined at right angles. The Abajo and La Sal mountains could be seen in distant Utah, while the great Sleeping Ute Mountain appeared to hug the Mesa Verde. To the north we could see the towering, snow-capped La Plata Range of the Rockies, to the south the Chuskas, and to the east dim Sangre de Cristos. Rivers weaving through the valleys, even the great monolith of Shiprock, seemed like miniatures from our promontory.

Mesa Verde was true to its name, a rich verdant green, cut by the deep canyons holding the ancient cities tight against their walls. The pristine, awesome beauty of the Southwest lay before us like a great painting by God.

As we walked around to the east, the beauty of Sun Temple was dwarfed by our first sight of the majesty of Cliff Palace, below and across from us on the east face of Cliff Canyon. From that distance, it appeared to be a westward-facing small city floating on perpendicular walls, with its stone structures impressive, well formed, and seemingly intact. The golden glow cast by the setting sun made it ethereal, unearthly. My imagination gave me the sensation of looking through a veil of light to people still alive in their world of hundreds of years ago. Here my fascination for these Anasazi, or ancient ones, was born, and so it has always remained.

Back at the "village," or Spruce Tree Camp, where we were to spend the night, we gratefully ate a hearty dinner. Collapsing after an especially memorable day, we rolled onto cots in our tents. However, it wasn't a particularly restful night. A terrific storm rolled in with thunder, lightning, and torrents of rain. The tent proved to be adequate, but the thought of lightning striking all around this wooded area made me pretty uneasy.

It was still dark when I woke up and decided to see the cliff ruins of Spruce Tree House by dawn. I threw on some clothes. Lots of them. It was mighty cold at 8,500 feet. As I came out of my tent, Steele called from his adjacent tent, "Hey, where ya going? Wait for me." We two were about to set off down a rough, winding path to the "village" of 114 rooms deep in the canyon when a young Navajo stopped us and asked where we were going. When he learned what we intended to do, he immediately warned us not to go alone and volunteered to guide us to Spruce Tree House. It was a good thing. Although the storm had passed, the rain had played havoc with the trail. It was a tough scramble, treacherously slippery. This taught me that Mesa Verde needed lots of work on trails as well as roads.

The sun cast its first peach-colored rays into the canyon while we remained in the shadows of the overhanging cliffs, ancient walls, and kivas. Standing deep in the ruins of Spruce Tree House, we were speechless. It was more incredible up close than from afar. The enormous size of the place, 216 feet long, was deceiving. Built in the thirteenth century, it had amazingly intricate masonry work and architectural details. No one could call this civilization a primitive society.

Returning to the top, breathless and muddy all over, we met Rickner, who was seething. He couldn't bawl us out, so he took it out on the young Navajo, blaming him for letting us go down and also for not reporting where we were. Apparently he had been scared that the acting director had wandered off some cliff. We quietly apologized but exonerated the poor Indian.

Later I got Rickner alone and gave him a few choice words of my own about treating his workers, especially his Indians, in a fair and civil manner. To calm things down, I suggested we work over proposed plans for the park in the few hours I had left before our train departed from Mancos.

"Few hours?" repeated Rickner. "Mr. Albright, you can't go anyplace. The storm made the Knife Edge Road impassable, and I ordered it closed. It's just a murky mess, slides, rocks still falling down. Neither you nor anyone else could go up or down." He went on to say that he had sent out every available person from the top and called for extra men from Mancos below to do an emergency cleanup.

Rickner enlightened me about "normal" conditions of this road. It was so steep that a quarter of the cars trying to come up to the mesa just couldn't make it. Next, it was so narrow that cars couldn't pass. So travel on this road was regulated by telephone in the supervisor's office. No cars were allowed to meet on the hill. They were held at the bottom or the top until the road was clear.

Before going any further, I should tell how we were finally able to fix that Knife Edge Road. I brought my photos taken after the storm around to friends on the Appropriations Committee, which resulted in a new road being started in 1918. However, we immediately ran into a problem.

Mesa Verde National Park had been created in 1906, and a vital addition, including Cliff Palace, was made in 1913. The Ute Indians traded this land for a much larger acreage of their own choice. At the time they were glad to get rid of the mesa land, for they rarely went near it, having a superstitious feeling that it was accursed. It was the land of the spirits. At this time the park was still pretty much surrounded by reservation. Another part of the deal was that the federal government had guaranteed annual supplies for the Utes' farms and homes.

Now we learned that the Indians had a good supply of gravel needed to lay a firm bed on the proposed road in Mesa Verde. Congress actually appropriated a sufficient sum to purchase it, but the Utes flatly refused to do business with a government they hated. Again and again they refused. Time passed, and finally Congressman Louis Cramton of Michigan came out to the park to see what he could do. There was a meeting of Cramton, Park Service men, and the Ute council. After hearing all the arguments, proposals, and sums of money offered, the council stood firm. No gravel.

But the curious old chief asked why the Indians had gravel and the United States government did not. A ranger explained that in ancient times a river ran through Ute valley lands and deposited the gravel there but not up on the mesa. The council adjourned to think about that. After some time, the chief returned to say they would sell the gravel "when the river ran across their land once more."

Cramton listened solemnly. He then explained that he was "chief of the council" in the United States Congress that decided how much money would be given for the annual Ute supplies. He added that, unless they sold the gravel to the park to make the road safe for travel, whether wet or dry, snow or sun, rain or dust, there would be no more money for supplies for the Ute tribe "until the river ran again across their lands."

The chief rose slowly and, with great dignity, withdrew once more with his council. This time he was gone only a few minutes. When he returned, he announced that the Ute council had reconsidered the "splendid offer" and desired to "help" the Park Service in its troubles. The gravel would be sold. And thus the Indians once more learned the ways of the United States government. But it must be added that the Utes received everything promised while the government finally got a new safe, well-designed, two-lane road. It even had parapets.

Seeing we were stuck in this fascinating place, we happily made the best of it. It was quite a day, and I couldn't possibly name or describe everything we saw. Our group never gave up until darkness forced us back to Spruce Tree Camp. After dinner the same young Navajo guide gave a fascinating talk at a large campfire to our group and maybe thirty campers, stuck like ourselves on top of the mesa. He was very poignant in his story of Navajo beliefs about the balance that should be honored between the land, nature and its creatures, and human beings. .

The next morning we were told by Rickner that the road was in desperate condition but that our car only would be allowed to navigate the treacherous way down. It was some experience. Several times we had to pile out of the auto. Our extra weight would have sunk it beyond all hope in the muck. Then there were the "flying rocks" unexpectedly showering down from the cliffs. We were terrorized when this happened, but we dodged them. Mudslides also added a little pepper to the descent. We arrived at Mancos and once more boarded Wadleigh's grand little car.

I left Mesa Verde with as much regret as I had felt when I left Zion. In both, I had gained a great deal of experience and knowledge in national park problems and administration. In Mesa Verde I had been confronted with a totally different type of park. The natural wonders Mather emphasized were certainly there, but the whole horizon of historical and scientific interests was even more pronounced and fascinating.

Wadleigh's original schedule had called for a narrow-gauge trip up the Animas River gorge from Durango to Silverton and a detour on the "Chile Line" to Santa Fe. The extra time in Mesa Verde had canceled them. Instead, we finished the segment of the Grand Loop through Cumbres Pass to Alamosa, in the San Luis Valley, and then on the Denver, where I stayed only a short time before boarding a train for Washington.

We had just completed one of the most exciting, spectacular "Grand Tours" I'd ever experienced up to that time—or maybe ever since. As I lay in my Pullman berth that last night, I went over every inch of it and tried to assess the results of the last week or so. I felt I had matured a lot, had gained a great deal of confidence by making far-reaching decisions on my own, though always trying to do what I felt Mr. Mather would approve. I certainly gained an enormous fund of knowledge about Colorado, the national park areas currently in the system, their condition, how they were operated, and what needed to be done.

Light at the End of the Tunnel
1917

Back in Washington on September 17, I was appalled by the stacks of mail, reports, *Congressional Records*, and other paper on my desk. One bright spot was three letters from Mather. This Colorado trip had cut us off from each other except for some postcards I had hurriedly scrawled along the way. Happily, his letters showed that he was in fine health and good spirits. His next one, written on September 20, really had great news: "Glad to know you are back on the job again after your strenuous summer. . . . I may get down to Washington next week for a day or so, stopping on the way in Philadelphia to see Dr. Weisenburg and get his o.k."

Mr. Mather arrived in Washington on September 27. Dr. Weisenburg had given permission for him to stay only until October 1, but he seemed to be in fine health, both mentally and physically. Actually, I didn't get to see too much of him during those three days. I set him up in a pleasant suite at the Shoreham Hotel. His many friends watched over him like mother hens, quietly entertaining him in small groups and avoiding any excitement or worrisome subjects. Grace and I usually accompanied him at dinner time along with other Washington acquaintances.

Mather made only one visit to the Interior Department, just an hour or so to inspect the new offices of the National Park Service. He was as delighted as a child with the location, the decoration of his office, and the brief meeting with his personnel. He did not ask to see Secretary

Lane. I don't think he ever did meet him on this visit, but he did talk to him over the phone. He didn't express any desire to step back as director.

It was just as well, for I guess Mather wasn't quite as well as Grace and I thought. Dr. Weisenburg wrote me on October 8:

As you know I had a long talk with Mr. Mather and had a very good opportunity to see just how much improvement he has made. I do not think that he is well enough as yet to assume charge of the department. He still lacks confidence in himself, has many fears about his health, etc., is quite frequently gloomy and is not capable of sustained mental effort. It would, however, be an excellent thing for him if it could be managed to have him in Washington where first of all he would be away from Mrs. Mather, who herself admits that it is about time for him to get away from her, and secondly it would be of the utmost benefit to him to be able to do some work, for he is capable of some mental effort. Of course it would be all wrong to put any responsibility up to him. If, for example, he could take charge of a department with the understanding that you should do the very important work and that nothing should be done without your approval, the plan could be worked out.

I answered the doctor on October 10:

Ever since I saw him in the West the latter part of August, I have been perfectly sure that the most advisable thing for him to do would be to come down here and undertake the easy ends of the National Park Service work. There is nothing in the world that interests him so much as the park work, and there is nothing that gives him so much pleasure. . . . I have worked very hard the past year and have got the administrative work of the National Park Service in such condition that I can handle it without any difficulty, and I can keep Mr. Mather from worrying and fretting over any phases of the work. . . . He doesn't know much more about the details of the Park Service work now than you do, and I don't propose to let him acquaint himself with them. . . . Secretary Lane is very anxious to have him down here, and he does not care whether he does any work or not. He knows, as all of us do, that Mr. Mather can accomplish more while he is enjoying himself at luncheons and is with his friends on automobile trips or around the club than he could accomplish in his office. It would have done your heart good to have seen him when he was here last week. He enjoyed his new office as much as a little boy does his new red wagon.

Temporarily Mr. Mather didn't choose to get back to Washington and pick up the reins in the Park Service. But I was optimistic that we'd have him back some time soon. Not so. Supervisor Lewis reported to me shortly thereafter that Mather had turned up in Yosemite apparently concerned with the Desmond Company, had a few secretive meetings with people associated with it, and went back to Chicago. I was told nothing and I made no inquiries. Sometimes I felt the less I knew about Mather's dealings with Desmond, the better off the service and I would be.

In the meantime, I only had a few days to finish the annual report of the Park Service and prepare the financial estimates for the upcoming year. Fortunately, I had asked all supervisors and custodians to send me their reports and data at the close of the fiscal year in June. I had many of these with me as I was traveling in the West. With the help of my little portable typewriter, I had been able to write up a rough draft of the annual report. Maps, statistics, and the polishing of the total project were completed back in Washington with the invaluable help of Isabelle Story, Arthur Demaray, and Bob Yard.

With the report out of the way, I tackled the financial situation for the next fiscal year. As I wrote a friend, "I am overwhelmed with the work of writing my annual report and preparing the estimates for the next fiscal year and really ought not to take the time to go home and sleep!" That pretty well summed up our lives. My dearest, long-suffering Grace cooked food that could be held and heated up when I finally got home. We managed some conversation while I ate, and then it was off to bed for me while she cleaned up alone. Some life my precious girl enjoyed, but she never once complained.

I wrote Mather on October 17: "I got the report in about an hour before midnight on the 15th and now have a little time to take up some of the matters that will be interesting to you." These included arrangements for him to return to Washington to live at the Shoreham.

But he wrote back: "I think I will be here for awhile. I do not see my way clear to come down for sometime yet." Well, I didn't take no for an answer and wrote him on October 24:

> Everything is fixed up for you here, including temporary quarters at the Shoreham with Mr. Bradley and tentative plans for your enjoying the morning gymnasium class on the top of the Powhatan with Secretary Vogelsang and a number of other officers high in official life.

However, if you do not care for the class, I have arranged to go into the gymnasium 3 times a week with you at 4:30. I am going to do this because the doctor tells me you need to continue your exercises.

However, Mather still wouldn't give me any date for his return to Washington.

I pored over the estimates for the next fiscal year and finally got them out of my way. With Mather in Chicago, apparently with no immediate plans to come to Washington, I had to focus my attention on policy-making problems, many of which arose from that annual report. There was widespread coverage of it by newspapers in areas adjacent to particular national parks or monuments. Some were hearty in their praise, others nasty and troublesome for us.

Our plans for a Greater Sequoia received the most publicity, which seemed terrific at the time although we later realized it had alerted all kinds of people to block us. Being young and naive, I wrote Jesse Agnew, a firm supporter in Visalia: "We are going to drive the Sequoia Bill pretty hard during the coming session of Congress. Most of the influential Forest Service men are in France and I think we can overpower those who are left here. . . . We are going to try to put the bill through before the opposition can get thoroughly organized."

We were also ready for a major push to enlarge Yellowstone, to make its boundaries conform more closely to the reality of what nature had delineated in the flow of waters and drift of the animals. It took over thirty years just to save the Jackson Hole, but the borders of original Yellowstone never have been rounded out as we visualized them at this time.

Organization in the Park Service was another thing that required some concentration during this quiet stage. The overriding concern with the war precluded implementation of most of my ideas and plans, but I felt standards must be set up immediately. As far as possible, uniformity must prevail throughout the system. Personnel of high caliber were impossible to recruit while fighting men were needed. However, I had gotten to know most of our top-ranking men. I knew which of them could handle their areas with more or less responsibility.

They, in turn, needed confidence and pride in their work and a uniformity in title. So on November 1, 1917, I ordered the designation of "superintendent" to cover all national park executives. I had never understood the matter of one park, like insignificant Platt, having a superintendent while another, like Mount Rainier, had a supervisor. The title of "custodian" remained for the national monuments.

Although most employees of the Park Service in Washington were covered by civil service, I held back pushing this for field personnel. Until Mather returned, I was hesitant to freeze some of them into the service. I knew he had likes and dislikes and would want to replace many. Actually, it didn't matter that much as there were so few personnel at this time in any park area. We'd have a lot of problems to solve before we could organize and hire large forces of rangers after the war. Among these would be applicants with little training or education in this naturalist field, lack of job security without civil service, lack of housing.

There was no housing for married men and little for bachelors. The latter usually got lodging in a nearby town, in a ranger station, or worse, in a tent or lean-to in the woods. For the time being, I would let well enough alone. Later, when the time seemed appropriate, I did step in to push through civil service status for our people.

Long hours were spent with various authorities interested in the national parks, listening to their ideas. I took their knowledge and recommendations into account when formulating future plans and then wrote outlines for discussions with Secretary Lane.

Lane was not a man of any great intellectual capacity, hated details, and was impatient with the pros and cons of a given subject. Unless it was political or directly concerned himself, he would form a tipi with his fingers, nod sagely, and say, "Verrry interesting. Verrry interesting. Why don't you just go ahead. See how it works out and let me know."

So my list of discussions to be held with Lane over future National Park Service plans came down to just one—the standardization of the uniform. Lane was most interested in that. He had to hear how each recommended article of clothing had originated, what the color was to be, who was to be the manufacturer. This really caught his attention, for he had various acquaintants in the clothing business that he suggested I contact. I reminded him that Mather had expressed his desire to settle those details. All I had to do was pass on a uniform—"uniform" meaning everyone in the field Park Service was to wear the same thing, thereby eliminating the wild assortment of boots, shoes, scarves, and hats with which our free-spirited men were now decorating themselves.

For the most part, they accepted a design by Mark Daniels, which was pretty much a combination of the Forest Service style and color with bits of the army here and there. For years, Mather and I could never totally quash the ingenuity of our various officials when it came to their uniforms. Especially Colonel John White, later superintendent of Sequoia. I'll bet Mather fired him ten times for his rakish hats and swishing baton. (Of course, he was hired back every time.)

In general, plans were made for the 1918 tourist season or for after the war. The uncertainty of the war as well as the almost total lack of money put much on hold. However, I plodded along, putting my plans on paper for uniformity in building and landscaping, campground rules, acceptance of gifts to the government of land, pay scales, wildlife problems, expansion of the system (especially Sequoia and Yellowstone), information centers for the parks, and programs for rangers to enlighten and aid the tourists. I kept a file in my desk and when an idea struck would pull it out and jot it down.

And then there was Enos Mills once more. Lordy, how I used to pray he would just get off my back for a few months. He had misinterpreted a few lines in the annual report about parks in the Denver area. What about the Mount Evans region? Why had I spent so much time in California instead of Colorado? And on and on. I spent more energy on explanations than I should have, but his influence was enormous, and he was a dangerous fellow to cross.

A few weeks later he seemed to have forgotten the original gripe and now took off after me about Bob Yard: "I find that a number of National Park enthusiasts throughout the country do not trust him. For very good reasons I have not for more than a year. If it ever comes to a show-down I shall say so to officials higher up and also denounce him before the public."

It took a few letters to discover that Mills regarded Yard as a secret agent for the despised Forest Service and believed that he was using his official position "to screen the insidious work of the Forest Service." It took more letters and a lot of soft soap to quiet him on this subject— temporarily.

Although Mills was bad news in my life, I had good news too. Absolutely joyful news arrived with the resignation of our old enemy, Congressman John Joseph Fitzgerald, as of December 31, 1917.

Ever since returning from the West, I had been attacking the problem Fitzgerald had created concerning troops in Yellowstone. My main argument centered on the war: that soldiers were badly needed in Europe to fight the Germans, not loll around a national park. On September 25 I persuaded Secretary Lane to write Secretary of War Newton D. Baker about the troops. I even sketched out a rough draft for him, so there'd be no mistake about our purpose.

Lane's letter stated: "The employment of troops in the protection of national parks, as you have again and again emphasized, is from every military point of view undesirable. . . . I propose to submit an estimate for an appropriation that will make possible the early withdrawal of the troops now stationed in the Yellowstone and the reorganization of the civilian ranger force. This estimate will be included in the budget of the National Park Service for the next fiscal year."

When Lane reached the next section of my outline, he looked up quizzically and asked, "Albright, don't you think we've gone far enough for this time?"

"Well, Mr. Secretary," I replied, "What have we got to lose? The generals over at the War Department have bigger things to think about. They may just accidentally overlook this demand." And so the memo continued: "Another question of policy that I believe we should submit to Congress through the medium of the estimates this year—should not the National Park Service, rather than the Engineer Corps of the Army, be charged hereafter with the construction and maintenance of roads in Yellowstone and Crater Lake National Parks? The Service has control of work of this character in all other national parks." As I wrote Mather the same day, "We are 'out for blood' this time."

My enthusiasm got ahead of events. Another letter to Mather on October 17 reported: "The Engineer Corps of the War Department double-crossed us on the Yellowstone and Crater Lake estimates. They did not give Secretary Baker a chance to look at Secretary Lane's letter until the day the estimates were to go in, and then it was too late for us to do anything with them. I hope I may never run across another body of men that I dislike as much as the Engineer Corps of the Army. They are the most determined and self-centered lot of men that draw salaries from the Government."

The end of Fitzgerald's reign of terror at the House Appropriations Committee and the elevation of Swager Sherley of Kentucky to his position brought about the removal of troops from Yellowstone and provided funds for the reorganization of the ranger force there. The last of the cavalry departed at the end of the 1917–18 fiscal year, and on June 10, 1918, Congress turned Yellowstone National Park over to the exclusive jurisdiction of the National Park Service, thus removing the Army Engineers from that park as well as from Crater Lake. It was the end of sharing administration of national parks with other sectors of the federal government. "I guess you could call it the 'separation of powers,'" I wrote Mather.

Without warning, Mr. Mather suddenly appeared in Washington on November 5 and stated that he would resume his normal activities as director of the National Park Service. On the surface, we all deferred to him and gave the impression to the public that he was completely back to normal, but we carefully screened his mail, his phone calls, and everyone who wished to see him. I also made sure Weisenburg's instructions were carried out to the letter: "Let him come to the office and play director but you keep all problems away from him and you do all the work." In view of that, Lane, with Mather's consent, kept me in the position of acting director.

After breakfast and a workout at the gymnasium, Mather would come into his office about eleven o'clock, read his mail (which I had already screened for any problems or disturbing news), and dictate letters to his secretary. Then he would call me in for maybe an hour of discussion, go to lunch with friends, usually at the Cosmos Club, and seldom return to Interior. A favorite pastime was to rummage in the scrapbooks the Albrights had made for him.

I'm not entirely sure what he did most of the afternoons. Various people filled me in that, after a leisurely lunch with him, they might then accompany him to the zoo or the Smithsonian, drive in the country, or stroll along the Potomac. In any case, I was satisfied that he was contented and not involved in anything that might upset his health. I was also careful in letters I wrote to people interested in the Park Service to add that Mr. Mather was back and had enjoyed "a complete recovery." Although I wasn't all that confident, physically he looked healthier every day and appeared to be mentally bright and cheerful.

However, just as suddenly as he had arrived in Washington, he departed. He simply called me in one morning and told me that he was returning to Chicago—"two weeks here, two weeks in Chicago." No reason, nothing the matter. Only three weeks after his arrival, he pulled out.

That same day I had written Dr. Weisenburg: "He has grown stronger and healthier and is taking a great interest in his work, although he gets the blues once in a while." I added that Mather had been immersed in Desmond Company affairs, and "it is hard to keep him from worrying about them."

Actually, he had gotten so upset over Desmond's affairs, not knowing details, that I finally broke down one day and gave him all the information I had. I feared that his fretting over Desmond's mess would be more detrimental than just plain letting him have the facts. Happily, he worked over the financial sheets, dictated a few letters to Dohrmann, and appeared to be the better for satisfying his curiosity. I took the precaution, though, of letting Weisenburg know what I had done in case Mather's reaction turned out to be adverse.

I was at a loss to know why Mather had gone back to Chicago. I never did get the answer. Mrs. Mather wrote me to say she was worried about her husband's health, his cough. And all I learned from Dr. Weisenburg was that Mather was doing just fine, but he cautioned me not to discuss his former illness. "He knows nothing of his old lung trouble." Lung trouble? I never did know what all that meant and never asked. I was simply too relieved that there was no problem with his mental and nervous condition.

The year 1917 was drawing to a close. I can't say I was sorry to put it behind me. It had been a brutal time in some respects: Stephen Mather's prolonged illness and gradual recovery, organizing the Park Service, fighting for appropriations, setting up policies, fighting the commercial interests' attempts to use our parks, traveling thousands of miles but learning an encyclopedia about the National Park Service, its individual unit problems, reclamation, wild animals, and on and on. I felt I had matured, had tried to pattern myself in the image of my chief, Mr. Mather, and had been rewarded by a credible performance for him and the National Park Service.

Probably the worst thing about 1917 was that my work had kept me away from my lovely Grace entirely too much. Looking back, I realize that I saw very little of her until near the end of the year. She never complained. She always understood my compulsive need to fulfill what I regarded as my duty.

Not until December, when Mather had gone back to Chicago and government work slowed to a crawl, did Grace and I finally spend time together. And did we have fun! We had snowball fights in Rock Creek Park. We went to the zoo several times. We had a lovely weekend in Annapolis. We even wrote an article for the *Northwestern Motorist Magazine* together. I contributed the facts, and, as she was a much better writer, she put it all together. It was really exciting when we saw it in print early in

1918. Although it included pictures of Mather and me, the editors deleted Grace's name as co-author. Such was the lot of women in 1918.

Over the holidays we spent many evenings catching up with friends, the Yards, the Marshalls, and the Gidneys. We went out alone to the theater, to dinner and dancing. On New Year's Eve we remembered Mather's dinner a year ago. We decided to splurge some carefully saved cash and go to the same hotel and celebrate.

And what did we have to celebrate? The main thing was that we had managed to survive this past year. We had overcome the strain of separation, the concern for Mather's health, and for me the stress of organizing the new Park Service and making the solitary crucial decisions affecting its future. Balancing all this was the fact that we had grown stronger through the experiences. Grace summed it up: "We're young. We're healthy. We have a love that just grows deeper as it gets tested by fire."

We were always confident about our future. Especially now, with Mr. Mather apparently recovered and eager to take over once more, we felt we would soon be free of Washington. So on New Year's Eve, had we had been drinkers, we would have had a toast in champagne to that.

Little did we know that 1918 would be nearly as much of a trial as 1917.

Park and Resource Preservation
1918

With the New Year, the primary issue for me was the Grand Canyon. I had spent many hours in the past year on the problem, but now I vowed to put the same kind of energy into this as I had in trying to have a park service created. It was essential, not only on general principles but to give Mather's morale a real boost. To make this incomparable chasm a national park was a long and difficult project.

It began on January 5, 1886, when Benjamin Harrison, then United States senator from Indiana, introduced a bill in Congress to make Grand Canyon a national park. It failed to pass. As our first great conservationist president (1889–93), Harrison set aside 17,564,800 acres of Forest Reserve in 1893 and placed its administration in the Department of the Interior. The Grand Canyon area was part of this.

In 1905 all the Forest Reserves were transferred from the Interior Department to the Agriculture Department. In 1906 the Antiquities Act was passed, enabling presidents to establish national monuments without the consent of Congress. In the same year President Theodore Roosevelt used this power to proclaim Grand Canyon a national monument, which he placed in the newly created Forest Service of the Department of Agriculture. In 1917 this was the status quo, the base from which the Park Service launched its attack.

At that time, Secretary of Agriculture David F. Houston was agreeable to a transfer of the Grand Canyon to Interior, but while not openly opposing the move, he was doing nothing to speed it along. His favorite trick was to say "yes" but stall or block us by haggling over boundaries. Mather and I had caught on to him and were determined not to let him keep us in limbo this time. But it turned out that a bigger stumbling block was Ralph Cameron and his claims in, around, and down the Grand Canyon.

Lured by accounts of adventure in the "Wild West" and visions of money-making schemes, Cameron and his brothers left Maine around 1880 and rode as far as the rails in the Southwest could take them at the time—Flagstaff, Arizona. They went into the sheep-herding business. Shortly afterward they visited the Grand Canyon and visualized its potential as a profitable tourist trap—the Niagara Falls of the West!

So the Camerons, plus some acquaintances around Coconino County, quickly filed claims along the South Rim of the canyon and down into the chasm. By the time the Grand Canyon was made a national monument in 1906, they had over one hundred lode, placer, and millsite claims from Grand View Point to Hermit Creek, the finest scenic area on the South Rim.

They wasted no time in working a few mining spots and improving an ancient Havasupai Indian trail from the rim to the Colorado River, calling it the Cameron Trail (later known as Bright Angel Trail). They took dead aim at the tourists, charging them one dollar each for use of the trail, whether on foot or on mule back. If they rode to the bottom of the canyon, there was an additional fee for the mules. Here the poor, stranded tourists were usually hit by their "guide" with another "four-bits" demand in order to get back up to the rim.

Halfway down, on their Indian Gardens claim, the Camerons set up a ramshackle place called a "hotel," which had the only drinkable water available. They even charged for the "comfort stations" along the way. What a deal, and it was all theirs!

But only until the Atchison, Topeka, and Santa Fe Railroad appeared on the scene. By an act of Congress, a small company had been granted a right-of-way for a rail line from Williams to the Grand Canyon. It had also been granted rights for the Cameron–Bright Angel Trail to the Colorado River. However, the project failed financially, when rails were completed only halfway from Williams.

The Santa Fe bought it out and finished the line. At the terminus on the South Rim, they constructed a railroad station and El Tovar, a large, luxurious, rustic-style hotel to be operated by the famous Fred Harvey

Company. At the turn of the century, conflict between the Santa Fe Railroad and Ralph Cameron was inevitable.

Ralph Cameron was a master politician, manipulator, and artful dodger. He threw up splintery shacks by the Santa Fe railroad station and put up signs on his claims nearby (one of which read "The Buttinski Mine"). The Santa Fe loudly complained to the United States government. The Forest Service was sympathetic and sided with the railroad. After a lengthy legal fight, the quarrel reached the Supreme Court, which canceled the Cameron claims. In 1906 Cameron's franchise for the Bright Angel Trail expired, and it reverted to Coconino County.

Did that make any difference? Not to Cameron. By now he had entered politics and was a member of the county's Board of Supervisors and controlled it. All these roadblocks were just flies in the ointment to Cameron. He blithely carried on as though the pot of gold at the end of the rainbow was beckoning him and nothing could get in the way of his plans.

Cameron next applied for a permit to build a scenic railway along the South Rim. Not only was it denied, but the Santa Fe was given permission to build roads, trails, and tourist facilities in that area. Cameron quickly hit on another scheme to fix those opposed to him. He used his claims, which bisected the Santa Fe's proposed road, to halt construction every time the road bumped into them. So here was a fine macadam road abruptly halting at a Cameron claim, turning into a dusty rut in summer and a murky mess in winter. Continuing on the other side, it became macadam once more until it met the next Cameron claim.

Now Cameron planned to set up a company to extract gold from the sands of the river. He crowed, "I have always said that I would make more money out of the Grand Canyon than any other man." But this scheme also failed for the simple reason that he didn't have title to the land.

Cameron shrugged and instantly became involved in a new scheme. He would dam the Colorado River and make a fortune from hydroelectric power. Someone said, "He could charm a bird out of a tree." I guess he did, because almost immediately he had a "pigeon," a fellow named C. Frank Doebler. Together they formed the Hydraulic Properties Company. Of course, they had title neither to the land where they planned to build the dam nor to the mighty Colorado River. The United States government hadn't given permission to do anything. To Ralph Cameron there was no problem he felt he couldn't fix.

Cameron had been the territorial delegate to Congress prior to Arizona's admission to the union in 1912. Now, in 1914, he decided he would simply run for governor. Of course, he would be elected. Then he would be in a position to make the dam a reality. But there was one stumbling block. He was defeated by George W. P. Hunt.

After many secret cabals, an agreement between the Santa Fe and Cameron interests was signed in 1916. Details remained vague and hidden in the mists. The railroad paid some forty thousand dollars to the Cameron group and thereby acquired all the claims along the South Rim and water rights at Indian Gardens. Somehow Cameron still kept the hydroelectric and mining rights as well as rights-of-way across claims deeded to the Santa Fe. Either the Santa Fe lawyers weren't careful enough or Cameron was too crafty for them. Representatives from various bureaus in the Interior and Agriculture Departments tried to unearth details of the deal, but they were efficiently buried. We never did learn the true facts.

It was at this point that the National Park Service was doing everything in its power to get control of Grand Canyon National Monument and turn it into a national park. But what sort of a mess were we faced with? There was opposition from stock growers wanting to have unlimited grazing rights. Reclamation and irrigation people were looking forward to future Colorado River dams. The Forest Service was trying to hang on to every foot of land they could. There were scores of legal problems, contradictory claims, and water problems.

Even though Indian Gardens was now in Santa Fe hands, Cameron's horses had polluted this sole source of clean water. Typhoid germs had been detected. His miserable, unsightly buildings, equipment, mining machinery, and other debris were scattered everywhere. His sheep and cattle had grazed both North and South Rims, almost wiping out the natural ground cover.

I was depressed and at a loss to know what could be done about it until we could get a bill through Congress to acquire jurisdiction. The laborious job would be to collar the key representatives and senators to introduce bills to make Grand Canyon National Monument a national park. Next the power brokers had to be assembled to settle differences and then see if the compromise bill could be passed by both houses.

Deep down I felt we were at a dead end until the war ended, but I was never one to quit when the goal was as vital as this one was. Mather desperately wanted this park. I felt it would be a tremendous boost to his health and well-being if I could push it through, so I put in an enormous amount of time and energy on the project.

At the instigation of President Taft, bills had been introduced in the Congress in 1910 and 1911 but had died in committee. At the present time we had fine support from influential individuals, publications, and organizations, including the Sierra Club, the Appalachian Club, and national magazines. Powerful interests in Congress were with us. With the admission of Arizona as the forty-eighth state in 1912, impetus had picked up with the strong backing of its new representatives in Congress, Senator Henry Ashurst and Representative Carl Hayden. We had pinned hopes on the fact that these Democrats would receive support from President Wilson, but this was one president that didn't care a fig for conservation.

A bill to create the Grand Canyon National Park was presented to the Sixty-fourth Congress, but it adjourned on March 3, 1917, without passage. As soon as the new Sixty-fifth Congress was seated in April 1917, another bill was introduced. Nothing came of it either until the third session.

Talking over the problem with Secretary Lane, I suggested he get into the fight. He was rather gun-shy of openly advocating controversial measures since Hetch Hetchy, so I suggested he could send a forceful letter up to the Capitol. He agreed to do that. On February 5, 1918, Lane signed a letter I had drawn up for him and sent it to Senator H. L. Myers, chairman of the Public Lands Committee. It was a strong statement, which reviewed the outstanding features of the Grand Canyon and urgently pressed for national park status. Shortly thereafter, on May 16, 1918, the Senate passed the park bill.

Well, of course, that wasn't the end of it. There were snags in the House and further negotiations with the Forest Service. Finally agreement was reached with a revised boundary map drawn up with the help of Ashurst and Hayden. The revised bill got through both houses and, on February 26, 1919, was signed into law. Grand Canyon National Park was a reality.

It wasn't all joy and light, though, for it came into the National Park System with boundaries still so limited and with so many strings attached that our relief was also mixed with concern for the problems ahead. As it turned out, our fears were justified. Worse troubles lay ahead of us, troubles just beginning in 1920 when Ralph Cameron was elected United States senator from Arizona. I still shudder thinking about it, but that's a story all its own.

On the morning of February 15, 1918, I woke up feeling sick and quickly found myself quarantined with a treasonable case of German measles. Informed of my incapacity, Mather wrote a most unsympathetic letter to me. "It certainly was too bad that you had to be laid up just at this time and not even be able to get in touch with the office except by telephone." Along with the pleasure of my wife's company during my incarceration, I continued to work on Park Service business via my little portable typewriter.

When I returned to the office, Sieur de Monts National Monument in Maine was the most important issue. It was the first national park area east of the Mississippi, created only a year and a half before. This was very important to me. I firmly believed our service should encompass areas throughout the United States. There were so many exciting and beautiful regions in the East that should be preserved. People living there should not be forced to travel thousands of miles to enjoy a national park. There was also the practical side of the issue. Most of the population of America lived in the East, and more representatives in the Congress came from this section. I reasoned that they would therefore pay more attention to the National Park Service and its needs, financial and otherwise. Aside from all these considerations, this particular monument was close to my heart because of George Dorr.

Shortly after I joined the Interior Department in 1913, a distinguished-looking gentleman quietly and rather timidly entered the office. He introduced himself as George Dorr of Bar Harbor, Maine. He wished to see Secretary Lane. I told him that this was Mr. Miller's office, that both were away in the West, but that I was authorized to make appointments for the secretary. He looked like the Washington heat had worn him out, so I suggested he sit down while I went for a cool drink. I brought back a pitcher of water. He gratefully drank several glasses and then related his reasons for wishing to see Lane. It was a fascinating story.

George Dorr came from New England aristocracy. His mother's ancestors had accumulated vast wealth from the China trade. He had a home on Mount Desert Island in Maine. Fearful of unchecked development in this scenic area, he started a movement in 1900 to save the rugged land around his island and Seal Harbor. A few years later this led to the formation of an organization under the leadership of Dorr and Dr. Charles W. Eliot, president of Harvard University. It was designed to hold in trust land donated by local citizens. Its purpose was "that all in the future might find in it the pleasure, health and inspiration we have found;

to save it from the encroachments of commercialism; and to conserve the wild life, both plant and animal, whose native habitat it was." I copied those exact words from a letter Dorr showed me to explain the dream he and his friends had. I was most impressed by the man and the ideals for which he stood. I made an appointment for him to see Lane when he returned.

Apparently Lane was also impressed, as were many influential people in the government to whom I introduced Dorr. Sieur de Monts National Monument was proclaimed on July 8, 1916, and Dorr was named custodian. It was a notable event because it was the first national park area created entirely by private donations (except for tiny Muir Woods in California).

The Hancock County Trustees, who had been holding the gifts of land, turned everything over to the federal government, but the House Appropriations Committee under Fitzgerald ignored this new monument as it had all our other neglected monuments. No money was allocated for two more years. That was the condition of Sieur de Monts at the beginning of 1918.

Secretary Lane, along with his wife, had stayed with Dorr at his home in Maine the previous summer, had enjoyed the visit immensely, and had become a true champion of the monument. When Dorr came down to Washington to see about the financial problem, I suggested he bombard the new chairman of the Appropriations Committee, Swager Sherley. Let him understand the history of the monument and its needs, show him appeals from important and influential people.

I assured him that Secretary Lane and the National Park Service would do everything in their power to help. Dorr and I also agreed that, while we were at it, we could try to change the status of the monument to a national park as I was doing with Mukuntuweap in Utah.

Around May 1918, Dorr sent me a little booklet containing a dozen or so printed letters written to Sherley by an assortment of men, including Theodore Roosevelt. Everyone pleaded for the fifty-thousand-dollar appropriation Lane had requested for the monument. I guess we all knew Sieur de Monts was never going to get fifty thousand dollars, but, by golly, it did get ten thousand.

What's more, bills were introduced in the Congress early in 1918 to make it a national park. On February 26, 1919, President Wilson simultaneously signed bills creating Grand Canyon National Park and Lafayette National Park. The name change was to honor the famous Frenchman who had fought alongside Washington in the Revolutionary War and for our soldiers who had recently served so bravely in France.

Dorr and I really didn't approve of the name, but we went along with it until I became director of the service in 1929. Then I pushed through the name we had chosen years before, Acadia National Park.

Shortly after I visited Mukuntuweap and trumpeted its beauty, newspapers and magazines joined me in promoting the idea of having it made a national park. Senator Reed Smoot of Utah took the first step toward that status by getting a bill through Congress in March 1918 that changed the name to Zion National Monument.

When I reported this news to Mather, he shot back a short but decisive note: "I know you, Horace! Don't go any further with this monument. There is to be no national park in the back of your mind until I see if it measures up."

Well, I ignored his warning, knowing he'd be as crazy about Zion as I was. I kept a low profile, but did everything I could to help the Utah congressional delegation. Their bill to create a greatly enlarged Zion National Park sailed through both the Senate and the House to become law in November 1919.

That same month Stephen Mather made his first trip to Utah's "Dixie." He was not only ecstatic about Zion but dazzled by its neighboring territory, Bryce Canyon. As a result he gave his wholehearted blessing to the new park, and within a few years Bryce also became a national park.

The foremost problem facing the Park Service in the early months of 1918 was a concerted effort by certain interests to make adverse use of the parks, excusing it as patriotism but, in reality, attempting to open them once and for all for commercial and money-making projects alien to the Park Service's organic act. Since the entry of the United States into the European conflict, this harassment had never let up.

As the war dragged on into the spring of 1918, pressure from the cattlemen and sheepmen, hunters, and water and power interests became more intense. One particularly nasty attack was contained in a western newspaper editorial, "Soldiers need meat to eat, not wild flowers!"

The Interior Department was flooded with all kinds of demands. Slaughter the Yellowstone elk herds. Kill the nearly extinct bison. Allow the organization of hunting parties to enter the parks to shoot wild animals for additional meat. And allow grazing everywhere.

Meeting unrelenting opposition, they switched the promotion of their agenda to the Food Administration, which operated under the capable and wise leadership of Herbert Hoover. First, he quashed the movement to suspend or modify the game laws by saying: "Any effort to weaken the present laws or in any way relax them in one locality would immediately lead to a demand for such relaxation of laws in all other localities, insuring a rapid breakdown of the whole legal structure of present game protection erected after efforts extending over numerous years."

This pretty well took care of some issues, but we were still faced with the grazing problem. There was a song going around the West. I think it was called "A Battle Cry of Feed 'Em," sung to the tune of the famous Civil War song. Out in Washington and Oregon I heard it, but with nasty lyrics that alluded to the national parks, grazing, and eating the wild animals. Feelings ran strong in the West.

Herbert Hoover saved us from further serious trouble. On January 9, 1918, he proved a staunch ally by issuing a memorandum: "The U. S. Food Administration concurs with the Department of the Interior that the Government's policy should be to decline absolutely all such requests." Unfortunately, even this wasn't completely able to halt the barrage of claims for resources in the parks.

I have already related how Walter Hansen saved Glacier and the Mountaineers Mount Rainier. Pressure from local newspapers did the same for Crater Lake. Yellowstone's organic act, with more than a little of our quiet, strong-armed tactics, carried it safely through. But still in 1918 requests drifted in for grazing cattle, sheep, or both in most of the great western national parks. They were fought fiercely and immediately by conservation groups, by magazine and newspaper writers, and locally by concerned individuals. As Emerson Hough wrote in *Forest and Stream* magazine: "I hate a goddamn sheep. I hate a ram. I hate a ewe. I hate a lamb. I hate their meat. I hate their tallow. I hate their hides. I hate their wool. I hate all goddamn sheep."

Although a lot of furor was created, we fortunately were able to hold the troublemakers at bay. I was absolutely adamant about wilderness intrusion by domesticated animals, and I firmly believe that our collective action during the war established a policy that remained unbroken into the future. Had we let our defense down in 1918, the national park areas might have been desecrated forever.

We had a great slogan someone put up in our Washington office at this time, a takeoff on John Philpot Curran's famous line. It went something like this: "Eternal vigilance is the price of don't let the bastards graze!"

Mr. Mather, who was out in California, kept sending me clippings about the grazing problems, although he offered no advice. He was sticking to his guns about not getting involved in park affairs. Happily, he had other interests and became immersed in the new Save-the-Redwoods League from the spring and on into the summer of 1918. Had he been involved in this grazing situation, it could perhaps have caused him too much mental stress.

In 1917 I had been asked to join Henry Fairfield Osborn, Madison Grant, and John C. Merriam for a tour of the land of the *Sequoia sempervirens*, the coast redwoods of northern California. To my everlasting regret, I had to beg off in order to continue my inspection tour of various parks and monuments. But these three men did travel the length and breadth of the redwood country. They were so impressed by the beauty of the old trees that they decided to form a society to buy groves for permanent preservation. They organized the Save-the-Redwoods League in 1918.

Mr. Mather had not forgotten this opportunity an official of the Park Service was forced to pass up. At the first chance he had, he made an inspection tour of this region in March 1918. He was horrified to see the destruction from massive clear cuts. Logging had been stepped up because of the war. The redwoods were even to be used for railroad ties.

When Mather heard this, he immediately contacted Osborn, who had been with him on the mountain trip in 1915, and offered his personal support as well as that of the Park Service. Mather wrote me from Santa Rosa: "Horace, it is stupefying to see what destruction man is capable of. I felt almost physically sick when viewing the mortal remains of these immortal trees."

Unable to be counted as "founders" of the Redwoods League, Mather and Congressman Billy Kent decided they would tour the region and see what help they could offer the fledgling organization. While they were cruising around the northern California redwood groves, they attended a meeting in Eureka to solicit contributions for the purchase of some choice redwoods. Typically, Mather got all excited about the prospect and spontaneously pledged fifteen thousand dollars. Then he enthusiastically pledged another fifteen thousand for Billy Kent, somewhat to Billy's dismay. Their donations plus appropriations from Humboldt County made possible the purchase of what was then known as Vance Bottom. It was deeded to the state of California in 1921.

A Creed for the Park Service
1918

Back in Washington, while Mather promoted the Redwoods, I launched into a project I had been thinking about for many months. I had been keeping a notebook with ideas, plans, statistics, and data taken in the field. They weren't all mine by a long shot, but they were all worthwhile and had given me much food for thought. Words and ideas of the famous and the unknown from Catlin to McFarland, Olmsted, and Colby, from men and women I'd talked to out in the parks, names beyond recall if I ever knew them. It was a hodgepodge of information if taken alone. But always in the back of my lawyer's mind, I wanted to organize it, codify it so to speak. Now that I had a little more time, I fell to the task of formulating a creed, a framework of ideological guidelines to which the National Park Service could aspire and grow into the future as time and conditions might change. Some years later a secretary of the interior called it the Magna Carta of the national parks. I don't know about that, but at the time I needed to rough out my thoughts and, I hoped, those of Stephen Mather. When I finished this draft, I took it to Secretary Lane to get his reaction.

As usual, he listened without interruption and then said: "Albright, that's a great idea. Put it down in full and let me see it on Monday. You know I'll be away for a week or so, so I'd like to mull it over during that time." I gulped at the thought of writing the whole thing up in three days, but I assured him I'd do my best.

Telling Isabelle Story not to disturb me unless the building was on fire, I closed the door to my office and set to work. I never was very good at dictation, so I had to write it out by myself on my little typewriter. I wrote and wrote and wrote. Whole sections would be finished and then I would think of something to add or change, so I'd start over again.

On Sunday I brought the work home, finished it to the best of my ability, then had Grace check it over for phrasing, spelling, and punctuation. Don't forget her grades were better than mine at Berkeley. On Sunday afternoon I took it over to Bob Yard's and asked for his comments and suggestions. He toned up some sentences and polished an idea here and there, but decided I had really covered the ground, offered no amendments, complimented me on the job, and stated that he was sure Mr. Mather would be happy with it. Aside from the many contributions made by thoughts and words from my notebook, Grace and Bob Yard were the only people who added to or subtracted from the finished product.

On Monday morning Isabelle Story typed it up in readable form, and I presented it to Secretary Lane. Instead of taking it with him when he went away, he read it immediately. In fact, he read it several times while I anxiously awaited his reaction. Then he smiled and nodded and, with no changes, approved it and said, "Good job, Albright. We'll use it."

Then I told him I had been giving a lot of thought to the form in which the "creed" should be released and offered the suggestion that it be as a directive from himself to Stephen Mather. It would carry more weight coming from the secretary of the interior, and it would promote and enhance the name of Director Mather, a phantom figure now due to his extended absence. In addition, I secretly felt that it didn't hurt to give Lane a little extra pat on the back. He gladly accepted credit for it and had it printed in the 1918 annual report of the National Park Service: *Statement of National Park Policy, May 13, 1918, from Franklin K. Lane to Mr. Stephen T. Mather.*

I had tried to write it in Mather's spirit—his ideas, what he would wish to say—but I didn't have time to show it to him until after Lane had approved it. When Mather did get it, he never criticized a word, just congratulated me on the effort.

Admittedly, I was relieved by Mather's acceptance of the manner in which the directive was addressed. I let it stand at that, never wishing to inject the truth. Then in 1925, unknown to all except Secretary of the Interior Hubert Work and Mather, I was asked to revise the creed. This also was presented as a directive, this time from Work to Mather.

A CREED FOR THE PARK SERVICE

There always remained argument and doubt among National Park Service historians and writers about who really wrote it. Franklin K. Lane? Stephen Mather? Finally Lon Garrison, superintendent of Yellowstone, stated openly that I had written it. He had pieced together the fact that Lane wasn't really able to have put together something like that and in 1918 Mather was not functioning. Garrison boxed me in at a Park Service conference of senior officials in Philadelphia in 1964 and made me tell this story. Although I had never cared for recognition of the work, I have privately taken great pride in promoting these standards for which our service has stood ever since.

There is no need to go into all of the sections of the creed. The underlying theme was to clarify and elaborate the ideas and goals set for the National Park Service in the brief organic act of August 1916. My ideas were meant to outline the future management of the parks. I also tried to delineate more closely the paradox of leaving the parks unimpaired and yet allowing their use and enjoyment as a "pleasuring ground" for the people.

In a speech I gave to a meeting of the General Federation of Women's Club around this time, I said: "There are four general functions fulfilled by the national parks: the development of physical health and the desire for outdoor life on the part of the citizens; the development of a broader mental horizon and the education of the people in the ways and habits of wild animals, birds, and natural history; the development of a national patriotism; the diversion of the tourist travel from foreign countries and the retaining of the money spent by American tourists abroad in this country."

Others may differ over the highlights of my directive, but I felt the following were very important:

1. The national parks must be maintained in absolutely unimpaired form, and every activity of the service is subordinate to the duties imposed upon it faithfully to preserve the parks for posterity in essentially their natural state.

2. The parks should be set aside for use, observation, health, and pleasure of the people.

3. The national interest must dictate all decisions affecting public or private enterprise in the parks.

4. It is necessary to restrict leasing of lands. In national parks summer homes and other private holdings should be eliminated. No

trees should be cut except for vistas, infestations, or hazards. Harmonize trails, roads, buildings, and other improvements with the landscape.

5. All concessioners should be regulated as to rates, have no competition, and yield revenue to the federal government. All types of accommodations should be provided either by the concessioner or by the Park Service, from free campsites with water and sanitation to luxury hotels.

6. Sports should be encouraged (except for hunting), but not to interfere with the enjoyment by other visitors or in any way to harm the natural environment. Educational use of parks, museums, and other attractions should be promoted.

7. The National Park System should not be lowered in standards, dignity, and prestige by the inclusion of areas that express in less than the highest terms the particular class or kind of exhibit they represent. Existing parks should be improved by the addition of adjacent areas that would complete their scenic or other purposes.

At the same time I was writing the "creed," I gave a great deal of thought to the future. Although I had promised Mr. Mather I would stay on to organize and operate the National Park Service until he could return, I was rapidly losing faith in the possibility that he would ever again pick up the reins of his office. He had stayed away from Washington for months, now stretching into years. Although appearing to be back to complete physical health, he still felt shaky about his mental and nervous condition. He seemed afraid to undertake responsibility for assuming the operation of the service, although he was mildly involved in routine concession problems, attempts to expand the boundaries of Yellowstone and Sequoia, and the publicity work that Yard was handling so well. We tried to keep him abreast of national park affairs, but at Weisenburg's insistence still siphoned off anything that might worry or upset him. The balance continued to be delicate.

Mather and I wrote to each other two or three times a week. My correspondence, along with official bureau papers, was mainly anecdotal, for he loved "inside" news. His warm, upbeat letters were full of his social activities and plans to come to Washington, which never materialized. Plans for Washington changed to plans for a long tour of the West that would take up most of the spring, summer, and perhaps September. On April 1, 1918, he wrote: "Oh, Horace, I just can't wait to get back where there are snow-clad mountains, winds fresh with scent of pines, lakes so calm you can see your face in them. And this is no April Fool's joke! I'm mapping out my trail west now and will let you know details shortly." Not too long after that he sent me an itinerary that included a visit to the northwestern parks, an extended trip in the Sierra, and then another long vacation at Charlie Thompson's Lake Tahoe home.

By May Mather's letters were coming from Yosemite. They were good news to me, for he was picking up threads of work, and it didn't seem to upset him. I had suggested to him that he settle on promotion and pay standards for Yosemite that could then be applied throughout the system. He and Dusty Lewis did a fine job on that. Then on May 31 he was to have a meeting in San Francisco with Will Colby and food administrator Ralph Merritt concerning cattle grazing. I was confident that his deft rapport in this sticky situation would prove valuable.

During all this time Mather never once mentioned stepping into the directorship, now or in the future. And he said nothing about my future either. My morale was hitting bottom with the long-range problems as well as the lesser but constant annoying situations. How often I wished I had just one man near me with whom I could discuss the park problems, just one more person to share in the decisions.

Now came "the rite of spring," the agony of appropriations. Although Joseph Swager Sherley, the honorable representative from Kentucky, was a lofty step above the miserable Fitzgerald, he was not known to be an easy touch when it came to allotting money. Furthermore, I had no personal knowledge of the man, so I was doubly nervous at testifying before him.

Although it was a tough session, the Park Service came out bruised but not beaten considering wartime and the scarcity of funds for civilian use. The outlook for continuance of the war into or through the next fiscal year weighed heavily against our financial needs. For the entire park system, only $754,195 was made available. There wasn't a cent for new roads and only a small amount for improving the existing El Portal road in Yosemite.

For fire fighting, not a penny was allocated. We were facing a brutally dry summer and had to end up using our reserve maintenance funds when disastrous fires erupted in Yellowstone and Glacier. From that time on, I fought for a separate fund to fight fires whenever they broke out in any park.

Throughout the federal government, the policy on fire was to fight it immediately and vigorously, and this was costly, for fire was a common occurrence in the West. For the national forests, the reason was that valuable commercial timber could be burned. For the national parks, the idea was the beauty of the landscape and the wildlife in them should be protected and left "unimpaired."

It was suggested that money could be saved by just letting the fires burn themselves out as the Indians had done. But Indians had been terrified of great fires and did everything in their power to keep from starting them. Only their angry gods did that. The more civilization crept across the land, the more fires were caused by man—especially in national parks with pack trains, campgrounds, and incidentals like machinery and cigars.

In the appropriations there also was no raise in pay for personnel. Despite my pleas for some recognition for the national monuments, not a cent more was set aside for "the orphans." This was terribly disturbing to me. I was fearful that many of them, particularly the Southwest historic ones, would further disintegrate, perhaps beyond hope of restoration, unless we could get even minor appropriations.

The saving grace was that authority was granted to various organizations and universities for scientific work in many monuments. Among those involved were Dr. Edgar Hewett of the School of American Research excavating the ruins of Gran Quivira, Dr. Clark Wissler of the American Museum of Natural History doing archaeological work at Chaco Canyon, and my old friend Neil Judd of the National Museum of the Smithsonian, who was hard at work restoring Betatakin cliff dwelling at Navajo National Monument.

During the war, Judd had been locked into what he called "a lifetime at an aviation concentration camp" in Oklahoma. During 1918 we exchanged ideas about my desire to create an archaeological division of the Park Service, both for scientific research and for restoration of ancient sites. I wanted Neil to be the chief of it, and he was as enthusiastic over the plan as I was.

Of course, it was the same old story of no money to start anything new. After the war ended, I lent what little weight I had to get him back into the Smithsonian, where he had been working when I first knew him in Washington. Even though our plans couldn't be carried out, in the years ahead he was always a great help to me and gave me an endless flow of free knowledge and advice as well as contributing invaluable work in our western archaeological sites.

Because of the tight fiscal situation, I was particularly upset about the newly created national parks. Lassen received no appropriation, no road or trail improvement, and was still being administered by the Forest Service, which was allowing grazing.

Of course, Lassen wasn't the only area to see zero new appropriations. Hawaii and Mount McKinley suffered that fate along with the Grand Canyon, which was included in the appropriations for the fiscal year 1918–19.

Probably one of the hardest things on the service was the Appropriations Committee's refusal to negate a 1917 ruling that admission fees earned in the parks could not be used in them. Revenues of the national parks were to continue to revert to the United States Treasury. We saw little of them after that.

One lovely Sunday in May, Grace and I adjourned to Rock Creek for a picnic. She suddenly blurted out, "Horace, I have no idea how to say this except we're going to have a baby." I was bowled over but thoroughly delighted. We eagerly began to make plans for the newcomer, whose birth was expected around February 1, 1919.

The glow lasted for me only until that night, when Grace slept peacefully and I couldn't sleep a wink. The euphoria had died down and was replaced with apprehension, doubts, and worries. I had to have a known future and a better-paying job. I was deeply concerned with the knowledge that Mather might never return to Washington, that I was stuck in this uncertain position of acting director, that I had made no real plans for my future as an attorney in San Francisco, that I not only had my beloved wife, but soon there would be another human being to care for. The whole thing overwhelmed me.

The responsibility for charting my own family's course was crushing enough, but to feel that whatever I did would have an influence on the course of the National Park Service now and into the future made it worse. I sat out on our tiny balcony half the night, chewing on my knuckles (a bad habit) and rolling all the alternatives around in my mind.

Unfortunately, in that day and age, it was supposed to be the sole responsibility of the male to decide family and career questions. Later I found that talking everything over with my beautiful and very intelligent wife was the real solution. Temporarily I just couldn't face up to a decision. I'd have to get the appropriations set up for the new fiscal year and then use my summer for an inspection trip of the parks, straightening out the worst problems there.

Sometimes I felt like getting down on my knees and praying that Stephen Mather would get well enough to pick up the reins of his office before our baby was born. I just had to leave the Park Service by that time. I vowed I had to.

I tried to maintain what little confidence I had that Mather might still return in 1918. I formulated plans to cover as much ground as possible in my summer inspection trip, to iron out field problems so the service would be in good shape should he be able to take over.

In the meantime, on May 24, Mather had set off for the West with his business associate in Chicago, Oliver Mitchell. He wrote that he would stay in Yosemite for a few days before going to visit Thorkildsen in Los Angeles. He sent no itinerary, no schedule, just a brief, "I will wire you from time to time, keeping you posted on my movements." There was nothing left for me to do in Washington with the adjournment of Congress and the operation of the government going into hibernation for the next few steamy months.

The frightening outbreak of the so-called Spanish Flu caused me to accelerate my plans for leaving Washington. Mortality was exceedingly high, especially for pregnant women. I had to get Grace to the West Coast, which was reported to be somewhat safer. On July 1, we boarded a train for Denver, where we separated. She went along to her parents' home in Berkeley while I began my travels.

Before I was diverted into major problems in the large national parks during that summer of 1918, I decided to further my knowledge of the national monuments. I had been deeply interested in these forsaken bits of our Park Service. Mather considered them beyond the pale, sort of nuisances for which we were legally responsible. He felt most were of poor scenic value, and he had little interest in historical areas. Furthermore, most were far from railroads or other means for tourists to visit them. That meant if there was no visitation, there would be no congressional appropriations.

Short acquaintance with Mukuntuweap (Zion), Colorado, and a few other monuments had whetted my interest in them. I had read everything I could lay my hands on about them, and now I decided to take an in-depth look to see how they could be brought up to the standards set for the national parks. I knew full well that it would be a tough job to get any money from Congress. But if I presented solid knowledge, with facts and figures coupled with enthusiasm and plans to lure tourists to the monuments—well, anything was possible.

After parting with Grace in Denver, I headed to the Southwest to meet Frank Pinkley, custodian of the Casa Grande Ruins. I had him join me at Grand Canyon for an inspection of the Southwest monuments.

Frank Pinkley was indeed a remarkable human being. He had come to Arizona to regain his health after contracting tuberculosis. Pitching a tent near the Hohokam ruins of Casa Grande, which had been set aside for preservation by President Benjamin Harrison in 1889, Pinkley made these his own. From 1901 until his death in 1940, he gave them, and many other sites in the Park Service, his devoted, loving care.

When Pinkley and I were about to leave the Grand Canyon, he wanted to use his car on our trip. I was shocked into silence when I saw this thing he called a car, which looked like it couldn't get out of El Tovar even rolling downhill. It was the most rattletrap auto I'd ever seen. It looked like a decrepit boiler with wheels, with rickety posts to hold the top on. He called it "The Baby." I knew he had constructed a house at Casa Grande out of junk he had found or had been donated, so I asked, "Had some leftovers from the home-building, huh?" He laughed at that, and I in turn admired him more every minute, for he had a great sense of humor.

Ford Harvey stepped in at this point and insisted that we borrow one of his nice touring cars. Mrs. Pinkley could take the family car home. Pinkley proclaimed that I had to drive because he wouldn't know how to handle anything that splendid.

Of the Interior Department's twenty-four national monuments in 1918, thirteen (not counting the potential Zion Park) were in the southwest corner of America. Who had ever heard of Montezuma Castle, Capulin Mountain, Natural Bridges, Rainbow Bridge, and most of the others? Or what they were or where they were? I had to admit that I was vague on a few until Pinkley shoved a map in front of me and lectured me on each, even the ones he'd never seen. But, by golly, he'd read everything available and knew them as though he spent his life in them.

It was a whirlwind trip, but we covered an enormous amount of territory. From Grand Canyon we headed south through Prescott to Phoenix. We planned to visit Montezuma Castle National Monument, an ancient five-story Indian cliff dwelling, but the road to it was obliterated by recent summer storms. We stopped overnight in the desert capital of Phoenix. It was one of the most fearsome nights

I ever spent, under a fiery hot tin roof that radiated the previous day's 120 degree heat. Pinkley and I gave up around 5:00 A.M. and headed for his Casa Grande.

When we arrived at Pinkley's home at Casa Grande, I was astounded. How he managed to exist in this home with a wife and children, I could never imagine. His house couldn't qualify as anything better than a shack. He had constructed it himself with remnants of materials he had scrounged up. I was shocked to learn that this was typical of the manner in which our national park people were existing in many places—almost like wilderness slums, living no better than animals. Fortunately, I had brought my camera along this summer to record my inspections, so that I could demonstrate at future congressional hearings exactly what the conditions in our parks were. I certainly snapped plenty at Casa Grande.

Our dinner was cooked on an outdoor fire and eaten at a table made of two rough planks resting on wooden boxes. Our seats were benches of the same. Pinkley anxiously awaited my last bite. Then he grabbed a flash-light and said, "Mr. Albright, how about a tour of my castle?" By the beam of his torch, we toured Casa Grande.

Of course, there really was not much left of the Hohokam enclave. But you would think you were gazing on one of the Seven Wonders of the World to see the affection and pride Pinkley had in his moldering ruins. It was beyond belief. He pointed out every spot that had been restored, every plan he had to complete his dream. To him it appeared a true *casa grande*, a magnificent house of the noble Hohokam rising toward the sun, not a melting mound of clay as we saw it.

After we had spent an hour or so looking over his domain and were slumped by the fire outside his home, we got to talking about long-range plans. I questioned him very carefully, not just concerning Casa Grande, but about other national monuments. What could be done about them? How could we arouse interest enough to get money for them? Where could we find other competent people like himself who had the love and devotion for these treasures being saved through the Park Service? Although he had given a great deal of thought to the problem, he honestly admitted that he really didn't have any answers. I remember one thing he said though: "At the rate attention has been given to our monu-ments, there'll be no need to remember them. Before long they will have been washed away or crumbled away by sun and rain or hoisted away by tourists and merchants."

His thoughts and spirit, his enthusiasm and practical knowledge, so impressed me that I spontaneously threw out the idea: "Pinkley, what would you think about taking on the superintendency of Grand Canyon when we get it—probably next year?" He didn't jump for joy as I expected. He didn't even act like he'd heard me for a few minutes. Then he replied: "I'm deeply grateful that you'd even think of me for the position. I've had so little experience in the National Park Service. But I'd just like to say that I'm at home with my little ruins. And if you feel I could help you, let me work on this one and perhaps other national monuments. They all need attention and help so badly."

As it turned out, when Grand Canyon did become a national park the following year, Pinkley's name was brought up to fill the superintendency slot, and I spoke up against it. I remembered this intimate conversation of a year ago. Not that I didn't think he could handle the position magnificently. I knew his wishes and that he was the only one available who could oversee the southwestern monuments with expertise and devotion.

Continuing our discussion well into the night, I listened intently to his ideas and was more impressed by the minute. I promised him that evening that one thing I would do was get Casa Grande out of the limbo it was in. Although under the Interior Department, it was neither fish nor fowl. It had been created in 1889 as Casa Grande Ruin Reservation. I immediately wrote Secretary Lane, extolling Pinkley's work and the need to publicize the monuments, and requested that he get Casa Grande's status formalized. On August 3, 1918, it was legally made a national monument by executive order. I wasn't with "Pink" at that time, but I know it had to be one of his happiest days.

Pinkley and I bounced around the desert roads of southern Arizona and gave special attention to Tonto and Tumacacori National Monuments. I kept asking myself, why should a national monument like Tonto be in the Forest Service, Department of Agriculture, instead of the National Park Service, Department of the Interior, when it was so like Casa Grande, Montezuma Castle, and others? The sad state of the old Spanish mission of Tumacacori prompted me to appoint Pinkley as custodian of this monument as well as his Casa Grande.

Our friendship, my confidence in Pinkley, and his brilliant and intelligent work eventually culminated in his appointment as superintendent of Southwestern Parks, which included fourteen units. "Boss" Pinkley proved to be one of the giants of the National Park Service.

Greater Yellowstone
1918

*Back in California, I had only one or two days in Berkeley with my precious wife.
She was blooming physically but joyfully, with the coming birth of our baby.*

*I spent most of the time on Sequoia and Yosemite matters, although I decided
there was no need to visit the parks at this time. Yosemite was in good shape, due
to the efficient administration of Superintendent Lewis. The concessioner mess was
put on hold for Mather's return. On May 28 the new power plant had finally
begun operation. On September 7 Secretary Lane and Mr. Mather formally chris-
tened it "The Henry Floy," in honor of its designer, Mather's recently deceased
brother-in-law.*

Mather had approved of a donation from the Sierra Club to install
iron posts, threaded with steel cables, creating a trail to the top of Half
Dome. This would replace an old unsafe rope-and-bolt device put in by
a sailor back in the 1880s.

Getting rid of the old was fine, but I was afraid we were going to
open a new kettle of worms. I always hated to interfere with a decision
Mather had already made, but I decided to write him about this matter:
"Mr. Mather, we are in agreement that the old Half Dome trail is
dangerous and folks should be kept off it but I am afraid of something
else. My fears are that a fine new one will encourage too many mountaineers and they will now want to go beyond the trail and begin all sorts
of climbing on the face of Half Dome and other landmarks in Yosemite.

That, to me, would be a desecration of the natural wonders our visitors come to Yosemite to see."

I received no answer to my letter, and the new trail was constructed in 1918. Many decades later climbers with pitons and ropes crawled on Half Dome, El Capitan, and other granite cliffs of the Yosemite while tourists watched the spectacle.

One person I had to see in San Francisco was Ralph Merritt, federal food commissioner for California. I had received a letter from him on May 9 in which he thundered: "I am counting on you to see that as many cattle as possible are admitted to the national parks in order that we may have sufficient carry over to leave us enough stock for next year. . . . Let me know how many head you plan to let in to each one of the parks."

I replied that we had tried to be "accommodating" with the cattlemen, but that I didn't like their implied blackmail: "to assume an attitude of opposition to our 'Greater Sequoia Park project' if we didn't open the parks to grazing." I wanted to make sure Merritt understood that grazing was unacceptable as Park Service policy, except in minor circumstances—war or no war.

I stated my argument that we were opposed to grazing for many reasons. The prime one, of course, was that sheep completely, and cattle nearly, destroyed the floor-covering nature had laid down to protect the natural environment. Then there was the matter of steep mountain slopes up which whole herds of cattle scrambled and dug their way, tearing up laboriously and expensively laid out trails and dislodging rocks. Finally, the hikers and horseback packers had to pass up desirable camping sites because the cattle had used them as "nightstands," as Emerson Hough had called them in 1915.

Stephen Mather, with his incomparable charm and persuasiveness, had used all these arguments and probably a lot more when he had seen Merritt a short time before. It had gotten him nowhere, so if Mather hadn't succeeded, I had no confidence I could. It was a moot question in any case, for Merritt was away on vacation and I never saw him.

On July 12 I headed north to check out the major parks. My job was made easier by the fact that Mather had preceded me on his inspection tour of the Northwest. Traveling in his own chauffeured car, he had visited Yosemite, General Grant, Sequoia, Crater Lake, Mount Rainier, and Lassen. As I followed Mather's trail, I was satisfied that Crater Lake and Mount Rainier were in good shape. The work on the rim road around Crater Lake was superb.

At Mount Rainier Superintendent Dewitt Reaburn and others told me how grand Mather had looked, how decisive he had been, how quiet and steady he had seemed. The only downside was that he had tired easily, but that wasn't out of line considering his long illness. My spirits soared at the thought that my chief seemed to be pretty much his old self. His taking hold of even small matters was reassuring, and it lifted some of the burden from my shoulders.

Because of Mather's inspection of Mount Rainier, I could move on quickly to Glacier. Even here, I picked up a few extra days as this park was also in fine condition. The arrangements I had made last year about grazing were holding up with few complaints. The east side road was just about finished, and my negotiations with the Blackfeet during the spring had settled most of their complaints.

Timber cutting, mining, summer residences, and other practices contrary to park principles were allowed in the act creating Glacier in 1910. Eight years later Lane forbade the construction of new residences but allowed old ones to remain. These were finally outlawed in 1931.

Privately owned lands were a real problem, especially summer homes on Lake McDonald. There seemed to be no solution to these until the war's end, when some money could be appropriated.

Gradually exchanges of lands near roads or other attractions were made for lands outside the park—usually Forest Service lands. Always regarding us with jealousy and fear, the Forest Service fought back, but by an act of Congress in the 1920s the secretary of the interior was authorized to trade private lands in the park for lands anywhere in Montana.

In June 1918 Thomas J. Walsh of Montana was one of the most powerful senators in Washington, and he owned a house on Lake McDonald. A bit later on, his fellow senator Burton K. Wheeler became a neighbor with a summer cottage. Trying for years to rectify the original mistakes in Glacier's organic act, we always had a war with Walsh, not just in this park but in many others. I always said that when Enos Mills left the battlefield for the grave, Walsh took his place with me.

Now I went on to Yellowstone, where I was looking forward to a prolonged stay in my favorite park and to the time I would have to investigate the Jackson Hole–Teton situation. When I was younger and homesick and had a hard time getting to sleep, I would close my eyes and imagine my Owens Valley and old Mount Tom and the neighboring Sierras protecting Bishop. It was always comforting, as I suppose I felt they were also protecting me. Once I had seen the Jackson Hole and its jagged, snow-topped peaks, serene valley, and lazy Snake River, I felt the same deep peace. But the fear was always with me that this beautiful spot might go the way mine had gone. Instead of having to provide water for thirsty Los Angeles, it could be ruined by commercialization and its water drained off for Idaho potato farmers.

Now when did the concept of adding the Teton area to Yellowstone occur, and whose idea was it? Well, Mather and I would have liked the honor, but the only credit we could claim was that we were the ones who finally forced action on it. The idea apparently germinated in the mind of General Philip Sheridan of Civil War fame. In 1882 he suggested that Yellowstone's size be nearly doubled in order to create a larger game sanctuary. No attention was shown to his idea or to various other proposals put forth from time to time.

Some interest was aroused in 1917 when a road was opened from Yellowstone down to Jackson Hole. It stretched twenty-six miles from the Snake River Ranger Station to Moran. Then in October of that year Emerson Hough, our old friend from Mather Mountain Party days, had sent me a manuscript of his that would appear on December 1, 1917, in the *Saturday Evening Post*. Its title was "Greater Yellowstone." Its themes were to preserve the elk herds and other animals from unlimited hunting, double the Yellowstone area for scenic enjoyment, and save Jackson Hole from timbering, mining, and other destructive practices. His punch line was "Greater Yellowstone; Greater Wyoming; above everything else, Greater America."

Hough's accompanying letter to me concluded: "Please let us get this thing through; that country ought to be a part of the Park."

And I replied, "It is not necessary for you to appeal to us for sympathy toward the idea of including the Jackson Hole country in Yellowstone Park. We have been boosting this project for two years."

So Hough deserves the honor of coining the phrase "Greater Yellowstone." I know I always used his words during the long fight to get the area into the National Park System. To this day it is still a rallying cry for conservationists when referring to areas outside the limits of Yellowstone.

Much as Mather and I had always been in agreement that this area must be acquired for the Park Service, he now instructed me not to waste my time on it because of the inherent opposition. He said: "Let it go for a while. Let things settle down after the war's upheaval." I rarely opposed

Mather, but I was the acting director, the person responsible for that service, with Mather assuring me time and again that I was to make all decisions. I did so at this time and was comfortable in proceeding with my plans for Jackson Hole.

When I had been here a year ago, I hadn't been able to get down there and had only gazed at the Tetons from Shoshone Point in Yellowstone, but I had made a strong statement in our annual report headed *The Tetons Should Be Added at Once*. Listed as necessary to the extension of Yellowstone were "the Teton range, Jackson Lake, all of the rugged scenic lands north of the Buffalo Fork of the Snake River, including the valleys of Pilgrim and Pacific Creeks to Two Ocean Pass." No piker, I added, "the canyons, lakes and forests of the Upper Yellowstone and the Thorofare Basin. Every foot of the area naturally belongs to Yellowstone Park."

A bill including this outline had been drawn up and introduced in the Congress by Wyoming's Senator Frank Mondell on April 24, 1918. Secretary Lane pushed it forward. Henry Graves, head of the Forest Service, reluctantly endorsed it, knowing he was relinquishing vast lands to the Park Service.

We attained one thing when, on July 8, 1918, as an aid to this pending legislation, President Wilson withdrew the land concerned from homestead entry, setting aside six hundred thousand acres of Teton National Forest.

Sadly, Mondell's bill was lost at the bottom of the Senate calendar, as it needed unanimous consent to climb to a spot where it could be considered before adjournment. Denial of this consent by Senator John Nugent of Idaho ended the park extension bill for 1918. Next the Forest Service switched positions after Wilson's executive order and became an antagonist, pulling the ranchers and cattlemen with it. Notwithstanding all this, the project seemed assured, and the bill would pass when the Sixty-fifth Congress reassembled for its third session in the fall.

To me this project was an example of the paradox within our Park Service organic act. We were charged to conserve the scenery, the natural and historic objects, and the wildlife. *But* at the same time we were to provide for the enjoyment of these by the people. *But* at the same time we were to leave them unimpaired for future generations. As one who had participated in the discussions and writing of that 1916 act, I remembered the difficulty of reconciling these opposite factors. We had finally come to the belief that, with rational, careful, and loving thought, it could be done.

Applying those principles to the Teton country, it went something like this. It should be an integrated whole with Yellowstone. A separate park wasn't considered at this time. The American people should be able to enjoy a totally different experience than the one that the original boundaries of Yellowstone offered. Aside from the natural wonders of geysers, a grand canyon, and hot springs, Yellowstone was a vast, untouched wilderness of lodgepole pine forest and rather ordinary mountains. In contrast, Jackson Hole was enhanced by its astounding Teton spires and jewel-like lakes, the imposing Gros Ventre range to the east, and the Hobacks to the south. Through the center flowed the aptly named Snake River, twisting and turning its way toward Idaho.

Along with this magnificent beauty, were we going to add something alien to Yellowstone's nearly pristine lands? Jackson Lake had long since been dammed where the Snake River exited southward. This had caused a ghastly eyesore of dead trees as far as the eye could reach and had polluted the water. There were ugly buildings at Moran, saloons near Jenny Lake, a rundown old town sprawling across the end of the valley, cattle everywhere.

Another consideration for Greater Yellowstone was the rounding out of the land to complete the watersheds, leaving nature alone, undirected and untouched. Already there had been talk about dams for Two Ocean and Emma Matilda Lakes. This would seriously interfere with the natural trails of the moose, bear, and the great herds of elk. The cattle ranchers of Jackson Hole counted on the friendly Forest Service to keep control over the great southern elk herd by bottling them up in restricted areas, leaving the rest for the grazing of their domesticated animals or good hunting.

To sum it up, the area was on its way to wanton commercialism and physical destruction if the Park Service didn't get it and get it soon. I wanted Jackson Hole saved, and I wanted Yellowstone not confined to a map of straight lines. This unity created by the natural courses of mountains, rivers, and animal migrations was my primary goal, along with preserving the Hole from commercial trashing.

The purposes of an inspection of Jackson Hole were to learn as much as possible to further Mondell's bill, to examine and get a thorough knowledge of the whole region, not just the part in which we were interested, and to get local support to accomplish our goal. What were the physical features? Roads? Towns? Who lived there? What was the economic situation? What about the animals, in particular the elk migration? How extensive were the water problems? What were the reclamation features, the sorry-looking Jackson Lake and dam? Who was in favor of, who against the extension?

When I arrived in Yellowstone, I was met by Arthur Demaray from our Washington office, a talented draftsman who had earlier served in the Geological Survey. He had brought his wife and young daughter, Elise, with him. On the morning of August 3, they joined me and we set out for Jackson Hole, again staying at Ben Sheffield's in Moran.

When the Demarays were settled and under the wing of Ben Sheffield, I set off for Jackson at the southern end of the Hole. I'll tell you, it was a jolt. Sheffield had made out that it was a town. Well, a town is not a city, but a town should be more than a haphazard crisscross of rutted streets, a cluster of shaggy buildings, with no hint of respectability except for an old church. I passed up the local rector and scouted around for the newspaper office. There always was one of those if there were two people to read the paper, and an editor of a newspaper always knew more about a place than anyone else. On foot I covered the town and finally hit on a nondescript little square building. It was nothing to look at, but it sure had a splendid sign over the door: "Jackson's Hole Courier" in flowery nineteenth-century-style print.

I opened the door and walked in. I saw a fellow about my own age over in the corner and asked him who was in charge here.

He replied, "I am."

Rather surprised, I next inquired, "Well, where's the editor of the paper?"

He said, "I am."

Still not feeling comfortable about this rather abrupt young man, I asked, "Well, then where is the owner of this paper?"

Again the reply, "I am."

That seemed to cover all the bases, so I introduced myself and explained why I was in Jackson. He put out his hand and said, "Well, I'm Dick Winger. I'm not sure whether you are welcome around here as we don't take to the federal government interfering in our affairs. But sit down and tell me about your Greater Yellowstone." So that's how I met Winger. We became fast friends and associates for many years to come.

After I had gone over our ideas for Jackson Hole, Winger suggested he walk me around town and introduce me to some of the old timers. "You'll have to get along with them or you might as well high-tail it back to Yellowstone," he said. Then he put a sign on his door that he had gone to lunch and wheeled me into one old place after another to meet one old duffer after another. When he introduced me, Winger let them assume I was just a casual visitor. He never mentioned my Washington job. In Wyoming you could be taking your life in your hands if you mentioned the W word. I'll bet their school history books even eliminated our first president.

Anyway, I tried to be extremely cautious, affable, and friendly with them, but gave out as little information as I could. I elicited their opinions about anything and everything from the war to the weather to the price of cattle, and of course how they felt about the future. What changes if any might come to Jackson Hole in the future? The answer was a menacing consensus. "Nobody better try to change this place." The statement proved prophetic. So the whole trip to Jackson bore no fruit at that time except for Winger's instant friendship and promise to keep in contact. Little did I know what an enormous plus that would be a few years ahead.

The next day Demaray and I spent four or five hours on horseback, covering the territory around Jenny and Leigh Lakes, which lie at the base of the Tetons. The local Forest Service man accompanied us. I don't remember his name, but he was tough and antagonistic. Of course, he knew who we were and could guess for what reason we were looking over his territory.

Maybe I've overdone this already, but let me give a little more background on the National Park Service versus the Forest Service. I don't think Mather and I ever had any idea of challenging the Forest Service for leadership of the conservation movement. We just wanted to round out the National Park System. We declined to consider Lake Tahoe, Mount Hood, Mount Baker, Mount Shasta, the Arkansas Ouchita Mountains, and many other beautiful areas because they did not measure up to what we regarded as national park standards or had too much commercial development or too many inholdings, or because the cost was prohibitive considering what the Congress would give us. Certainly Mather and I weren't trying for a power base, as we both planned to leave the government as soon as we could accomplish our initial job of organizing the Park Service on a firm and lasting basis, trying to build a system that would stand up for all time and not be in danger of absorption into some other bureau, probably the Forest Service.

Although we recognized that this branch was only ten years older than ours, it had acquired a reputation and a political clout through men like Theodore Roosevelt and Gifford Pinchot. If the latter had not been fired by Taft in the Ballinger-Pinchot controversy of 1910–11, the Forest Service would probably have succeeded in swallowing the national parks before our bureau could have been created.

From the moment an independent Park Service was organized, the Forest Service was jealous of it and never failed to fight it whenever their land was involved. But look at it this way. For new parks or additions to old ones, the Park Service had few places to acquire land in the public domain unless it dipped into holdings of the Forest Service. They stood for use of anything within their borders: water, minerals, forests, and other commercially attractive enterprises. They allowed hunting, dams, summer homes, and unlimited roads for lumbering. Their beliefs contradicted all of ours.

I'll admit that Mather and I gave little thought and had less concern when reaching out for their land because we were so philosophically opposed to them. We genuinely believed we were preserving while they were destroying. The antagonism continues to this day.

Demaray and I spent that long day with the sullen Forest Service man. We accomplished a tremendous amount of fact-finding. Demaray's notes and pencil drawings were invaluable when we returned to Washington to push our agenda. Furthermore, our companion from the rival service was so angry underneath his frozen, surly exterior that he accidentally gave out a stream of information that we could and did use in the months ahead.

It was an unpleasant day in some respects, but a glorious one in others. If you have ever stood at Jenny Lake and looked across to Cascade Canyon weaving its sinuous way toward the summit of the Tetons, you will know the joy of being in a sacred place, designed by God to be protected forever. This may sound juvenile and presumptuous, but then I took it personally. I really felt I had a mission to preserve the Grand Tetons in the only way I knew, through the National Park Service.

Another day or so was spent alone with Demaray gathering data on the Jackson Lake mess, scouting out the Buffalo Fork region, and learning a great deal about the drift of the elk to the valley's winter refuge. No matter how much we had read about this area, we had been pretty ignorant. Now we felt we had a real store of useful knowledge to work with when we got back to Washington. So we packed up and returned to Yellowstone.

On August 12 I went up to Bozeman to meet our engineer, George Goodwin, and the Gallatin County commissioners. The Park Service was now responsible for our own roads in Yellowstone after the army engineers were relieved of this duty on July 1. This meeting was to reach an agreement on a scenic highway through the Gallatin Canyon into the northwestern corner of Yellowstone. Mather had recently been in touch with these people, had given general approval to the project, but had left decisions to the commissioners.

Their plans met with my opposition. I was very precise in spelling out my overall policy on roads even though I knew it clashed with some of Mather's. He promoted the idea of improved "highways" to and in the parks to encourage more visitors. As the American people owned the national parks, I felt they deserved not only good roads but safe roads. These should be improved to eliminate dangerous grades and curves, with parapets erected, and, most of all, should be paved. This had been one of the reasons for establishing the landscape and engineering department.

I had already set a policy for roads to be limited to two lanes, only wide enough to safely accommodate ordinary cars and trucks, with parapets to be erected where necessary. This was a safety measure, but it was also my quirky opinion that it made tourists slow down enough to enjoy the parks more. Previously I had ordered no more wagons or stagecoaches after a nasty fight in Glacier in 1916, when a stagecoach company challenged us and demanded the right to compete with the auto coach service.

To the commissioners I especially emphasized the dangers of a highway near or in a national park. This encouraged a diversionary network of smaller roads in the parks and would result in an invasion of wilderness areas not intended to be trampled by crowds of tourists.

Worst of all in my mind was that highways spelled too many people. This is where Mather and I visualized the future quite differently. Mather never gave up on the idea that rail passengers would always make up a large segment of tourists. And furthermore, there never could be too many tourists for Stephen Mather. He wanted as many as possible to enjoy his "treasures."

Many of us who were in the younger generation, such as Howard Hays and Dusty Lewis, could already see that the automobile would create a huge increase in visitors, and we worried whether too many might overwhelm our parks in the future. There never was a quarrel on the topic because all of us loyally followed Mather's philosophy of encouraging tourists no matter how they got to the parks.

At this time, I was making the decisions, and I told the commissioners that for the time being, and probably the foreseeable future, Yellowstone would get along just fine with General Chittenden's army roads. Improve them, yes, but we wouldn't encourage any more. All the wondrous sights were on Chittenden's loop route, which left the vast majority of the park in wilderness. That could be visited on horse or on foot.

On August 14 Chief Forester Henry Graves came to Bozeman to talk over an agreement on sharing costs for this Gallatin road from Bozeman to West Yellowstone, which would enter both the national forest and the national park. Our discussions were pleasant even when Graves questioned me closely about my trip to Jackson Hole. His man down there had written a rather nasty report, poor-mouthing Demaray and me. Among the nicer things he called us were "arrogant, snoopy, and high-handed." Fortunately, Graves knew me quite well, discounted the letter, and accepted my honest answers to his questions. In fact, later in the year, in discussions with Mather, he produced notes he had taken in Bozeman that had helped him decide not to openly oppose Mondell's extension bill.

On August 17 I climbed on a train at Cody, made a quick stopover in Denver, but avoided Chicago except for changing trains. When I arrived back in Washington on August 23, because of the flu epidemic, I walked all the way from the station to my apartment on California Street where it joined Columbia Road and Connecticut Avenue. Here was a statue of Civil War General George McClellan. Propped up against it was a sign warning, "Your cough may kill."

When I finally climbed the four flights to the Albright apartment and opened the door, my spirits plummeted. It was just a hot, musty, empty place with no beautiful Dacie-girl. No smell of her wonderful cooking. No laughter, no music from the piano. It was overwhelming to think I hadn't seen her in months and had no idea when I would see her again. Most of the time I put it to one side, but this night was tough and I really wondered if all our sacrifice was worth it.

CHAPTER
23

"I'm Coming Down to Washington"
1918

Mather spent the remainder of the summer of 1918 in California. With Huston Thompson, he explored the Kearsage Pass area of the Sierra, then went to Yosemite to dedicate the new power plant and the new Glacier Point Hotel. On September 9, Mather wrote me that he planned to come east, visit Chicago and his home in Darien, and then "come down to Washington."

Come down to Washington. To read this was like Gabriel blowing his horn. My chief was well and could take over the service, and I would be free to go home to California to Grace. Hallelujah!

Before all these wonderful events could take place, I had to get out the annual report for the fiscal year ending June 30, 1918, a report ostensibly written by Stephen Mather to Secretary Lane. As I wrote Lindsley on the day I returned to my office, "The trip did me a world of good. . . . I am getting down to the annual report and other matters of this kind that will occupy me for the next month, and, as I am director, assistant director, and chief clerk, you can well imagine that I am going to be rather busy."

Last year my report had emphasized the origin of the National Park Service, the state of the units it comprised, and an outline of our plans for its future. For the 1917–18 report, my main thrust was to show that the Park Service had not only survived the "war exigencies" but had produced "important achievements in the development of the national park and monument system." I emphasized the "statement of policy" (the creed) in an opening paragraph and then had a footnote that it was printed in full in the appendix. Privately I took pride in the creed and gave myself full credit for it, but in the actual report Lane got all the credit.

When I finished the report and had Secretary Lane's approval, the biggest problem left was Bob Yard. I didn't want to get involved in this and had avoided any decision until Mather could take charge, but fate was pushing an immediate decision. When Mather hired Yard and brought him to Washington, he was managing the magazine section of the *New York Herald*. Mather put him on the Geological Survey payroll at a dollar a month, so he could obtain an office in a government building and use the franking privilege. Gradually the government pay rose to three hundred dollars a year. Mather, of course, was augmenting this with six hundred a month. On July 1, 1918, however, the Congress passed a new law prohibiting the paying of government employees from private funds such as Mather did for Yard, certain clerks and secretaries, and of course myself.

This new law came about because Senator John D. Work of California was a Christian Scientist. He had discovered that the Bureau of Education was employing many experts for one dollar a month. They were being paid by the American Medical Association to write pamphlets on school hygiene and treatment of children for distribution in the schools as well as to give advice on prenatal care. So Work put an amendment on one of the appropriation bills to prohibit the payment of government employees from private funds. That meant you either took Mather's money and cut all ties with the government or kept your job but no longer accepted his monthly checks. The law was to be effective July 1, 1919.

When I received notification of the new law, I went to each of the office workers to whom Mather was paying a gratuity and explained the situation. I wanted to make sure they understood they had until July 1919 to receive his checks and make plans for the future. Most groaned but took it with a shrug of their shoulders.

Bob Yard was another proposition. I went over to his home, sat down with him out of earshot of his ladies, and carefully outlined the law. He was instantly hostile and said, "I won't leave. I'm too old to go back to magazine and newspaper work. Steve promised me a lifetime job, engaged me for life, and is obligated to take care of me financially to the end."

That was pretty blunt and positive, so I replied, "Well, any agreements you and Mr. Mather made are between the two of you. That's not my business. However, my business, as acting director, is to see that the law is obeyed. You have been heading the education and information section of the National Park Service, have a government office, and enjoy federal privileges. All these must be relinquished by July 1, 1919. You have one year to make new arrangements."

He stared me down. I didn't want to hurt this old friend, but there was no alternative for him, so I tried to soften the blow by adding, "Bob, of course, you'll continue to receive your regular check from Mr. Mather's account until you two can have a talk, settle your problems, and receive new instructions from him. How's that?" Bob just sat there, sadly nodding his head and staring vacantly out the window.

After Mather returned to Washington, they had it out. The result was that Bob stuck to his position. Mather denied he had ever made any long-range commitment. The estrangement between the old friends flared to the point that Mather was ready to cut Yard off without a nickel. Fearful of Mather's fragile health, several of us who were close acquaintances of both men tried to cool the situation. Nothing worked.

Mather even sent me over to Horace McFarland of the American Civic Association with an offer to slip him thirty-six hundred dollars a year to put Yard on the association's payroll. The understanding was to be kept a secret from Bob. But McFarland had never liked Bob and didn't want him in his outfit, so he refused Mather's request.

Attempting to make an appearance of friendly separation, Mather was persuaded to praise Yard publicly for his national park publicity work and pay his salary (now $650 a month) until the law went into effect in 1919. He also made a deal with Yard for a cash settlement of ten thousand dollars to start Bob's pet project, later known as the National Parks Association. When this organization was formed, Mather went so far as to lend it his name and prestige even though he wasn't happy. He feared it would directly compete with his friend McFarland's American Civic Association. However, at that time it seemed the only solution for placating Yard.

A few years later the two men parted forever. Mather became so angry with Yard's often rash criticism of Park Service policies, especially opposition to a Grand Teton National Park, that he withdrew his name and support from the National Parks Association.

Next I turned my attention to something to which I'd given a lot of thought. After this summer's tour of the parks, I had come to the conclusion that an architecture and landscape division should be created within the Park Service. We had finally been able to assume full jurisdiction over the roads in park areas. Mather and I had talked about this many times and felt that roads in a national park should have exceptional consideration. Obviously, top priority would be given to construction and safety, but esthetic values came next. Within park areas this covered buildings, gateway entrances, overlooks for scenic vistas, and other architectural and visual components.

Consulting with several people, including Frederick Law Olmsted, Jr., I set up a new landscape division, outlining its duties to plan, design, approve, and direct construction of all park structures by the government or the concessioners. I wanted to ensure that the natural scene be kept as close as possible to what it was when found and, from then on, kept unimpaired into the future.

As for the natural features of the parks, I stated that only the outstanding ones, which were the prime reasons for the creation of a park, would be considered for development. The remainder, usually seventy-five percent or more of the total, were to be reserved as wilderness areas.

One day a telegram arrived: "Horace. Get out the flags. Dust off my desk. I'm coming back. Ogden September 15. Chicago September 23. Washington September 25. In between have date in Darien for graveyard dedication on September 22. Hooray. Stephen Mather."

On September 25, 1918, Mather strode into the office. He looked marvelous with his white hair and brilliant blue eyes accentuated by a deep, healthy tan. I'd never seen him look better, so robust, so exhilarated, so charming. He settled right down to the job as though he had never been away. We spent the next few days catching up on park business, mainly items that I had been careful to keep from him, long-range problems, and controversial matters.

I had good news for him too. The previous day, September 24, Katmai National Monument had been created by proclamation of President Wilson. I had barely mentioned to Mather how Gilbert Grosvenor of the National Geographic Society and I had hatched a plan for Katmai. It is an example of how we got things done in 1918. Grosvenor merits ninety-nine percent of the credit for its success.

One day Grosvenor called me up and asked if I'd meet him for lunch. That would be fine. He appreciated good food, so we usually went to some fine restaurant. However, on this day when I walked into his office lunch was there—a large tray of sandwiches, some pie, and beverages. Across a huge oak conference table, a desk, and assorted open spaces were large Geographic Society maps, papers, and stacks of photographs. In an open arms sweep-of-the room gesture, he greeted me with: "Horace, look at all this. I have a new Park Service unit for you. This is Katmai National Park or, if you wish, the Valley of Ten Thousand Smokes National Park!"

I already knew quite a bit about Katmai and about the eruption in June 1912 of Novarupta volcano, located on the Alaskan mainland close to the string of Aleutian Islands. The giant explosion had been ten times more powerful than the modern Mount St. Helens eruption. Shortly afterward, the National Geographic sent an expedition to the region, led by Robert Griggs. He reported: "The whole valley as far as the eye could reach was full of hundreds, no thousands, of smokes curling up from its fissured floor." He named it the Valley of Ten Thousand Smokes. Grosvenor was deeply interested in the area and, in his January 1917 *National Geographic*, devoted almost the entire issue to Katmai.

Grosvenor had spoken to me about taking Katmai into the Park System, but at the time we had enough problems with Mount McKinley. To Congress, the whole Territory of Alaska was some far-off place like Mars. It was really only the forceful work of the Boone and Crockett Club members (one of whom was Theodore Roosevelt) that brought McKinley enough recognition to make it a park.

Also, we had already pushed Lassen from national monument to park status so that Billy Kent would support our Park Service organic act. In that same year we acquired more volcanoes when Hawaii was made a national park. We had taken a great deal of criticism for letting some of these become national parks. We weren't very pleased that Congress had created them while allowing certain obnoxious practices like mining and hunting in McKinley, summer homes in Hawaii, and railroad lines and reservoirs in Lassen. Of course, these developments had been planned and legislation was rolling before our Park Service was created, so we felt we didn't bear any shame. When new park areas were proposed and we noted that these practices and others even worse were included, however, we tried to wave a red flag. Where commercial interests were involved, it was really safer to avoid Congress and settle for a national monument.

I followed up with Grosvenor on the project. He had done a superb job of assembling maps and material, which he brought over to our offices in the Interior Department along with Robert Griggs, who knew and explained every inch of the proposed monument. We added experts from various bureaus in our department to the National Geographic people, and after several meetings we had a finished product. The boundaries, the financial issues, the expectations for wild life, and all other issues that the members of Congress or the Interior Department might raise seemed to have been settled.

Then I asked Grosvenor: "Well, now what'll we do? This really isn't the best moment to ask for a national park."

Grosvenor replied: "As long as you are satisfied, Horace, leave the rest to me. We may not get a national park, but by George at least we'll get a national monument."

So I said: "You're undoubtedly right. Because McKinley was such a long, hard pull, I think we'll have to settle for Katmai as a national monument."

This project wasn't exactly typical. Most proposed areas came out a lot differently, or at least with a lot more worry, time, and trouble. But Katmai does show how a prime area, studied carefully, and presented almost as a *fait accompli*, could become a part of the Park Service. Especially when no one in the Congress had an ax to grind or was paying much attention.

We didn't take it up with anyone. Nobody cared much about it. We just did it. We got the Geological Survey to take their fine maps and convert them to official Interior maps. As an attorney, I drew up the legal proclamation, as I did almost all legal papers for our bureau. I had it checked out by the department's solicitor general, and then I presented it to Secretary Lane. He never asked a single question except whether it was worthy of being in the Park Service. I said, "Yes." So he approved the project and sent it over to President Wilson, who signed the proclamation making Katmai a national monument.

I should add here that President Woodrow Wilson was totally uninterested in conservation, national parks, or anything that pertained to the great outdoors. Whatever fine things occurred during his administration, like creation of a National Park Service, came through Secretary Franklin Lane. Neither of them should be counted as conservationists, but Lane let us have free rein for the most part and in general didn't care to interfere with our judgments. Wilson just wasn't a conservationist in any sense of the word.

Mather was understandably excited about Katmai. He loved mountains and he loved volcanoes. He immediately wrote out his own personal check to Grosvenor to help with further scientific work at the new monument. This also whetted his appetite to investigate the question of more park areas, especially the ones proposed in Colorado. Unfortunately, they all were connected with Enos Mills.

There had rarely been a peaceful day between Mills and the National Park Service since its creation. The quarrel became of vital importance in 1918.

Mills was one of the prime spokesmen and writers in the fledgling conservation movement and was in a position to wreak havoc on the Park Service. Earlier, he had been in the forefront in promoting a park bureau and had led the fight for the creation of Rocky Mountain National Park. After 1916, however, relations had gone downhill like a toboggan. His antagonism focused on his belief that our service was becoming just like the Forest Service, and his venom was aimed mainly at me. After all, there wasn't anyone else around in the Park Service to jump on. Many the time I gnashed my teeth but kept my temper while trying to placate him without giving in to his unreasonable demands.

In November 1917, when he was all riled up about the grazing situation, Mills used the national press to vilify our policies and egg us into a fight with the Forest Service. I tried the iron fist in a velvet glove:

> I want you to know that I personally regard you as one of my best friends and that I also regard you as a most devoted friend to the cause of the national parks, and, furthermore, that I regard your accomplishments in the promotion of the national park movement as so important and far-reaching that only the lapse of time will afford opportunities to see them in their great proportions and value them correctly. . . . You may attack any forces whenever and wherever and in any manner that you choose . . . but it is ridiculous to even think of one executive department, or one of its bureaus, openly attacking another department or subdivision thereof, or even an individual officer of another department or bureau. It has therefore not been our policy to make any public references of any kind to the Department of Agriculture or to the Forest Service in regard to the national parks.

Mills paid no attention to my letter and others that followed. Instead he stepped up his attacks. In newspaper articles and letters, he stated that I had "sold out to the Forest Service." Evidence of this was manifest, he said, because of the slow progress in Colorado parks, especially Mount Evans, which lay in the middle of a national forest. Well, practically the whole western half of Colorado lay in some national forest, and we had already carved out quite a chunk for national park areas. With his monumental ego, Mills couldn't see any point of view except his own, couldn't or didn't want to understand the problems we had all over the West with the Forest Service.

Finally the matter came to a head. Mills wrote Secretary Lane in May 1918, thanking him for a copy of "your National Park Platform," and saying, "This platform should be epoch making." Not knowing I had written the platform, he added, "The Acting Director is a menace to the entire cause of the National Parks." Lane replied on July 22: "You undoubtedly mean Assistant Director Albright. I can not quite understand why you consider him a menace to the national park cause; on the contrary, he has been a conscientious and indefatigable worker in every phase of Interior Department activity looking to the advancement of the parks."

Mills kept up the attack from that time on. In August 1918, while I was inspecting the Fall River Road in Rocky Mountain with a Denver parks committee and a few of our park people, including my own assistant, Arthur Demaray, Mills never stopped delivering a tirade against the Park Service and me. Here's a sample of his rhetoric: "Albright's a crook who has sold out to the Forest Service" to further his own "cheap political interests." Demaray recorded this and similar sentiments and sent them on to Washington.

Mather read the reports carefully. Then he grilled me on every aspect of the various park areas in question and Mills's feud with the Park Service and me. When he seemed to be satisfied that he had digested the facts, he said: "Horace, you've got to get out to Colorado immediately and clean this whole thing up. Not just Mills. He's like a nasty little mosquito buzzing around waiting to draw blood. But we can't let all these important men and organizations believe we are passing them by, ignoring them, cozying up to the Forest Service for our own ends. That Mount Evans question is primary. Go there. Investigate it and make a decision on it. In the meantime, I'll straighten Mills out."

I packed my suitcases and caught a night train out of Washington on September 30. It was a depressing, heartbreaking trip. The train was overcrowded, mainly with men in uniform going to troop reception centers. We were packed in like sardines, and because of the flu the railroad provided masks and insisted we wear them at all times. That was pretty frightening, but cold as it was I spent as much time as possible standing up in the fresh air between the cars.

When I arrived in Denver, I kept my train mask on, as the mayor had ordered every person in public to wear them. He also had forbidden the assembly of more than five people, so meetings with the Chamber of Commerce, the Hotel Men's Association, the Tourist Bureau, and other groups scheduled for me had to be canceled. Instead, a tedious round of small conferences was held, often outdoors. The few inside scared me to death, for the disease was rampant in Denver.

However, it was vitally important that I meet with these groups. Denver was a beehive of activity with its so-called Denver Parks. Eleven thousand acres of them were easily and quickly accessible, and this didn't even count our Rocky Mountain National Park. Everyone from the governor to a shopkeeper seemed to be vitally interested in them, so of course we had to be too.

Trying to avoid crowds, I stayed with Roe and Jeanette Emery. Waiting for me was a copy of Mather's letter to Mills. In part it read: "Your astounding statement that Mr. Albright is a crook is particularly remarkable, coming from a man of your standing. Mr. Albright's record is as clean as a hound's tooth, and, in and out of season, he has given of himself without stint to the exacting duties of his office, carrying a particularly heavy burden during the period when my own illness threw everything on his shoulders. I simply will not stand by in silence and have slanderous statements of this kind go by without protest." Mather had a little note to me attached, which said, "I fixed Mills up with Lorimer [editor of the *Saturday Evening Post*]. If he doesn't be quiet, his income is going to suffer!"

Everywhere I went I heard more accounts of Mills and his comments about Albright, the Park Service, and now Mather. I inwardly boiled for hours. Finally that night, when I was as mad as a hornet, I typed out a letter to Mills. I intended to mail it as soon as I got out of Colorado, but I ended up reading it to him in person a few days later. My letter advised him that I knew all about his vitriolic attacks and added: "Evidently, in your opinion, Secretary Lane and Mr. Mather, under whom I have worked for years, are not as competent to pass on my fitness for this position as you are. I would not like you to believe that, under a few more pricks of your unjust and untruthful pen, I will get discouraged and quit. That is not my disposition nor my intention. . . . I shall see you there [Rocky Mountain], but not to ask advice, consent or instructions from you."

At about 14,260 feet, Mount Evans was the most prominent peak seen from Denver, though not so much different from any number of others along the Front Range of the Rockies. Its surrounding region greatly resembled Rocky Mountain National Park. So why was Mather so desirous of adding it to that park or creating a separate one? I'm not sure. He loved Rocky Mountain and felt Mount Evans would enlarge the experience of visitors. Of course, the two would not be connected because a vast area would lie between them. But deep down, I knew he held Mills in high esteem, even being a bit afraid of him and the power of his pen.

From my standpoint, I wanted to go over the region carefully because I had serious doubts about it and wouldn't think of disputing my chief unless I had good reasons. With so many wonderful areas on our list for acquisition, like Greater Sequoia and Greater Yellowstone, I wasn't sure that duplication of this mountain scene and getting into another war with the Forest Service was worth it. Although the whole Mount Evans project was only eight percent of Pike National Forest, and with so much above timberline as to have no commercial value to speak of, you could bet that they'd still fight like cats over letting us have it.

Besides these considerations, the Denver backers wanted many other nearby areas in the Park Service, areas that mainly attracted people from Denver. These didn't really have a national appeal. I always was thinking of this factor, having had to beat back or discourage countless plans eager congressmen had for some little place in their district to help the local economy and pat themselves on the back come reelection time. I believed the Park Service should never be diluted with sites that did not measure up to the highest standards for all the people, that were not of national significance. As I put into the "creed" earlier that year, "The National Park system as now constituted should not be lowered in standard, dignity, and prestige by the inclusion of areas which express in less than the highest terms the particular class or kind of exhibit which they represent." Mount Evans wasn't in a lower class, and it was of national significance. But it was a question of duplication, being superfluous.

From October 5 to 9 Superintendent Way, two experienced mountain climbers, and I reached the summit of Mount Evans and then explored various cirques and buttresses around the peak to work up a proposal for a national park. It was an extraordinary experience. I came to the conclusion that Mount Evans was definitely worth fighting for and should be made a national park, whether by extension of Rocky Mountain or on its own. I had gone up there a doubting Thomas and had come down completely sold on acquiring it. The only reservation I still had was the highway to the top of the mountain, which was already under construction. Nothing could be done about that anyway.

"I'M COMING DOWN TO WASHINGTON"

From Mount Evans, I went on to Rocky Mountain National Park for a quick but thorough inspection, carefully avoiding Enos Mills until I was ready to leave for California.

On my last day at Rocky Mountain, at about the last hour, I let Way inform Mills that if he came to the Park Service office I could arrange a short time to see him. Well, I think he must have done the one-minute mile from his place, for he rushed in with tie askew and panting like a hound after a fox. Of course, he was anything but gentle and contrite. He ranted on about the park, but mainly confined himself to chastising me for not paying attention to the Mount Evans region. He said I was in cahoots with the Forest Service to let them keep that area, and on and on.

I didn't have the time or the inclination to listen to much of this, so I cut him off with a few curt sentences about my recent trip up Mount Evans and the possibility of recommending its inclusion in our service. Then I read my letter addressed to him, as mentioned above. With that I picked up my coat, put on my hat, told Way we were leaving, and exited. Mills apparently was too stunned to open his mouth. He never got a chance to say a thing before we drove off to Denver.

I wrote Howard Hays a few days later, telling him about the meeting, and closed with, "I am done with the fellow unless he comes around with an apology." Well, he never did, but we lived to meet on more battle-grounds until 1922, when he died.

Earlier I quoted Roe Emery about Mills's death, but here's another remark to me from Jack La Gorce, an editor of the *National Geographic* magazine: "I cannot tell you how happy and pleased I am to hear of the death of Enos Mills, and I hope that he is in the nethermost of the seventy hells of Confucius for that's where he deserves to be."

I wrote back, "It is hardly necessary to tell you that I was considerably relieved when I heard that the undertaker was attending to him instead of a doctor."

All in all, Colorado had afforded a marvelous, worthwhile visit. However, I was very careful not to commit the Park Service about the Mount Evans region (known locally as the Denver National Park) until a final decision could be made in Washington. I stated in the Denver newspapers that I could not discuss the project except from my personal impressions, which were favorable, that I was here simply to observe and gather facts for a report to be given to Mather and Secretary Lane.

Shortly after this, a bill sanctioned by the Interior Department was introduced in the Congress but never made it out of committee. It was smothered before a full vote could be taken. In a letter to the Denver Mountain Parks Commission in December 1918, I somewhat bitterly wrote: "The time has come when the choice must be made between the Forest Service and the Park Service in matters relating to recreation service. Henry Graves and his powerful lobby defeated the National Park Service efforts to get the Mount Evans area."

CHAPTER
24

A Step Backward
1918

After a nostalgic visit with my dad and mother in Bishop, I went to Berkeley. I had decided to use this time to make a break with the Park Service and find a position with a law firm in California. Grace and I were finally together and looking forward to months of happiness.

Our "months" lasted one day. A telegram from Secretary Lane arrived, which stated: "You must return at once. Matters here make it imperative." I left immediately, only stopping in Chicago long enough to learn from Harold White, Mather's close friend and financial advisor, that Mr. Mather was suffering a mental relapse. It was a different twist from his earlier illness. This upset was marked by irrational check-writing for political purposes, seizure of hotel and transportation concessions in Yellowstone to make them public corporations, and appointing a man outside the Park Service as superintendent of Yellowstone. Badly shaken by this information, I wondered if something worse had happened to warrant Lane's orders to me. I hurried on to Washington and arrived on October 31, 1918.

At the Interior Department I went directly to Secretary Lane. He was anxiously waiting for me. Usually placid and calm, he greeted me with: "Albright, thank God you're here. I've got a wild man on my hands. You're the only one that can handle him. Get him out of Washington. Get him to a doctor. Just get him away from this department before all hell breaks loose."

I quickly assured the secretary I'd do my best, but I had to know what Mr. Mather's problem was. He gave me a rundown of events that chilled my bones. Mather was not in any form of the depressive and physically weakened condition of January 1917. He now exhibited a frenzied euphoria and extreme aggressiveness, considering himself infallible. He was apparently riding the crest of a wave. He was just as big as all outdoors, the mightiest man in the world.

Spending the rest of the day carefully avoiding Mather, I talked with almost everyone else associated with him to get a clear, unbiased account of his actions. They all loved the man so much that no one wanted to say anything detrimental. Isabelle Story was more open and frank, suggesting that he probably wasn't as well as he had appeared, that he hadn't really regained his confidence to go it alone. My departure, so soon after he had returned to office, had thrust more responsibility on him than he could take. It sounded reasonable, but that didn't solve the problem.

Before the day was out, I was dealt another blow. Mather had appointed a new Yellowstone superintendent, Emerson Hough. I simply couldn't believe my ears that Mather had actually appointed that old curmudgeon, who couldn't get along with Santa Claus, the superintendent of Yellowstone.

Hough himself broke the news to me. Mather had been grateful for all the articles he had written on behalf of the parks, all the help he had given the Park Service, so he offered him the job. Hough was pleased and proud and accepted the offer.

Late in the afternoon Hough reappeared and informed me that Mather had told him he could use my apartment until he got out of the army and could set off for Yellowstone. At this time he was serving as a captain in the intelligence division. After announcing that, he looped his arm through mine saying, "Well, let's go pick up my things and get settled over at your place." No one would enjoy living with Emerson Hough with his cigars, clacking typewriter, and foul moods. A few days out in the Sierra Nevada was one thing, but holed up in a tiny apartment was something else.

November 1, 1918, was a day to remember. I went down to our office early that morning. Before I could even plan what to do about Mather's situation, I received instructions to go to school. School? Mather had ordered every member in his bureau to meet in the basement at 9:15 A.M. Not only that, but he had summoned the other bureau chiefs of the Interior Department to attend, including Geological Survey, Indian Affairs, and so forth. Even more astonishingly, Secretary Lane had been instructed to attend. Mather stated that he would lecture the class on "principles of government."

Needless to say, the other bureau chiefs politely declined Mather's summons, and I never heard what Lane's reply was, if there even was one. The "school" was the talk of the department. Of course, those under Mather's control obeyed and were dutifully assembled. Mather presided like a schoolteacher. He wouldn't allow any whispering. Everyone just sat there, listening to his rambling, disconnected, but very enthusiastic sermon on the future of the National Park Service and its mission. I'm sure every one of us felt the same: grimly silent and obviously distressed to see our chief in such a condition.

After Mather let us out of school, he and I were alone in his office. I asked, "What is all this you are doing?"

"Don't you like it?" he replied.

I answered, "No, I don't, and we can't have this kind of thing, Mr. Mather."

His answer was short and to the point: "You are fired. You can't interfere with what I am doing. I am back here now taking up the reins, and either you agree with what I do or get out."

I was not going to get into an argument with him or get him more excited, so I simply nodded and left. First of all I went to Lane and reported the incident. I told him that I just wasn't going to challenge Mather anymore in his fragile state of mind, that Lane would have to handle it. I probably overstepped myself by emotionally saying, "You'll have to do the dirty work yourself."

Fortunately, Lane recognized that I was overwrought, so he ignored my words and answered quietly, "I just don't want him around here anymore. He's messing in politics. He's messing up my department. Just get him out of Washington."

That sobered me immediately. I was fearful that he would summarily replace Mather, so I asked him directly if that was his plan. He didn't answer me immediately, just seemed to give some real thought to the question. Finally, he said, "I don't want to lose Steve, but I can't have a repetition of his breakdowns disrupting my department. So have him take another rest, and in the meantime I'll reappoint you acting director."

Much as I hated the thought, I quickly decided it was better that I had the position than that Lane should appoint someone else or just remove Mather permanently. I assured the secretary that I would get

Mather out of Washington immediately but asked him please not to tell Mather I was to be acting director.

Then I called Chicago and spoke to Mrs. Mather and Harold White. They informed me that the amount of the checks Mather had been writing for the election of senators and congressmen was increasing. He had donated thousands and thousands of dollars so far. Now another disturbing thing had cropped up. He planned to go "on the road" to campaign for his favorite candidates before the upcoming election. He especially wanted to work for his good friend Representative Julius Kahn of San Francisco, one of those who had no opposition.

I went back to see Mr. Mather, who had apparently forgotten I was fired. I was very quiet and agreeable no matter what he said. I pulled the conversation around to the elections, and he eagerly told me how he wanted to campaign for friends. Picking this up with great enthusiasm, I proposed that we head for Chicago. "Let's get out of Washington, move back to the heartland of America, and plan strategy." He thought it a splendid idea and proposed that we leave that very night. Quickly calling on a railroad friend, I secured a drawing room on the first train for Illinois.

We pulled away from Washington and were comfortably settled in for the night. Mather was in the lower berth, I in the upper. Suddenly he jerked me awake with, "You get down out of there. We've got work to do. We have to sharpen a lot of razor blades." He was standing there with a handful of his straight-edged razors. My heart pounding, I jumped down, not bothering to put on a bathrobe, and relieved him of his blades. I advised him to get some rest, that I'd sharpen them. And I honed razor blades most of the night. Every time I would try to quietly leave these things in the little bathroom and sneak back to the upper berth, he would pop out and question how I was doing or volunteer to do it himself. I wasn't going to trust him with the razors, so I would get him back to bed and start stropping the darn things myself.

We pulled into Chicago the next morning. Mather was bright as a button but still wired as though tied to a battery. I was drained from no sleep, worry, and probably loss of blood from my multiple cuts. I had never handled these antique nineteenth-century weapons before.

When I got Mather in a cab and gave the address of his home at 5638 Dorchester Avenue, he flatly refused to go there, insisting on the Athletic Club instead. Mrs. Mather had warned me not to cross him in any way, so we went to the Athletic Club, where I signed him in. Then I quickly called Harold White for help.

A STEP BACKWARD

Before White could get to the club, Mather decided he was leaving immediately for Denver and ordered me to make reservations. When Harold arrived, we tried to talk Mather out of his Denver destination. He was adamant, so we three went down to the station. When it was time for the train to go, we had to tell him he couldn't leave. We took his suitcase away and checked it. At the same time, White hissed at me, "Get out of Chicago and leave this to me."

I didn't need a second warning so immediately headed back to Washington to start unraveling what Mather had done. Of course, I did not know the extent of the damage. When I reported to Lane on the outcome in Chicago, he was so relieved that I feared he was about to kiss me for spiriting Mather away, saving him from taking action himself.

For the next several weeks, Mather made a short visit to Darien, then went on to Henry Fairfield Osborn's Hudson River estate for several weeks, and finally entrained for Hot Springs. At Dr. Weisenburg's suggestion, and with Lane's consent, I assigned Joseph Cotter and Frank Griffiths from the Interior Department to stay with my chief.

On November 20 Griffiths reported: "STM is wrought up much as he was a few weeks ago. He is all worked up over the Child–Yellowstone Hotel matter." I settled this problem by suggesting to Child that he join Mather at Hot Springs and talk to him man-to-man.

Child arrived in Hot Springs and joined Mather at a bath house. As they lolled in the warm mineral waters, Harry tossed off, "Hey, Steve, I want to thank you for taking those damn, money-losing hotels and buses off my hands. They were killing me and I wasn't making any money anyway." Mather jumped at this opportunity, conceded he'd made a mistake, blamed it all on Harry's son Huntley, and practically begged Harry to take his white elephants back.

Now I had to figure a way to get rid of Emerson Hough's superintendency of Yellowstone. First, on November 21, I wrote Mather:

I hope you will do or say nothing about the matter of appointing Mr. Hough to the Yellowstone until I have a chance to talk to you. There are a good many angles to this matter which we ought to go over together before any final steps are taken. You know he is disliked cordially in the Jackson Hole, and Mr. Mondell [Wyoming's congressman] has no use for him. We must go slowly on these accounts until the Greater Yellowstone bill is brought up. Furthermore Mr. Lindsley has a right to some consideration in this matter. It is hardly right to put a man in just to give prestige to an office while another man has to do all the work at a lower salary.

Mather's reply was more than a little discouraging: "I am still following up the matter of Mr. Hough taking the superintendency of Yellowstone. Mrs. Hough expresses herself as thinking well of it and is willing to accompany him and live in one of our stone houses."

Now there was only one way to go. I had to disenchant Emerson about the job. Sometimes in the evening when we were sitting around my apartment, we would "chew the fat," as he called it. Every opportunity I got I threw in the disadvantages of his being superintendent of Yellowstone. He would lose his identity as a writer. He would be required to remain in the park all year—even during the long months of those terrible winters. His yearly salary would be peanuts compared to just one serial in the *Saturday Evening Post*. And, of course, that was a moot question because he'd never have time to do any writing for the *Post* or anything else.

Hough was a complete hypochondriac, so I gave him food for thought about the terrible time we were having to recruit a doctor for Yellowstone. No doctor worth his salt would take the job. I worried out loud a lot about how we'd "end up with some doctor we used for treating sick bison."

Remembering what Mather had written, I casually mentioned the superintendent's house. It certainly would be hard for Lottie to keep up that enormous four-story house. That was a brilliant stroke and the one I think did the trick. It was a terrifying idea that he would be isolated in a huge, drafty old stone house with snow piled up to the windows and no one but Lottie and the French maid to keep him company. The Airedale would even have to stay in the kennels in Chicago.

If I ever needed a job, I guess I could be a snake oil salesman because it worked. Eventually Hough backed out with apologies and thanks to Mather. Later, when I became superintendent of Yellowstone, Mather accidentally let Hough know about my effort to squash his appointment. Hough never let me forget that he believed I had eased him out of the job so I could have it. That was very embarrassing, but I guess he forgave me because he and Lottie came for an extended stay at our home in Yellowstone in 1919 before we had our suitcases unpacked.

In the meantime, the best of all possible news burst on the nation. The war finally ended on November 11, 1918. The town went crazy. About

6:00 P.M. I went downtown to the corner by the Treasury Department, 15th and Pennsylvania. The place was pandemonium. Every vehicle that could be commandeered—trucks, cars, bicycles, even some horses and wagons—milled around. Horns on the vehicles were blown. There were cowbells and drums. The noise was unbelievably loud and raucous. I stood there on the corner, wondering if I wanted to celebrate, mix with the crowd. I admit to being a coward when it came to the Spanish Flu. Instead I went to dinner with an old friend from California with a mixture of joy and thanksgiving. When Spanish Flu cases plummeted almost from the hour of the armistice, Americans breathed a sigh of gratitude and prayerful thanks to God for these two miracles.

With the conclusion of the war, Mather apparently recuperating in Hot Springs, and the Park Service operating smoothly in Washington and across the country, I had to weigh my options for the future carefully. I must say I was very unhappy. I had never felt so unsure of the future. For almost two years I had been positive that when Mr. Mather came back full-time as director I would be set free. I could return to California, go into a legal firm in San Francisco, and settle down with Grace. Now Mather's renewed collapse was a blow to all my hopes. I was depressed, unhappy, and in a dreadful quandary.

I could simply resign and leave the Park Service. But I was appalled at the thought of deserting this fledgling bureau and the goals we had set for it. Most of all, I couldn't fail Stephen Mather. There were whispers all over the Interior Department that Lane was ready to ease Mather out. With the directorship open, he could of course appoint someone new. The end of the war would open a floodgate of men looking for jobs in government, men with money or influence in the Democratic administration. Lane had only feeble political clout, so it seemed probable that those close to Wilson could pick the man.

I could find out nothing concrete about my chief. I simply had gotten to the point that I couldn't face an endless future of uncertainty. I'd been forced to assume all responsibility for the Park Service for two years, and now I felt like I had to fish or cut bait. Was Mather in or out? If I had to keep taking his place, would I be appointed director should he resign? Or was I always to be doing the work of a director but having the title of assistant? What exactly was my real authority and my future, if any, in the National Park Service?

It boiled down to the fact that, under current conditions, I couldn't abandon Mather and the Park Service. On the other hand, I couldn't stay under these conditions, never knowing what my future was. After agonizing over the pros and cons, I came to the conclusion that I must bring the entire question of Mather and Albright directly to Franklin K. Lane and have it out in the open and settled.

With Hough in my apartment, I set up my typewriter late at night in the office. I wrote a letter to Lane that was succinct and unemotional, just a request to see him to ascertain Mather's future. But after I went home and lay in bed, I couldn't sleep. Suddenly I looked at the whole problem in a different light. I got up, dressed, returned to the office about 3:00 A.M., and wrote a very long letter to Secretary Lane, presenting every fact I could muster as to why I should be appointed director of the National Park Service should Mr. Mather be unable to continue in that position. My new letter tried to convince Lane to keep Mather as director, but if he decided against that, to offer every reason I could think of why I should replace him.

The formal letter was followed by a seven-page legal-like brief entitled "Confidential Memorandum for the Secretary." I began with a long summation of Mather's brilliant success since coming to Washington in 1914. Next I turned to my qualifications for the position of director if he were no longer holding it.

On November 26 I received a reply to my letter. It had been mailed to me the day before, not hand-delivered as was the custom in the department. It was brief and to the point: "Dear Mr. Albright: I hope Mather will be able to return soon to take charge of his work. In the event that he can not I have in mind one or two men who I would put into his place; and if you would find it impossible to remain as Assistant Director of course you could resign, much as I would dislike to see this because of your identity with the work, your interest in it, and the good work you have done. Cordially yours, Franklin K. Lane."

I was stunned, hurt, and humiliated. His abrupt words and what seemed to be callous indifference shook me to the core. His use of "Mather"—not Mr. Mather or Steve, as he always called him—hit me as an insult to my chief. It was as if he had brushed this incomparable man and his accomplishments aside like a worrisome fly.

I read and reread those few lines. First anger, furious anger, replaced shock. Then I began to feel wounded, rejected, and dismayed. I had succeeded in everything I had ever tackled and felt I had accomplished a great deal in my twenty-eight years. Now Lane, with a few blunt sentences, had badly undercut my self-confidence.

A STEP BACKWARD

I couldn't understand at first why he had dismissed my proposals out of hand. Why couldn't he have offered a kindly explanation? Or why couldn't he have waited to talk it all over with me in person? The main point was that Lane was obviously through with both Mr. Mather and me. It was now only a question of when, not if, a new man would be taking over the National Park Service.

But the more I thought about it, the more I decided there was something beneath the surface. Lane was a very insecure man. He often referred to the fact that he was chosen for his position not because of ability to run the Interior Department but because he could pull off the Hetch Hetchy deal. Wilson needed that to secure the support of the San Francisco political machine. Lane also frequently complained that he wasn't "in" with the president, wasn't consulted on many issues outside his own department, was ignored at cabinet meetings.

Could my comments on Mather's and my success at the University of California been construed in Lane's mind as a reference to his inability to graduate? Furthermore, references to Mather's success in business and his wealth might have rubbed Lane the wrong way. He complained about not being able to keep up a style commensurate with his social position. He was always scrounging for money and let people pick up tabs at dinners, hotels, and so forth. He had a deferential, almost humble, attitude toward powerful and wealthy people.

I remember a clash Lane and Mather once had when the secretary expressed his opinion that he was in favor of the federal government preserving wilderness. After a pause, he added, "as long as convenient." While Mather's blood pressure rose, Lane went on to explain why the government should aid economic growth. He gave the impression that he would go along with conservation of parks and forests as long as it didn't interfere with economic expansion or private business making money from public resources. We found that out in 1919 when Lane came out strongly for water and power interests in Yellowstone.

Lane always helped big oil companies while he was secretary. He was in favor of government support of them through tax benefits and letting them make good profits from the public domain while paying very little to the United States government. He endorsed disputed private claims within the Elk Hills naval oil reserve and was in favor of large firms receiving tax write-offs. He resigned as secretary of the interior to become vice-president of Edward Doheny's Pan-American Oil Company at a salary of fifty thousand dollars a year. Later Albert B. Fall, another interior secretary, was jailed for accepting a loan from Doheny tied to the same oil fields in Wyoming. Fall always claimed that the shenanigans surrounding Teapot Dome had started during World War I under Lane.

All these ideas were neither here nor there because the conclusion was basically the same. Secretary Lane was preparing for a change in the National Park Service that would eliminate Mather and Albright. I was heartsick. For myself, I really wanted a new direction for my life out in California with Grace and our new baby to be born in a few weeks. For Stephen Mather, a man I had grown to care for more than any other, I could hardly bear the thought of what an abrupt dismissal might do to him. I tried to console myself by believing I had done everything I could to spare him the pain.

I had my meeting with Lane. I was cold and polite while he was pleasant and normal as always as though no correspondence had been exchanged. He never brought it up, and I was still so angry that I knew it was the better part of valor to keep silent. He asked me offhand if I would be around during the holidays and I replied, "Well, I could, Mr. Secretary, but with Washington practically closed down from the Christmas holidays to the new session of Congress, I'd like to go West and tackle problems out there."

Lane agreed to that. He added that my first concern should be to have the California Legislature remove the state's authority over Yosemite. He casually remarked that of course I'd remain as acting director. He also requested that I stay in Washington until after the New Year to see how Mather was doing and what his schedule was going to be.

In Hot Springs Mather decided that a relaxing trip to the West Coast was just the thing. In December, accompanied by his friend Herb Gleason, he traveled through the Northwest. By the end of the year, he was back in Chicago and felt he would pick up the reins in Washington soon. Quick action this time had saved him from a serious and lengthy relapse.

In Washington I was preparing for the coming summer season. In view of the war's end, we anticipated a flood of tourists to the parks, which required endless, precise planning. I was also responsible for projecting the budget for the upcoming fiscal year and for testifying before Congress to support my recommendations.

Christmas came and went like every other day, except that I didn't go to the office. New Year's Eve, December 31, 1918, was just as bad, the most miserable I had ever spent in my life. No gay, whirling evening at a grand Washington hotel. No romantic toasts to the New Year. No beautiful wife to waltz around a dance floor. I took out my little pocket diary and, with mounting depression, added up the dismal score: I had only been with Grace four days in the last six months! I made a New Year's resolution right there that 1919 was going to be different, and we were never going to be apart that much again.

25

A New Year and a New Future
1919

On January 6, 1919, I celebrated my twenty-ninth birthday by pulling out of Washington. Just before I left, I received a telegram from Mr. Mather. He was in Albuquerque, New Mexico. "Congratulations on your birthday and for what you have accomplished in this relatively short span of years. May the next 29 be ever more fruitful." He added that he would meet me in South Chicago.

Lane had issued my travel orders and had assured me Mather knew all about them. That was not true. Mather had only been told I was going west for a short time, and it was implied that I'd be back in Washington soon. When we sat down together in Chicago and he learned Lane had consented to an indefinite stay in California, his ill-concealed anger at Lane turned into smooth talk to convince me that my place was in Washington.

Not this time, I protested. My orders were from Lane, and I couldn't do a thing about it. Of course, he knew that I could easily get those changed if I wanted to, but I had absolutely no intention of doing so.

I was delighted to note that Mather appeared to be as good as new. Instead I felt I was the one who was beaten up. I reminded him of the last two years, of the stress and work, the separation from Grace. He listened and kindly sympathized and thanked me profusely, but he came back with the argument that he simply couldn't stay in Washington too long at a time. It damaged his health. I would have to take over when he wasn't there. I almost told him I couldn't and wouldn't, but Lane's letter came back to haunt me. I had deliberately kept our correspondence away from Mather.

Mather then happily told me about the proposed trip to Hawaii that he and his family were going to take right after the first of the year. He pointed out that it would be necessary for me to be back in Washington while he was gone. His purpose was clear. Get me to Washington and then keep me there when he returned. My reaction was that he was again thrusting on my shoulders the burden of keeping him healthy and seeing that the Park Service was running smoothly even though he was back as director.

It was just too much for me. For the first time since we had been a team, I refused his request. Not only that, but I added that I had to go to California to look for a new job, that I had to leave the Park Service for the sake of my wife and the baby. And I blurted out the gist of my letter to Lane and his response. There just was no future for me in the service.

Momentarily I was afraid I had gone too far, for he slumped back in his chair, put his hands over his face, and said nothing. Just as I was about to try to soften my abrupt declaration, he quietly said, "I understand, Horace. You go on out to San Francisco and stay there for a few months with Grace and the baby. I know how hard it's been for you and how tired you must be. Go ahead and open an office out there and clean up our problems on the West Coast. But I'll ask one thing of you. Please don't make any hasty decision. Take care of the service while I'm gone and give me a little time to ease back into my job."

His pathetic words and my deep concern for him forced me to agree to his plan. You could almost hear our sighs of relief that an impasse had been avoided—at least temporarily.

I stayed over in Chicago for a day with him, going over matters I would attend to on the West Coast, especially Yosemite concession problems. On the train I had a few days of reading and relaxation before arriving in Berkeley on the clear and sunny morning of January 11, 1919.

As usual, my girl was her bubbling self and looked as beautiful as ever. I want to say right here that she wasn't just beautiful on the outside, for she certainly was, but she had an inner beauty. It just shone like an aura around her. Approaching motherhood had added to her already gentle and compassionate warmth, her desire always to do something for someone else and to make my life as smooth as she could. Each reunion seemed more precious than the last.

The next day, January 12, I set up my headquarters in an office of the United States Public Health Service in the Call-Bulletin Building on New Montgomery Street near the Palace Hotel. As Grace and I were living with her parents on Ellsworth Street in Berkeley, I commuted daily back and forth to the "City" via the ferry boat. Those quiet, lazy ferries were a wonderful invention for a person to catch up on the news in the morning paper going over and calm down at night with the wind, the foghorns, and the gentle dipping and swaying of the boat as it plowed its way to the East Bay.

Instead of what I had planned, my California relaxation period turned into a buzz-saw. Of course, there was the business Lane had assigned me of getting a bill through the state legislature turning over California police jurisdiction of Yosemite, Sequoia, and General Grant parks to the federal government. Then there was another crisis with the concession in Yosemite. On top of these, Mather opened up an explosive situation with changing our Sequoia extension project into a promotion of Roosevelt National Park, as he renamed it.

Since Mather's two mountain trips in 1915 and 1916, we had gained a great deal of support for the extension of Sequoia. The so-called Greater Sequoia would include the existing Sequoia and General Grant Parks but would add the Kern River Canyon, Mount Whitney and surrounding area, and most of the Kings River and its watershed. Of course, we also wanted the Tehipite section to the north of the Kings. In Yosemite we never let up asking for the restoration of the magnificent Minarets and Mount Ritter areas, which had been taken away in 1906. Our dream was to create a great swath of wilderness through the "The Range of Light," as John Muir called the Sierra Nevada.

The American Civic Association, the Sierra Club, the national and local press, and many prominent men in Washington had joined our crusade. Bills had been introduced in the Congress but were dangling in the wind. From the beginning, we had been grimly opposed by the Forest Service, by the people who had grazing rights, by hunters and fishermen, and finally by the water and power interests, including the juggernaut Los Angeles, which was also gobbling up the lands on the east side of the Sierra.

The Park Service had made one step forward when, on July 8, 1918, President Wilson signed an executive order temporarily withdrawing from entry, sale, and settlement all lands described in the latest extension bills before the Congress. However, in December our adversarial secretary of agriculture, David F. Houston, issued an unfavorable report, claiming that he hadn't had time to study the whole situation in his forests (which, of course, constituted most of the lands we coveted). Our Greater Sequoia appeared stalled.

Then came news of Theodore Roosevelt's death, on January 6, my birthday. To Mather this was a terrible blow. A few days later he read in the paper about a dinner in New York where a group of Boone and Crockett Club members had met to decide on a fitting memorial for their most famous member, Teddy Roosevelt. Someone had suggested that a national park in his honor would be perfect. Of course, said Mather, and he knew where that park was located and how to promote this splendid idea.

Even though Roosevelt was one of his heroes, Mather didn't give a darn about memorializing his name. He had instantly recognized a way to get his Greater Sequoia. Although another park had been proposed at the same time, by the same name, in the Badlands of North Dakota, Mather played that one down. He publicized Roosevelt's connection with California, knowing full well that the state wasn't prominent in TR's life. He had visited the state a couple of times, and he had received only 174 votes more than Wilson in the 1912 presidential election, splitting the electoral vote.

But Mather knew how to exploit a situation and never missed an opportunity for publicity. He had Yard and other media contacts pump out reams of copy about creating a great Sierra Nevada park in honor of the late lamented president, Roosevelt National Park.

Honoring a favorite president by a great national park captured the fancy of Americans and was received with warm approval. There already was a bill concerning Greater Sequoia pending in the Congress, so Mather planned to turn the grief of a nation into a golden opportunity to get this passed.

Mather ordered me to get busy on the situation in California while he drummed up support in Washington. The result was swift. A Senate bill creating the Roosevelt National Park by enlarging the present Sequoia Park passed unanimously, but it still had to face the House. As it turned out, it was defeated by the tactics of Representative Denver Church of Fresno, a Democrat. He had no intention of glorifying any Republican president. At the same time, he did want to satisfy his agricultural friends with irrigation water that would be denied to them with this enlarged park. He pulled the old stunt of pleading illness. He was too sick to be present for a vote and requested the House delay the vote until he could return. As a gesture of sympathy, his wish was granted and the bill died aborning.

Before I could jump into this fray, I got a telegram from Lane, needling me to get going on the job he had asked me to do for him. I dropped everything else and headed for Sacramento, where I spent a great deal of time for the next several months.

California still retained law enforcement authority over the national parks in the state. The Park Service wanted to have complete jurisdiction within its borders. We had gotten the soldiers out of our lands. We had the army engineers off our road construction. Now we wanted federal judges to have the power to punish lawbreakers, federal commissioners in the parks who could try cases rather than have the state try them outside the parks.

Although the matter had been brought to the attention of state officials, it had been ignored. Voters were apathetic, and consequently politicians did nothing. Then I noticed in a newspaper that a college friend, Charlie Kasch, was in the state assembly from Ukiah. I hurried back to Sacramento and got in touch with him. He immediately picked up the ball and ran with it. He introduced a bill in the assembly on January 16, giving full police powers to the federal government. Next he got me together with Senator Evans, who started the bill through the Senate. It still took many trips to Sacramento before the bill finally passed on April 15, 1919. It was most successful and covered everything we wanted, except that the state retained the right to tax and issue fish and game licenses. On June 2, 1920, Congress accepted California's cession of jurisdiction over all lands within Sequoia, General Grant, and Yosemite.

Before I could turn to the Yosemite situation, Mr. Mather returned to Washington. Many people wrote me about how grand he looked and how he had really taken hold in his masterful and exuberant style. He approached every problem there with contacts in person or a deluge of letters. His charm and persistence brought results. If he couldn't move people by verbal or written arguments, he coaxed them over to the Cosmos Club for lunch or took them out for a leisurely dinner at the Willard and perhaps an evening at the theater afterward. They usually came around to his suggestions.

Now that I felt the work in Sacramento was basically wrapped up, I turned to Yosemite. On December 12, 1917, the name of the Desmond Service Company had officially been changed to the Yosemite Park Company and leased to Richard and Harold Shaffer.

These brothers had been doing business in the valley before there was a Park Service. When the "blunt-nosed mechanical beetles," as John Muir called the automobiles, were permitted into Yosemite, they were required to stay in a special auto camp. When that filled up, all other motorists had to leave their cars at a certain garage for space or repairs. These averaged twenty-five dollars per car.

So along with this business the brothers Shaffer now operated the Yosemite Park Company from April 1 to October 1, 1918. They did just fine, better than anyone had before. In fact, they actually made money, all of sixteen thousand dollars. This profit inspired them to ask A. B. C. Dohrmann and associates to sell the company to them. Negotiations went well for a while. The Shaffers raised the amount they understood was necessary, but Dohrmann raised the ante. He now wanted $450,000, more than the Shaffers could come up with.

In December 1918 Harold White had written me that he expected Dohrmann in Chicago the next day. He was not going to allow Mather to see him and intended to refuse any further refinancing of the Yosemite Company through the issue of additional bonds.

When it became apparent that there was no money to see the company through the 1919 summer season, the Reorganization Committee under Dohrmann came to the conclusion that the only way out of their dilemma was to renegotiate the franchise contract with Secretary Lane. The company simply had to make more profit.

In December 1918 Dohrmann and Lane agreed on general terms. Then they directed me to negotiate the final contract. That's what used up a good portion of my time through the winter and into the spring. It was a well-trodden path from San Francisco to Yosemite, from Dohrmann to Lewis, to my typewriter or the telegraph office with messages for Lane and Mather. Terms simply couldn't be reached. Later on in the year Lane appointed an arbitration committee, people outside both parties, and final terms were agreed upon, although never really settled until 1923.

To remove the company from receivership, Dohrmann and his associates reorganized the Yosemite Park Company, raised one million dollars from San Francisco and Los Angeles businessmen, and talked the original stockholders (like Mather) into a voluntary sixty-percent assessment on their stock. Stock in the new organization was exchanged. A twenty-year lease was signed with the government for the former Desmond concessions, including general transportation, garage operation, and the camps and hotels. The Desmond dairy, saddle horse services, and store operation received a franchise for ten years.

Now the shock came. White sent me a surreptitious letter letting me know that Mather had contributed more money to the Dohrmann group. That seemed to fit the sixty-percent levy on original stockholders. I never knew for sure the exact amount of the new contribution, but it was somewhere around $200,000.

Why did Mather keep slipping deeper into this quagmire? There seemed to be two reasons. First, he was violently anti-Curry. He felt he couldn't allow the Curry Company to get too powerful and cut into the profits of the Yosemite Park Company. Second, Mather was intent on promoting the development of his "new Yosemite village." He felt it was imperative to have the financial backing of this consortium of San Francisco and Los Angeles businessmen to accomplish his goals of developing Yosemite Valley with the new northern village and a luxury resort hotel.

I was torn between telling myself it was none of my business and fearing for the future of Mather and the Park Service should this leak out in the public press. I passed White's letter along to Lane without comment. Lane's reply was close to explosive. He told me he had warned Mather long ago about a conflict of interest and his involvement in government affairs using his own money. He had discussed every angle of the case with him. After a crisscross of telegrams between Lane and me, Lane insisted I write Mather saying that "Lane and I" felt he should back out of any further connection with the Yosemite Park Company.

I didn't want any part of telling my chief what to do, felt it was none of my business, and didn't want to appear to be in cahoots with Lane. But I was afraid this situation might cost Mather his position, so I reluctantly agreed to do it. I kept the letter short, used Lane's opinions almost entirely, and concluded with, "I hope you will take the Secretary's words as friendly advice, for he cares deeply about you and fears for you should the company go into bankruptcy."

No matter how careful White, Lane, and I were, it seemed everyone in Yosemite heard rumors. Even the Currys heard about it but kept silent, fearful that Mather might turn on them and cut them off with no lease at all. The matter was temporarily dropped. Mather simply ignored Lane's arguments, blandly assuring him that when he made the additional loan he wasn't trying to make any money. After all, he was only charging five percent interest. As far as I ever knew, Lane must have been baffled and let it go at that. A few years hence, with a different interior secretary, a forceful showdown occurred.

. . .

On February 2, 1919, our son, Robert Mather Albright, was born. He was a handsome, healthy little fellow who weighed in at eight pounds, ten ounces with a mop of very dark hair like his mother's and the potential for her dancing brown eyes. Once more the National Park Service had kept me from her even during the birth of our son. Of course, my work kept me away from her most of the time she was in the hospital too.

First, I received a wire from Congressman Mondell that his Greater Yellowstone extension legislation had sailed through the House and looked good for the Senate. He suggested that I immediately get busy rounding up support, get the Sierra Club and others to bombard California's senators and other advocates to push the bill through the Senate. Unfortunately, there was a full-blown filibuster in the Senate, and the bill died for that session. Reintroduced in May 1919, it was never reported out of committee because Senator John Nugent of Idaho blocked it. He couldn't seem to get it through his head that the west line of our proposed extension of Yellowstone was the summit or backbone of the Tetons. He believed we were bringing the extension to the state line, thus including much sheep-grazing land used by his Idaho constituents. While we had been so near our goal in February, we never came close again for thirty years. It was controversy and bitter warfare from 1919 until a separate national park, Grand Teton, became a reality in 1950.

On February 17, when Grace and Bobby had only been home from the hospital two days, I left for Fresno to attend a meeting of the supervisors of the Seventh Congressional District. It was of vital importance concerning the Sequoia extension or, as it was currently called, the Roosevelt Park.

On February 19 advocates and opponents met at the Fresno County Courthouse. As the Fresno paper reported, "Before a crowd that overflowed the large room and stood around the walls, senators, congressmen, attorneys, army officers, and representatives of chambers of commerce and civic organizations favored and opposed the enlarging of the Sequoia park to contain 1,025,000 acres or 1,600 square miles to preserve its vast resources for future generations."

The paper further stated that "the most heated debates ever heard here" were witnessed that day. That was true. Opposition was immediate and vociferous. Grazing and lumber were the prime considerations. Proponents were ardent. Both sides were out of order time and again, interrupting when an argument didn't suit them.

Our opponents clearly carried the day. The upshot of the hearings was a wire from the supervisors of the county to Washington: "It was the sense of the mass meeting at Fresno today that the passage of S.B. 2021 and H.B. 10929 be deferred until National Park and Forest Service further investigate as to boundary lines and varied interests." The stalemate was exactly what I had figured the Forest Service and their allies would accomplish.

Sequoia was put on hold while I switched to a new pet project of Mather's. He had visited Yosemite in the fall of 1918. Accompanying him was Rudolph Spreckels, one of the wealthiest and most prominent men in San Francisco. They had become excited about the possibilities of a "winter season" for the park. They envisioned an all-year, seventy-mile concrete-surfaced road between Merced and El Portal that would open Yosemite to winter sports as well as summer sightseeing. Another purpose, as quoted in California newspapers, was "to give employment to thousands of our out-of-work service men, some of whom are now being cared for at public expense and whose idleness is rapidly becoming a menace to the industrial security of the nation."

Spreckels was so fired up by Mather's idea that he went to work to raise money for the project. He arranged a luncheon conference on February 28, 1919, at the Hotel Fresno to iron out details for financing the construction of this "winter gateway" to Yosemite. Attending were representatives of chambers of commerce, the newly powerful California automobile clubs, other commercial interests, the "good roads" advocates, and highway officials from all levels of government.

To my surprise, Mather had instructed me to offer a method of raising the money through the Park Service: "Tell the conference to issue $5 certificates of membership which will be exchanged for park permits. As a permit is worth $5, the purchaser of a certificate will lose nothing by advancing the money to build the road as there is no fixed time limit when the certificates must be redeemed. He can use his certificate (permit) to come to the park at any time."

I did as ordered but asked myself: Wasn't the Park Service paying for this road instead of private capital? How were we to explain the loss of permit revenue to the United States Treasury? Or worse still, the congressional appropriations committees? I never got an answer to my questions from Mather. To my chagrin, the local newspapers attributed this idea to me, saying I originated it.

More business concerning the Sequoia area had me rushing back to San Francisco for a conference on March 4. I was greeted with a pile of congratulatory telegrams concerning great news from Washington. On February 26, 1919, Grand Canyon had finally been made a national park.

My ebullient mood evaporated when I received a telegram from Mather: "In view of my Hawaiian trip, please be in D.C. by March 15." He had obviously chosen to forget our conversation in Chicago in which he promised to let me stay in California to rest up, be with my family, and plan my future. Of course, I hadn't been with my family and I hadn't rested up. I'd been running around like a chicken with my head cut off. But the one thing I had done was interview for positions in various San Francisco law firms, and I had been offered two fine opportunities that promised bright futures.

This telegram had brought me to a fork in the road, and a major decision had to be made. There could be no more shilly-shallying, no more procrastinating, no more grim determination to leave the Park Service mixed with painful regrets in cutting the umbilical cord. I had to make up my mind once and for all where I was going.

I chose to resign from the National Park Service and put that part of my life behind me.

Up to this time, I had tried to keep my increasingly depressed state of mind and the problems I was wrestling with to myself. But this was a decision that affected our whole family. I told Grace that we had to have a talk, so we took a long walk up on the Berkeley campus. When we finally sank down on the grass, Grace said, "All right, darling. What is it you have to tell me? I read the telegram from Mr. Mather. I know it upset you badly, but I wanted to let you tell me about it when you were ready."

As I poured out all my doubts and uncertainties, all the depression and discouragement of the situation with Mather, Lane, and what I felt was my future in the Park Service, my precious wife sat there with quiet tears streaming down her face. She was overwhelmed by the thought that I had kept all this to myself, hadn't let her share my agony.

It was a relief to talk things over with her. As I related my feelings about the months and years of strain, of difficult decisions, of loneliness, of concern over Mather and the Park Service, of relentless, unending work, I began to realize just exactly how depressed and exhausted I was. Grace understood and felt that resignation from the Park Service was the only answer. We agreed that we owed each other and our baby a life together, that I just couldn't be responsible for carrying the type of burden I had carried for the last two years. Mr. Mather's health was an uncertain question at best. Lane's reply to me had cut any hope I had to step into Mather's position should be become ill again and be replaced. Our income after July 1, when Mather's payment to me had to cease, would be impossible for the three of us to live on.

When we went home, I got out my typewriter and wrote a letter of resignation to Mr. Mather, dated March 9, 1919. The next few days I was very sick with what I called a bilious attack, so the letter didn't get mailed until March 14. It was just as well because, in those five days, I added a few extra pages that changed the course of our lives forever.

My original letter began with and repeated throughout my love and admiration for Stephen Mather, "the one man that I am mighty nearly as fond of as I am of my own parents." "You shall ever remain our (Grace and my) ideal of Christian manhood, our highest conception of a public official, our personification of all that is good, kind, gentle, thoughtful, and unselfish in modern man."

My regard for Mather as a father-figure made the original section of the letter an emotional reiteration of my own hopes and despairs, my deep concern for him, my agonizing over this decision I felt I had been forced to make in view of Lane's attitude, financial concerns, and love for Grace.

I concluded the letter of March 9 with:

I do not know what I will do as yet, but I am not afraid of this old world. It has never had me guessing, and I think I can weather any storm that hits us. Grace is a brave girl, and will back me up night and day. . . . It is hardly necessary for me to say that I shall never get into any line of work that will interest me as much as national park work. . . . You and I know more about the parks than any other men on Earth; the National Park Service is our child. We gave birth to it and we will love, cherish and protect it as long as we live."

With that last paragraph, I signed the letter and put it in an envelope. I felt my career in the National Park Service had been put behind me forever, but fate stepped in and turned my life around. There is no more logical answer than that.

The unmailed letter kept torturing me like a cat playing with a mouse. I couldn't get the thought out of my head that I was making a terrible mistake. Every bit of logic told me that the choice was correct, but every fiber in me cried out not to accept it. I knew I couldn't face a future along the same path I'd been traveling the last few years. I simply refused a life of uncertainty, total responsibility for operation of the Park Service, and, it seemed, Mr. Mather, and unacceptable separation from Grace.

My dilemma seemed insurmountable until a thought began to worm its way into my consciousness. Why not be a field officer like superintendent of Yellowstone and also be available as a troubleshooter? This would keep me with my family and in the Park Service but away from Washington most of the time. I could still help Mather on park and administrative problems. Would a proposal like this satisfy both of us? I went back to the typewriter and added four more pages to the existing five.

My proposal began with: "If I could have my wife and my baby and my home, and, at the same time, continue in my beloved National Park Service, I should ask for little more in this world. Wealth I have never craved, but home life is as dear to me as anything can be, and this I do crave. This I must have."

Then I came to the crux of the issue: "For several years, I have hoped that circumstances might make the superintendency of the Yellowstone available to me. Back in 1916, when Colonel Brett left, I wanted the place, but I felt that I could help you more in Washington then; I have thought longingly of the Yellowstone ever since." And then, in typical legal fashion, I proceeded with paragraph after paragraph promoting the idea and then presenting arguments against it.

I suppose I thought I was being very straightforward in offering suggestions for a person who could fill the position of assistant director to Mather, but I quickly dismissed each one of them offhand or found serious faults with each. I made the flat, blanket statement: "There seems to be nobody in the Department that could fill the job."

Conclusion: "You need personal representatives in the field constantly . . . somebody in the far West and in the Rocky Mountain region to keep tab on all movements that affect the parks, just as I am watching everything out here now. . . . With me in Yellowstone, in the winter time, you could call me to Washington for a couple of months to help with legislation, or any other work that even now comes within my sphere. . . . It is absolutely impossible for you to think of making the entire round of the parks, and still look after the promotion of Roosevelt Park as you plan." I believe it was the first time that the idea of Park Service regions with their own officials was put forth.

I didn't have long to wait for an answer. Instead of the multipage, handwritten letter I had expected, I received an immediate reply in the form of a short and to-the-point telegram from Mr. Mather in Washington. He simply asked me to defer any precipitous action until he returned from his Hawaiian trip and to assume the position of acting director in Washington until that time. I agreed to do this, but I pointedly did not take back my resignation.

It was mighty frustrating to be back in Washington on April 2. I pushed thoughts of my future aside to focus attention on the upcoming tourist season. We anticipated greatly increased visitation, which would lead to road, concession, and numerous other problems. One on the top of the list was finding topnotch personnel for the parks. We needed numerous rangers, but most of all we were looking for superintendents of the Dusty Lewis variety. And fortune smiled on the Park Service, as we acquired many a fine leader as they emerged from wartime service.

There was the case of Roger Toll. I had been acquainted with him through my work in Colorado and had extensive communication with him before he left for Hawaii to study the volcanic mountains. I gave him letters of introduction to officials in the islands and suggested he look up Mather while both were there. Then I wired Mather about him. I praised his knowledge and ability and suggested he be appointed superintendent at Mount Rainier.

When the two men did meet in Hawaii, Mather was most impressed by Toll and wired me to get Lane's approval for the appointment. Toll took over Mount Rainier on May 29, 1919.

Then one day a jaunty, red-haired Air Corps colonel named John White came into my office and asked for a job. His background was that of a soldier-of-fortune, but I instantly liked him and offered him a ranger position at Grand Canyon. He snapped it up and, within a year, became superintendent of Sequoia and General Grant Parks.

Sandwiching in work on next year's budget and outlining the 1919 annual report, meeting with congressmen about park legislation, especially the Sequoia and Yellowstone extensions, and handling the day-to-day operations, I faced some interesting decisions.

There was a flurry of bills regarding various parks and monuments. Introduced or reintroduced were extensions of Yellowstone, Sequoia, Crater Lake, and Hawaii. Members of Congress had a field day proposing new areas to add to the system, including Pajarito (New Mexico), Mississippi Valley (Iowa and Wisconsin), Mammoth Cave (Kentucky),

Grand Coulee (Washington), and Killdeer (North Dakota). The list of national monuments was endless, including a tract of land in California to save the *Washingtonia filamentosa* (palm).

Opportunity arose to accept gifts of land: a section of the beautiful Great Smoky Mountains in North Carolina and equally attractive acreage in the Green Mountains of Vermont. These offers excited me, for I felt eastern parks were the wave of the future. Most of our population lived east of the Mississippi, most of the Congress represented them, and appropriations would be more generous if eastern areas were included. Above all, Americans deserved to have every section of the country represented in their heritage. Year after year in our annual report, I encouraged the idea that the National Park Service should consist not only of scenic parks, but of historic areas transferred from the War and Agriculture Departments.

Even though I considered my time in the service probably coming to an end, I actively promoted our extension plans for Yellowstone and Sequoia and a few new ones, including the California *sempervirens* redwoods and Great Smoky Mountains. I considered most of the other new proposals rather facetious, not up to our standards, or out of reach financially. However, I didn't discourage or promote them, but left them for Mather's consideration.

Although I left decisions on less vital issues for Mather, I was dead serious, firm, and decisive about others, especially the effects on the parks due to the conclusion of the war. The most immediate problem that arose was Secretary Lane's enthusiastic endorsement of a program to reward our returning war veterans with public lands, farms, and ranches to start new lives.

On the surface this idea sounded fine, but it quickly turned into something else when suggestions were made as to how these lands could be made more productive by providing more water for irrigation. At the top of the list for proposed irrigation projects was Yellowstone Park, including Lewis, Shoshone, Yellowstone, and Heart Lakes as well as the incomparable Falls River Basin in the southwest corner.

Dams were projected for all of them that would flood huge sections of timberland, bringing wholesale desecration to these vast wilderness areas. Not only were dead trees a blot on the landscape, but they were a source of serious water pollution. In the National Park Service annual report of 1919, I deplored the utilization of the lakes and the Falls River Basin for irrigation. The loss of this precious land, I wrote, would only be "for the benefit of a few individuals or corporations."

This situation couldn't wait for Mather's return. Perhaps because I believed I would be out of the Interior Department soon or because I no longer had as much awe and respect for Secretary Lane, I openly crossed swords with him about Yellowstone. I wrote a eight-page "brief" arguing that these irrigation dams would destroy a wilderness that was ordained by law to be kept "unimpaired." He read my paper and, right in front of me, angrily tore it in half, threw it in the wastepaper basket, and, without a word, signaled me to leave his office.

There was obviously nothing more to be done at the Interior Department, so I turned my attention to the Capitol. I sought out conservation friends here, passed out a one-page version of my arguments to Lane, and especially warned them to be on the lookout for the bills when they were brought before committees. This was just the start of the Yellowstone irrigation confrontation, and within a few months I was deeply embroiled in it once more.

Mr. Mather didn't come back to Washington immediately after he returned to Chicago from Hawaii. I was on pins and needles until the morning he did show up. He dropped an orange paper lei around my neck, clapped me on the back, and laughingly said, "All right, Horace, the time has come for a showdown!"

We were closeted in his office for hours. He started off by telling me that Secretary Lane had assured him that it was our decision, that he'd go along with whatever we decided. But then he never got to the central issue, never directly referred to my letter. It seemed as if he was stalling as we discussed mundane park problems, including a new superintendent for Glacier, the Yosemite road, and other like matters.

I finally blurted out, "Mr. Mather, I have resigned from the Park Service, so I really don't know why you are bothering to go over all these things with me."

This must have startled him, for he immediately became serious: "You're not really going to leave me in the lurch, Horace, are you? You yourself said that we were a team, that we would be in this thing together."

From there the conversation quickly picked up steam, and all the arguments were exchanged. Mather purred like a cat in his most charming and persuasive style while I was in my best legal form. Of course, it ended as we both knew it would. He proposed the exact thing I wanted, and, by my acceptance, he gained what he wanted.

I would assume the superintendency of Yellowstone National Park on July 1, 1919, along with a house, official car, and raise in salary to thirty-six hundred dollars per annum. Chester Lindsley would become my assistant superintendent. I would relinquish my title of assistant director. We agreed that together we would pick out a new assistant director, who would remain in the Washington office constantly, so that Mather could also get away most of the time.

Instead I would be designated assistant to the director. In this capacity I would continue to oversee all the field operations as well as come to Washington for a few months in the winter when Yellowstone was closed. I would still be responsible for the budget, working up appropriations and testifying about them before the congressional committees, and promoting legislation concerning the parks.

With this settled, Mather wasted no time in outlining things he wanted me to work on until it was time to go to Yellowstone. Then he grinned at me and said, "Horace, I'm going to start your new salary before then, so you'll have a little extra to move on." He arranged this by getting Lane to appoint me as of June 10 and start my new salary on that date.

Before the law shutting off private payments to government workers went into effect on July 1, Mather gave Grace and me a personal check for one thousand dollars. It was an awesome sum to us, and we were eternally grateful to this kind, thoughtful man. His note that accompanied the check read: "You may have to keep your little Washington apartment for awhile with some necessities, and Grace can't live with all that old army furniture in Yellowstone. You'll need something better—and a lot more of it—for that huge, old stone barn you're moving into. At least I want a better bed than Brett's iron monster when I come to visit—which will be often!"

Shortly after our agreement was reached, Mr. Mather and I came to a decision about a new assistant director for the Washington office. It was to be Arno B. Cammerer.

Cammerer was born in 1883. Financial problems in his family forced him to quit high school, and he left Nebraska and came to Washington. Here he took secretarial courses, finished high school, and went to Georgetown University Law School by night. He worked as a clerk in the Treasury Department by day. In 1916 he was chosen assistant secretary to the National Commission of Fine Arts and first secretary of the Public Buildings Commission of Congress. In this position he prepared annual budgets, testified before Congress, handled financial accounts. The commission was in charge of the District of Columbia parkway system, the construction of the Lincoln Memorial, and the care of other structures.

Although we both knew Cammerer casually, Mather made some in-depth, discreet inquiries. From these, we came to the conclusion that he would be perfect to handle the bureau, allowing both of us to be absent from Washington a good deal of the time.

Of course, we recognized that he knew nothing about national parks, but his administrative ability, extensive financial work, supervision of office staffs, and knowledge of congressional budget and legislative processes made him the perfect man for Mather. He was very intelligent and would pick up park affairs in short order. Above all he was hard-working, amiable, and even-tempered, with a great sense of humor and an opti-mistic, businesslike devotion to duty. Mather and I liked him immediately and immensely.

Mather offered Cammerer the position of assistant director, and he took his place on July 3, two days after my appointment as superintendent of Yellowstone was activated. "Cam," as we always called him, proved invaluable, and through the years we regarded ourselves as a triumvirate.

The Washington situation was in good shape, so I headed back to California once more. I wanted to be sure of Grace's reaction to the deci-sions reached in Washington. Of course, I'd written her all the details. I was sure they met with her approval, but it wasn't until I arrived in Berkeley and saw her excitement and happiness that I was completely ready to face my new challenge.

Grace felt her life had been turned around. We would be together most of the time, although she knew probably better than Mr. Mather and me that I'd be away on park affairs more than imagined. But in the meantime, the Albright family would enjoy a real home. She loved Yellowstone.

On June 10, 1919, I received a beautifully engraved parchment docu-ment signed by Secretary Lane proclaiming me superintendent of Yellowstone National Park. With this was a formal letter from him confirming the appointment.

In view of the strained relations between Lane and me since the preceding November, I was astonished to see that there was a four-page note attached by a paper clip. It was scrawled in pencil on five-by-eight-inch official Department of the Interior stationery. It was in Lane's hand-writing but unsigned: "I want you to understand that we part with you here with great regret and because of your sure knowledge of the parks we shall feel free to call upon you to do some larger work than others in your position. From time to time Mr. Mather will call upon you to give him your opinion on phases of administration in the other parks but this must be done in such as way as to keep from any semblance of subordinating other superintendents to you and I know that your tact will not permit this impression going out."

• • •

The Albright family arrived in West Yellowstone on July 14, 1919, and occupied our huge stone house the next day. As I was exploring my new office, Jack Haynes, who had the photographic concession in the park, sent a fellow over to take some pictures of me on my first day as superintendent of Yellowstone. I was delighted, as I had my full-dress National Park Service uniform on.

Before going outside for the picture-taking session, I studied myself in the mirror. The uniform was fine. With fear and trepidation, I had ordered it by mail, but it fit perfectly. My puttees were polished, my hat was squarely on my head, but I still looked too young.

Although my age had never handicapped me, I was always so conscious of it. This particular day I was especially bothered that I not only was twenty-nine, but looked twenty-nine. After considering the problem, I decided my pince-nez glasses would do the trick. I pinched them on my nose, straightened my tie, and assumed my pose on the bottom step of my headquarters. Solemnly staring at the camera for my first official photograph as superintendent of Yellowstone National Park, I felt a surge of happiness go through me. All the doubts, depression, and fears were gone. There was nothing but opportunity to make this land, the size of Rhode Island and Delaware, into a shining example of what a national park could be. I was filled with anticipation of work to be done, goals to be reached, and years of sunshine ahead in this strange and beautiful wilderness.

I always remembered this day as one of the proudest moments of my entire life.

Suggested Readings

Albright, Horace M., as told to Robert Cahn. *The Birth of the National Park Service: The Founding Years 1913–33.* Salt Lake City: Howe Brothers, 1985.

Albright, Horace M., and Marian Albright Schenck. *The Mather Mountain Party of 1915.* Three Rivers, Calif.: Sequoia Natural History Association, 1990.

Dilsaver, Lary M., ed. *America's National Park System: The Critical Documents.* Lanham, Md.: Rowman & Littlefield, 1994.

Everhart, William C. *The National Park Service.* Revised edition. Boulder, Colo.: Westview Press, 1983.

Foresta, Ronald A. *America's National Parks and Their Keepers.* Washington, D.C.: Resources for the Future, 1984.

Haines, Aubrey L. *The Yellowstone Story.* Yellowstone National Park, Wyo.: Yellowstone Library Museum Association in cooperation with Colorado Associated University Press, 1977.

Hartzog, George B., Jr. *Battling for the National Parks.* Mt. Kisco, N.Y.: Moyer Bell Ltd., 1988.

Ise, John. *Our National Park Policy: A Critical History.* Baltimore: Johns Hopkins University Press, 1961.

Morrison, Ernest. *J. Horace McFarland: A Thorn for Beauty.* Harrisburg: Pennsylvania Historical and Museum Commission, 1995.

Rettie, Dwight F. *Our National Park System: Caring for America's Greatest Natural and Historic Treasures.* Urbana: University of Illinois Press, 1995.

Rothman, Hal. *Preserving Different Pasts: The American National Monuments.* Urbana and Chicago: University of Illinois Press.

Runte, Alfred. *The National Parks: The American Experience.* 2d edition. Lincoln: University of Nebraska Press, 1987.

Sellars, Richard West. *Preserving Nature in the National Parks: A History.* New Haven: Yale University Press, 1997.

Shankland, Robert. *Steve Mather of the National Parks.* 3d edition. New York: Alfred A. Knopf, 1970.

Swain, Donald C. *Wilderness Defender: Horace M. Albright and Conservation.* Chicago: University of Chicago Press, 1970.

Wirth, Conrad L. *Parks, Politics, and the People.* Norman: University of Oklahoma Press, 1980.

Index

References to illustrations are printed in italics.

CPSIA information can be obtained
at www.ICGtesting.com
Printed in the USA
FSHW04n1532170318
45799FS